ASEAN and East Asian International Relations

ASEAN and East Asian International Relations

Regional Delusion

David Martin Jones

Senior Lecturer, School of Political Science and International Studies, University of Queensland, Australia

M.L.R. Smith

Reader in War Studies, Department of War Studies, King's College, University of London, UK

Edward Elgar
Cheltenham, UK • Northampton, MA, USA

Published by
Edward Elgar Publishing Limited
Glensanda House
Montpellier Parade
Cheltenham
Glos GL50 1UA
UK

Edward Elgar Publishing, Inc.
136 West Street
Suite 202
Northampton
Massachusetts 01060
USA

A catalogue record for this book
is available from the British Library

Library of Congress Cataloguing in Publication Data

Jones, David Martin.
    ASEAN and East Asian international relations: regional delusion/
by David Martin Jones and M.L.R. Smith.
        p.   cm.
    Includes bibliographical references and index.
    1. Asia, Southeastern—Foreign relations—East Asia. 2. East
Asia—Foreign relations—Asia, Southeastern. 3. Regionalism—Asia.
4. ASEAN. I. Smith, M.L.R. (Michael Lawrence Rowan), 1963– .
II. Title.
DS525.9.E18J66   2006
909'.09823083—dc22   2005049478

ISBN-13: 978 1 84376 491 5 (cased)
ISBN-10: 1 84376 491 1 (cased)

Typeset by Cambrian Typesetters, Camberley, Surrey
Printed and bound in Great Britain by MPG Books Ltd, Bodmin, Cornwall

Contents

Acknowledgements

This work came about as a result of our encounters with the East in its Singaporean manifestation and Australia in its Keatingite and post-Keatingite form, both of which raised a perplexity in that the world that Asian and Australian elites described did not fit with what we observed taking place on the ground. We found, moreover, that to question the notion of an evolving East Asian community was to invoke either ridicule or embarrassed silence.

The puzzlement was fuelled by the willingness of many western academics, themselves the beneficiaries of open and pluralistic societies, to endorse the illiberal consensus sponsored by the variety of authoritarian regimes in the region. It is from this perplexity that the essays that came to shape this book first arose. Dating from the mid-1990s our thoughts appeared in a series of scholarly articles and shorter pieces in journals and newspapers, including the *Australian Financial Review*, *Contemporary Security Policy*, *Intelligence and National Security*, *International Affairs*, *Jane's Intelligence Review*, *Orbis*, *The Round Table*, *Studies in Conflict and Terrorism* and *The World Today*. This book draws on some of this initial research work and we would like to thank these periodicals and their editors for their willingness to publish material on what has turned out to be an ostensibly contrarian project.

Our persistence was further invigorated by the rejections we received from grant-giving organizations like the ARC (Australian Research Council) and the ESRC (Economic and Social Research Council) to fund any part of this project. These agencies busied themselves instead with projects promoting an appreciation of ASEAN, its admirably diverse strategic cultures, the Asian economic miracle and the inevitable regionalization of the global order (which this book contests). We would like to acknowledge, though, the generosity of the Ford Foundation who – in theory – awarded us several thousand dollars to study 'non-traditional security issues in Southeast Asia'. However, for reasons best known to the Director of the Institute of Defence and Strategic Studies (Singapore), who administered the Ford Foundation bequest, our payment never materialized. Given the current predilection amongst Aseanologists for the discursive construction of imagined communities, imagined regions and imagined futures, we can safely claim that this is the first instance of an imagined grant. Nevertheless, we suppose it's the thought that counts.

We have been encouraged in this endeavour by Luke Adams, our commissioning editor, whom we would like to thank for his patience as we both struggled to complete this book while swimming through the glue of bureaucratic sclerosis that characterizes allegedly research-led universities in Britain and Australia.

Abbreviations

ABC	Australian Broadcasting Corporation
AFTA	ASEAN Free Trade Area
ALP	Australian Labor Party
ANZUS	Australia, New Zealand, United States
APEC	Asia–Pacific Economic Cooperation
ARF	ASEAN Regional Forum
ASEAN	Association of Southeast Asian Nations
ASEM	ASEAN–Europe Meeting
ASIO	Australian Security Intelligence Organization
BBC	British Broadcasting Corporation
BOI	Board of Investment
CCP	Chinese Communist Party
CEPT	Common Effective Preferential Tariff
CGDK	Coalition Government of Democratic Kampuchea
CLOB	Central Limit Order Book
CNN	Cable News Network
CPF	Central Provident Fund
CPP	Cambodian People's Party
CSIS	Centre for Strategic and International Studies
DFAT	Department of Foreign Affairs and Trade
DPR	Dewan Perwakilan Rakyat
EAEC	East Asian Economic Caucus
EAEG	East Asian Economic Grouping
EAS	East Asian Summit
EC	European Community
EDB	Economic Development Board
EEC	European Economic Community
EPB	Economic Planning Board
EPZ	Export Processing Zones
ESB	Economic Stabilization Board
EU	European Union
FBI	Federal Bureau of Investigation
FDI	Foreign Direct Investment
FKI	Federation of Korean Industries
FPI	Front Pembela Islam

GAM	Gerakan Aceh Merdeka
GATT	General Agreement on Tariffs and Trade
GDP	Gross Domestic Product
GIA	Groupement Islamique Armé
GNP	Gross National Product
HCIP	Heavy and Chemical Industry Plan
HICOM	Heavy Industries Corporation of Malaysia
HPAE	High Performing Asian Economies
IBRA	Indonesian Bank Restructuring Agency
IIRO	International Islamic Relief Organization
IMF	International Monetary Fund
ISA	Internal Security Act
ISD	Internal Security Department
ISEAS	Institute of Southeast Asian Studies
JI	Jemaah Islamiyah
KLSE	Kuala Lumpur Stock Exchange
KMM	Kumpulan Mujahideen Malaysia
KMT	Kuomintang
KPRP	Kampuchean People's Revolutionary Party
LDP	Liberal Democratic Party
MCI	Ministry of Commerce and Industry
MILF	Moro Islamic Liberation Front
MINDEF	Ministry of Defence
MITI	Ministry for Trade and Industry
MMI	Majlis Mujahideen Indonesia
MNE	Multinational Enterprises
MNLF	Moro National Liberation Front
MOF	Ministry of Finance
NAFTA	North American Free Trade Area
NBER	National Bureau of Economic Research
NDP	National Development Policy
NEP	New Economic Policy
NGO	Non-Governmental Organization
NIE	Newly Industrialized Economies
NTUC	National Trade Union Congress
NWC	National Wages Council
OAU	Organization of African Unity
OECD	Organization for Economic Co-operation and Development
ONA	Office of National Assessment
OPEC	Organization of Petroleum-Exporting Countries
PAN	Partai Amanat Nasional
PAP	People's Action Party

PAS	Parti Islam Se-Malaysia
PDB	Philippine Development Bank
PDI	Partai Demokrasi Indonesia
PDI-P	Partai Demokrasi Indonesia Perjuangan
PECC	Pacific Economic Cooperation Council
PKB	Partai Kebangkitan Bangsa
PKS	Partai Keadilan Sejahtera
PLA	People's Liberation Army
PNB	Philippine National Bank
PPP	Partai Persatuan Pembangunan
PRC	People's Republic of China
PRK	People's Republic of Kampuchea
PULO	Pattani United Liberation Organization
SARS	Severe Acute Respiratory Syndrome
SEANNWFZ	Southeast Asian Nuclear Weapons Free Zone
SEATO	South-East Asia Treaty Organization
SEP	Strategic Economic Plan
SEZ	Special Economic Zone
SLORC	State Law and Order Restoration Council
TAC	Treaty of Amity and Cooperation
TNI	Tentara Nasional Indonesia
UMNO	United Malay National Organization
UN	United Nations
US	United States
USSR	Union of Soviet Socialist Republics
WTO	World Trade Organization
ZOPFAN	Zone of Peace, Freedom and Neutrality

Introduction: the age of delusion in the Asia–Pacific

The dominant international relations paradigm of the late 1980s and early 1990s assumed that regions represented the necessary structures that under-pinned an emerging post-Cold War global order. This regional re-ordering, it was asserted in works like Paul Hirst and Grahame Thompson's *Globalization in Question* (1996) and Susan Strange's *The Retreat of the State* (1997), would occur at the expense of the nation-state. These authors, and many others like them, believed that a complex web of transnational processes that spanned the activities of non-governmental organizations, corporate and media conglom-erates on the one hand, and international institutions on the other, would continue to erode state sovereignty from above and below. In scholarly and media commentary the perception and description of this apparent shift towards regionalization was often accompanied by the overt promotion of multilateral arrangements as the necessary corollary to the new post-Cold War order.

Nowhere was the enthusiasm for building multinational institutions that reflected the seemingly inexorable transition of the international system from a state-centric into a regionally based order more noticeable than in the Asia–Pacific. In particular, scholarly zeal focused on the Association of Southeast Asian Nations (ASEAN) as the exemplar of this evolving regional emphasis. ASEAN, and its expansionist offshoots, the ASEAN Free Trade Area (AFTA) and the ASEAN Regional Forum (ARF), together with the Australian initiative of Asia–Pacific Economic Cooperation (APEC) and later the ASEAN Plus Three framework embracing China, Japan and South Korea, represented the building blocks of a distinctive Asian trading region and secu-rity community. Prior to the financial crisis of 1997 many of these arrange-ments, it was also maintained, intimated a shift in the global order towards a new Pacific Century premised on multilateral practices of cooperation and dialogue that reflected a regional diplomatic culture of consensus and non-interference. Indeed, multilateralism based upon what Ken Booth and Russell Trood in *Strategic Cultures in the Asia–Pacific* (1999) deemed a sensitivity to the strategic cultural preoccupations of this evolving region would facilitate a burgeoning and largely benign interdependence. Even relatively recent works like Mark Beeson's edited volume, *Reconfiguring East Asia* (2002), continue to maintain that an East Asian region, as opposed to individual states, is 'increasingly consequential in political practice [and] economic decision making' (Beeson 2002, pp. 2–3).

The regional economic crisis of 1997–98, followed by political breakdown in Southeast Asia, regime change in Indonesia, the recrudescence of suppressed ethno-religious tensions and the emergence of a regional terror network with links to al-Qaeda, along with the region's conspicuous inability to coordinate a coherent response to transnational threats in the form of diseases like SARS (Severe Acute Respiratory Syndrome) or natural disasters like the 2004 tsunami, challenged many of these regionalist and multilateral-ist assumptions, exposing them as fallacies. The multilateral orthodoxy which sustains these fallacies has strongly resisted reasoned counter-argument (see Öjendal 2004, pp. 519–33). Instead, it maintains faith in the regional verity, despite evidence to the contrary, which regional commentators repeatedly played down, overlooked, misunderstood or just ignored. Analytical weak-ness, combined with ideological faith, we shall show, sustained a delusion that became entrenched in the field of Asian international relations.

How this delusion came to dominate the study of the Southeast Asian, and the wider East Asian, region forms the central theme of this book. It will assess how it achieved the status of an intellectual orthodoxy and explain its persis-tence, which continues to impede an accurate understanding of regional affairs. Furthermore, this study suggests that the aftermath of the Asian finan-cial crisis, along with the new agenda posed by the forces of economic glob-alization and the low intensity conflicts that bedevil Southeast Asia and the wider Pacific region more generally, require us to re-evaluate radically both the political economy and the security arrangements in Pacific Asia that are essentially the product of the Cold War and immediate post-Cold War era. This work, therefore, specifically examines the failure of ASEAN to address the political and economic problems that became increasingly evident after 1990. In order to scrutinize these failings, ASEAN's weakness is set in the context of the broader economic and political incoherence that afflicts the Asia–Pacific region more generally and which, according to Gilbert Rozman, always rendered the promotion of regional interdependence flawed (Rozman 1998). In other words, we shall analyse the economic, political and ethno-reli-gious tensions that beset the wider region through the distorting prism that is ASEAN.

This study begins with an examination of the manner in which an ASEAN scholar-bureaucracy and its western fellow travellers promoted flawed region-alism in the course of the 1990s. Having revealed the limitations of a variety of liberal, idealist and post-modern theorizing and their distorting conse-quences for understanding the historically contingent factors that shaped threat perception in the Asia–Pacific, we shall proceed to examine the post-1945 evolution of international relations in Southeast Asia, and their implications, if any, for the wider Pacific Rim. Subsequent chapters thus examine the curious dispensation through which ASEAN rose to international prominence. In particular, we shall assess how ASEAN erroneously came to be seen in the 1990s as a new form of security cooperation that could, in its extended version of the ARF, apparently effortlessly embrace Northeast Asia. We shall then analyse how rising levels of low-intensity conflict generated by the forces of globalization threaten to undermine irrevocably Southeast Asia's economic and political integrity.

As an imitation community rather than an imagined one, we shall further show that the competing forces of economic integration and identity politics have exposed ASEAN's constituting ambivalences that leave it ill-equipped to serve as the template for a post-Cold War regional order. Furthermore, the seemingly insoluble Cold War flashpoints in Northeast Asia, coupled with Chinese irredentism and American ambiguity towards both the People's Republic of China (PRC) and Japan, render a balance of power in Northeast Asia both complex and uncertain. It will be the further contention of this work that as the processes of globalizing trade and internetting markets continues this will have a centrifugal rather than a centripetal impact on the region. These processes will be further exacerbated by the impact of the 'war on terror' and its spillover into Islamic radicalism in both Southeast and South Asia.

Globalization premised on state security will afford opportunities for stronger states to quell internal dissent while exploiting comparative advantage. As a result, the United States, China, Japan and Australia will exercise increasing soft power in the Southeast Asian region. The downside to this process will see the less adaptable Asian developmental states eroded both at the global level by difficulty in adapting to post-meltdown market requirements and at the sub-state level by a global black market in guns, drugs and people smuggling that facilitate the activity of sub-state actors working through diaspora communities to sustain long-standing separatist movements. Thus the region's weaker states, like Indonesia, Burma, Malaysia and the Philippines, will either federalize or fragment. China, meanwhile, will constitute an evolving problem: on the one hand, seeking to re-establish a tributary relationship with its pre-eighteenth century area of regional influence in the *Nanyang*,[1] on the other, guarding internally against separatist Islamic forces and pressures to democratize both from within and without which impels it towards new authoritarian and anti-Islamic groupings like the Shanghai Five.

Finally, it will be argued that the notion of Asian values, manifested organizationally in shared ASEAN values during the 1990s, constituted an illusion that both masked emerging tensions between Asian states and actively obscured political and economic weaknesses, with ultimately disastrous consequences. Ironically, the extent to which Southeast Asia and the broader Asia–Pacific more generally can sustain the status quo and avoid a possible Middle Eastern fate will reflect the balancing role played by the west, in the shape of the US across the Pacific region and Australia in Southeast Asia.

DEALING WITH DELUSION

The main argument put forward in this work is that many of the acknowledged experts on Southeast Asian and Pacific affairs have consistently misread regional prospects, their assessments and prognostications consistently undermined by the subsequent turn of events. The contention, though, is not that these analytical errors were, despite the best of intentions, the product of the simple inability to predict the future. The point this study seeks to make is that many of the key assumptions that underpinned the study of Asia–Pacific relations were themselves delusions: seriously flawed understandings of regional developments that produced a systematic misreading of the character of international relations that inevitably disfigured any attempt to discern the trends and patterns in regional affairs.

The notion of delusion, then, forms the principal motif running through this work. Delusions are defined here as 'mistaken beliefs that are maintained in spite of strong evidence to the contrary' (Huffman, Venoy, Williams 1987, p. 552). What gives rise to a delusion is a question that is a good deal more complicated than this straightforward definition might imply. The term itself derives from psychoanalysis and denotes various dichotomous conditions where internal beliefs fail to conform with any wider, more objective or intersubjectively understood ideas of reality.[2] Hence, the term is associated with psychiatric disorder: delusions of grandeur, delusions of persecution or delusions of reference.[3] In these respects, the idea of delusion is often located within states of extreme narcissism (see Jung 1983, pp. 14–41). In psychiatric practice, for instance, a chart of questions is used to locate personality types and, if an individual forms a cluster around a certain spread of responses, they are more than likely to be delusional.

One of the interesting aspects of the delusive personality as a psychiatric phenomenon is that, while it may cover neuroses that encompass modes of aberrant behaviour, it does not of itself necessarily delineate mental illness. The condition can be observed in, say, the business or academic type who, despite corruption, mismanagement and incompetence, demands that his board or faculty feed his or her delusion. This is called monosymptomatic delusion and manifests itself in ego-driven behaviour and a tendency to intellectual hubris, and can be found in some degrees in many walks of life and most modern universities (Beary and Cobb 1981, pp. 64–6; Walter 1991, pp.

283–4: see also Kagan and Segal 1992, pp. 502–4). In the monosymptomatic understanding, the world must fit *my* view of it. The delusive personality, therefore, cannot face the reality principle without the ego feeling threatened. A consensual group maintains and reinforces belief systems, no matter how misguided they may be. Such a mentality is unable to withstand contradiction without descending into fragmentation, which also explains the tendency in narcissistic personalities towards paranoia.

Interesting and potentially fruitful though a psychoanalytical approach may be, we somewhat reluctantly reject it as an explanatory tool in this analysis. As authors we do not possess any formal psychiatric training. Further, while we can note the valuable attempts to scientificize understandings of aberrant behaviour, it is recognized that psychoanalytical approaches are themselves open to question. Psychoanalysis rarely yields itself to decisive external veri-fication. This has led political philosophers, and sociologists like Ernest Gellner and Karl Popper, to argue that it is inherently speculative and its conclusions ultimately unfalsifiable (Gellner 1985; Popper 1985, pp. 127–8, 363–5). Such accusations inevitably intimate a degree of controversy in any field of study that seeks to define and ascribe mental disorder and social deviance. Specialists in psychiatry and psychology do, needless to say, acknowledge the severe difficulties in discerning what constitutes abnormal behaviour (Kagan and Segal 1992, pp. 482–3). What the problematic and contested nature of such debates clearly suggests, however, is the inapplica-bility of psychoanalysis as a viable investigatory method in the social sciences. This is reinforced by the obvious abuse of psychoanalytical terms that have made their way into political and sociological discourse that claim the right to detect 'phobic' or 'philiac' tendencies in ideological and intellectual positions. The imputation of mental illness or disorder to others is itself a form of intol-erance that is the enemy of scholarly inquiry. Such imputations should have no place in any wider discussion of the humanities and social sciences, a theme to which this introduction will return later.

Despite the difficulties associated with psychoanalysis, there are neverthe-less strands of thought evolving from group psychology that legitimately inter-sect with themes in the realm of political science and which possess analytic utility. These notions arise out of concepts like 'groupthink' and concentrate on the empirically observable (see Janis 1982; 't Hart 1990; 't Hart, Stern and Sundelius 1997).[4] Thus it is possible to discern evidence of systemic predic-tive and analytical error and seek explanations in ideas that relate to the forma-tion of orthodoxies and the attraction of individuals to consensus-seeking activities. It is the establishment of orthodox modes of understanding that can result in a collective tendency to screen out discrepant information that might diverge from it. This, in turn, inhibits alternative appreciations of develop-ments that might more thoroughly accord with the available evidence. In this way shortcomings of certain forms of intellectual activity can be properly tested without ascribing psychiatric dysfunction.

Therefore this study sets out to examine the evident empirical failure of Southeast Asian regionalism, despite the confident claims of regional experts concerning its emergence. Consequently, we are dealing with a body of analytic opinion, framed in terms of a specialist knowledge of the politics of the region and as such invested with an authority disported in academic and journalistic forums. This authoritative voice seeks to describe and explain the emerging patterns in regional affairs, but, more often than not, has failed to do so with either accuracy or coherence. None of this implies that there exists a single truth about regional developments and that it is only the blinkered nature of academic consensus that blinds people to it. Such a view would itself be a sign of delusion. Debates in the social sciences should properly exist as a contest of perceptions based on considered assessments of the evidence. However, the spirit of open-minded inquiry so necessary for understanding has been notably lacking in the realm of Southeast Asian studies. Indeed, the very idea of 'debate' in regional academe has become problematic. The free exchange of contending views concerning regional developments became in the course of the 1990s characterized by a refusal to consider more plausible alternative explanations because they clashed with the prevailing orthodoxy.

FASHIONABLE DELUSION

The focus of this study, then, is the observable and potentially explicable, not what is wished or willed. There are, though, two further related questions that need to be raised at this point. The first is: what is the nature of the intellectual orthodoxy on regional affairs that has distorted understandings of Southeast Asian international relations? The second is: what is the principal delusion that may be said to underpin this orthodoxy?

The premise which informs this book is that a contradictory understanding grew up around the various security dilemmas that ASEAN was originally designed to address. Over time, ASEAN's approach came to exercise an attraction to an eclectic assortment of scholarly opinion both within Southeast Asia and beyond, ranging from soft-realists and liberal-institutionalists on the one hand to post-Marxists, constructivists and post-colonialists on the other. This broad and inclusive church gained particular currency in the immediate post-Cold War era, developing into an orthodox understanding of regional relations where ASEAN's unique style of multilateral diplomacy became seductively modish. This consensus, we argue, was based on a delusion.

An investigation of the recent history of Southeast Asian international relations, in this respect, reveals an interesting case study in teleology. This teleology held that the post-Cold War world would witness increasing global interdependence based on multilateral cooperation in which the consensual practices of consultation and dialogue would forge shared regional values and identities that would render established patterns of inter-state relations redundant. Most notably, during the 1990s, a time in which theories of multilateralism, constructivism and strategic culture proliferated in the previously theoretically bereft study of international relations, ASEAN's international profile grew on the back of its appeal as the prototype of such forms of regional, economic and security cooperation. This fashionable delusion, however, obscured major fault lines in ASEAN's theory and practice that misread its past, overestimated its capacity to manage the region's affairs and ignored or underestimated new threats and challenges to the regional order.

ASEAN came into being in 1967, after a series of faltering attempts at regional security cooperation among the non-communist states of Southeast Asia. Few hopes were invested in ASEAN's formation. Its agenda was vague and its direction uncertain. As Singapore foreign minister S. Rajaratnam observed after an ASEAN ministerial meeting in 1974: 'You may recall at the first meeting in 1967, when we had to draft our communiqué, it was a very difficult problem of trying to say nothing in about ten pages . . . we ourselves, having launched ASEAN were not quite sure where it was going, or whether it was going anywhere at all' (quoted in *Business Times* 1992, 15 January). The Association was rescued from this road to oblivion by a series of fortuitous international events that would change the security dispensation in Southeast Asia and boost ASEAN's profile.

The first major turning point was the enunciation of the so-called 'Nixon doctrine' in 1969 (Kissinger 1995, pp. 707–9). Looking towards the day on which the United States extricated itself from its Indochinese quagmire, President Richard Nixon sought to clarify the outlines of future American foreign policy in the post-Vietnam era. Recognizing that it could no longer expect to impose its will on the character of emerging states (like Vietnam) Nixon, nevertheless, reiterated that the US retained global interests and would be prepared to back those states prepared to defend themselves against the threat of Communism, not through direct intervention, but through less direct forms of military, economic and diplomatic support. It was this doctrine that provided for the continuing, but less intrusive, commitment to maintaining its interests in Asia that afforded ASEAN the space to define the rudiments of a regional consensus after 1969 defined primarily as a shared resistance to Communism, which, at this time, was diagnosed as the common root of internal instability.

The Nixon doctrine proved to be a more viable basis for the US to build stability in Asia. The semi-detached US security presence enabled the still fledgling ASEAN states to pursue domestic consolidation and regional cooperation largely free from the direct interference of the major powers outside Southeast Asia. Thus, from 1971 onwards, ASEAN's diplomatic profile as a cohesive regional security organization began to take root. Yet it was the reformulated nature of the American security commitment to Southeast Asia that formed the vital backdrop to nearly two decades of unparalleled political stability and economic growth in the region which permitted ASEAN the illusion of international significance: an illusion, as this study will seek to demonstrate, that it was not necessarily in the interests of the benign American hegemon to dispel.

The second pivotal event from which ASEAN benefited was the ending of the Cold War. At the dawn of the 1990s, having outlasted the Soviet Union and experiencing rising levels of prosperity that appeared to challenge conventional, and – given the then downturn in the US and European economies – apparently moribund western models of growth, the collapse of the bipolar world enabled ASEAN politicians and scholars to promulgate what they argued was a distinctively Asian approach to economic and political development. The years of the so-called 'economic miracle' in the Asia–Pacific between 1985 and 1995 had, in the minds of some observers, propelled Asian states into the 'first rank' and engendered 'greater cultural self-confidence' (Kausikan 1993, p. 32). According to one ASEAN scholar–bureaucrat, 'East and Southeast Asian countries are increasingly conscious of their own civilizations and tend to locate the sources of their economic success in their own distinctive traditions and institutions' (ibid., p. 34).

Growing regional self-confidence consequently displaced the long-term impact of the Nixon doctrine as the chief explanation for the region's success. A uniquely Asian cultural disposition perfected by ASEAN's regional diplomacy over the previous 25 years, it was now maintained, rather than economic growth and political stability engendered by a benign American hegemony, foreign direct investment and access to global markets, had established regional stability and order. Those who extolled the supposedly harmonious and consensual practices of the Asian way believed that the character of Pacific Asia's political culture would provide the basis for a regional dynamic that would solidify East Asian cohesiveness. ASEAN, it was asserted, would evolve into a 'security community' in which conflict amongst its membership would be banished through the creation of a diplomatic milieu of multilateral arrangements in which regional problems 'either do not arise or can be readily managed' (Leifer 1995, p. 34).

Furthermore, the success of ASEAN's diplomacy would be the cornerstone of a new Pacific order in the twenty-first century (see Naisbett 1995). Pundits predicted that a confident and prosperous East Asian region would occupy an increasingly dominant place in the global trading and political order (see Chia 1994; Bell, R. 1996). The forces of regionalization would be extended through pan-Asian forums like the ARF and AFTA, which would consolidate regional confidence as former or market-oriented communist regimes in China, Pacific Russia, Vietnam, Laos and Cambodia experienced the beneficial consequences of foreign direct investment and export-driven growth.[5] Through such means regional trade and cooperation would be further facilitated. The utopian vision mapped out for the region emphasized Pacific Asia's seemingly effortless capacity to sustain economic growth founded on its distinctively shared regional values.

It is here that we see the seeds of delusion being sown. For the curious Asian hiatus, extending from the end of the Cold War to the financial crisis of 1997 and beyond, provided an attractive, but ultimately deceptive, locale upon which an eclectic mix of analytical perspectives – ranging from pan-Asianists, post-modernists, cultural conservatives, constructivists, multilateralists and strategic culturalists – alighted. Liberated from the constricting straitjacket of Cold War power politics, many analysts saw in the ASEAN region both the practical validation of their methodological preferences and the harbinger of the future regionalization of the global order. The 'ASEAN way', therefore, united various shades of opinion into a fashionable orthodoxy. But it was an orthodoxy built on contradiction.

Officially endorsed opinion emerging from Southeast Asia during the 'miracle' decade often explicitly sought to contrast the distinctively consensual and managerial approach to problem solving of ASEAN to what was deemed the rigid, legalistic, treaty-oriented, confrontational power political norms of western diplomacy (Mahbubani 1995a, pp. 105–20; Sopiee 1992, p. 131). This thesis found willing adherents beyond Asia, most notably in western academia itself, which conceived the attractively diverse multilaterism of 'Asian way' regional cooperation within the broader context of the rejection of realist, Eurocentric, inter-state and balance of power ideas that were held to characterize the western strategic–diplomatic process. Thus a curious intellectual concurrence evolved during the 1990s that brought together western liberals and post-modernists on the one hand, with an assortment of autocratic Asian governments on the other, that came to exert a powerful hold on analytic opinion about regional developments.

Yet, in practice, the hopes invested in the ASEAN way (both by Southeast Asian governments in the post-Cold War and by their western academic followers) as the forerunner of a new and excitingly different form of international diplomacy suffered from a gap between rhetorical aspiration and the underlying realities of Southeast Asian diplomacy. ASEAN's origins did not, in fact, spring from any deep commitment to the principles of inclusive multilateral cooperation, but from very traditional security concerns to stabilize inter-state relations in Southeast Asia and the pursuit of internal consolidation (Leifer 1989, p. 4). In particular, the formation of ASEAN was premised on two overriding security issues: (1) to present a unified anti-communist front towards the spread of Communism across Indochina, and (2) to lock Indonesia, the biggest and most powerful state in Southeast Asia, into a diplomatic system that had at its core the recognition of accepted sovereign borders, thereby curbing its destabilizing ambitions which sought territorial expansion through a policy of 'confrontation' with its neighbours (Leifer 1996, p. 13). These concerns represented a thoroughly 'realist' understanding of international relations with its emphasis on Cold War imperatives and a security commitment to maintaining a regional balance of power that reflected distinctly Eurocentric understandings of a 'concert' of powers. The fashionable orthodoxy that arose in the post-Cold War years obscured or ignored the fact that ASEAN was essentially a supranational arrangement that functioned as a mechanism to strengthen the new states of Southeast Asia. Over time, this realist commitment to the state as the major actor in a local concert of powers was conflated with an anti-realist framework that extolled multilateral interdependence, shared norms and the cooperative management of a 'security community' (Acharya 1991, p. 176). The post-modernism of the early 1990s that embraced somewhat incoherently both ethical relativism and western self-loathing further enhanced the capacity of Southeast Asian scholars and diplomats to disregard the underlying realist logic of ASEAN. This approach rejected the ethnocentric and patronizingly Orientalist assumptions assumed to be embedded in western political discourse while elevating the distinctive diplomatic and strategic norms of non-western cultures (Booth and Trood 1999; Krause and Williams 1997; Krause 1999; Robison 1996; Turner 1994).

However, as the rhetoric of regionalization reached its zenith both in official discourse and in the groves of academe, the onset of the Asian financial crisis rendered these same 'norms' redundant. The ASEAN norms of consensus, harmony, multilateralism and regional managerialism now stood condemned for promoting corruption, cronyism and opaque government–business dealings that had engendered regional meltdown. Why had ASEAN's allegedly 'unique from of multilateralism' whose 'remarkable economic dynamism' constituted the basis for a progressive 'culture of cooperation' (Leifer 1996, pp. 53–7) suddenly mutated into a feeble concert of imitation states incapable of addressing the effects of the regional economic crisis and its devastating political consequences? At the turn of the new century ASEAN was revealed as an organization of political, economic and security contradictions. The Association's purpose, it seemed, had been to shield fundamental differences amongst its membership from public scrutiny under the guise of consensus. It succeeded in this somewhat limited objective for most of the Cold War. However, the post-meltdown era, where defensive ethnic and religious fundamentalism represented a growing response at the sub-state level to the uncertainties generated by the processes of globalization at the supra-state level, exposed the unsustainable nature of the Asian Cold

War model of building national and regional resilience. And what sustained this delusion was fashionable orthodoxy.

THE DELUSION OF DETACHMENT

The possible reasons why certain explanations of political development in Asia meshed into an 'accepted' orthodoxy are likely to be many and varied. But the question remains, what was delusive about this orthodoxy? To address this area of debate will help provide some understanding about whether there exists a fundamental delusion that accounts for the formation of this orthodoxy. While the prevailing orthodoxy was a composite of diffuse influences, nevertheless this study evinces that it had one overriding characteristic, namely, that its adherents believed it represented a neutral and objective understanding of Asia. It was a delusion of detachment.

Effort in most scholarly disciplines is devoted to the attempt to establish rigorously formulated intellectual positions based on investigation across the range of available source material and the development of analytical frameworks in order to generate theories and arguments that appear to accord with a comprehensive reading of the evidence. This is, of course, exactly how academic inquiry should proceed. To achieve knowledge, however, a theory can only provide a testable hypothesis. All explanations can be improved upon or overturned by new and maybe better data and/or the development of new interpretations. For any mode of explanation to have meaning it must be refutable, or, to use Karl Popper's formulation, it must be 'falsifiable' (Popper 2002, pp. 120–32). A vibrant field of inquiry is, therefore, characterized by a continuously evolving debate between different, contending arguments.

Nevertheless, the danger is that, in attempting to work out dispassionate positions through the weighing up of facts and figures, this fixes the limits of 'acceptable' knowledge about any given subject. The nature of inquiry renders the analyst prone to the conviction that they see things 'as they really are' and come to believe that they purvey the only accurate, balanced and neutral assessment of events. Once a broad network of opinion accepts a particular interpretation as the most balanced and accurate, it can promote concurrence and this can result in the 'hardening of the categories' where all attempts to challenge a settled paradigm are consciously ignored or dismissed as unreasonable or partisan (see Makinda 2001, p. 319). The orthodoxy becomes the only valid explanation and the single truth (Jones and Smith, 2003, pp. 131–41).

A variety of factors facilitate the delusion of detachment. The condition might arise from a bland empiricism that holds that 'facts speak for themselves' and require no further embellishment. Or it might derive from the cynical view that a balanced assessment results from taking a middle point between two contending arguments. Alternatively, it may stem from the attempt to apply the principles of rational scientific method to the landscape of the social, an approach particularly attractive to American political science, which classically presumes that, once the 'dependent' and 'independent' variables are settled, situations will yield objective results (Walt 1999, p. 12). Additionally, there may be notions that appeal to a more post-modern mentality. For example, ambivalently drawing from the writings of the conservative political philosopher, Carl Schmitt, who argued that the concept of the political required the friend/enemy dyad, which demands an adversarial 'other', many post-modern thinkers and critical theorists convince themselves that they can unmask the 'othering' process and are thereby endowed with a unique sense of impartiality and independence (Schmitt 1996, pp. 19–79).

In all these instances, commentators of whatever methodological provenance persuade themselves that they see events independently and without prejudice. Collectively, this adds up to the conviction that they can stand outside 'the political'. Consequently, analysts conclude that they are merely neutral observers who exist above the fray of conceptual conflict between contested viewpoints. Having transcended all the difficult epistemological questions, they see little need to justify their own 'neutral' and 'objective' positions, and in this state of grace feel able to pronounce with Olympian detachment on those who challenge their objectivity. The effect of this delusion of detachment, evident in the theory and practice of scholarship in the Asia–Pacific, has been to close down avenues for debate while denouncing counter-arguments that disturb settled opinion as polemical.[6]

But as writers and philosophers from Orwell to Schmitt have noted, no-one can stand outside the political (Orwell 1948, pp. 1261–8). To argue that the contestability of viewpoints in the academic realm is somehow uncouth and that politics should be exiled from the humanities and social sciences is itself a political statement. To assert that there is a neutral understanding of events is inherently subjective. To maintain that only you can unmask the 'othering' process is merely to 'other' those you deem to be guilty of 'othering' themselves. To accuse someone of being polemical is itself an act of polemicism. In Schmitt's words:

> Above all the polemical character determines the use of the word political regardless of whether the adversary is designated as nonpolitical (in the sense of harmless), or vice versa if one wants to disqualify or denounce him as political in order to portray oneself as nonpolitical (in the sense of purely scientific, purely moral, purely juristic, purely aesthetic, purely economic, on the basis of similar purities) and thereby superior. (Schmitt 1996, pp. 31–2)

One aspect of this delusion that came to predominate in Asian political affairs was that it united an amalgam of scholar-bureaucrats operating on behalf of a variety of authoritarian governments, whose job it was to propa-gate the virtues of the ASEAN way, and western scholars who functioned in ostensibly liberal environments. How these two seemingly very different bedfellows came to share a common agenda is one of the more peculiar aspects of the regional delusion. The dilemma for those scholars working in the auto-cratic political arrangements of Southeast Asia in the 1990s is one readily familiar to anyone who possesses any experience of living and working in an illiberal polity. It is the dilemma articulated by writers like Czeslaw Milosz, who, in *The Captive Mind*, described how intellectuals in newly Stalinized Eastern Europe after World War II were systematically worn down by author-itarian duress and who, despite their independence of mind and spirit, were eventually subordinated to serve the formal goals of the state (Milosz 1990, pp. 191–222). Ultimately, the intellectual predicament in Eastern Europe or Southeast Asia was the same – conform or be crushed.

Less easy to appreciate, and far more curious, was the mentality of the western scholar of Asian politics who faced no such dilemma. Their path to delusion, unlike those who existed in the 'guided democracies' of the Asia–Pacific, was self-chosen. Comprehending western intellectualism's encounter with Asian authoritarianism is less to do with Milosz's captive mind, and more to do with Mark Lilla's identification of *The Reckless Mind* (2001). Western academics enjoy the luxury of being able to take extreme or outlandish intellectual positions without having to accept responsibility for them, and certainly not incurring any of their consequences. In this context, the reckless mind is attracted to the 'Lure of Syracuse' – the yearning of the intellectual to be taken seriously, to have influence, to be relevant, to make a difference. In other words, to have power (Lilla 2001, pp. 193–216).

The attraction of some western thinkers, who benefit and flourish under a liberal dispensation, to illiberal solutions is not peculiar to thinking about Asia. However, the concept of 'Asia' has traditionally presented particular problems for western social and political thought, the Asian 'other' often seducing a variety of European commentators into sympathizing with forms of Oriental despotism (Jones 2001a, pp. 1–13, 143–203). The concurrence of thinking that emerged between western analysts and ASEAN scholar-bureaucrats offers an interesting continuation of this phenomenon. Those that embraced the ASEAN way could expect to be lured to Syracuse, enabling themselves to feel empowered within an officially endorsed consensus that embraced scholars in sub-ministerial meetings and confer-ences and a patronage network that could dispense jobs, grants and other forms of preferment.

The consequence of this contract with Syracuse, however, was a severe form of groupthink. It reduced academic debate on Asian developments to a self-perpetuating consensus that disallowed dissenting viewpoints, and at best permitted only the cautious nuancing of received wisdom. Closed scholarship occasions sclerosis and the inability to think or move outside self-censoring boundaries. It is a regressive construct that loses the ability to test its ruling assumptions through sceptical inquiry. Indeed, 'scepticism' is the enemy of the paradigm. The result is an orthodoxy that ceases to be a theory with explanatory value. Rather it is a self-reinforcing ideological preference that mistakes its own belief in balance and neutrality for a valid methodology.

The irony is that when any mode of thought, be it Asia–Pacific studies or the wider study of international relations theory, becomes closed in this manner it becomes irrelevant to practice. When a discipline suffers from a misguided belief in its own neutrality it becomes delusional, mistaking its own relevance and importance. Eventually, it stands revealed as the provenance of a sect that talks only to itself, yet hovers on the edges of the *classa politica* acting as pliable supporting counsellors to political agendas, usually in the service of authoritarian regimes, but losing all pretence to rigorous inquiry.

NOTES

1. A Chinese word meaning 'southern ocean'. The term commonly refers to the areas in Southeast Asia that contain significant numbers of ethnic Chinese, most of whom, in countries like Malaysia, Singapore and Indonesia, are descendants of migrants from the southern provinces of China, and sometimes also known as the 'overseas Chinese'.
2. According to the current compendium, *Diagnostic and Statistical Manual of Mental Disorders* (latest edition DSM-IV) published by the American Psychiatric Association, the formal definition of delusion is 'false belief based on incorrect inference about external reality that is sustained despite what almost everyone else believes and despite what constitutes incontrovertible and obvious proof or evidence to the contrary'.
3. Delusions of grandeur are 'mistaken beliefs of being important persons'; delusions of persecution are 'mistaken beliefs that others are plotting to harm or destroy you'; delusions of reference are 'mistaken beliefs that give special significance to unrelated events' (see Huffman, Venoy, Williams 1987, p. 552). These are only a few of the diagnosed conditions of delusion, amongst many others such as delusional parasitosis, an erroneous belief of infestation by parasites or bacterial infections (see Freinhar 1984, pp. 47–53).
4. The concept of groupthink is a useful tool to aid understanding of concurrence-seeking activity. Groupthink was initially developed by Irving Janis to provide a social psychological explanation for serious failures in foreign policy. Other analysts have critiqued the concept (see t'Hardt et al. 1997), suggesting that it does not sufficiently take account of the politico-bureaucratic conditions that confront decision makers faced with stressful decision-making tasks 'that have serious consequences, are unusually complex, and divisive or controversial' (Neves 2005, p. 30). Felipe Ortiagão Neves argues that the key idea behind groupthink is 'collective, stress relieving uncritical concurrence seeking' or 'stressed groupthink' for short (ibid., p. 33). As a criticism of the explanatory power of groupthink to fully explicate failures in political decision making these arguments have some force. Accounting for 'intellectual' failures is, however, likely to conform far more to the original conception of groupthink as envisaged by Janis. Scholars are rarely challenged by collective stressful decision making. The stresses, such as they are, in the academic realm that lead to concurrence seeking are more likely to be self-induced through a susceptibility to peer pressure resulting

in a generalized timidity in questioning fashionable orthodoxy. Concurrence seeking in academia may in these respects be reinforced by deference to dominant figures in a particular discipline or the methodological preferences of leading journals, along with a predisposition to be bureaucratically guided towards officially endorsed goals and agendas through the grant-giving machinery. All these factors can provide powerful incentives towards concurrence, rewarding with financial and professional preferment those who conform to the orthodoxy, while punishing, by exclusion, those who dissent. For a profession that supposedly is governed by the ethos of scrutinizing given assumptions, this is deeply paradoxical. It is, in part, aspects of this paradox that this book is intended to address.

5. AFTA envisaged the creation of a common effective preferential tariff scheme of between 0 per cent and 5 per cent across the region. In order to facilitate a regional free trade area, ASEAN Economic Ministers in Phuket, Thailand in 1994 agreed to implement the scheme by 2003. As yet this has not happened.

6. The marginalization, exclusion or denunciation of arguments because they are allegedly 'polemical' (i.e. challenge the orthodoxy) is something that it is possible to encounter on a regular basis in the field of Southeast Asian studies, notably in the journal review process. For example, one commentator asserts that criticism of ASEAN may be credible so long as it does not degenerate 'into polemics', though what is meant by polemics is, as is often the case in the rhetoric of Southeast Asian international relations, rarely spelt out (see Acharya 2003, p. 336).

1. The delusions of Aseanology: exploring the Sovietology of Southeast Asian studies

It may seem curious to initiate a study of post-Cold War Southeast Asia, and the wider relationship with East Asia, with a comparison with the former Union of Soviet Socialist Republics (USSR). On the surface their respective geopolitical and historical settings would seem to offer no basis for comparative evaluation, yet a similarity does exist, not in any straight like-for-likeness, but in the way each area was studied by scholars. For what characterized inquiries into both areas was a prevailing academic ideology that deeply influenced the way that scholarship was conducted.

The potential for comparison becomes more fruitful when one considers that within the space of 10 years both subjects experienced a crisis that undermined many former assumptions that held sway in these academic areas. In Cold War Soviet studies, the crisis was the sudden disintegration of the Soviet Union and the collapse of Communism in Europe between 1989 and 1991, which ended the Cold War. In Southeast Asia, it was the financial crisis of 1997/98 and its political ramifications that exposed the 'Asian miracle' and the prospects for the much-vaunted 'Pacific Century'. In both cases the crises were largely unforeseen within the disciplinary mainstream that studied the political, security, economic and international relations of each area. Analysts failed to predict or even identify the causes that provoked the cataclysms that afflicted their respective fields of inquiry. Therefore it is possible to compare the way both disciplinary inquiries approached their objects of study and consider why they overlooked the underlying determining processes and practices.

This chapter will first attempt to outline the shortcomings that were seen to afflict Sovietology in the light of the end of the Cold War and trace its similarities to and differences from the study of the domestic and international politics of contemporary Southeast Asian studies. The intention will then be to explore the implications of these comparative failings for the understanding of regional affairs and the general social science endeavour to 'explain, predict and test' the practices of illiberal political systems (Popper 1959, p. 133).

In the first instance, it is necessary to define what is meant by Southeast

Asian studies and Sovietology, respectively. To define Southeast Asian studies, in particular, is not without difficulty when the term 'Asia' is itself such an amorphous and ambiguous idea, expanding as it does from the Bosporus to the Pacific Ocean. Additionally, as with any field of inquiry, Southeast Asian studies is many faceted. In the social sciences and humanities alone one can approach with a bias towards political science, economics, sociology, anthropology or history. For ease of comprehension this analysis will use the term 'Southeast Asia' to denote the geographical area encompassed by members of the Association of Southeast Asian Nations (ASEAN), namely, Brunei, Cambodia, Indonesia, Laos, Malaysia, Myanmar, Philippines, Singapore, Thailand and Vietnam. 'Southeast Asian studies' will be used to refer to the scholarly community that focused on the contemporary politics, security and international relations of the region primarily in the years after the end of the Cold War.

Similarly, defining 'Sovietology' is equally difficult since it embraced not just those who were concerned with domestic Soviet politics but a spectrum of analytical opinion interested in the wider issues affecting superpower relations during the Cold War. Therefore the term 'Sovietology' will be applied in its broadest sense to encompass those specifically with an interest in Soviet politics and foreign policy as well as those who focused on the general security implications of Cold War confrontation and who themselves obviously had to develop reasonably sophisticated views about the Soviet Union and its conduct. Although the term 'Sovietology' may seem rather broad and complex, the key point is that Soviet specialists themselves accepted the term and, in the aftermath of the Cold War, conducted assessments into what was considered the relatively poor performance of the discipline in terms of adequately comprehending the myriad forces that led to the demise of the Soviet Union. In 1993, Peter Rutland published a critique, 'Sovietology: notes for a post-mortem', which identified a series of problems inherent in Soviet studies. From this it is possible to distil a number of shared characteristics to illustrate the epistemological shortcomings that confronted the study of ASEAN.

FAILING TO PREDICT THE FUTURE

The starting point for any assessment of Sovietology and Southeast Asian studies is simple: that regional specialists got their predictions wrong. Despite the resources devoted to the study of the Soviet Union the vast majority of Cold War commentators failed to forecast the collapse of the Eastern bloc in Europe. Worse, their predictions before 1989 seemingly contradicted every event that subsequently happened (Rutland 1993, p. 109). American graduate

schools constructed theories of hegemonic rivalry which were developed
explicitly to anticipate change (Wohlforth 1994, p. 103), only to discover that
the change they envisioned failed to eventuate. Paul Kennedy, like many
others, postulated that the US was suffering from 'overstretch' and in decline
(see Kennedy 1989, pp. 564–92). As William Wohlforth remarked: 'The
debate focused like a laser beam on US decline, even when the Soviet Union
was entering its final stages of collapse' (Wohlforth 1994, p. 103).

Taken by surprise by the Cold War's impromptu end, scholars remained
reluctant to believe that superpower competition had resulted in victory for
one side. The belief persisted that somehow the Soviet Union had unwittingly
dissolved itself (see Kolodziej 1992a, p. 5; Lebow 1994, p. 262) rather than
imploded in the face of unsustainable rivalry. The sense was that the USSR's
demise owed nothing to any innate American superiority and that US decline
had probably been exacerbated by that very effort to contain the Soviet threat
because both superpowers had become 'overburdened by military spending'
(Booth 1991a, p. 2).

Consequently, despite the US's victory against the Soviet Union, the late
Cold War *mentalité* continued to haunt post-Cold War scholarship. In other
words, the end of the Cold War in international relationsthink merely presaged
further US decline. On the eve of the 1991 Gulf War, Ken Booth claimed,
somewhat obscurely, 'In countering talk of declinism it [the US] is actually
showing how much it had declined.' In this view, the very fact that Iraq had
invaded Kuwait proved that US deterrence had failed because Saddam
Hussein felt he could disregard western threats. Furthermore, 'the relative
decline of the United States' was 'reflected in the call for financial support
from its allies', thus proving that the US was 'neither as independent nor as
authoritative an actor as hitherto'. If war in the Gulf was to break out, Booth
posited, 'it will be the clearest signal yet of the decline of US power in the
region; the use of force will demonstrate that the US lacks power'. Indeed,
Booth further asserted: 'Some if not all Americans know that a conflict against
war-bloodied Iraq is not likely to be a "three day turkey shoot" ' (Booth 1991b,
pp. xii–xiii).

In one respect, Booth was right. The land war was a four day turkey shoot.
In all other respects, we now know these prophecies to be entirely wrong. The
emphatic American-led victory in the Gulf war merely underlined how far the
United States stood unequalled as a military superpower and engine for world
economic growth. Yet the misunderstanding of the nature and dynamism of
American power also contributed to the misreading of power relations elsewhere in the world, particularly in Asia, for if US power was declining, the
'rise of Japan and Western Europe as economic superpowers marked major
milestones in international politics'. The projected growth in the political
influence of these powers intimated a 'significant shift in the international

political economy towards the Pacific Basin' (Booth 1991a, p. 2). This shift, it was contended prior to 1997, was one that would presage the formation of 'an axis of power, wealth, knowledge and culture' that was 'likely to shape world history as decisively as the North Atlantic Community has for the last several centuries' (Perry 1985, p. 41).

The governing paradigm of international relations theory, like western government itself, needed reinvention in the light of this change 'in the structure and balance of economic power' (Bosworth 1991, p. 113) The impressive growth rates in the Asia–Pacific, evident for the best part of two decades (see World Bank 1993; Wong 1977) compared favourably with the economic sluggishness in Europe and North America in the immediate post-Cold War era. The informal, consensus-oriented relationships within and among Southeast Asian states helped smooth the way for harmonious economic and political development. In contrast, the otiose individualism and rule-bound governance of western societies were seen to produce welfarism, stagnation and moral decay (see Kausikan 1993; Mahbubani 1994a, 1994b, 1995a, pp. 105–10). Added to this ASEAN itself was seen as an authentic survivor of the Cold War. Having both overcome the trauma of the US military withdrawal from the region after 1975 and outlasted the Soviet colossus reflected regional resilience and lent weight to the image of a tidy Cold War *fin de siècle* that announced the end of European and American dominance and the beginning of an Asian Age (see Naisbett 1995).

As with the collapse of Soviet power, we know with the benefit of hindsight that this optimistic prognosis for the region failed to anticipate the devastating economic meltdown of 1997–98. Analysts initially maintained that the meltdown was merely a blip. As the blip evolved into a fully fledged recession the various miracle, tiger and dragon economies of the Asia–Pacific came to require one. Currencies, together with stock markets, imploded. No less remarkable was the degeneration of ASEAN's much-vaunted consensual style of diplomacy into bickering and mutual recrimination. Internal tensions rose and regimes tottered. In Indonesia, the largest and most important state in the regional grouping, an unstable coalition and a disintegrating periphery replaced Suharto's kleptocratic New Order that had ruled the archipelago between 1966 and 1998.

Clearly, the collective inability of Southeast Asian studies to recognize the fissures in the pre-meltdown regional order suggests a discipline suffering problems analogous to those of Sovietology, the most obvious similarity being a shared lack of insight into the region, culminating in a woeful record of predictive ineptitude. However, to attain a more complete insight into the deluded worlds of Sovietology and Southeast Asian studies, it is necessary to examine the reasons for their systemic failure.

SURFACE IMPRESSIONS

The preoccupation with the newsworthy rather than historical research into long-term trends represented an additional analytical weakness in Sovietology. During the 1980s the obsession with contemporary events seduced scholars 'into the role of media pundits and soothsayers' which 'left paltry incentives for careful empirical research' (Rutland 1993, p. 112). Particularly disturbing was the overconcentration on the role and personality of the somewhat inept Mikhail Gorbachev, who was elevated as the efficient cause of the USSR's transformation.[1] As Rutland notes, Gorbachev was neither 'genius, arch-villain, nor superhero' but merely an 'above average product of the *nomen-klatura*' who wished to preserve the Soviet system (ibid., p. 112). Yet, as a result of the media's preoccupation with celebrity, 'Gorbymania' commentators ignored other more critical factors that accounted for the USSR's slide into oblivion. Analysts largely overlooked the fateful legacy of the war in Afghanistan that overstretched Russian resources and eroded public confidence in both the political elite and socialist internationalism. Likewise, Sovietologists underestimated the impact that the Chernobyl nuclear accident had in stimulating popular dissent, which re-made *glasnost* 'from a sterile political campaign into a genuine movement for change' (ibid., p. 110).

Southeast Asian studies evinced a similar infatuation with short-termism, the object of contemporary enthusiasm here being, not a personality but an apparent economic and political phenomenon, the 'Asian way'. Observers became transfixed with what was seen as 'one of the most successful experiments in regionalism in the developing world' (Acharya 1993, p. 3), which would provide 'a model for emulation by other states in Southeast Asia' (Chalmers 1997, p. 53). This was a widespread, but highly tendentious, view of regional developments. In this respect, Southeast Asian studies shared Sovietology's tendency to overlook deeply embedded political, economic and cultural tensions in favour of fashionably current anti-Orientalist media and academic approaches.

The governing assumption pervading much commentary upon ASEAN during the 1980s and 1990s was that the grouping had been making steady progress towards the achievement of a 'security community' (Acharya 1991, p. 176). ASEAN had, it was contended, developed shared norms of diplomatic behaviour that were 'operationalized into a framework of regional interaction' based on 'a high degree of discreetness, informality, pragmatism, expediency and non-confrontational bargaining styles' (Acharya 1997a, p. 329). The ASEAN model was seen to offer 'the prospect of long-term stable peace in the region' (Chalmers 1997, p. 53) This had already provided the platform for the 'spectacularly successful' economic growth that so mesmerized the scholarly community (see Krasner 1996, p. 123).

If, in Rutland's assessment of Sovietology, Gail Sheehy's biography of Gorbachev, *The Man Who Changed the World* (1990) represented the acme of misplaced intellectual enthusiasm, a similar uncritical spirit influenced quasi-academic potboilers dedicated to Southeast Asian growth like Jim Rohwer's *Asia Rising* (1996), John Naisbett's *Megatrends Asia* (1995), and François Godement's *The New Asian Renaissance* (1996). If Gorbachev was the precursor to an optimistic vision of Soviet renewal, the ASEAN way, by 1996, was the outward and visible sign of a new multilateral economic and political order. The serendipitous conjunction of market economics with specifically Asian values of thrift, harmony and consensus encouraged both economic interdependence and innovative multilateral security practices. So, while the end of the Cold War had led to disorder elsewhere, in Southeast Asia, analysts effused, 'it has led to increased domestic tranquillity and regional order' (Acharya 1997b, p. 310).

Such understandings, however, were superficial and fundamentally flawed readings of the underlying dynamics of Southeast Asian affairs. The Sovietology of Southeast Asian Studies had exaggerated the economic performance and political stability of the region. It consistently understated the nature and extent of bilateral tensions and intra-state fragility that existed beneath the surface of regional tranquillity, and which was to so rupture that surface calm in the wake of financial meltdown in 1997 (see Tan 2000a, p. 1). In the same way that unbounded faith in Gorbachev's abilities to lead the Soviet Union out of its Brezhnevite sloth militated against scepticism, so euphoria about the coming 'Pacific Century' helped foster an intellectual environment inimical to empirical investigations and the rigorous evaluation of assumptions that might have yielded a less attractive picture.

Just as the fixation with Gorbachev blinded Sovietologists to the parlous Soviet condition, the beguiling combination of exponential growth with equity and apparently harmonious regional relations inhibited critical examination of the Southeast Asian political economy. Like Sovietology's 'Gorbymaniacs', students of Southeast Asia became cheerleaders for ASEAN. Instead of exposing the limitations of Asian financial and business practice, academe directed its attention to discovering the secret of the miracle economies, and the lessons to be derived from the 'Asian way' (see World Bank 1993, pp. 1–25).

INSIDERS VERSUS OUTSIDERS

In any intellectual debate there is bound to exist a tension between the received wisdom of accumulated opinion and those who seek to question ruling assumptions. The academic profession relies on this tension to give it meaning by providing it with the capacity to achieve progress in knowledge and under-standing through argument. In theory, intellectual life is congenitally disputa-tious. This requires mutual recognition that participants in 'conceptual combat' can legitimately maintain healthy debate between arguments that derive from different knowledge, different perspectives, different evidence selection and different experience (Baldwin 1997, p. 11).

In practice, however, scholars often seek conditional 'resolution' by aiming for a synthesis of antagonistic viewpoints. Sometimes the search for synthesis can lead to concurrence seeking, which subsequently inhibits the free exchange of ideas. Concurrence mutates into consensus. Consensus is taken as resolution, that in turn announces the closure of debate. Thereby the conjunc-tion of a powerful academic consensus can effectively silence dissenting voices. Those who seek to challenge the consensus are dismissed as maver-icks. The act of questioning the orthodoxy creates a *prima facie* case for marginalization and official suppression. From the perspective of an increas-ingly bureaucratized social science in many western countries that in effect can have their research agendas dictated through the major and often govern-ment-sponsored grant-giving agencies, the idea of healthy scepticism, once considered the *sine qua non* of dispassionate investigation, is dismissed as mere polemic. This worrying practice occurs in the physical sciences as much as the humanities and social sciences (see Waldmen 2000). In the 1980s and 1990s, it came to define both Sovietology and Southeast Asian studies.

In any discipline there are those whose work in hindsight affords a more accurate interpretation of its object of concern. Given the difficulty of forecast-ing events in the social sciences, the issue is not, as Rutland argues with regard to Sovietology, who accurately forecast the demise of the USSR but 'Who was asking the right questions?' (Rutland 1993, p. 110). William Wohlforth, for example, acknowledges the writings of sociologist Randall Collins whose examination of the potential for international change led him from the 1970s to predict the collapse of the USSR from geographical overstretch and resul-tant institutional exhaustion (Collins 1978, pp. 1–34, 1986). Likewise, Rutland singles out Zbigniew Brzezinski, Alexander Shtromas, Morton Kaplan, Richard Burks and A.A. Fedoseyev as analysts who could legitimately lay claim to having got it more or less right (Rutland 1993, p. 111). Brzezinski argued consistently from 1962 that the Soviet system was unreformable and therefore inherently brittle (Brzezinski 1962, 1966, 1976). Shtromas and Burks, meanwhile, identified the creeping political and bureaucratic break-down of central Communist Party authority (Rutland 1993, p. 113).

These writers, however, represented a small handful who went against the grain of conventional thinking. Interestingly, Shtromas and Kaplan's edited volume, *The Soviet Union and the Challenge of the Future* (1988), one of the very few texts to foresee the collapse of Soviet power in 1989–91, was the

result of a conference sponsored by the Unification Church. Somewhat worryingly for the social sciences, as Rutland observed, it would appear that 'the
Moonies got it right when the CIA, Brookings, RAND, Harvard, Columbia
and the rest got it wrong' (Rutland 1993, p. 111).

But why did these analysts who successfully identified the fault-lines in
the Soviet system reside at the disciplinary margins? Partly, this was because
none of them were, strictly speaking, Sovietologists. Rather, they were for
the most part specialists in Eastern Europe. More precisely, in the case of
Brzezinksi, Shtromas, Fedoseyev and others who expressed doubts about the
Soviet Union's long-term viability, like Vladimir Bukovsky, were themselves exiles from Communist Eastern Europe. While *émigré* scholars as a
whole did not necessarily achieve any greater accuracy in terms of forecast-
ing the end of the Soviet Union (Krasnov 1988, pp. 387–9), the discipline
often denied their insights into the Soviet system through the persistent
dismissal of their views by established academics in the west (Rutland,
1993, p. 112). Ken Booth's disquisition on the difficulty of area studies illustrates how easy it was to disparage *émigré* scholarship. Area specialists,
Booth opined,

> should not be listened to uncritically. This is especially the case when an area falls
> into the hands of a particular group with deep emotional commitments, such as the
> way US sovietology fell into the hands of Eastern European *émigrés* after World
> War II . . . Area specialists (other than *émigrés*) usually have the reputation of being
> smitten by the country or region which they study. This is a justifiable warning in
> some cases, but even where it is there is much to be said for having one's own
> nationals explaining with conviction the outlook of those foreigners with who one
> has to deal. (Booth 1987, p. 49)

We might, of course, dispute Booth's characterization of Sovietology as
having been dominated by *émigrés* when in fact they were marginalized. We
can also lament the fact that Booth and his ilk did not pay more attention to
what East European exiles actually said about the underlying state of the
Soviet empire. However, what emerges clearly in such remarks is how one set
of views became discursively privileged over others. *Émigré* scholars were
deemed incapable of objective judgement because of their presumed animus
toward their object of study. From this rationalistic perspective a lived experience of Communism inexorably poisoned a true, objective, neutral understanding. Therefore their views could be dismissed as in any way constituting
part of the national 'outlook of foreigners' that required explaining to western
policy makers. Their assessments could be discounted as mere distortions
caused by living and working (and sometimes no doubt suffering) under a
system they despised. The consequence was often that uncritical evaluations
of the authoritarian Soviet system were favoured in western scholarship over

judicious scepticism, which, as Booth's comments indicate, invariably incurred academically licensed censure as excessively partisan. This reflected a curious inversion of the insider–outsider syndrome in academic debate. Those thought to possess empathy, but less direct knowledge of the Soviet Union and Eastern Europe, were bestowed with reputations as authoritative 'insiders'. Yet those with direct experience of those very same communist societies were judged to be intellectually compromised and thus considered as 'outsiders'.

We should, perhaps, be grateful to those like Booth for articulating openly the, albeit misplaced, assumptions that informed international relations scholarship during the Cold War. One will find no similar candour in Southeast Asian studies. The failure to detect the fissures in the regional order leading up to the economic crisis of 1997 provoked little in the way of disciplinary self-examination. Conversely, Soviet studies spanned the best part of three-quarters of a century and, despite its consensus-bound deficiencies, a diversity of opinion did eventually emerge. Contending and, ultimately, prescient views did come to light even if they were not given the recognition that they should have warranted at the time.

By contrast, Pacific Rim enthusiasm, which began in the aftermath of the Vietnam war (see Cumings 1997, pp. 3–4) and reached a disciplinary crescendo between 1990 and 1997, provided even less room for contending views to emerge. Indeed, Southeast Asian studies possess an even less distinguished record for predicting the collapse of the Asian 'miracle' than Sovietology does for anticipating the end of the Cold War. In a way not dissimilar to Sovietology, those who voiced alternative interpretations of Southeast Asia's political and economic development often struggled to be heard. Between 1990 and 1997, those who questioned the dominant discourse of an unstoppable Asian growth model premised upon harmonious inter-ASEAN relationships were principally confined to the academic twilight of book reviews, working papers, unpublished dissertations and unpublishable submissions to academic journals.

In assessing the disciplinary orthodoxy that took hold of Southeast Asian studies, we must initially distinguish between criticism of the Asian growth model first promulgated by a small band of economists, and the more general avoidance of the incoherences in the political institutions of the ASEAN way. Interestingly, a number of economists disputed the view advanced by both Asian statesmen and their scholar-bureaucrats that Asian growth reflected a specifically Asian cultural disposition (see Zakaria 1994, pp. 109–13 and Mohamad and Ishihara 1995). Significantly, those who challenged the economic sustainability of the Asian growth model made some impression before the currency crisis took hold in the latter part of 1997. Paul Krugman and Alwyn Young in particular observed significant weakness in the input mobilizing model of Asia prior to 1994 (see Krugman 1994; Young 1992).

Krugman's scepticism represented the first expression of doubt concerning the sustainability of economic growth in the region of the kind officially espoused by regional governments, regional scholars and the World Bank in its report, *The East Asian Economic Miracle* (1993). Over the same period journals like the *Economist* and the *International Herald Tribune* and the occasional scholar like Kunio Yoshihara and Christopher Lingle (Lingle 1996; Yoshihara 1988), identified a number of problems with the Asian model of growth generally and the Southeast Asian variety in particular. These included, inter alia, long-term growth funded by short-term loans, burgeoning current account deficits, lack of financial transparency and an inadequate fiscal machinery, a speculative property boom and the uncertain future facing the ersatz economies of Southeast Asia as low cost/low value added manufacturing and financial centres ('States of denial', 1996).

Significantly, then, a small band of scholars committed to empirical rigour and not tied to Asian banks or institutions pointed to flaws in the Asian economic model. By contrast, scepticism towards an evolving ASEAN multilateralism was far more muted. Instead social scientists and international relations experts lined up to support the view that ASEAN had become the 'hub of confidence building activities and preventive diplomacy in the region' (Almonte 1997, p. 80) which offered 'the model of inter-state cooperation' that 'would be a key-building block for a new global community' (ibid., p. 90).

In the multilateral glow that initially inspired the 'New World Order', few analysts demurred from this cheery consensus. The potential ethnic, religious and intramural fault-lines in Southeast Asia received scant attention. Superficially, with the conclusion of the Cambodian peace process (1991) and the expansion of ASEAN after 1993, relations among the states of Southeast Asia appeared harmonious. Increasing regional self-confidence fuelled by high growth rates provided the platform upon which analysts erected the notion that ASEAN's successful model of cooperative security could be extended across the Pacific. Several scholars pointed to the continuation of intramural tension within the ASEAN community, suggesting for example the existence of a 'precarious balance in Singapore–Malay relations' (Huxley 1991, pp. 204–13). Nevertheless, even those who expressed mild scepticism over the new regionalism did so in deliberately ambivalent terms either in deference to local sensibilities or to avoid prosecution.

Just as the Sovietological consensus dismissed *émigré* scepticism an analogous process inhibited the emergence of contrarian views in Southeast Asian studies. The academic review process, and the grant-giving machinery, actively discounted countervailing views. Merely to question the inevitability of the Pacific Century earned reproof. To outward appearances relations among states in Southeast Asia were harmonious. They were unified in a common developmental path that was reaping the fruits of economic success. ASEAN was the focus of this unity and optimism. Increasing regional self-confidence constituted the basis upon which analysts conceived that ASEAN's successful model of cooperative security could be extended across the Pacific. However, the ramifications of the meltdown for regional order and domestic stability rapidly became apparent. Long-suppressed hostilities rapidly eroded ASEAN's outward harmony. By the end of 1998, a number of states had degenerated into bilateral feuding over the causes and consequences of the economic slide. Even the generally tame regional media considered the Association 'only marginal in warding off the worst effects of some members' economic and social collapse' (*Straits Times*, 11 December 1998).

Even more worryingly, the collapse of the miracle economies and the fracturing of ASEAN failed to generate any disciplinary introspection. The lack of any substantive body of work that critiqued existing assumptions about the region meant there was no real set of counter-arguments by which the discipline could measure its shortcomings. Therefore regional experts could move unproblematically, and with uncanny speed, from pre- to post-crisis mode with minimal self-examination. Thus pre-1997 academics who once heralded the achievements of ASEAN multilateralism shifted position accordingly, leading to a flurry of articles which, *ex post facto*, sought to expose the Association's weaknesses (see Henderson 1999; Dibb et al. 1999, pp. 5–20; Acharya 1999a, pp. 84–101; Leifer 1999, pp. 25–38; Cheeseman 1999a).

THE EMERGENCE OF TACIT CONCURRENCE

What were the forces at work that permitted a consensus to flourish in a way that inhibited the emergence of a diversity of opinion? An examination of this question again indicates a parallel between the two disciplines. One of the charges against Sovietology was that ideological polarization inhibited intellectual and predictive capacity. Each side accused the other 'of manipulating Soviet studies to serve its domestic political agenda' (Rutland 1993, p. 112) to the detriment of objective inquiry. Scholarship of a left-wing provenance set itself against what it saw as the prejudice of the right that was intent on demonizing the Soviet Union, playing down the specific historical conditions that explained the rise of Communism and why it might enjoy a wide measure of acceptance in the USSR. This view suspected right-wing politicians and scholars of wishing to impose an Anglo-American liberal democratic value system on a country that did not share these values in the first place (ibid.). Conversely, to the right, such empathetic views were the product of indulgent thinking that eschewed moral engagement by assuming that the Soviet system behaved just like any other (namely, to mediate and respond to popular demands for social betterment within its own cultural frame of reference). The ethical relativism of left-leaning Sovietologists meant they refused to see the flaws and injustices of the Soviet state that were to lead to its disintegration.

However, as Rutland observed, the notion of a simple left/right cleavage in Sovietology, while superficially attractive, is actually misleading, arguing that ideological partisanship was far less evident in contemporary Soviet studies than in many treatments of Soviet history. Rather, Sovietology rejected conflicting viewpoints, which might have yielded contested, but falsifiable, academic interpretations as biased. It instead favoured a scholarly neutrality. Thus scholars of a liberal disposition repressed their political intuitions in order to try to 'analyze the USSR in a "non-judgmental fashion" ' (ibid., p. 113). This attempted neutrality succeeded only in deflecting attention away 'from glaring inefficiencies in the Soviet system – flaws which Western Marxists and conservatives alike found it much easier to recognize' (ibid.). In other words, purported academic objectivity required the suspension of ideological difference. As a result, tacit concurrence developed across the discipline to abstain from divisive rhetoric, which ultimately shaded off into punch pulling and fence sitting.

Several egregious consequences followed from this tacit concurrence. First, it constructed informal barriers to entry for anyone who promulgated heterodox views. For new work to receive approval, scholars had to conform to these unstated rules. Second, tacit concurrence further curtailed intellectual exploration by fixing the limits of useful knowledge. This problem was most apparent where Sovietology met Cold War international studies. Here, intellectual energy focused upon 'East–West bipolarity, defined by the US–Soviet balance of terror and the confrontation of two massed armies in central Europe' (Kolodziej 1992b, p. 425). Thereby, those like Halliday could write in 1989 that the 'great contest' between the superpowers was 'permanent and global' (Halliday 1989, p. 264). By concentrating attention at the international level, the discipline largely ignored those domestic events which would have revealed a crippled Soviet economy where many of the answers for the sudden end of the USSR, and the Cold War, resided.

A similar tacit concurrence established itself in Southeast Asian studies. The Asian version of concurrence derived from the fact that the Asian economic paradigm served ideological agendas of a social democrat and economically liberal provenance in Europe and North America. For those of an interventionist disposition, the title of former President of Singapore, C.V. Devan Nair's edited volume, *Socialism That Works* (Nair 1976) best summed up the attraction of the Asian economic success story. From this perspective, state regulation of the market had promoted economic and political development from Seoul to Singapore. The state technocracy picked economic winners and established the market-friendly preconditions for long-term economic growth. At the same time, the state management of housing, health and education ensured the equitable redistribution of the economic profits. Technocratically planned development thus had the benign effect of generating growth with equity.

Reinvented socialists and Marxists, now re-described as social democrats and neo-Keynsians, ranging from Will Hutton (1995) and Anthony Giddens (1998) in Britain, to Richard Robison (1996) and Mark Latham (1998) in Australia, and Clinton advisers like Robert Reich (1991) and William Galston (1991) in the US found much to admire in the Asian model. Indeed, it particularly influenced those Anglo-Saxon academic policy advisers helping to shape a new left response to the republican and conservative-inspired economic liberalism of the 1980s. These writers found in the apparent socially cohesive and community-sensitive Asian model a plausible alternative to the exuberances of an uncaring and, more particularly, uncommunitarian free-market casino capitalism. The Asian model therefore constituted a corrective to the excesses of finance capital excoriated by Will Hutton in *The State We're In* and John Gray in *False Dawn* (1998). In so doing, it constituted the foundation for the elaboration of a 'third way' that offered post-Cold-War socialist proponents of big government the seductive prospect of a future after Communism and Thatcherism.

Paradoxically, at the same time, the Asian model also appealed to a curious collocation of moral conservatives, free marketeers and economic rationalists. From William Rees-Mogg (1997) of the *Times* to the *National Review*, conservative pundits and think tanks applauded the deregulation and market openness of many Asian economies (see Garnaut et al. 1994). They noted with satisfaction 'that East Asia has prospered over the past forty years largely because it had small, pro-business governments which have refused to offer much public compassion for the unfortunate or improvident. This has been hard on unlucky or feckless individuals, but it has created exceptionally strong and resilient economies' (Rohwer 1996, p. 44).

The Asian model possessed a further seductive blandishment both for neo-conservative and third way democrats in that it promoted family values against the depradations of market libertarianism. Patriachs of single parties or military juntas like Lee Kuan Yew or Chun Doo Wan emphasized the Confucian family unit as the cornerstone of society and the antidote to dependence on state welfare. Economic thrift and family-induced 'responsibilitarianism' reinforced a virtuous cycle that enabled government to reduce welfare spending and taxation and promote high domestic savings, that in turn afforded the resources for productive investment in infrastructure, education and health. The Asian model, unlike its Anglo-Saxon alternative, therefore, appeared morally as well as economically justified. It offered a prophylactic against the western dependency syndrome which insisted on overtaxation, overregulation and a too ready willingness to throw money at 'teenage mothers in ghettoes' (ibid., p. 34). In contrast to the dynamic communitarianism of Asia, the degenerate welfare states of the west appeared effective only at producing growth in crime, disorder and social alienation.

Ultimately, the resolution of the paradoxical appeal of the Asian model to all sides of the western political spectrum may be explained by its constituting ambivalence. It offered to reformers of both left and right the Oriental solace that their reformist programmes were correct (Jones 1990, p. 462). As both neo-liberals and third way social democrats looked at only those aspects of the Asian miracle that reinforced pre-existing opinions, they established an ambivalent but tacit concurrence that set the boundaries of useful knowledge. Western commentators, in their often highly negative assessments of Thatcherism and Reaganomics, accepted uncritically the growth-strewn path of the Asian way. Scholarly inquiry thus devoted itself to divining the wider meaning of the miracle. After its meaning had been identified, all that remained was to discern the particular western ideological creed it vindicated. Whether there was a miracle at all constituted the truth that dare not speak its name. Such an approach, of course, could identify neither the long-term causes of economic growth nor the reasons for its incipient financial meltdown.

In the aftermath of the meltdown, it went largely unremarked that former Asian economic virtues transmogrified into Asian vices. Long-term planning now became market distortion; high savings equalled a drag on consumption; and government–business links facilitating long-term planning mutated into financial opacity hiding cronyism and corruption (see Jones and Smith 1999, p. 18). In a similar vein, tacit concurrence pervaded the discussion of the Asian security dispensation. The regional stability provided by ASEAN's apparent success as a conflict resolution mechanism, it was ubiquitously maintained, underpinned Southeast Asia's two decade-long economic expansion. This assumption again curtailed the scope of analytical inquiry. The prevailing multilateral orthodoxy concentrated its focus on process-oriented assessments of ASEAN's diplomatic style in order to demonstrate ASEAN's success as a regional experiment. The fashionable post-Cold War deconstruction of privileged western realist understandings added further academic legitimacy to an uncritical acceptance of ASEAN's distinctive consensual style which emphasized non-interference in the domestic affairs of member states and effortlessly sustained good interpersonal relations between Southeast Asia's political leaders (Acharya 1997a, p. 329). This orthodoxy radically curtailed understanding of 'what was important to study', restricted debate and obscured the severe fissures in the regional order that belied its superficial harmony. Indeed, to identify weaknesses convicted the critic of the crime of Orientalism in the first degree.

SYSTEM STABILITY

Ironically tacit concurrence, which sought to demonstrate a scholarly value neutrality, merely depoliticized the academic space in a way that proved deleterious to conventional scientific standards of scholarship. Scholarly neutralism increasingly considered sceptical questioning of the prevailing orthodoxy a mixture of bad manners and polemic, which raises a largely unexplored methodological question: what is it that inspires different shades of opinion and opposed ideological perspectives to reach tacit concurrence? Once again, it is possible to turn toward the inquest performed upon Soviet studies to illuminate the methodological flaws of Southeast Asian studies.

Thomas Remington argues that it was pointless to criticize Sovietologists for failing to notice the disintegration of the Soviet Union. They could no more have predicted the collapse of the USSR 'than seismologists can say when the next great earthquake will strike the San Andreas fault'. 'Instead of blaming Sovietology for failing to predict a particular event,' he continued, 'we should ask how well students of the Soviet political system understood the underlying tectonics' (Remington 1992, pp. 240–42). Remington concluded that ultimately Sovietology promulgated an underlying faith in the stability of the Soviet system that overestimated its capacity to adapt to change (ibid., p. 258).

In other words, the dominant functionalist paradigm, particularly in American social science, required the Soviet system to be considered inherently stable. Functionalists assumed the system worked. It aggregated popular demands and incorporated them in a social contract between the people and the state (Rutland 1993, pp. 116–18). System stability was necessary because analysts further assumed the Soviet political machinery possessed the capacity to evolve. American social science during the Cold War and after assumed a necessary and universal correlation between modernization and progressive democratization. Hence it presented the uncertain shifts from Leninist and Stalinist totalitarianism, to Brezhnevite managerialism and Gorbachev era reformism, in terms of a progressive teleology (Bialer 1986, pp. 32, 169, cited in Rutland 1993, p. 117). In particular, Gorbachev's reforms seemed to support the view that the Soviet system possessed the functional capacity to modernize and liberalize itself. Western social science consequently averred: 'Together, *perestroika* and *glasnost* have put the Soviet Union on the road to becoming a more "normal" country, defined broadly in Western terms (multiparty and market-orientated)' (Booth 1991a, p. 3).

This bias towards system stability had the further deleterious consequence of encouraging the 'Sovietological community' to go native, 'accepting Soviet categories at face value' (Rutland 1993, p. 116). It was this academic disposition that provided the intellectual rationale for presenting Gorbachev as an agent of adaptation, change and normalization. A similar preoccupation with system stability and gradual change in a progressive direction equally informed scholarly accounts of Southeast Asian political economy and international relations in the course of the 1990s. For different but comparable reasons, Southeast Asian studies unquestioningly accepted the official terms of Asian economic success and regional order.

Here again the ruling social science assumption of an inexorable liberal democratic end of history promoted the comfortable acceptance that, Asian values notwithstanding, economic progress inevitably presaged eventual liberalization and democratization (see Hewison 1989, p. 214). Western social scientists accepted uncritically that the Asian way promoted the system stability that had facilitated regional order and economic progress. Academic endeavour consequently focused upon the contradictory task of unravelling those aspects of Asian values that both guaranteed continuing stability and facilitated progressive change.

The assumption of system stability thus constitutes the fundamental commonality between Sovietology and Southeast Asian studies. This predilection further reinforced the academic self-disciplining instinct. For the lack of an agreed heuristic framework of explanation promoted the consensus-seeking tendency in order to overcome the inherent methodological insecurity in the field. The consequence was ' "disciplinary groupthink" that either ignored or discouraged alternative thinking' (Rutland 1993, p. 116). In this way, powerful orthodoxies took hold. Once entrenched, they could only be negated by the wholesale collapse of the functional system they ostensibly studied, but, in effect, only mythologized.

A SOVIETOLOGY OF SOUTHEAST ASIAN STUDIES?

Although the intellectual approaches of the two disciplines reveal striking parallels, a number of crucial differences also emerge. Thus a defining feature of Sovietology was its difficulty in terms both of the level of language and research skills required, and of access to data in a decaying but essentially closed society. To an extent, these difficulties excuse some of the discipline's shortcomings.

Such excuses are not, however, available to students of Southeast Asia. The despotisms of Myanmar and Communist Indochina prior to 1995 notwithstanding, information gathering in this region was far less onerous. Certainly, the ASEAN states restricted access to government records and discouraged a too intrusive foreign press, yet information gathering in general was not an issue. Centres of higher education in Southeast Asia and institutes specializing in regional affairs maintained a continuous output of scholarly publications. Equally, student and academic specialists found access to the region for field work broadly encouraged. Regional universities and institutes often employed expatriate teachers and researchers or welcomed visiting scholars from abroad. Western university departments specializing in Southeast Asia maintained close links and even established offshore faculties in the region. The fact that English, ironically, constituted a common *Bahasa* across ASEAN further facilitated the flow of information.

This quantitative difference in accessibility to Southeast Asia raises the question: why did Southeast Asian studies fail so miserably to generate either predictive capacity or a plurality of opinion? Three related factors that both distinguish Southeast Asian studies from its Sovietological counterpart and collectively constitute a distinctive Southeast Asian Sovietology, account for this failure.

The Scholar and the State: the Bureaucratization of Academia

The first important difference can be seen in the rather peculiar relationship that grew up between scholarship and the state in Southeast Asia. Historically, western social science has maintained a necessary distance between the intellectual and the policy-making professions. Academics engage in sustained and long-term observation of events in order to reveal patterns of behaviour and theories of explanation that yield insights into the wider truths of any given situation. Policy makers by contrast are far more concerned with practical, hands-on issues that require functioning under constraints of time and limited resources to work out a viable plan of action (Newsom 1995, p. 55). In theory, one profession intellectualizes, the other operationalizes.

But what are the consequences for a discipline if the operationalization of policy determines the terms of its analysis? For this is precisely what happened in Southeast Asian studies during the 1980s and 1990s. This academic mutation reflected both the sociopolitical character of the ASEAN states themselves and the alliance structure of the Cold War that discouraged critical analysis of the internal mechanisms of authoritarian allies.

By the early 1980s, a number of commentators, such as Robert Wade, Alice Amsden, Stephen Haggard and Chalmers Johnson, had identified how the ruling bureaucratic elites in Northeast Asia governed their markets, picked industrial winners and established an iron triangle of bureaucracy, industry and ruling party, which then exploited the Bretton Woods trading order to generate export-oriented growth. Southeast Asian states copied this model belatedly and more ineffectively. They depended on external investment and internal political repression. The model was one of enterprise association wherein the state mobilized all resources towards economic growth while maintaining political stability (Cotton 1998, pp. 17–21). Mahathir Mohamad, explaining the nature of the project in 1987, termed the state that he increasingly dominated 'Malaysia Incorporated'. This evolving corporatism required modification of the post-colonial constitution, abrogation of the independence of the judiciary, and 'money politics' to oil the cumbersome machinery of single party rule. As these countries modernized, moreover, the media and academe were drawn into the bureaucratic web that defined the collective project, popularizing its goals and promoting the ruling ideology.

This reduction of the academy to a department of government in an organically incorporated body politic had critical implications for the understanding of both domestic politics and international relations in the Asia–Pacific. In the wake of the Cold War, the ASEAN states endlessly advertised the virtues of their consensual, interpersonal and non-binding cultural arrangements for maintaining peace and security. To the extent that the regional arrangement possessed a governing principle it embraced, somewhat equivocally, the idea of non-interference in the domestic affairs of member states (Leifer 1989, p. 69). To explore the operation of this practice, ASEAN governments, aided by substantial donations from western governments and non-governmental organizations like the Ford Foundation, established research institutes that in practice functioned as ideological proponents of the ASEAN way. Institutes like the Institute of Southeast Asian Studies and the Institute of Defence and Strategic Studies in Singapore and their Malaysian, Indonesian, Thai and Philippine equivalents have nurtured a generation of scholar-bureaucrats that gave ideological specificity to the region's distinctive approach to security and economic growth.

Like the region's political economy, regional scholarship functioned in terms of a cronyist maintenance of good interpersonal relations oiled by nepotism and the money politics of large grants. The scholar-bureaucrats' role was not to question, but to give intellectual credibility to distinctive values and practices that enabled the developmental state to sustain its inexorable economic expansion. Consequently, scholarly assessments of Southeast Asian international relations primarily attended to narrowly focused accounts of the successful procedural application of the ASEAN way, and their shared values (see Acharya 1997a, p. 329; Snitwongse 1998, p. 183). Titles such as 'Asia's different standard', 'Go east young man', 'The Pacific way' (see Kausikan 1993; Mahbubani 1994a, 1994b, 1995a, 1995b) and studies of the internal arrangements of the developmental state like Stella and Jon Quah's seminal work on the Singapore police, *Friends in Blue* (1987), indicates the extent to which scholars suspended critical judgement in order to gain official approval and career advancement.

The fact that the most influential analysts of Southeast Asian international relations enjoyed careers as prominent civil servants in the foreign ministries of their respective states illustrates how far the state had bureaucratized academia and set the rules of permissible study. David Newsom has observed that 'Scholars find that bureaucracies are seldom open to assessments that cast doubt on current policies ... The scholar ... who challenges policy and the conventional wisdom is unwelcome' (Newsom 1995, p. 55). In Southeast Asia this tension disappeared as the bureaucracy and the local scholarly community became indistinguishable. The fact that authoritarian single party rule directed the developmental state in Southeast Asia meant that state agencies regulated and extensively intervened in the civil space where independent association and alternative views might flourish (see Gomez 2000, pp. 33–53). Scholars who harboured differing opinions from those of the state refrained from airing them in public, knowing that their careers would come to a rapid and humiliating conclusion if they did.[2] One consequence of this was a local *samizdat* culture of joke-telling that at least enlivened the table talk at the official conference dinners of otherwise unremarkable academic gatherings.[3] On the rare occasions that an academic publicly articulated dissent, he necessarily anticipated prosecution for libel and sedition, and punishment that minimally entailed a humiliating and widely publicized retraction of his 'incorrect views' in the state-owned media.

Coercion and Cooption: the Role of Outside Academics

Ostensibly, the subordination of academe to the requirements of nation building in Southeast Asia resembles the experience of Soviet academics who were similarly expected to promulgate the official party line. However, there was a critical difference: Soviet scholars were not considered 'Sovietologists'. Sovietology was the preserve of western analysts observing the system from the outside. This was not the case with Southeast Asian studies, where indigenous scholarship played an increasingly influential role in framing the discipline and methodology, especially towards the end of the Cold War. By contrast, the closed system of the Soviet bloc, together with the linguistic barriers and mutual suspicion generated by superpower hostility, thwarted any meaningful dialogue between Soviet scholars and western Sovietologists.

Southeast Asian scholars, of course, have every right to study their own locale. Ideally, local scholarship would contribute to the diversity of opinion within area studies. Even the bureaucratization of scholarship in Southeast Asia might have been overcome if scholars beyond the region had defended the principle of independent inquiry more vigorously. Unfortunately, this did not happen. Rarely did western scholars of Southeast Asian states or their international relations subject regional values to critical scrutiny. Instead, they reinforced the indigenous scholar-bureaucrats' claim to articulate the authentic voice of the region, when they merely mouthed the views of their political masters.

This process of cooption both extended and externalized the bureaucratic orthodoxies of local scholarship. The evolution of this incestuous relationship represents a second critical difference between Sovietology and the Southeast Asian variety. The propensity of the western specialist to overidentify with his or her chosen area is, as Ken Booth observed, not uncommon. Sovietologists rarely challenged the tenets of Marxism–Leninism. 'It was not that these writers were convinced Marxists,' Rutland contends, 'It was simply assumed Marxism–Leninism shaped Soviet reality, so that was the logical place to begin' (Rutland 1993, p. 116). The difficulty of access to the USSR to some extent explains this scholarly passivity. No such excuse is available to Southeast Asianists who appeared exceedingly willing converts to the norms of the Asian way. Why did this happen? Ironically, instead of enhancing disciplinary pluralism, the links between local and western scholars actively undermined it. Curiously, the barriers that impeded exchange between western and eastern students of Soviet affairs preserved the integrity of the discipline by maintaining a diversity of views in a way that Southeast Asian studies did not.

The reason why Southeast Asian studies developed as it did reflects the manner in which the Asian pursuit of the bureaucratization of academia extended beyond the region and fitted into a related process of growing bureaucratic control in the west. In an increasingly bureaucratized academia, western scholars depended upon access to local research institutions for information and networking. To preserve *guanxi* (networks of personal relationships) meant refraining from controversy and endorsing official ideology (Leifer 2000a; 2000b). The fact that western intellectuals who criticized regional economic and political practice suffered the regional equivalent of excommunication reinforced this tendency. In Singapore and Malaysia, periodic purges of expatriate political science lecturers and journalists deemed to have expressed unacceptable views (see Lingle 1994), reinforced the reluctance to engage in academic controversy.

Fear of exclusion, however, was not the only reason for this growing academic subservience, for Southeast Asian governments explicitly garnered the support of foreign academics. Influencing external opinion reflected Asian elite conceptions of the political arena, which accentuated harmony, consensus and conformity. As Catherine Jones explains:

> Arguing on public issues, taking sides on the basis of rival points of view, engaging – heaven forbid – in open pressure group activity . . . are still more likely to be viewed as proofs of government failure than political maturity. Successful government, in this context, is government with least appearance of politics. The proper

place for politics is behind the scenes, out of sight, absorbed into the administration
. . . People who matter will as far as possible have been recruited, co-opted or assiduously cultivated, as appropriate, by the ruling establishment. (Jones 1990, pp.
451–2)

Interestingly, external scholarship proved as cultivable as indigenous
scholarship. At its most direct, the cultivation of what is commonly referred to
in Southeast Asia as 'big names' took the form of lucrative visiting professor-
ships for eminent scholars in return for an endorsement of the local managerial practice. More often, ASEAN states achieved the depoliticization of a
potentially critical, external, intellectual environment through the subtle induc-
tion of foreign academics into the norms of the prevailing regional orthodoxy.
The evolving political correctness of western institutions and grant-giving
agencies from the late 1980s, which considered any criticism of Asian practice
'Orientalist', facilitated the process. This was most evident in the sphere of
Southeast Asian international relations. The economic boom from 1985 to
1997 and the swelling international profile of ASEAN further promoted this
development. The perceived success of the Association in managing regional
relations inexorably influenced the formation of other ASEAN-inspired groupings like the ASEAN Regional Forum (ARF). The regional practice of cooperative security engendered a profusion of sub-ministerial workshops,
meetings, seminars and exchanges intended to promote ASEAN's informal,
consensus-oriented diplomacy (Chalmers 1996, pp. 152–9).

Participation in the plethora of discussion fora socialized academics into
ASEAN norms. The belief that they were contributing to the development of
a non-western, and fashionably post-colonial approach to peace building
sustained the involvement of academics from outside Southeast Asia in what
became known as 'Track II' diplomacy (see Acharya 1991, p. 176; Higgott and
Nossal 1998, pp. 281–6). In practical terms, there could be little pretence that
such gatherings offered any critical evaluation of regional relations.

The capacity of Track II discourse to induce acceptance of official
'ASEANthink' manifested itself in the shared vocabulary of scholar bureaucrats, on the one hand, and western scholars of Southeast Asia, on the other.
Thus claims by indigenous scholars that the 'process was more important than
any eventual agreement' (Almonte 1997, p. 81), found a responsive echo in
statements from western regional specialists who argued that the 'process is
always held to be . . . more important than the product. ASEAN multilateralism is process-orientated, rather than product-orientated' (Acharya 1997a, p.
329).

This process of cooptation contributed to the depoliticization of Southeast
Asian studies as scholars from outside the region merely parroted official
rhetoric in their discussions of the region's international relations. This
explains why much academic writing on ASEAN during the 1990s became

preoccupied with bureaucratic and procedural detail that extended even to the discussion of seating arrangements at ASEAN intergovernmental meetings (see Leifer 1996, pp. 32–3). This obsession with process at the expense of empirical analysis obscured the fault-lines in regional relations that emerged with devastating consequences after 1997.

Intellectual Regimes in International Relations

Finally, the distinctively Southeast Asian process of academic cooptation did not occur by accident. Asian academic managerialism serendipitously coincided with a growing trend towards the bureaucratization of research in British, American and Australian institutions of higher education. Driven by performance management targets, western academics were coopted because they functioned in an academic structure already predisposed to bureaucratic guidance.

Wider intellectual trends at work in the 1990s, which from the end of the Cold War systematically assaulted the traditional 'western' realist-oriented and empirically based paradigm in international relations, further reinforced a predisposition to Asian-style groupthink. The new theoretical approaches that sprang up after 1990, which emphasized relativism, multilateralism, post-structuralism and constructivism, tended to maintain that balance of power politics and the dominance of state-centric concerns had over-determined Cold War international relations thinking (see Booth 1995, pp. 328–49). The dominant assumption within Sovietology of system stability, which left the discipline poorly placed to diagnose Soviet ills between 1989 and 1991, gave substance to post-Cold War revisionism.

The new post-Cold War dispensation, consequently, encouraged those who considered security a 'discourse' capable of construction and amenable to re-thinking in novel and culturally sensitive ways. The fashionable assumption of the early years of the New World Order that state sovereignty was in the process of being overtaken by a system of complex interdependence arising from rapid globalization reinforced the propensity toward this kind of theorizing. According to one analyst: 'The result of such diffusion of power above and below the state level would be a dense global mesh of norms, rules and decision-making structures, complex economic interdependence, non-territorial as well as territorial communities, and overlapping identity patterns' (Booth 1990, p. 541). From a slightly different perspective, those informed by understandings derived from post-colonial theory and post-modern deconstruction found multilateral approaches conducive to the cultural sensitivity necessary in a new world order that promoted both a globalized 'McWorld' and a worrying propensity to *jihad* (holy war) (Barber 1996).

In the early 1990s, ASEAN became the beneficiary of this conjunction of alternative security approaches. Seemingly, it embraced a post-colonial capacity to be with the 'other', accentuating as it did 'a sense of shared common interests and values, even if still limited, and belonging together' (Snitwongse 1990, p. 40). ASEAN's emergence into the international relations limelight can be traced to the initial western scholarly uncertainty that marked the end of the Vietnam war. This period (1975–90) witnessed an emerging concern with regionalism at the expense of specialist area studies, giving rise to what Bruce Cumings called 'Rimspeak'. The term 'Pacific Rim', he observed,

> was the post-1975 artistry, an era of forward movement and backward occlusion, as Americans sought to 'put Vietnam behind us.' 'Pacific Rim' thus heralded a forgetting, a hoped for amnesia in which the decades-long but ultimately failed U.S. effort to obliterate the Vietnamese revolution would enter the realm of Korea, the 'forgotten war'. But more importantly, it looked forward: suddenly the rim became the locus of a new dynamism, bringing pressure on the mainland of Asia. (Cumings 1997, pp. 3–4)

Rimspeak, initially, sought to explain Asian development according to the canons of modernization theory, which looked with 'curiosity if not disdain upon anyone who did not privilege the market'. 'Organized into the new inventory,' Cumings noted, 'were "miracle" economies in Japan, South Korea, Taiwan, Hong Kong, Malaysia, and Singapore, with honorable mention for Thailand, the Philippines, Indonesia, and post-Mao (but pre-Tiananmen) China' (ibid., p. 4).

In this way, the concept of regionalism was formalized in Asian studies generally. Subsequently, during the 1990s, a developing regionalism adumbrated by notions of strategic culture and multilateralism enabled a collocation of local and western theorists to articulate the view that ASEAN states had pioneered the notion of a security community (see Acharya 1998a, pp. 207–13; Booth 1991c, pp. 317, 319). From this perspective, ASEAN had successfully forged new collective regional identities through 'the deliberate creation of, and adherence to (indigenous) norms, symbols, and habits' (Acharya 1998a, p. 218). Promiscuously assembled from elements of modernization, post-modernist and multilateral theories, the 'ASEAN experience' challenged 'the neorealist preoccupation with anarchy and the inevitability of war as well as the rationalist and materialist foundations of cooperation assumed by the neoliberal institutionalists' (ibid.).

Whenever momentum builds behind an intellectual trend, no matter how incoherent, research grants and career opportunites inexorably follow. As Newsom comments, to outsiders, 'much of the process of modern scholarship seems [and indeed is] incestuous' imbricated in a web of self-promotion (Newsom 1995, p. 62). Intellectual endeavour represents not a search for wider meaning, but a process designed to fashion labels and categories 'intended to gain the kind of academic identification with a theory or equation that will lead to professional advancement' (ibid., p. 63). This was particularly the case in the international relations of Southeast Asia. Here voguish theoretical approaches, lubricated by large grants, promoted a self-fulfilling groupthink where, 'Resarchers arrive . . . with their analytical engine as part of their baggage, their chief mission being to feed the engine the evidence it needs' (Johnson and Keehn 1994, p. 17). There is no doubt that, prior to the economic meltdown, the analytical engine operated at full throttle, producing a disciplinary orthodoxy, pervaded by a post-modern, multicultural sensitivity to the Oriental 'other' that made it *de rigueur* to extol the ASEAN way, and a bad career move to question it.

A FAREWELL TO SCEPTICISM

Three further consequences stemmed from this bureaucratization of academe and the scholarly trends in post-Cold War international relations theorizing that further distinguished Southeast Asian Studies from its Sovietological equivalent.

First, Southeast Asian scholars confined attention almost exclusively to the regional level, thereby neglecting the domestic, intramural and intra-state tensions that deeply affected regional behaviour. By contrast, Sovietologists devoted much time and effort to uncovering the domestic sources of Soviet conduct. During the Cold War, for instance, alternative defence theorists like Ken Booth acknowledged that the search for 'cognitive consistency' permeated academia. To 'minimize this problem,' he maintained, 'we must act as our own devil's advocates'. This meant that those who took a more relaxed view of the Soviet threat 'must remind ourselves about Soviet ideology, the suppression of human rights, the Gulag, the episodes of adventurous Soviet behaviour in the past . . . and all those negative aspects of Soviet behaviour which make the prospect of living together a bumpy prospect' (Booth 1987, p. 59). Indeed, as Booth reiterated, the 'study of security would always benefit when it engages [*sic*] with the problems of those, at this minute, who are being starved, oppressed or shot' (Booth 1997, p. 114).

Curiously, however, Booth and his culturally relativist fellow researchers jettisoned such considerations when they turned their attention to Southeast Asia. Thus, while perfunctorily acknowledging the existence of internal conflicts in the region, they insisted, on the basis of questionable data, that the end of the Cold War in Southeast Asia 'led to increased domestic tranquillity and regional order' (Acharya 1997b, p. 310). This triumph of politically correct hope over scientific rigour (ibid.) found expression in unstinting praise for the workings of ASEAN and the growth of processes that 'embedded conflict management into the culture of [its] members' (Trood and Booth, 1999, p. 354).

These enchanting visions of domestic and regional tranquillity would have come as something of a surprise to all those being shot, starved or otherwise oppressed in an authoritarian pact that ran the spectrum from curtailment of free speech and harassment of opposition politicians to child slavery in Myanmar and genocide in East Timor. This all-consuming enthusiasm for ASEAN's conflict management technique explains why international relations analysts ignored the underlying ethnic and religious tensions that made a mockery of regional harmony and consensus after 1997.

The academic disposition to a politically correct enthusiasm for multilateral 'region building' had the additional countervailing effect of negating both scholarly scepticism and the capacity to 'weed out false theories' (Popper 1959, p. 133). Indeed, the scepticism with which Booth and others greeted inflated projections of the Soviet threat during the Cold War, and which contributed to the diversity of opinion within Sovietology, was entirely absent from Southeast Asian studies. In an area where post-colonial theorizing increasingly dominated the field there developed an unspoken injunction against scepticism towards the post-colonial regime. Hence scholarly enthusiasts of ASEAN multilateralism claimed that, whilst it might be 'easy to be sceptical of the ASEAN way', in fact the 'ASEAN brand of "soft regionalism" ' was a 'symbol of collective uniqueness' and 'source of considerable satisfaction and pride for ASEAN members'(Acharya 1998a, p. 212).

Prior to 1997, it was virtually impossible to examine critically the postulates of the new ASEAN-inspired multilateralism. Instead, analysts circumvented criticism on the simplistic grounds that 'ASEAN members' were proud of it. Second, the problem with much contemporary social science is that it has been vitiated by a post-Marxist and post-modernist hermeneutics that presents 'truth' and 'reality' as socially constructed norms. This severely restricts open debate by promoting an 'extreme form of relativism which holds that objectivity and the ideal of truth are altogether inapplicable in the social sciences where only success . . . can be decisive' (Popper 1959, p. 16).

The preoccupation with deconstructing European enlightenment notions of truth and the inauguration of an anti-Orientalist discourse that privileges the 'subaltern' voice has enabled a post-colonial cadre with a politically correct view of the development of the new world order to dominate academic discourse of both an Asian and a western provenance. The generous disbursement of grants to those who follow the ASEAN line or its multicultural western equivalent further facilitates deference to 'Asian difference'. If money politics corrupts due process across Southeast Asia, an equally disturbing 'money political science' corrupts the discipline and lends credibility to a bureaucratic managerialism that further erodes scholarly pluralism.

This suffocation of critical inquiry contributed a final defect to the study of Southeast Asia. For scholars, like the governments they studied, increasingly observed the principle of 'non-interference'. Indifference to country specialist expertise obscured internal conflicts, intra-regime tensions and a variety of domestic religious and ethnic instabilities. Scholars rationalized this indifference on the modish grounds that an anachronistic empiricism had vitiated Southeast Asia area studies during the Cold War (Khong 1997a, pp. 294–5). By contrast, culturally engaged scholars in the post-Cold War era were facilitating the emergence of an 'exciting' 'cooperative security discourse' that mitigated the confrontationalist tenets of realist-oriented balance of power diplomacy (ibid., pp. 298–9). Ultimately, what resulted was an intellectual culture of self-censorship that kept regional studies within tacit and self-regulated boundaries.

THE SOVIETOLOGY OF SOUTHEAST ASIAN STUDIES

Pronouncing his verdict on Sovietology, Rutland contended that it had failed to confront the magnitude of its failure, and that in the years after the end of the Cold War academics were more interested in 'damage control' in order to preserve their research funding and falling student enrolments. Ultimately, such practice was 'not conducive to a frank discussion of the intellectual flaws in the discipline' (Rutland 1993, p. 122). Even so, the fact that Rutland and others could expose Sovietology's pretensions at least suggested a discipline ready to accept and respond to criticism. At the same time, even its critics realized that some of the discipline's failings were attributable to the constraints of data gathering (Remington 1992, p. 241).

Southeast Asian studies, as we have indicated, shared many of the shortcomings of Sovietology. Significantly, it did not share either the restraints upon its data gathering or a willingness to accept, let alone respond to, criticism. The problems of Southeast Asian studies, moreover, were largely self-induced, not structural. Its theoretical incontinence dated from the end of the Cold War and the assault upon the realist/empiricist paradigm of international politics. Post-Cold War revisionism contended that the realist understanding of the state as the main actor in international relations was both redundant and responsible for the erroneous belief in system stability. This flaw, it was maintained, had hindered diagnosis of the internal symptoms of Soviet decay. However, the constructivist turn towards allegedly more diverse perceptions of the international system that emphasized multilateralism, strategic culture and cooperative security failed to improve matters. Instead, it rendered Southeast Asian studies vulnerable to cooption by the putatively multicultural Asian 'other'.

Yet it would be wrong to ascribe all the incoherences that arose in Southeast Asian studies to the increasing bureaucratization of Southeast Asian academia. The role of scholar-bureaucrats in promoting the ideology of regional developmentalism was, after all, quite transparent. Consequently, the onus fell upon western scholars to uphold academic independence and integrity. This the majority of regional analysts signally failed to do. As a result, Southeast Asian studies failed more completely than Sovietology. The unwillingness even to recognize its limitations is the starkest manifestation of this failure. Even now, years after the meltdown and the effective disintegration of ASEAN as a multi-lateral engine of regional security, there has been no inquest into the state of the discipline and consequently only limited appreciation of the region's growing instability.

A distinctive feature of the academic reaction to the events of 1997 is a conveniently Orwellian amnesia about previous panegyrics to the Asian way. Whilst financial analysts lost their jobs for being irrationally exuberant about Asian capitalism, their academic equivalents moved from praise to blame without missing either a promotion, a new book contract or new research funding opportunities. After 1997, even some of the most uncritical admirers of ASEAN were moved to assume a more sceptical approach towards regional institutions (see Acharya 1999a, pp. 84–101). However, this by no means entailed a recognition of any hubris. Such collective amnesia can only be sustained by policing the journals, research schools and the grant-awarding agencies of higher academe. For a post-mortem of Southeast Asian studies would reveal not only the predictive weakness of social and political scientism but also the extent to which academe welcomed a progressively sclerotic bureaucratization that played into the hands of a variety of plausible but deeply authoritarian governments.

In its evolution, moreover, it might be further argued that the Southeast Asian case represents a particularly egregious variety of a more systemic problem of conformity across international relations and its sub-fields. It might be said that academia, like politics, 'is being reduced to yet another middle-class career option' where salary scales and promotion ladders predominate (Rankin 2000). In this respect, universities and academic departments increasingly resemble corporations. And in corporate life, as Rankin observes, 'individualism and independence of mind are obstacles to progress' (Rankin 2000). Contemporary post-modern international relations theorizing that privileged incoherence and considered 'cutting edge' the chameleon ability to reflect new mutations in the academic undergrowth further reinforced this tendency to conformity in Southeast Asian studies.

International theory generally demonstrates little capacity for theoretical consistency. As Richard Ashley has noted, international relations exudes a willingness 'to hightail it across the surface of historical experience . . .

seldom pausing to dismount and explore any locale, eschewing all commit-ments, always moving as if chasing some fast retreating end or fleeing just ahead of the grasp of some relentless pursuer' (Ashley 1996, p. 240). Indeed, international relations 'is a language that enables us to shift and manoeuvre, outflank and charge, turn tail and run, retreat into historical ambiguity, commandeer resources where we find them, shed one uniform and don another, and return to fight another day' (ibid.). The sovietology of Southeast Asian studies offers an extreme example of this propensity to the extent that it ceased to offer a theory that was capable of achieving progress through the continual testing of its ruling assumptions, and thus learning from its errors (Popper 1959, p. 87), and mutated instead into an ideology dedicated to its own perpetuation.

NOTES

1. Rutland cites the obsessive distracting focus on Gorbachev in Gail Sheehy's biography, which put Gorbachev's attempt to reinvigorate the Soviet Union down to the male menopause (see Sheehy 1990, cited in Rutland 1993, p. 110).
2. In this context the experiences of former Singapore academic Chee Soon Juan are instructive. Dr Chee lost both his job, his house and his savings and is regularly denounced in the state-directed press as a 'cheat' and 'a liar' for standing against the Prime Minister during a general election and criticizing official statistics. Chee is perhaps the most prominent academic dissi-dent who, because of his refusal to apologize for his differences of opinion, has been deemed to show a lack of remorse and therefore deserving of no concession.
3. One example would be the endless jokes about Lee Kuan Yew and Mahathir. For example, Lee and Mahathir decide to have a fishing competition. They start fishing from opposite sides of the causeway. At the end of day, there is a pile of fish caught by Mahathir but none caught by Lee. The punchline follows: 'even the fish are afraid to open their mouths in Singapore'.

2. An imitation community for imitation states: ASEAN and the region that never was

The political philosopher, Michael Oakeshott, coined the term 'imitation states' to describe the incomplete nation building of many newly formed countries in the post-colonial world. Riven by ethnic, social and economic fissures these states struggled to establish themselves in a decolonized world. Developing this line of thought, Oakeshott's colleague at the London School of Economics, Elie Kedourie, argued that leaders of imitation states 'labour under strong feelings of insecurity generated by their lack of legitimacy. The product of fake elections or military coup d'état their unrestrained power does not rest on the loyalty of those whom they rule' (Kedourie 1975, p. 351). Such insecurity, translated to a regional level, it may be contended, also produces imitative institutions that are essentially rhetorical shells that give form but no substance to domestic and international arrangements.

Applying this understanding, this chapter shall investigate the extent to which the Association of Southeast Asian Nations (ASEAN) resembles an imitation community. For much of the 1990s, political scientists extolled ASEAN for its successful management of regional affairs. It was maintained that ASEAN had done much to promote stability, which, in turn, underpinned the impressive economic growth rates in the region during the period that extended from the 1970s until the Asian financial crisis of 1997/98.

By contrast, the argument advanced here is that in the years prior to the economic crisis ASEAN's supposedly multilateral security architecture masked a series of structural faults evident to anyone who cared to probe the basis of regional security. Disturbingly, the constraints of regional scholarly practice, regional *amour propre* and a fashionable intellectual orthodoxy in international relations theory combined to distort ASEAN's role in the course of the 1990s and ignore its constituting weaknesses. Furthermore, if, as the editor of *Foreign Policy* observed in 1998, 'a theory's value is proportional to its predictive power', this dominant orthodoxy proved woefully inaccurate (Naim 1998, p. 2). In this chapter we shall trace the curious path of ASEAN's development from its inauspicious beginnings in 1967. Moreover, by critically examining the actual impact of its many treaties, forums and ministerial meetings, we shall further assess the extent to which its purported achievements in generating regional peace, order and economic growth were more imagined than real.

ASEAN AND THE NATION-BUILDING STATE IN SOUTHEAST ASIA

According to admiring commentators in the early 1990s, ASEAN's successful experiment in regionalism had enabled Southeast Asia to attain unparalleled levels of stability (Acharya 1993, p. 3; Chalmers 1997, p. 53). The basis of the organization's apparent success resided in its identification as one of the pillars of Pacific stability that had facilitated the impressive economic growth rates witnessed in the region after its formation in 1967. By managing relations among a highly disparate set of states and preventing the outbreak of conflict, it was claimed, ASEAN enabled its members to devote their attention and resources to both nation building and economic development (Chalmers 1997, p. 36). 'ASEAN's achievement is all the more impressive', declared one analyst, 'because it was born thirty years ago, out of conflict', and yet 'peace has been maintained throughout its existence' (Snitwongse 1998, p. 183).

The secret of this conflict management formula lay, it was asserted, in a series of procedures that came to be collectively known as the 'ASEAN way'. This entailed consensus building and non-binding dialogue among government elites, which rested, in turn, on the principle of non-interference in the internal affairs of member states. The approach purportedly built trust among political leaders and led to the settlement of disputes away from intense media scrutiny. These practices were embodied in the Treaty of Amity and Cooperation (TAC) agreed by the founding members of ASEAN – Indonesia, Malaysia, Philippines, Singapore and Thailand – in 1976, which gave official form to these informal norms. Subsequently, enthusiastic proponents extolled the 'uniqueness' of the ASEAN way in diplomacy whereby 'norms were operationalized into a framework of regional interaction' that 'contrasted with the adversarial posturing and legalistic decision-making procedures in Western multilateral negotiations' (Acharya 1997a, p. 329).

With the seemingly inexorable economic growth of the Asia–Pacific littoral after 1975, many analysts conceived that a prosperous and confident region would increasingly occupy a dominant place in the global trading order and lead to the 'ASEANization' of Australia and East Asia (Chalmers 1997, pp. 40–43). The growth of a variety of pan-Asian arrangements like the ASEAN Regional Forum (ARF), the ASEAN Free Trade Association (AFTA) and Asia–Pacific Economic Cooperation (APEC) seemed to reflect the extension of the Association's model of cooperative security. By the mid-1990s ASEAN commentators perceived that the Association had a 'major opportunity . . . for re-shaping the regional order' (Acharya 1993, p. 3) in the evolving *Pax Pacifica*.

From the outset, ASEAN's significance extended beyond the management of regional relations. ASEAN's diplomatic practice lent credence to the internal promotion of nation-building strategies amongst the insecure, imitative states that constituted post-colonial Southeast Asia. ASEAN legitimated the pursuit of state-led economic development and political consolidation. In this respect ASEAN, despite its anti-communist roots and authoritarian characteristics, came to be viewed in the voguish constructivist idiom of post-Cold War international relations as a distinctively 'Asian way' to regionalism that emphasized an attractively different approach to regional security blissfully unencumbered by the rule-governed constraints of western rationalism (see Krause and Latham 1998). Ultimately, ASEAN offered 'an authentic and successful model of multilateralism' (Acharya 1997a, p. 341).

In this understanding, while ASEAN stabilized external relations, the regional ideology of Asian values saw the ruling elites overcoming internal vicissitudes and their lack of legitimacy by crafting states conceived as 'enterprise associations', rather than civil associations (Oakeshott 1975, pp. 114–15). In this they sought to forge cohesiveness and resilience by eroding autonomous associations and integrating heterogeneous populations into a collective enterprise mobilized towards economic goals. The management of this pursuit required a suitably modernized collective identity that, in turn, necessitated the inculcation of paternalistic traditions paradoxically amended to serve the developmental process. So it was that in the 1980s President Suharto's Indonesian New Order came increasingly to propagate *bapakism* – paternalism and deference – in the state-inculcated ideology of *pancasila* (five principles). Similarly, in Singapore, programmes to promote, somewhat incoherently, both Confucianism and shared Asian values became an urgent matter of political and educational policy in the same decade. Meanwhile, in Malaysia, the politically dominant United Malay National Organization (UMNO) sought to revitalize and purify traditions drawn from the golden age of the Malacca Sultanate, but adapted as *rukun negara* (national pillars), to support the untraditionalistic leader, Mahathir Mohamad, in his quest to build 'Malaysia Incorporated'.

Central to these elite inspired totalizing visions was an anxiety about the potential for instability posed by perceived internal and external threats. For three decades Communism supplied the threat that justified the corporatist controls in Thailand, Malaysia, Indonesia and Singapore. The Communist Emergency of the 1950s and the inter-ethnic riots of the 1960s also justified the extension of draconian internal security legislation to curtail political dissent. Analogously, in Thailand, the external threat of Communism legitimated monarchy, nation and the Buddhist religion in becoming the symbolic features of national unity (see Jackson 1991, chap. 7). In Indonesia the bloody trauma of the transition from Sukarno to Suharto in 1965/66 warranted the armed forces' official *dwifungsi* (dual function) to maintain order and protect the decolonized archipelago.

Foundational myths derived from the dread of disorder, and fear of a communist and communalist 'other', generated the imperative for internal unity and provided the rationalization for nation-building ideologies amongst these disparate imitation states. These legitimized autocratic single party rule, state control of the media and the suppression of political and religious freedoms. For example, Singapore's official history, as expounded by Lee Kuan Yew in his memoirs, maintained that the inter-ethnic riots of 1964 and the subsequent expulsion of the predominately Chinese city state from the Malaysian Federation in 1965, justified the enforcement of racial harmony and social cohesion (see Lee 1998). This overwhelming need further necessitated the transformation of the judiciary, trade unions and parliament into essentially mimetic institutions. A similar, but more fitful, process shaped Indonesian, Malaysian, Thai and Philippine political development.

At the state level, therefore, state ideologists selectively interpreted events such as the expulsion of Singapore from the Malaysian Federation and the 1963–66 *Konfrontasi* between Indonesia and Malaysia, to establish the threat that ratified the antidote of strong leadership by 'men of prowess' like Suharto, Mahathir and Lee. At the external regional level, however, these fundamental differences were shelved and the ruling elites in Indonesia, Malaysia, the Philippines and Singapore stressed, instead, the virtue of non-interference, consensus and good interpersonal relations. These developments also inspired the doctrine of 'national resilience' as a prophylactic against domestic opposition and external criticism (Acharya 1998b, p. 70). This strange contract, posited simultaneously on constituting difference but shared values, facilitated the common pursuit of export-oriented growth and the illusion of a unique approach to regional security (see Mahbubani 1995a, pp. 105–20; Acharya 1998b, pp. 55–85). Let us then examine the consequences of this strange contract and the regional delusion it engendered over time.

THE AMERICAN SECURITY CONNECTION

Given the failed cooperative ventures that preceded ASEAN, the mere fact that it survived intact for more than a decade testified to some sort of minimalist success. Even minimally, however, the fact of its survival was largely fortuitous, owing little to anything the Association itself did, and far more to the changing nature of the US military commitment to Southeast Asia between 1969 and 1975. Interestingly, the retreat of US forces from Indochina prompted as much anguish amongst the non-communist states of Southeast Asia as it did amongst the Americans themselves. The US role as an external guarantor was considered vital to the security of a part of the world where the non-communist countries alone did not possess the resources or collective will to ensure the defence of either themselves or the region. The great fear in the late 1960s was, as Wayne Wilcox observed, that the 'inherent disparity of power [between Southeast Asian states] coupled with very salient regional quarrels and disputes and the absence of external balancing forces would leave Asia not unlike it was in 1945' (Wilcox 1968, pp. 29–30).

America's disengagement from South Vietnam, although traumatic, ironically constituted a useful corrective, which far from weakening the US commitment to Southeast Asia actually stabilized and, ultimately, enhanced it. As Henry Kissinger subsequently observed, the US withdrawal from Indochina acknowledged that the simplistic assumptions of Cold War ideology founded on the global containment of Communism did not readily apply to Asia (Kissinger 1995, pp. 710ff). In fact, the US ground commitment destabilized and distorted the emerging character of Southeast Asia, obscuring nationalist impulses in a region where the appeal of Asian communists resided not in 'their revolutionary élan but in their orderly vision of a disorderly world' (Wilcox 1968, p. 26). As one analyst maintained in 1973, 'American influence in Asia has never been commensurate with the level of military involvement because will and weaponry have different currencies' (Darby 1973b, p. 210).

Despite the protracted engagement in Indochina, the United States government since the early 1950s had not conceived regional engagement primarily in military terms. Instead, it had seen economic aid as a vital currency of influence and stability. Net US foreign assistance between 1945 and 1967 to those countries that became the founding members of ASEAN amounted to US$2.4 billion.[1] Not only did US aid help the new states of Southeast Asia consolidate themselves economically, it was also critical in negating Moscow or Beijing-inspired initiatives to fill the vacuum left by retreating European empires. Although the scale of direct American aid declined after 1968, indirect economic assistance in the form of debt relief, inward investment and preferential access to US markets remained crucial to the development of the region. In other words, the United States militarily disengaged from Southeast Asia after 1969, but did not withdraw. Instead, it fell back on its economic strength and its naval and air power, projected across the Pacific from Hawaii via Guam and its huge bases at Subic Bay and Clark Field in the Philippines.

It was Richard Nixon who clarified the character of the emerging regional dispensation during his visit to the island of Guam in July 1969 (Kissinger 1995, pp. 707–9). The 'Nixon doctrine', as his Guam speech became known, undertook to maintain existing United States treaty commitments and to counter any aggression against its allies by providing military assistance short of direct intervention with ground forces (Yahuda 1996, p. 132). The doctrine not only defined the specific policy of 'Vietnamization', it also outlined a vision of future US foreign policy as a coherent strategic construct. While the Nixon doctrine recognized that it could no longer impose its will on the internal character of emerging states, it nevertheless asserted that the United States retained global interests and the capability to defend them. The new doctrine manifested a more subtle and realistic basis upon which to build regional stability in Asia, and one that maximized rather than diminished US influence.

This is not to say that regional faith in the American security guarantee did not falter. In the aftermath of the collapse of Indochina to Communism in 1975, the credibility of the US commitment was questioned openly by some ASEAN member states (Khoman 1976, pp. 613–17), and induced a short period of temporizing before the victorious Vietnamese communists. In July 1976, President Marcos sought to distance the Philippines from the United States and commended the Hanoi regime for teaching 'the whole world one of the most important lessons in human history' (*Far Eastern Economic Review*, 23 July 1976, cited in Gordon 1978, p. 596), while Thailand found it politic to comply with Vietnamese demands to close US military installations without consulting its US ally (Khoman 1976, pp. 619–20).

Yet, notwithstanding the initial loss of influence suffered by the Americans after Vietnam, US power and the US market remained central to the preservation of the nascent security order in Southeast Asia. The significant difference was that American power was now exercised at a distance. It was this covert rather than overt US commitment to Asia, in both military and economic terms, that provided the ASEAN states with the necessary space to pursue both domestic consolidation and extremely limited regional cooperation largely free from internal and external threats. Indeed, to the extent that ASEAN could begin to define the rudimentary outlines of a regional consensus after 1969 it consisted primarily in a shared resistance to Communism, diagnosed as the common root of internal and external insecurity.

THE NIXON DOCTRINE AND THE BIRTH OF DELUSION

Serendipitously, the altered state of the US security presence in Southeast Asia from 1969 onwards would, over the next two decades, afford the region a hitherto unknown degree of stability. One of the outcomes of the semi-detached American presence was that it gave the ASEAN states a new latitude in policy formulation, thereby affording the insecure member states the illusion of international significance.

Illusion went hand in hand with the evolution of ASEAN's international profile. Indeed, it was the condition for its emergence. One of the earliest examples of ASEAN's growing profile was the November 1971 joint declaration of sovereignty by Indonesia and Malaysia over the busy sea lanes of the Straits of Malacca. The declaration indicated the increasing assertiveness of ASEAN states. Indonesia in particular, as the largest member of ASEAN and aspiring to regional leadership, wished to stake out its various interests in the area. In practical terms, however, the declaration was an empty gesture. The Singaporeans, who also controlled part of the Straits of Malacca, opposed it; the major naval powers ignored it; and the two governments lacked (and continue to lack) the means to enforce it (Leifer and Nelson 1973, pp. 190–203).

More representative of ASEAN's growing flair for engaging in the politics of the grandiose but nebulous gesture were the various proposals to establish regional neutrality. In November 1971, a meeting of ASEAN foreign ministers adopted a declaration to secure 'the recognition and respect for South-East Asia as a zone of peace, freedom and neutrality, free from any form or manner of interference by outside powers'. Despite its idealism, ZOPFAN, as it was known, became a constant theme in ASEAN diplomacy for the next 20 years. In theory, ZOPFAN might have provided a basis for ASEAN to assume more responsibility for its own security. Indeed, the Malaysian Prime Minister, Tun Razak, suggested as much, explaining that 'The premise of neutralization is regional and national resilience. Southeast Asia must stand on its own feet. We – individual countries as well as the region as a whole – must be self reliant if we wish to survive' (quoted in Simon 1978, p. 429).

In practice, however, the concept, as Michael Leifer observed, 'assumed the quality of a political chameleon', because it appeared 'in a different hue according to the interests of the particular South-East Asian governments concerned' (Leifer 1973, p. 601). To the Malaysians, neutralization represented part of a broader design to normalize relations with China. ZOPFAN, in this view, would coincide with the Chinese desire to eliminate superpower influence in Asia. This, it was hoped, would convince Malaysia's ethnic Chinese-dominated communist party that it could no longer expect any support from the People's Republic for its ailing insurgency. By contrast, the Thais, who enjoyed close military ties with the United States, were distinctly lukewarm and (like the Philippines) went along with ZOPFAN, even though, at that time, it had no intention of closing the US bases on its territory. Meanwhile the Indonesians, who were sympathetic to the notion of zonal neutrality, were reluctant to accept the assumption inherent in ZOPFAN that neutralization would require undertakings from states like the United States, the Soviet Union, and perhaps even China, to guarantee the region's neutrality. Yet such a role for outside powers would clearly undermine Indonesia's regional pretensions (ibid., pp. 601–7).

This predication upon external guarantors exposed ZOPFAN's ambiguous mix of fantasy, idealism and pragmatism. The zone was designed to exclude major powers, but its existence actually assumed the continuing presence of those powers. In fact, had the ZOPFAN ideal been implemented in the 1970s it would have had ramifications diametrically opposed to those envisaged by the scheme's proponents. ASEAN states would have been compelled to cut off all sources of counter-balancing power and accept the position of supplicants to their foreign guarantors (Darby 1973b, p. 216). This would only have further exposed ASEAN's continuing inability to take responsibility for its own security, frozen Southeast Asia in a Cold War vacuum and destabilized the region. Thus, while acknowledging the regional aspiration for a 'new equilibrium', the Singaporean Prime Minister, Lee Kuan Yew, in March 1973, pragmatically observed that 'until this equilibrium is established Southeast Asia's security can only be provided by an American presence in the region' (quoted in Leifer 1973, pp. 604–5).

The fall of South Vietnam, Laos and Cambodia to Communism in 1975 did, however, provoke doubts over the US security guarantee, which, for a while, concentrated ASEAN's collective mind. At the Bali summit in 1976, the five ASEAN heads of state agreed to the Treaty of Amity and Cooperation (TAC). This treaty reaffirmed the territorial integrity of member states, and made this the basis of an explicit code of conduct for the peaceful resolution of regional disputes (Leifer 1989, p. 69). The Kuala Lumpur summit in 1977 further boosted the Association's international standing when Australia, Japan and New Zealand for the first time participated in post-summit consultations.

Both the TAC and the Kuala Lumpur summit implied ASEAN's collective solidarity and opposition to the newly established communist bloc in Southeast Asia and raised its international stature as a result. Yet both initiatives again revealed the inadequacy of ASEAN's earlier attempts to accommodate the Indochinese states. With the end of the Indochina conflict, the ASEAN states in fact sought to placate Vietnam. Both TAC and ZOPFAN were initially designed to conciliate the victorious communist regimes by announcing a self-denying regional ordinance. This, it was hoped, would appease these states and persuade them to join ASEAN in establishing a collaborative regional environment.

Significantly, the government in Hanoi spurned ASEAN's overtures, viewing both the Association in general, and ZOPFAN in particular, as vehicles for American security interests to contain Vietnam. The only way Hanoi could be reconciled to ASEAN was by the complete withdrawal of US forces in Southeast Asia (see Simon 1978, pp. 432–3). Yet, because ASEAN remained dependent upon the American security and economic guarantees, this precluded any rapprochement with the Indochinese communists.

ASEAN initiatives between 1969 and 1977 served, therefore, to reveal the organization's constituting ambivalence. On the one hand, the component members desired neutrality, self-reliance and the exclusion of non-regional powers. On the other, the largely autocratic post-1967 regimes that ruled the ASEAN states remained ultimately dependent upon the continued American security commitments and the American inspired GATT trading order that offered both Foreign Direct Investment (FDI) and a huge market for ASEAN's increasingly export-oriented economic development.

THE 'RESOLUTION' OF THE CAMBODIAN PROBLEM AND ITS DELUSIONAL CONSEQUENCES

Central to ASEAN's seeming longevity was the fact that it avoided serious disagreement between members that might have fractured the Association. Consequently, in 1975, Tun Razak argued that ASEAN had evolved 'a structure of regional co-operation which over the years had proved itself constructive in promoting regional understanding'. This structure, moreover, was 'nurtured with care to maintain its non-antagonistic, non-military and non-ideological character' (quoted in Simon 1978, pp. 418–19). That ASEAN had apparently been able to stabilize relations amongst its member states gave the organization, in the eyes of its supporters, the capacity to enhance its role on the regional scene. Tun Razak contended: 'I think today we can truly say that ASEAN's independent and progressive nature has won admiration from many quarters – large and small powers alike.' The Association now had the 'opportunity to extend the scope of regional co-operation throughout Southeast Asia' (quoted in Simon 1978, p. 419).

The optimistic view that ASEAN constituted an embryonic multilateral community, able to embrace the whole region, animated the Association and continued to generate adherents well into the 1990s (Hoan 1996, pp. 78–9). The translation of ASEAN's regional machinery from what were essentially pious hopes in 1975 into a tangible, if deeply ambiguous, form by the 1990s can be attributed largely to ASEAN's role in resolving the Cambodian conflict after 1978.

Far from calming Indochina by exorcising the demons of old-style Cold War conflict, the victory of Indochina's communists in 1975 succeeded merely in re-igniting, in a more radical form, ancient antagonisms. Internecine communist feuding, reflecting historic ethnic animosities between the Chinese, Cambodians and Vietnamese, replaced Cold War rivalry in Indochina. After 1975, the Vietnamese extended air and naval base facilities to the Soviet Union at Da Nang and Cam Ranh Bay. Ever suspicious of both Soviet and Vietnamese motives, the Chinese soon fell out with the Hanoi regime. Using their Kampuchean allies, China embarked on a mission to undermine Vietnamese influence in Indochina, which involved supporting

Khmer Rouge guerrilla raids as far as the Mekong Delta. Fearing that Kampuchea (Cambodia) was the 'cat's paw of China' (Turley and Race 1980, pp. 100–101), the Hanoi government ordered the invasion of Kampuchea. The Vietnamese army overran the Khmer Rouge in December 1978, and replaced the genocidal Pol Pot regime with a pro-Vietnamese regime under Heng Samrin's Kampuchean People's Revolutionary Party (KPRP). Under Vietnamese occupation the country was re-named the People's Republic of Kampuchea (PRK).

The invasion provided an immediate security issue for ASEAN. Vietnam's invasion violated Cambodia's territorial integrity, thereby constituting a breach of ASEAN's public philosophy elaborated in its founding declaration and reiterated in the TAC. Thailand in particular resented the extension of Vietnam's Indochinese hegemony to its borders (Alagappa 1993, pp. 450–52). An emergency meeting of ASEAN foreign ministers in January 1979 formally insisted upon 'respect for national sovereignty' and denounced 'changes of government brought about by military intervention across internationally recognized borders' (Leifer 1989, pp. 90–91). In ASEAN's collective view Vietnam's occupation of Kampuchea, with Soviet support, constituted both a dangerous precedent and an intolerable threat to regional stability.

In the aftermath of the invasion, ASEAN played a leading diplomatic role in denying international recognition to the new, Vietnamese-installed, PRK government. This was particularly evident at the United Nations, where ASEAN convened a conference on Kampuchea in 1981 which demanded the withdrawal of all foreign military forces from the country and the restoration of the right of self-determination to its people. The Association also played a significant role in forming and supporting a Cambodian government in exile, the Coalition Government of Democratic Kampuchea (CGDK) under the presidency of the former ruler, Prince Sihanouk. The CGDK was an uneasy coalition of three opposition factions that included the Khmer Rouge, which continued to wage guerrilla war against the Vietnamese occupation along the Thai–Cambodian frontier (Chanda 1989, pp. 25–43; Doyle 1995, p. 17).

Successful ASEAN lobbying secured UN recognition of the CGDK as the legitimate government of Cambodia in 1982, even though it controlled barely a fifth of the country. ASEAN capitalized on this diplomatic success by insisting on an explicit role in the negotiation of a UN-brokered political settlement (Leifer 1996, p. 16). In fact, the ASEAN viewpoint largely prevailed in the agreement on Cambodia, signed in Paris in 1991. The Paris accords provided for an interim Supreme National Council under UN auspices led by Prince Sihanouk prior to all-party elections in May 1993 (Doyle and Suntharalingam 1994, pp. 118–20).

ASEAN's success in mobilizing the international community against Vietnamese rule in Kampuchea signalled its apparent arrival as a mature regional organization, marking the Association's passage from an inchoate and vulnerable collection of states to effective international partnership with a growing impact on the regional security order. Even the United States, reluctant to involve itself directly in Southeast Asian affairs, endorsed the ASEAN line on Cambodia (Colbert 1984, p. 140). Not only did the Cambodian crisis boost ASEAN's international profile, it also cemented its internal cohesion. In Leifer's words, the Cambodian conflict 'was the critical episode over and during which the Association attained and demonstrated the quality of a diplomatic community able to conduct itself, up to a point, as a unitary actor' (Leifer, 2000c, pp. 84–5).

However, closer inspection of ASEAN's actual contribution to the Cambodian settlement reveals its role to be both ambiguous and ultimately limited. The guiding principle governing ASEAN policy towards the Cambodian crisis stressed territorial integrity and the inviolability of internal political arrangements. This non-negotiable position, however, conveniently overlooked Indonesia's invasion of East Timor in 1975 and China's abortive invasion of Vietnam in 1979. ASEAN took no action in either of these cases of territorial violation. This exposed ASEAN to the charge of dissimulation in selectively applying its own edicts, a charge that was to haunt the organization in its dealings with Indochina throughout the 1990s, and later with East Timor as the New Order disintegrated after 1998.

Furthermore, ASEAN's actual diplomatic practice undermined central features of its official rhetoric, compounding this ambivalence. Thus, although ASEAN appeared to take the diplomatic initiative against Vietnam's occupation of Kampuchea, in effect, it fronted an anti-Vietnam coalition that served the interests of powerful external actors as much as those of ASEAN. By aligning itself against Vietnamese domination in Indochina, ASEAN instead aligned itself with China and the United States in their geopolitical conflict with the Soviet Union and its allies (Kissinger 1995, chap. 28; Colbert 1984, p. 146). In seeking to limit the spread of Soviet power and influence in Southeast Asia, ASEAN's strategy violated its commitment to a vision of regional neutrality.

Moreover, not only did ASEAN promote the regional aspirations of China and Thailand, who both felt threatened by Vietnam's hegemony in Indochina, it also implemented a strategy 'of complete moral cynicism', by resurrecting 'the nearly devastated Khmer Rouge' (Solarz 1990, p. 102). By aiding Khmer Rouge guerrillas operating near the Thai frontier, 'Pol Pot's forces became the lever for removing Vietnam from Cambodia' (ibid.). There was no doubt that the long-term strategy of the Khmer Rouge was to regain its genocidal grip upon Cambodian politics, subsequently demonstrated by its boycott of the May 1993 UN-sponsored elections and its continued but increasingly desperate insurgency against the newly elected government thereafter. ASEAN's promotion of the CGDK disguised the presence of the Khmer Rouge, thus avoiding 'the annual embarrassment of supporting Pol Pot' at the UN (Colbert 1984, p. 143).

Despite ASEAN's high, but clearly problematic, diplomatic profile, it played only a secondary role in the events leading to the Paris agreement in 1991 and the actual resolution of the Cambodian crisis. Indeed, the eventual settlement of the Cambodia issue represented an archetypal manifestation of great power politics, in this case, the Soviet retreat from Empire. In July 1986, Soviet premier Mikhail Gorbachev began re-evaluating Soviet relations with Asia. Soon after, in 1987, Hun Sen, who after a series of factional struggles had emerged as the leader of the KPRP, initiated contacts with Sihanhouk's exiled coalition in Paris. In August 1988, the Soviets also started discussions with Beijing with a view to normalizing relations (Kissinger 1995, p. 792). As a result, in April 1989, Hanoi agreed to withdraw its combat forces from Kampuchea in order to achieve a political solution (Mackintosh 1993, p. 24). In practice, Vietnam's Soviet patron had disappeared, leaving Hanoi to find the best terms it could. This fact, combined with a more active United States regional diplomacy, having shrugged off its post-Vietnam malaise, along with an emergent China wishing to rehabilitate itself internationally after the Tiananmen Square massacre of 1989, opened the road to settlement (Doyle and Suntharalingam 1994, pp. 129–30).

In other words, the normalization of Sino-Soviet relations and the withdrawal of Vietnamese forces from Kampuchea rendered the Association's sinuous diplomacy largely peripheral. Moreover, ASEAN's intransigent attitude towards Vietnam further marginalized it during the Paris peace talks (Alagappa 1993, pp. 462–4). As a consequence of ASEAN's intractable stance the Paris negotiations initially floundered. It was only a joint American–Australian proposal (opposed by ASEAN), giving the UN a central role in the administration of Cambodia in the interim period between the signing of the agreement and the holding of elections, that eventually resolved the deadlock and paved the way to the 1991 settlement (Solarz 1990, pp. 101–9).

In retrospect, then, analysts exaggerated ASEAN's diplomatic role in resolving the Cambodian conflict. The Association appeared effective because its actions coincided with superpower interests. Seemingly at the forefront of events, ASEAN was actually a convenient front for external actors and interests. This role, moreover, contradicted ASEAN's stated principles on zonal neutrality. The fact that China and the USSR effectively solved the problem through bilateral diplomacy once again illustrated the region's continuing dependence upon external actors and the illusory character of ASEAN's attempt to erect a *cordon sanitaire* around Southeast Asia. Furthermore, when the superpowers eventually resolved the conflict, ASEAN largely failed to influence the course of the settlement.

Moreover, the fact that ASEAN's diplomacy played a key role in reinventing the discredited Khmer Rouge revealed a disconcerting void in the official philosophy of ASEAN ('Bad deal in Cambodia' 1996). Whilst, for a time, the conflict galvanized the Association, gave it cohesion and enhanced its international standing, it also violated those principles of 'non-antagonistic', 'non-ideological' independence which the Association officially proclaimed. This, by itself, made the Association's aspirations to play a greater role in regional affairs based on a unitary set of principles hard to sustain. This was subsequently demonstrated in ASEAN's diplomatic contortions in dealing with Hun Sen's ouster of Prince Ranariddh as Cambodia's 'first' democratically elected prime minister in July 1997.

A COMMUNITY OF EVOLVING AMBIGUITY

In examining ASEAN's role since its inception it could be maintained that the Association 'succeeded for its first ten years by doing nothing and can thank Vietnamese actions for a second decade of success' (Emmerson 1987, p. 16). It might be added that ASEAN's prospects were sustained for a third decade thanks to the collapse of the Soviet Union. The end of the Cold War gave impetus to the idea of ASEAN as the nucleus of a new security framework. In this context, the acclaim heaped upon the Association for its largely rhetorical role in resolving the Cambodian conflict convinced *jejune* analysts of Southeast Asia that ASEAN had been presented 'with a major opportunity for reshaping the regional order' (Acharya 1993, p. 7; see also p. 3).

After 1991, therefore, ASEAN sedulously embellished its economic and security role in an effort to fulfil the original desideratum of ZOPFAN, namely, regional integration 'free from . . . Great Power interference' (Sopiee, 1992, p. 131). This vision moved closer to realization with the decision at the fourth ASEAN summit in Singapore to create AFTA, the ASEAN Free Trade Area, within 15 years. The Singapore Declaration (1992) announcing the formation of AFTA constituted, in the words of the *Straits Times*, a 'milestone leap' that would 'engage member states in new areas of co-operation' (*Straits Times*, 19 January 1992). AFTA envisaged the creation of a Common Effective Preferential Tariff scheme (CEPT) of between 0 and 5 per cent across the region. In order to facilitate a regional free trade area, in 1994 it was agreed at an ASEAN Economic Ministers meeting in Phuket to implement the scheme by 2003 (ibid.).

Alongside this strategy of deepening the economic integration of the member states, ASEAN also embarked on a policy of widening its membership to include Vietnam in 1995 and Laos, Cambodia and Myanmar by July 1997. In addition, ASEAN sought to broaden its economic and security ties, extending these across the Pacific and even to Europe. By 1996 ASEAN played a key role in biannual Asia-Europe Summits (*Straits Times,* 4 March 1996) and in creating a prospective open trading Pacific region through the evolving machinery of Asia–Pacific Economic Cooperation (see Ariff 1994; Mack and Ravenhill 1994). Even more ambitiously, ASEAN expanded its distinctive non-conflictual diplomatic style across the region by initiating a 'security dialogue with external powers' through the medium of the multilateral ASEAN Regional Forum (Leifer 1995, p. 34). The first meeting of the ARF took place in Bangkok in July 1994 and involved the ASEAN states and its 12 dialogue partners, including China, Japan, the United States, Australia, Canada and the European Union. ASEAN scholars and diplomats, along with a legion of western academic adherents, contended that the ARF's policy of preventive diplomacy, dialogue, confidence-building 'workshops' and cooperation would ultimately secure regional harmony. The ARF, therefore, reflected ASEAN's preferred strategy of gradually building regional consensus through interpersonal ties and the avoidance of open confrontation.

Burgeoning regional self-confidence during the Asian boom decade 1985–95, further advanced the belief that the character of Pacific Asia's cultures would increasingly determine the basis of economic progress, political development and regional order in the twenty-first century. Pan-Asianists claimed, prior to the economic meltdown of 1997, that a curiously syncretic blend of neo-Confucian ideas, adumbrated in Malaysia, Indonesia and Thailand by a mixture of post-Islamic and Buddist values, provided the basis of regional prosperity. These 'Asian values', it was maintained, felicitously blended social cohesion, consensus, harmony and the subordination of the individual to the supervening collective good of family, hierarchy and order with the requirements of the market, thereby forming the ideological foundation of Asian development (*Economist*, 6 October 1994). In this sense, the translation of traditional high cultural values of Confucian, Islamic and Buddhist provenance into programmes of mass education and bureaucratic practice offered the prospect of an enduring, yet distinctively Asian, modernity (Gellner 1994, chap. 2). Hence, according to ASEAN proponents, Asian values explained successful regional development between 1985 and 1995 while at the same time offering an ideological critique of the perceived failure of the advanced economies of Europe and North America. These western economies founded, it was alleged, on an otiose individualism, had promoted welfarism, equal rights and civil liberties that produced only economic stagnation, moral decay, high levels of crime, inner-city chaos and monstrous regiments of single-parent families (see *Straits Times*, 22 August 1994; Mahbubani 1994a, pp. 6–7; Mohamad and Ishihara 1995).

A notable feature of this period was the determination of the leaders of some newly industrialized Asian states to resist what they considered a new and insidious form of colonization masquerading as democratization, which made for some acerbic exchanges between the advocates of Asian values and their critics. Influential Asian statesmen like Lee Kuan Yew and Mahathir Mohamad considered the individualistic assumptions of the American media particularly hypocritical and offensive (see Acharya 1993, p. 29). The Clinton administration's foreign policy, which in its early years veered from being inattentive to obsessive over issues linked to trade and human rights, further facilitated this essentially rhetorical clash of civilizations (Harding 1994, pp. 57–74). Responding to what regional leaders perceived as colonialism under the guise of human rights, ASEAN responded with its own Bangkok declaration in 1993, that emphasized both the 'rights [*sic*] of the community' and the principle of non-interference in the internal affairs of states.

In order to give additional institutional credibility to this incipient pan-Asianism, Malaysia in particular promoted the idea of an East Asian Economic Caucus (EAEC), explicitly excluding the United States and other non-Asian countries in the Pacific, that would include ASEAN together with the East Asian economies of South Korea, China, Japan and Taiwan. Plainly, 'economic success has engendered greater cultural self-confidence', according to the Singaporean scholar–bureaucrat, Bilhari Kausikan (Kausikan 1993, p. 32). As a result, he continued, 'East and Southeast Asian countries are increasingly conscious of their own civilizations and tend to locate the sources of their economic success in their own distinctive traditions and institutions' (ibid., p. 34).

In these respects, the end of the Cold War was a catharsis for pan-Asianism, liberating it from the shackles that had determined allegiance to the anti-communist 'west'. The collapse of the bipolar world afforded ASEAN politicians and scholars a new space to advocate a distinctively Asian approach to problem solving and, at the same time, expose the limitations of the western diplomatic process. Thus Noordin Sopiee, Director of the Malaysian Institute of Strategic and International Studies, declared that the western method of security 'emphasizes legalistic forms, agreements, contracts, institutions and structures'. The Asian way, by contrast, 'relies more on the meeting of minds and hearts, on consensus building, peer pressure, and on unilateral good and proper behavior' (Sopiee, in *Straits Times*, 1 September 1991; see also Sopiee 1992).

Whilst Asia possessed no supranational institutions comparable to the North Atlantic Treaty Organization or the European Union, it had, instead, according to Kishore Mabubhani, informal 'networks that are inclusive rather than exclusive' (Mahbubani 1995a, p. 107). Asian values and the inclusive networks of confidence and cooperation they promote had, it was asserted, made possible the advent of a new Pacific community (ibid.). The emergence of what Singapore's then Minister for the Arts, George Yeo, termed a 'common cultural area in East Asia' heralded a 'return to the time when Asia was the cradle of civilization' (quoted in *Straits Times*, 14 September 1992).

The region's 'moment in history' (Mahbubani 1995a, p. 106), it would seem, had finally arrived and the widening and deepening of ASEAN represented its outward and visible sign. The development of the ideology of shared Asian values and the felt need to promote a distinctively ASEAN way constituted the next phase in the construction of a delusion.

When we examine more closely the nature of ASEAN's expanding economic and security role, once again we find that several unacknowledged inconsistencies appeared long before the meltdown that should have exploded many of ASEAN's pretensions. To the dwindling number of sceptics in the field of political science, it was immediately apparent that the security of this supposedly 'autonomous, integrated, exemplary and purposeful' (ibid.) new actor in world affairs continued to rely upon the economic and naval presence of a morally debased United States (Zakaria 1994, pp. 109–13). Thus, in 1992, George Yeo (currently Singapore's Minister of Foreign Affairs), maintained that the United States 'must remain engaged in the region both in economic and military terms in order to complete a new triangular balance of power in East Asia that is vital for the continued prosperity and stability of the region' (*Straits Times*, 14 September 1992).

However, this 'new triangular balance' between Japan, China and the United States required America not only to adopt the Asian way in international relations but also to 'absorb the best of Asian civililization' both to reform its decadent society and to build a 'two way street' across the Pacific (Mahbubani 1995a, p. 107). As Don Emmerson observed, Asian values seemed to assume that 'economic co-operation begins at home while military security involves including powers from abroad including partners such as the United States who can in the long run balance China and Japan' (Emmerson 1995, p. 19; see also *Straits Times*, 2 May 1994). Illustrative of this gap between rhetoric and reality was the example of committed pan-Asianist, Prime Minister Mahathir of Malaysia, who consistently denounced western and particularly American influence in the region. After 1990, Mahathir emerged as a leading sceptic on APEC and promoted instead an East Asian Economic Caucus of Pacific states designed to keep out the United States, an idea subsequently modified to the desire to create an 'ASEAN Plus Three' (ASEAN plus China, South Korea, Japan) after 1998 (Nagatomi 1995, pp. 206–11). Yet, in practice, it always remained far from clear whether the Malaysian desire to limit American influence in the economic sphere extends to the security realm. In fact, much of the rhetoric about regional non-alignment to 'prevent hegemonism whether it be Soviet, Chinese or American' (Deputy Prime Minister Datuk Musa Hitam, quoted in Simon 1987, p. 23) disguises Malaysia's *de facto* support for the US military presence (ibid.), evidenced by the revelation in April 1992 of a secret agreement, concluded in 1984, to provide high-level defence cooperation between Malaysia and the United States (Acharya 1993, p. 57).

A similar ambivalence characterized ASEAN's economic initiatives and the problematic attempt to deepen regional economic cooperation. As the World Bank noted approvingly in its own paean to the region's supposed economic miracle, ASEAN growth since the 1960s has been largely export-led (World Bank 1993, chap. 1). Southeast Asia's growth has been notable for its success-ful cultivation of foreign direct investment, largely from Japan, Taiwan and South Korea and the export of cheap, labour-intensive manufactured goods to the North American market. Southeast Asian capitalism, as Kunio Yoshihara observed, has been largely 'technologyless' (Yoshihara 1988, pp. 125–6). To sustain growth, the ASEAN economies depended upon the continuing open-ness of the North American market and the post-GATT World Trade Order. Despite AFTA and the much-vaunted integration of the regional economy, inter-ASEAN trade remained substantially less in the 1990s than it was before 1939.

The deepening of inter-ASEAN trading links has proved more symbolic than real, illustrated by the failure of the purported Batam–Johore–Singapore growth triangle and the continual renegotiating, notably by Indonesia and Thailand, of 'sensitive' trade items that will require protection after 2010 ('Par for the course', 1995). Indeed, despite the impressive growth rates sustained by the ASEAN economies in the period 1985–95, it became increasingly apparent that, in their haste to industrialize, the mounting foreign debt incurred by Thailand, the Philippines, Malaysia and Indonesia, together with their uncertain futures as low-cost/low-value added manufacturing bases for the Japanese *keiretsu* and South Korean *chaebol* (industrial conglomerates), left them highly exposed to the vagaries of the world market, especially the finan-cial market in globally traded derivatives. Subsequent exposure to the elec-tronic herd of globalized finance culminated in the economic meltdown of 1997 from which these economies have yet to recover and whose causes ASEAN's various forums have done little to address, as we showed in the preceding chapter (Yoshihara 1988, chap. 6; 'States of denial', 1996, pp. 56–7).

Equally incoherent was ASEAN's post-1993 attempt to promote the notion of both regional stability and autonomy in the new world order, by encourag-ing the assimilation of former communist states in the region, whose threat in the 1960s constituted the raison d'être for the organization's formation. In a landmark event for the Association, Vietnam joined the grouping in 1995. The culmination of the vision of a stable region united through ASEAN was timetabled to occur at the Association's thirtieth anniversary meeting of foreign ministers at Kuala Lumpur in July 1997, when the organization would formally embrace Laos, Cambodia and Myanmar in an 'ASEAN-10'. The attempt to establish this expanded regional group, however, was particularly to reveal the implausibility of ASEAN's philosophy.

Contradictions in the ASEAN way to security in Southeast Asia were most readily apparent in the Association's dealings with the State Law and Order Restoration Council (SLORC) regime in Burma/Myanmar and Hun Sen's Cambodian People's Party's (CPP) *de facto* government of Cambodia after July 1997. In the early 1990s, ASEAN predictably employed its non-interventionist and non-confrontational style in dealing with Burma. ASEAN consistently refused to condemn the military junta in Rangoon and, instead, followed a path of 'constructive engagement' through dialogue and economic investment ('Asian help for Burma weakens sanctions', 1996). Accordingly, Burma was inducted into the ASEAN fold at Kuala Lumpur in July 1997. The entry of Burma/Myanmar into ASEAN was premised on the desire to fulfil the founder members' vision of a politically stable Southeast Asia encompassing the region from Indochina to Indonesia. Central to this endeavour was, of course, the principle of non-interference and territorial integrity, which SLORC, naturally, found agreeable and willingly respected.

The pragmatic vindication of the principles of constructive engagement and non-interference, however, were almost immediately overturned by the ASEAN member states themselves when, at the same meeting, they refused to countenance the entry of Cambodia. The Association had, of course, taken a keen interest in the resolution of the Cambodian crisis and member states had contributed significantly to the interim UN peacekeeping force in Cambodia prior to elections in 1993. In the aftermath, Hun Sen overthrew the unhappy coalition, of which he had formed a key part, in 1997. ASEAN in particular felt it had 'lost face' as a consequence of the coup. ASEAN's response to the coup and its call for new elections in Cambodia violated its own often stated principle of non-interference which, if applied to other member states, would have required the expulsion of both Burma and Indonesia from the organization. Subsequently, new elections held in 1997, characterized by a mixture of vote buying and intimidation, afforded a facade of respectability to Hun Sen's regime that enabled Cambodia to meet the increasingly flexible criteria necessary for ASEAN membership in 1998.

By 1997, the fundamental difficulty confronting the Southeast Asian states, therefore, was that, while they were increasingly unwilling to accept US hegemony and the liberal post-Bretton Woods trading order it facilitated, there were insufficient indigenous resources to uphold a *pax Asiana*, which, in turn, condemned ASEAN to continued dependence upon either the US hegemon or some more complex arrangement that involves a balance of Chinese, US and Japanese interests ('The Pacific needs pax Americana', 1996). Prior to 1997 sustained economic growth, which induced a large degree of complacency about the efficacy of regional structures to resolve security problems, obscured this paradox at the core of ASEAN. Nevertheless, the unwillingness to recognize that this paradox existed indicated the disjointed nature of both security and economic relationships in the region. Indeed, the Association's raison d'être has been to obscure fundamental differences of view between its members under the guise of consensus and non-interference. In achieving this somewhat limited goal it has been mostly successful, particularly during the Cold War. In the post-Cold War era, however, the underlying ambiguities became increasingly exposed.

THE ERSATZ DIPLOMACY OF PRE-MELTDOWN SOUTHEAST ASIA

In certain respects some ASEAN statesmen implicitly appreciated the limits of ASEAN's role in an age of uncertainty prior to 1997 (see Foot 1996, p. 29). The very formation of the ARF, for example, recognized that the Association was by itself insufficient to promote regional security. By creating a broad dialogue group encompassing states with an interest in Pacific affairs, the ARF is intended primarily, according to Michael Leifer, 'to educate an irredentist China in the canons of good regional citizenship and to sustain the active engagement of the US in regional affairs' (Leifer 1995). The ARF, however, mirrors its ASEAN progenitors' emphasis on a consensual 'step by step' approach to regional problems (Jusuf Wanandi, *Far Eastern Economic Review*, 3 August 1995; see also Lee 1992). In other words, despite being more inclusive, the ARF simply projected ASEAN uncertainty into the wider Pacific basin. In its formal meetings the ARF has spent its time avoiding confrontation ('Terrific Pacific', 1996; 'Pointless?', 1996). Moreover, even in its informal South China Sea workshops where ASEAN was slightly more outspoken in its dialogue with China, China seemed notably reluctant to learn the lessons of 'good regional citizenship' when it affected issues of irrefragable sovereignty. Indeed, the fact that China refused to address issues of sovereignty within a multilateral framework rendered confidence-building measures limited in effect ('East Asia wobbles', 1995).

Since the ARF strategy is unlikely to shape a new Pacific Asian community, and given the emerging threat posed by Chinese irredentism, it is not surprising that states in the region sought solace in more traditional security arrangements, namely, national self-defence and balance of power politics. Between 1984 and 1995, all ASEAN members, with the exceptions of Vietnam and the Philippines, significantly expanded their military capabilities, especially in sea and air power (*Straits Times*, 21 February 1994). Increasing insecurity across the region has seen Singapore granting US naval forces extra facilities, the

Philippines re-negotiating its US security links, and it even prompted staunch proponents of regional neutrality like Malaysia and Indonesia to enhance their military ties with the Americans.

Most surprisingly of all, in January 1996, Indonesia surprised its ASEAN colleagues by concluding a security treaty with Australia, much to the consternation of pan-Asianists like Mahathir (*Economist*, 5 Janaury 1996). Although the treaty committed both countries only to consult each other in the event of a crisis and to explore avenues to enhance joint security (*News and View Indonesia*, January 1996, p. 2), it indicated considerable underlying scepticism towards the ARF, and by implication ASEAN. Subsequent events, as we shall show, rendered the treaty effectively stillborn. Nevertheless, this departure in ASEAN relations suggests that Southeast Asian states were somewhat aware of the underlying frailty of regional structures and were, as a result, reluctant to place all their faith in Asian values as a path to security.

In fact, what was particularly notable about the security debate of the early 1990s in the ASEAN region was its striking resemblance to the debate nearly three decades earlier when the US faced its Vietnamese nemesis. In 1968, Coral Bell observed that the 'characteristic pattern of American policy in Asia is one of ambivalence, of swinging between what may be called the assumption of an American protectorate in Asia and a reassessment of the costs of implementing that assumption' (Bell 1968, p. 9). Over 35 years later the security equation has remained largely unchanged, illustrated in the 1990s by anxiety about a dwindling US presence in an era of superpower retrenchment, and fear that the declining credibility of the American security commitment would create a political vacuum, thereby abandoning the region to an unknown fate (Shiina 1995, p. 220).

What this fate might entail necessarily raised questions about the emergence of China and its hegemonic aspirations. As one regional commentator asked, 'will it [China] become a country that values harmony within the international community, or will it emerge as a major power seeking primacy, if not hegemony in the Asia Pacific?' (Shiina 1995, p. 220). Analogous questions were being posed in the late 1960s (see Buchan 1966, pp. 271–81; Bell 1966, pp. 151–60). Moreover, the continuing speculation about regional structures, which over three decades ago were, it was believed, set to evolve (Darby 1973a, p. 29), but probably not to a level where any collection of Asian states would be able to afford their own security (Darby 1973b, p. 208), demonstrated that the position of the US remained crucial as the 'only country that can function as a power balancer' (Shinyo 1995, p. 224). The 'question Asians are asking today,' declared former Thai Foreign Minister, Thanat Khoman, in 1976, is, 'what do you think the United States can and will do in Southeast Asia?' (Khoman 1976, p. 313). The question, over 30 years later, remained the same.

Gerald Segal has perhaps come closest to explaining the intrinsic difficulty of a mutlilateralist arrangement like ASEAN in post-Cold War Asia. The problem resides in the very notion of the 'Pacific' as a geo-political entity (Segal 1992, pp. 407–9). The Pacific area is not a unitary bloc. The 'Asia–Pacific', and sub-regions like Southeast Asia, are essentially Eurocentric geographical contrivances (see Osborne 1995, pp. 4–5; Huxley 1996, pp. 203–4). Pacific Asia encompasses huge diversity. There is no common or dominant cultural, religious or ethnic identity and, as a consequence, no shared set of social, political or security values. This, together with the globalization of finance, information and technology, which the ASEAN economies must necessarily embrace, further inhibits the maturation of cohesive regional identities like ASEAN (Segal 1992, pp. 414–17).

In 1973, Michael Leifer considered the development of ASEAN at that time to be distinguished 'by resolutions rather than resolve' and 'a general, if unstated, recognition that the association has neither the sense of common interest nor the resources to shape the future pattern of regional order' (Leifer 1973, p. 607). Although the pretensions of ASEAN grew exponentially in the subsequent two and a half decades, the organization remained beset by the absence of common interests beyond survival or the resources to sustain regional order.

Despite, or perhaps because of, the inability to develop the joint force structure necessary to give its enhanced regional status credibility, ASEAN has nevertheless maintained, across three decades, a number of incoherences: it is committed to regional neutrality, most recently symbolized by the declaration at the fifth ASEAN summit (1995) of a Southeast Asian Nuclear Weapons Free Zone (SEANNWFZ), and yet this non-aligned neutralism requires the semi-detached presence of the United States; ASEAN believes in the inviolability of territorial boundaries and the refusal to comment upon the internal politics of member states, but any attempt to deepen or widen the Association necessarily entails political or economic 'interference', as illustrated by events in Cambodia and Myanmar.

The paradox remains why, given the contradictory character of many ASEAN initiatives since 1971, has ASEAN succeeded in the promotion of itself as a regional solution to regional questions rather than a regional delusion? The paradox is easily resolved if one reflects that at various times ASEAN has served as a convenient front for the needs of external actors. After 1971, it served the interests of the Nixon doctrine. In the run-up to the Cambodian settlement it served both United States and Chinese interests. And in the early 1990s, it served as the focus of an emerging Japanese regional foreign policy (see Khamchoo 1991, pp. 7–10; Hughes 1996). It has, moreover, been in the interest of both external actors and ASEAN itself to conceal these facts.

Events after the economic meltdown of 1997, however, exposed the devastating consequences of this post-Cold War regional delusion and revealed this imitation community to be not only irrelevant, but also detrimental to addressing the issues of corruption, ethnic separatism and religious fundamentalism that rapidly transformed Southeast Asia from a purported economic miracle to a region desperately in need of one. In the following sections we shall explore the negative impact of ASEAN upon regional stability after 1997.

THE IMITATION COMMUNITY AND THE POLITICAL CONSEQUENCES OF MELTDOWN

While countries with decidedly different, and often competing, security perceptions formed ASEAN, analysts maintained that the organization attained its international stature through an ability 'to manage regional problems rather than solve them' (Leifer 1995). Yet its constituting indifference to the domestic affairs of neighbouring states meant that the Association had remarkably little impact on unresolved inter-state disputes dating from the era of decolonization. The failure to deal with these differences during the Cold War has further implications for ASEAN's current ineffectiveness in tackling low-intensity religious and ethnic conflicts, not least because it reveals the fundamentally imitative quality of ASEAN itself.

Unresolved territorial conflicts include the Philippines' outstanding claim to Sabah; competing Malaysian and Indonesian claims to the islands of Litigan and Sipidan; and the contested ownership of the island of Pedra Branca by Malaysia and Singapore. Meanwhile, personal rivalries between regional men of prowess, like that between former Prime Minister Mahathir and former President Suharto, perennially erode informal interpersonal ties. Simmering suspicion has always characterized relations between Malaysia and Singapore. Singapore's defence posture offers the most graphic illustration of this. As Tim Huxley maintains, the Singapore Armed Forces' order of battle 'appears to be designed for the possibility of war with Malaysia' and he speculated that the Singaporeans would 'aim to disable' the Malaysian armed forces by 'a brutal and fearless pre-emptive strike' (Huxley 1991, p. 204).

Elsewhere in the region, unremitting communal attachments have always conflicted with the nation-building process in Southeast Asia. In this context, the Malaysian government's tacit support for Muslim separatist organizations, notably the Moro National Liberation Front (MNLF) in Southern Mindanao which organized training camps in Sabah in 1980, and the Pattani United Liberation Organization (PULO), has consistently aggravated relations with both Buddhist Thailand and the Catholic Philippines (Tan 2000a, p. 40). Likewise, Thailand has a legacy of difficult relations with both Burma and

Vietnam that ASEAN has done little to alleviate (ibid., pp. 43–52; Chalk 1997, pp. 41–54). In fact membership of ASEAN seems only to have deepened conflict along the Thai–Burmese border and encouraged the Rangoon regime's emergence as the world's largest supplier of illicit heroine and *yabba* (methamphetamine) (see 'Thailand wages battles against border smugglers', 2000).

Moreover, the post-Cold War era has not only altered the character of international relationships in the region, it also disrupted the previously delicate internal balance between ASEAN members, further revealing the organization's constituting ambivalence. The end of the Cold War ushered in a fluid political environment in Asia which, while not threatening to erupt into open conflict, has complicated ASEAN's security calculations. The collapse of the Soviet position in East Asia removed a natural counter-weight to Chinese irredentism. In addition, the reductions in US forces once more raised anxiety about the certainty of American commitment. Meanwhile, China's seemingly inexorable economic rise has enabled it to display long-neglected irredentist claims to the disputed Paracel and Spratly island chains in the South China Sea, and indulge, after 1995, in periodic confrontations with its purportedly 'rebellious province' of Taiwan.

Prior to the economic meltdown of 1997, the post-Cold War security situation in Asia revealed that the ASEAN states were increasingly divided in outlook, with no coherent strategy to address the challenges that confront the region. Polite, but nevertheless increasing, dissension emerged in ASEAN between those states, such as Singapore and the Philippines, which perceived a security vacuum in the area and sought after 1995 to bolster the American presence, and those like Indonesia and Malaysia that wanted to distance the ASEAN region from outside interference (see Acharya 1993, pp. 57–9).

After 1997, it became increasingly clear that an official multilateralist orthodoxy committed to shared ASEAN values had distorted the underlying realist characteristics of ASEAN in the immediate post-Cold War period. This in turn meant that it became impossible for the regional grouping to acknowledge let alone address the 'new wave of identity politics' related to 'the process of globalization' (Kaldor 1999, p. 7) that swept the region in the course of the 1990s and intensified in the wake of the financial meltdown of 1997. At the same time an alarming mixture of ideological distortion and structural change in the external environment rendered the post-colonial attempts at nation building, the resilience of which ASEAN was intended to guarantee, subject to increasing pressure from above and below the state.

One of ASEAN's basic problems is that it has suffered from a gap between rhetorical aspiration and regional reality. As Leifer noticed, ASEAN's origins reflected a security commitment to a balance of power within the framework of a distinctly Eurocentric 'concert' of powers (Leifer 1996, p. 13). Such a realist 'concert of Southeast Asia' not only constrained Indonesia, the largest member of the grouping, it also assumed a commitment to internal 'national resilience' and the need, as Suharto explained in 1967, to conceive 'the development process of a nation' as an enterprise (Leifer 1989, p. 4). In the 1970s, ASEAN and its institutionalized scholarship found it useful to obscure the inherent contradiction that a regional arrangement, which implicitly transcended the state, actually constituted a mechanism to consolidate the insecure imitation nations of Southeast Asia. In other words, the Treaty of Amity and Cooperation recognized that internal arrangements of member states remained sacrosanct in their inviolability. Yet this realist commitment to the state as the major actor in a concert became, over time, elided into an anti-realist framework of multilateral interdependence, shared 'norms' and the cooperative management of a 'security community.'

In this context, analysts who praised the virtue of Asia–Pacific multilateralism deliberately neglected the weaknesses inherent in the enterprise associations of Southeast Asia by enveloping them in the rhetorical cloak of an imitation community. Despite, or more precisely because of, its incoherence, this thesis won warm endorsement from ASEAN's ruling elites. In practice, Southeast Asia's regimes coopted the discourse of multilateralism to sustain the fiction of a harmonious regional community that obscured its constituting ambivalence. In so doing, political elites deflected analytical attention from both existing tensions among ASEAN states and the internal divisions within their states that reflected unresolved ethnic and religious dissonance and opaque networks of corruption and patronage.

Even at the height of the enthusiasm for the 'ASEAN way' in the mid-1990s, as we have shown, a number of unacknowledged contradictions were already apparent within the dense web of ASEAN-style casuistry. Mounting evidence after 1997 that ASEAN statesmen ultimately had little practical interest in pursuing multilateralist ventures in cooperative security further exacerbated ASEAN's ideological confusions. Increasingly they promulgated classic realist understandings of the balance of power as the primary guarantee of stability, especially the need to retain US influence in the Asia–Pacific to offset the rising power of China. As Lee Kuan Yew stated in late 2000, 'the role of the United States as the balancer is crucial if Asian countries are to have elbow room for themselves' (Lee 2000).

A similar incoherence permeated ASEAN's economic initiatives and the largely rhetorical attempt to deepen regional trade cooperation. The very patchy regional recovery from the 1997 meltdown, during 1999 and 2000, demonstrated both the irrelevance of inter-ASEAN trade to regional growth and the worrying emergence of China as a direct competitor for foreign direct investment rather than a partner in a shared future of cooperative Asian capitalism.

At the start of the Pacific Century, therefore, a variety of political, economic and security contradictions confronted ASEAN. Further, the Association's purpose was to conceal fundamental differences of view between its members under the guise of consensus and non-interference. It succeeded in achieving this somewhat limited goal during the Cold War. However, in the post-meltdown era, defensive ethnic or religious fundamentalism represented a growing response at the sub-state level to the uncertainties generated by exposure to an inexorable process of globalization at the supra-state level, which rendered the Asian Cold War model of building national resilience increasingly friable. It is ASEAN's inability to address these centrifugal tendencies that we shall explore next.

POST-MELTDOWN TENSIONS

As the depth and severity of the economic recession engulfing the export economies of Indonesia and Malaysia intensified in the course of 1997, the contradiction between domestic nation-building ideologies of the Southeast Asian imitation state and a supposedly shared value system came to the fore, brutally exposing the limits of multilateralism and the illusory character of ASEAN.

Prior to the financial meltdown, analysts declared that ASEAN's preoccupation with process delivered real, if not apparent, benefits which rendered the organization something more than an obsolescent anti-communist collective. Events after 1997, however, revealed precisely the opposite. Without an external communist threat the Association lacked any common purpose, while its process-oriented diplomacy appeared unequal to the challenge.

Recession-related factors quickly frayed the always volatile relations between Singapore and Malaysia, with both countries congenitally unable to refrain from comment on each other's internal affairs. Malaysia's officials criticized Singapore banks for aiding capital flight out of the country, threatened treaties guaranteeing Singapore's water supply and banned Singaporean military flights over its airspace. In Singapore, the ruling People's Action Party's nervous propensity to advertise its concerns over the policies responsible for the region's recession only fuelled bilateral tensions. Lee Kuan Yew's undiplomatic observations upon the fraught nature of the Indonesian political succession in the course of 1998 further strained the 'good' interpersonal relations central to ASEAN-style diplomacy. The subsequent failure of Singapore to disburse $3 billion in trade credit guarantees promised the previous April prompted a newly anointed, and short-lived, President Habibie to dismiss the city state as a mere 'red dot on the map' that was unresponsive to a 'friend in need' (quoted in *Financial Times*, 21 August 1998).

The volatility in diplomatic relations continued with Prime Minister Mahathir coming in for criticism from President Joseph Estrada of the Philippines and Indonesia's President Habibie for the arrest and trial of former Malaysian Deputy Prime Minister, Anwar Ibrahim ('Habibie, Estrada rethink KL visit', 1998). By the end of 1998, the economic crisis had seen the ASEAN spirit dissolve to a point where there was 'more name-calling than handshaking' ('Fightin' words', 1998).

Interpersonal bickering amongst ASEAN members heightened the paralysis at the heart of the imitation community. Predictably, ASEAN commentators dismissed the economic crisis as 'no more than a bump' (Almonte 1997, p. 86). In reality, however, the manifest lack of elite cohesion and legitimacy in conditions of economic recession released the fear that for so long dared not speak its name, namely, ethnic and religious or 'communalist', tension. Significantly, the crisis has highlighted the continuing vulnerability and separatist aspirations of ethnic and religious minorities that form substantial populations within the imitation states that created ASEAN.

The months following the 1997 economic crisis again emphasized the uncertain status of the overseas Chinese in the Southeast Asian region. Since the colonial era, when economic migrants from Southern China occupied an ambivalent comprador role in the European empires, indigenous leaders in both Indonesia and Malaysia have suspected the loyalties of the Chinese trading class. The continued ascendancy of Chinese business interests in postcolonial Indonesia and Malaysia caused both states to introduce official distinctions between indigenous and non-indigenous subjects. Yet, despite their political and cultural marginalization, Chinese entrepreneurs remained central to the rapid growth of these tiger economies after 1970. The prominence of the Chinese in Indonesian commerce made them an obvious scapegoat for economic failure, exemplified by the events of May 1998, when Suharto's fall was accompanied by the organized pillaging of Chinese districts in Jakarta and East Java ('Jakarta admits 76 rapes in May riots', 1998).

The Chinese have always represented the most obvious minority in Southeast Asia, and thus, traditionally, the obvious target when times become interesting. However, attempts at political consolidation since decolonization have spawned wider and increasingly intractable intercommunal tensions. During the Cold War ASEAN members tried to resolve the problems of nation building posed by the host of ethnic minorities within their borders by turning themselves into ethnocracies of various descriptions, which discriminated against minority groups. Consequently, the aftermath of the 1997 economic crisis witnessed increasing interethnic violence involving non-Chinese minorities. In March 2001, Kuala Lumpur saw the most serious interethnic violence in Malaysia since 1969, which left nearly a dozen people dead, but this time the conflict involved Indian and Malay communities. Somewhat differently, in

Kalimantan after 1998, an escalating regional propensity for ethnic cleansing prompted the indigenous Dayak communities to launch brutal assaults on Madurese incomers, moved to Kalimantan under the auspices of the Indonesian government's transmigration programme.

Elsewhere, in the Maluku islands and in the Philippines, violence has flared between Christians and Muslims, whilst in Thailand there is constant tension between the Muslim minority and the officially Buddhist state, and, in the Northeast, Isan ethno-regionalism remains a potent centrifugal force. Further, Burma's recent membership of ASEAN has failed to mitigate historic Thai–Burmese tensions exacerbated by the Karen separatist struggle. As Walker Connor observed in the 1970s, nation building during the Cold War was also a nation-destroying activity (Connor 1972, pp. 319–55). In the aftermath of the Cold War and the painful adjustment to globalization, the previously suppressed ethno-religious differences that gave purported resilience both to the nation-building states and to the overarching imitation community have returned with a vengeance to wreak havoc upon both.

The assumption that the low-level conflicts that racked Southeast Asia since decolonization would wither away as the Pacific Century matured has, since 1997, proved unfounded. In fact the growing influence of Middle Eastern fundamentalism on the formerly moderate, sometimes syncretic, 'civil Islam' practised in the region, has exacerbated intramural tensions and threatens to undermine the arduous post-colonial work of nation building (Pererira 2000). Towards the end of the twentieth century, increasingly chiliastic Islamic sects like *Al Ma'unah* (Brotherhood of Inner Power) in Northern Malaysia and *Abu Sayyaf* (Father of the Sword) in Southern Mindanao threatened the security along the Thai–Malaysian and in the Philippine–Malaysian maritime frontier zone (see Hamid 2000).

The post-Cold War conflict between what Benjamin Barber identified as 'Jihad versus McWorld' (see Barber 1996, esp. chap. 6) and the importation of Islamic radicalism from Libya, Iran and Pakistan since 1979 accentuated the appeal of Islamic separatism as well as feeding the growing Puritanism of the Parti Islam Se-Malaysia (PAS) opposition in Malaysia. In Mindanao, despite the signing of a peace accord between the Libya-sponsored MNLF and the Philippine government in 1997, the conflict between the Catholic Philippine army and the equally militant Moro Islamic Liberation Front (MILF) has escalated dramatically since 1999.

One of the most disturbing of all the post-meltdown consequences in Southeast Asia has been the uncertain transition to democratic rule in Indonesia, the largest and most significant member state of the ASEAN grouping, which has been plagued by 'dark forces' that threaten the 'national resilience' so assiduously cultivated by Suharto's 'New Order' between 1965 and 1997. Across the archipelago issues of identity and religion often provoked by dissident elements in the Indonesian armed forces have beset the post-New Order settlement of Indonesia. Since East Timor achieved its independence after what Xanana Gusmao termed 'the dreadful destruction of September 1999' (Hill and Saldanha, p. xvi) undertaken by Indonesia-backed militias, the post-New Order regime appeared increasingly powerless to contain the dissolution of the Indonesian periphery in Aceh and West Papua. Indeed, with the partial abrogation of the Indonesian military ethic of *dwifungsi*, the central government in Jakarta possesses even fewer resources to sustain the internal resilience of a disintegrating Javanese empire.

ASEAN has floundered in its attempts to manage both the regional economic crisis and its legacy of intercommunal violence and separatist struggles. Moreover, the foundational ASEAN doctrine of non-interference in the internal affairs of member states has only intensified the failure. Indonesia, Malaysia and Singapore, the core states of ASEAN, retain an inflexible commitment to this stance despite the fact that it is obviously obsolete. The murder of a *Gerakan Aceh Merdeka* (Free Aceh Movement) faction leader in Kuala Lumpur by 'Indonesian agents' in June 2000, and the attempted assassination of the Philippine ambassador in Jakarta by Moro secessionists in August 2000, followed by the exposure of the activities of *Jemaah Islamiyah* (Islamic Organization) in 2001, graphically illustrate the fact that violent ethno-religious separatists will interfere in the internal affairs of member states.

THE CONSEQUENCES OF A FAILED REGION

ASEAN's patent irrelevance to the evolving security disorder in Southeast Asia cannot be attributed solely to the effects of economic meltdown. ASEAN's founding contradiction was the assumption that its studied informality and consensus-driven approach provided a dispute management process whereby 'Divisive issues are simply passed over for later resolution' (Almonte 1997, p. 81). Curiously, ASEAN was a conflict resolution organization, without any conflict resolution mechanism: its own *modus operandi* precluded it from having one. Far from pointing out this incongruity, analysts made a virtue out of the fact that the 'ASEAN way involves a commitment to carry on with consultations without any specific formula or modality for achieving a desired outcome' (Acharya 1997a, p. 329). This was completely self-deluding. The 'ASEAN way' did not deal with underlying tensions. It simply ignored them.

Since 1997, the security situation in East Asia reveals, in fact, that the ASEAN states possess no clear strategy to respond to the challenges the organization currently faces. ASEAN, of course, possesses all the paraphernalia that regional organizations require: media-attended ministerial meetings, a secretariat, a bureaucracy and even a new 'troika' to take the lead in dealing with regional problems. Yet it can make no decisions and enforce no rules. ASEAN is, then, an imitation community. ASEAN, moreover, is not a modish constructivist project, as its apologists often claim. It cannot even sustain an 'ideational' discourse of regionalism, which believes that only to 'imagine' a community is to have it somehow materialize. It is an anti-constructivist project. The inviolable canon of non-interference negates the expression of a region. It merely denotes recognition of a collocation of independent sovereign states.

In this crucial respect, ASEAN is a declaratory contradiction. It purports to describe a regional arrangement that gives expression to the geo-political entity of Southeast Asia. But the terms of accession to ASEAN require the explicit recognition of the principle of non-interference in the domestic affairs of member states. It is a *non sequitur* to build a community among neighbouring states on the basis of official indifference to those neighbours. Only the rigid maintenance of an ASEAN-sponsored scholarly doublethink, memorably defined by George Orwell as 'the capacity to hold two contradictory views in one's mind simultaneously and accept both of them', prevented the exposure of ASEAN's constituting ambivalence. The essential contradiction embodied in ASEANthink, then, is that, while it is intended to establish the notion of a region called Southeast Asia, in effect, it calls on its members to accept that there is no region.

Finally, an imitation community, and how to address its deluded membership, clearly pose a challenge to foreign policy makers outside ASEAN who have had to deal with the consequences of its inability to tackle regional problems. Until quite recently, moreover, both the Australian Department of Foreign Affairs and Trade (DFAT) and the US State Department crucially underestimated the long-term causes of regional weakness, together with the destabilizing political and economic factors of more recent vintage. This neglect, of course, reflected an overreliance on imitation scholarship. Between 1986 and 1996, DFAT, in particular, propped up by academic advisers in a variety of well-endowed university departments and think tanks, wasted its energies on 'enmeshment' and engagement with a region that was essentially an illusion. Only since 1997 has Canberra begun to reassess how it stabilizes a disintegrating Southeast Asia rather than ingratiates itself with what it assumed to be the new Asian-model El Dorado.

Somewhat differently, US foreign policy assumed an untroubled ASEAN-led Southeast Asia as the inexorable corollary of the Nixon doctrine. Only since the débâcle of East Timor have both Canberra and Washington realized the centrality of a proactive Australia and a supportive United States coordinating policy to maintain regional balance ('Security plan built on solid ground', 2001). Ultimately, the uncertain collocation of fragile states that connote the failed delusional entity of Southeast Asia require a US and Australian presence far more than the latter require ASEAN. This has been especially evident in the stabilization of East Timor, where ASEAN proved ineffectual.

The recognition of ASEAN's irrelevance, in turn, necessitates a reassessment of bilateral arrangements with the very different individual states and their distinctive interests that compose this imitation community. At a bilateral level Australia and the US may plausibly educate the more pliable and market-oriented states like Singapore, Thailand and the Philippines in the formal and rule-governed formulas that regulate relations between states or sustain international arrangements like the World Trade Organization, while maintaining a sceptical distance from the inflated rhetoric of an ASEAN Plus Three or some other equally vapid scheme for pan-Asian renewal. Furthermore, Canberra and Washington should pursue these foreign policy goals without paying lip service to the pieties of an Asian way, a Pacific Century and a regional arrangement sustained only by its delusions.

NOTE

1. US financial aid to the rest of Southeast Asia (Vietnam, Laos, Cambodia and Burma) between 1945 and 1967 totalled US$4.134 billion, while total US aid to Asia as a whole in the same period amounted to US$24.915 billion: figures compiled from Government of the United States (1968) *Statistical Abstract of the United States 1968*, Washington, DC: Government Publishing Office, pp. 798–9 (cited in Wilcox 1968, p. 21).

3. Asia rising (again): ASEAN and the illusion of an Asian model of economic development

ASIA FALLING, ASIA RISING?

Over the past decade students of East Asian Political Economy will have been struck by the rapid mood swings affecting the formerly dismal science. A wander through Borders bookshop in Orchard Road, Singapore in 1997 would have presented the prospective student with titles like *Asia Rising: How History's Biggest Middle Class will Transform the World*, *The New Rich in Asia: Mobile Phones, McDonalds and Middle Class Revolution* or *The New Asian Renaissance*. A year later the same student in the same bookshop would have found these volumes, if not on special offer, replaced by new titles like *Asia Falling? Making Sense of the Asian Currency Crisis and its Aftermath* or *The Downsizing of Asia*, often written by the same authors (see, for example, Godement 1996, 1999; Henderson 1998; Robison and Goodman 1996; Rohwer 1996). Despite a brief, but unsustained, recovery in 1999, the bursting of the new economic paradigm in the United States and the ensuing tech wreck that occasioned a global economic slowdown between 2000 and 2003 only reinforced the view that East Asia in general and Southeast Asia in particular lacked the capacity to recover the economic dynamism of the early 1990s.

However, as the global economy began to recover from the paralysis that gripped it in the aftermath of September 11, the Asia–Pacific surprisingly re-emerged as the destination of choice for foreign direct investment. By late 2003, academic, newspaper and electronic media commentators once again enthused over the economic dynamism of the region and its impressive growth prospects. The 1997 financial crisis, it was now maintained, merely represented a pothole on the road to deeper regional political and economic integration. Indeed, a prevailing understanding of the political and economic dislocation of the period 1997–2003 now assumes that it was a cyclical adjustment exacerbated by the unnecessary panic of primarily western speculators adumbrated by the electronic herd mentality of an incoherently regulated global market in currency and derivative trading. Thus, in April 2004, the *Economist* busily dusting down the clichés it had circulated a decade before, pronounced *ex cathedra* that, 'call them tigers or dragons, write of thunder in the east or a shining India: whichever image you prefer, the Asian economic miracle is exactly that'. Although there had been the odd financial and political difficulty, the remarkable thing was 'how quickly most of the Asian economies had bounced back from them' (*Economist*, 24 April 2004, p. 11).

Yet the optimism that characterized commentary upon the political economy of the Asia–Pacific in 2004, like the global recovery more generally, seems somewhat brittle. The double-digit growth that caused economists, journalists and investment fund managers to salivate emanated from China and India, not from the miracle High Performing Asian Economies (HPAEs) previously celebrated by the World Bank report of 1993. Interestingly, it is the huge pool of low-cost and adaptable labour in China, combined with the comparative cheapness of Asian currencies, rather than any technological advantage that fuels the latest version of an economic miracle and attracts hot money and foreign direct investment. Ironically, a similar 'astonishing mobilization of resources' had, as we shall show, accounted for the miracle growth in Southeast Asia prior to 1997 (Krugman 1994, p. 8; see also Young 1995, pp. 655–80).

Moreover, amidst the excited claims that China and India have emerged as global economic players and that economic recovery in South Korea, Taiwan and Japan portends the development of an integrated economic region, there is relatively little attention given to the ASEAN economies as a significant factor in the latest instalment of the Asian economic growth drama. Indeed, a number of commentators both within and beyond Southeast Asia have wondered what, if anything, the grouping brings to the latest pan-Asian economic party. This contrasts dramatically with the mood that prevailed in the early 1990s. For, in that heady decade, it was the rapid development of Southeast Asia, the premonitory snuffling of a process to form an ASEAN Free Trade Area (AFTA) by 2008 (later revised to 2003) and the rapid expansion of the group to embrace Vietnam, Laos, Burma–Myanmar and Cambodia by 1999 that seemed to presage what then Singapore Home Affairs Minister George Yeo described in 1995 as a vital 'new East Asian Co-Prosperity sphere' (Yeo 1995, p. 75).

In order to clarify recent developments in the political economy of the Asia–Pacific, this chapter explores the rise of the Pacific Rim economies during the Cold War and considers the role of the ASEAN states in pan-Asian economic development before 1997. This will be followed by an account of the role of regional arrangements like ASEAN and, after 1989, Asia–Pacific Economic Cooperation (APEC) and AFTA in forging ever closer regional ties, together with the manner in which the region and its institutions responded to the 1997 financial crisis. We shall subsequently evaluate what role the ASEAN states and broader regional groupings like ASEAN Plus Three (Japan, South

Korea and China) play in the post-meltdown regional and global economy together with their future role in an increasingly interconnected but by no means integrated global economy.

THE POLITICAL ECONOMY OF PACIFIC ASIA, 1960–97

Curiously, given the media and academic emphasis on an emergent East Asian regionalism, any attempt to explain the economy of the ASEAN states and the role of ASEAN, AFTA, APEC or ASEAN Plus Three has to begin with a state-led model of development, sometimes termed the Asian developmental state. This in itself is paradoxical given that, alongside its role in purportedly securing stability in Southeast Asia after 1967, ASEAN's other claim to international and regional significance is its role in establishing the conditions for regional economic development and subsequent integration. Yet the distinctive political economy of the Asia–Pacific littoral that stretches from Japan through South Korea, Taiwan and Hong Kong to the Southeast Asian countries and which during the 1990s also embraced rapid development in the formerly autarchic economies of China and Vietnam, is essentially a state-driven enterprise characterized by cheap, flexible and docile labour, protected domestic markets, and export-oriented growth to developed markets outside the region guided, in varying degrees, by an apparently autonomous technocratic elite.

Since at least the early 1960s the majority of Pacific Asian economies discussed in this chapter have experienced prodigious rates of growth. The World Bank pronounced the achievement of Japan, South Korea, Taiwan, Hong Kong and the ASEAN economies of Singapore, Thailand, Indonesia and Malaysia an 'East Asian Miracle' (World Bank 1993). Meanwhile, states in the region that seemed more developed economically at the start of the growth era, like the Philippines, or had already achieved high gross domestic product (GDP) by the early 1950s like Australia, which during the 1980s made a conscientious effort to enmesh itself in the Asia–Pacific, were conspicuously less successful in securing rapid growth in the period 1966 to 1996. Yet other states, like the People's Republic of China, until it created special economic zones in the course of the 1970s, together with Southeast Asian states like Laos, Cambodia and Vietnam, until they joined ASEAN between 1995 and 1999, were immured in an iron rice bowl of a Maoist–Stalinist design. The economies of Pacific Asia, therefore, offer an interesting laboratory for investigating what we understand by economic development, the politics associated with such development and the role, if any, that pan-regional arrangements like ASEAN, ASEAN Plus Three and APEC play in this process.

In order to examine the political economy of East Asian development, and the role of the ASEAN states within it, we need first to consider the manner in which the Newly Industrialized Economies (NIEs) developed in the Cold War, beginning with Japan, the paradigmatic example of the developmental state. This will be followed by brief case studies of the later developing Northeast Asian and former Japanese colonies, of South Korea and Taiwan, and the Southeast Asian economies of Singapore, Thailand, Malaysia, the Philippines and Indonesia. These cases will be contrasted with those of the Philippines, which lacked the necessary elite guidance to sustain growth, and communist East and Southeast Asia which from the late 1940s to the late 1970s developed variations upon a Maoist–Stalinist developmental theme.

THE JAPANESE MODEL: GROWTH WITH EQUITY OR THE DUBIOUS VIRTUES OF LONG-TERMISM

In the essentially contested domain of developmental economics, post-war debate over the most effective manner of generating growth in underdeveloped countries focused upon the relative merits of protective import-substituting industrialization versus open trading in liberalized markets. By the 1980s, a number of neo-classical economists claimed that the emergence of Japan and the various dragon and tiger economies spawned along the Pacific littoral represented a victory for the competitive advantage generated by open markets and a potentially economically borderless world. If so, it was a curious victory for, as a number of less doctrinaire analysts showed, although export-oriented, the rise of the Pacific Asian economies demonstrated a high degree of market-governing, state intervention (Chan and Clark 1994, p. 33).

In this context, Japan was the first Asian 'tiger' economy both to sustain high rates of economic growth and to achieve membership of the Organization for Economic Co-operation and Development (OECD) in the post-war period. It has served as an example to later developing Asian economies, and originally constituted the distinctive Asian developmental model. It was in the 1960s that Japan began attracting international attention because of its rapid post-war recovery and successful industrialization. By the late 1980s, as Japanese industrial production, manufacturing, technology and, consequently, GDP overtook that of most western industrialized nations, Japan became a model not only for other late developing economies, but even for reforming western managerial and industrial practice.

Whilst historically industrialization in the United States and the United Kingdom occurred in the context of individual entrepreneurial enterprise, Japan's late modernization significantly subjugated individual interest for the sake of the group. In fact Japan pioneered what Chalmers Johnson identified in his seminal study of the Japanese Ministry for Trade and Industry (MITI), and termed the 'plan rational' state, where 'the government will give the greatest precedence to industrial policy, that is to a concern with the structure of domestic industry and with promoting the structure that enhances the nation's international competitiveness' (Johnson 1982, p. 19). This policy required a goal-driven view of trade to achieve long-term growth with relatively equitable distribution. In particular, MITI influenced investment and directed the principal Japanese producers to adopt the latest technologies. The explanation of Japan's dramatic growth resided in its ability to stimulate exports across a number of sectors (Yoshihara 1994a, p. 78). The development of one industrial sector after another, like 'flying geese', as the Japanese economist Kenichi Akamatsu described it, required technocratic guidance, overseeing links between government, business and finance (Akamatsu 1962, pp. 3–25). Meticulously organized industrial strategy, rather than any evident comparative advantage, thus explained Japan's emergence by the early 1980s as the world's second-largest economy.

In the period after 1951, the Bank of Japan and Ministry of Finance (MOF) kept the *yen* undervalued, domestic savings high and inflation low, thereby facilitating export-led growth. In this context MITI could plan the rise of Japanese manufacturing. In 1951, MITI designated automobile manufacture as a strategic industry and arranged loans for the Nissan and Toyota marques (Matthews and Ravenhill 1994, p. 46). Simultaneously, the government manipulated protective tariffs and restricted foreign direct investment to shelter the industry from foreign competition. This protection was nonetheless 'time-bound' and the threat of future competition spurred the industry to expand productive capacity and avoid excessive price competition. When domestic demand slackened from the early 1970s, these measures helped facilitate a decisive government-sponsored drive into foreign markets. The American market, in particular, became 'the engine that drove the growth of the Japanese auto industry' (Dunn 1989, p. 165). Similar strategic planning explains Japanese dominance of the world television and video tape recorder markets. The focus on generic technologies with broad applications distributed amongst competing domestic firms constituted a crucial ingredient in the strategy for promoting high value added products.

Developments in Japan's business and political culture further promoted an iron triangle of bureaucracy, government and business. In particular, the Liberal Democratic Party (LDP) that, apart from a brief hiccup in 1992–93 has governed Japan uninterruptedly since 1952, facilitated the rule of an elite, highly trained bureaucracy. Administrative guidance required a 'special measures' law that gave a bureaucratic elite the authority to issue directives, requests, warnings, suggestions and encouragements 'to the enterprise ... within a particular ministry's jurisdiction' (Johnson 1982, p. 265). The concept of *Amakaduri*, the procedure of appointing retired bureaucrats to the boards of companies they had previously guided, furthered bureaucratic guidance, whilst the legislative and judicial branches of government confined themselves primarily to deterring demands from the 'numerous interest groups in society which if catered to would distort the priorities of the developmental state' (ibid., p. 315). One particular interest that this iron triangle successfully managed was labour. The unique style of Japanese management that offered, until recently, lifetime employment, seniority-graded wages, seniority-based promotion, group decision making, group responsibility and the minimization of status differences between managers and workers facilitated smooth relations and company loyalty (Yoshihara 1994a, p. 151).

Before examining how later developing states in Pacific Asia utilized this plan rational model, 'the prototype of the capitalist developmental state' (Johnson, in Fallows 1994, p. 252), it should be noted that, as it evolved, the role of government leadership became subject to domestic, industrial and external fiscal constraints. In the view of Daniel Okimoto, the relationship between business and government modified bureaucratic autonomy over time into a 'network' state. In such an arrangement, 'strength is derived from the convergence of public and private interests and the extensive network of ties binding the two sectors together' (Okimoto 1989, p. 145). Such networks not only permeate business and government relations, but business itself functions on the basis of established ties between distributors and manufacturers and between small and large-scale producers, or between companies through cross-cutting share holdings. This loose conglomeration of firms is known as the *keiretsu* structure. *Keiretsu* further facilitated the successful promotion of Japanese trade while at the same time making it extremely difficult for those without access to such networks to penetrate the Japanese domestic market.

Easy access to finance through banks within the *keiretsu* structure meant that growth rather than profitability constituted both the measure of success and a growing moral hazard. Critical analysis of the *keiretsu*'s exploitation of domestic and foreign markets together with their non-performing loans, in fact, questions the state's capacity to direct an autonomous industrial or fiscal policy. Kent Calder contends that *keiretsu* borrowing has generated 'circles of compensation' combining public and private actors with common interests in a particular public policy endeavour. In this assessment, 'rather than picking winners . . . in a flexible fashion across the political economy as a whole, the Japanese state has allocated benefits, including industrial credit, through these established circles, which have, in turn, provided diversified support to the bureaucracy' (Calder 1993, p. 246).

Moreover, the dual impact of domestic clientalistic claims and external pressure to open the domestic market to western and, particularly, American goods profoundly affected the Japanese economy in the course of the 1990s. Ironically, the very success of protecting domestic markets while single-mindedly capturing overseas ones has, in combination with the revaluation of the *yen* after 1985, produced both a wave of overseas investment followed by domestic recession and a deflation of Japanese assets from which the economy has only just begun to emerge.

Hence the Japanese developmental model, as it came to be understood elsewhere in East and Southeast Asia, consisted of a number of interrelated features which we shall consider thematically: a benign trading environment; a high degree of state autonomy to devise and implement policy; the appointment of specific ministries to pick industrial winners and through corporatist strategies promote indigenous conglomerates, export-led growth policies and recourse to aid or foreign direct investment to promote growth; high rates of domestic savings; and educated, cheap, docile and flexible domestic labour. A further feature of this model requires the state both to move up the technology ladder and to respond, as the economy matures, to growing pressures both from within the state for greater access to decision making and from without as a deregulated trade in global finance, which evolved after 1990, required greater financial accountability and the removal of trade barriers. Successful though it evidently was, the developmental model encountered difficulty in establishing transparent procedures both in financial services and in government–business relationships that rendered the model open to serious question after 1995 as an integrated global economic order began to take shape.

THE DEVELOPMENTAL MODEL PERMEATES THE ASIA–PACIFIC LITTORAL

Across Pacific Asia state bureaucrats selectively applied Japanese management theory to the development of their fragile, post-colonial economies. The pre-World War II colonial experience and the post-war protectorate afforded by the American hegemony in Pacific Asia gave the post-independence elites that inherited the bureaucratic structures of the pre-war period considerable scope for initiating industrial policy. The experience of colonial or, in the case of Japan and Thailand, monarchical and military–bureaucratic-style development prior to 1945, the survival in attenuated forms of regional traditions whether Confucian, Hindu or Islamic that favoured state paternalism, together with the capacity of the post-colonial order to mobilize national unity against the external communist threat, gave the new states a high degree of governmental autonomy.

Throughout the Cold War period the apparently 'virtuous' rule of one man or one party, mediated by an elite cadre of highly qualified technocrats, guided the process of socioeconomic transformation. Development followed what Singapore's ageing patriach, Lee Kuan Yew, terms 'the step by step approach' where no aspect of economic or political life is left to chance.

Indeed, successful economic planning ultimately justified the rule of the autocratic generals or quasi-Leninist parties that governed 'developmental capitalist states' (White 1993, p. 5) of South Korea, Taiwan, Singapore, Indonesia and Malaysia. Even Hong Kong, the regional exception in terms of its *laisserfaire* economic development in the post-war period, had an autonomous, albeit colonial, bureaucratic administration

In order to implement planned economic and political development, guidance, often militarily imposed, had first to be achieved. This required the often brutal suppression of opposition, whether industrial or political. In *South Korea* the government broke radical trade union activity in 1946 and successive regimes subsequently controlled labour through state-sponsored organizations (Park 1987, pp. 903–12). The coup that promoted General (subsequently President) Park Chung Hee, into power in 1961 also witnessed the abolition of all political parties and organizations and restrictions upon the press. Certainly in the Park era (1961–79) South Korea possessed a state that was a 'cohesive actor with enormous strength, autonomy and capacity' (Moon 1994, p. 145). Although the relationship between government, bureaucracy and business changed with the assassination of Park and the seizure of power by General (subsequently President) Chun Doo-Hwan in 1980, the state-licensed technocrats at the Economic Planning Board continued to dominate the developmental process throughout the 1980s.

In *Taiwan* the martial law regime introduced by the *Kuomintang* (KMT), which arrived like an occupying army in 1948 and lasted with some modification until 1987, effectively suppressed all industrial and political opposition to planned development. The Leninist organization of the KMT and its insulation from indigenous Taiwanese aspirations further facilitated state autonomy. After 1987, and primarily in response to external pressure, the ruling party sought to legitimate its political authority through a process of democratization leading to the first direct election of President Lee Teng-hui in 1996. Despite growing accountability, state-appointed technocrats remain in control of the developmental process.

Somewhat differently, and chronologically later, in *Singapore* the People's Action Party (PAP) under the first-generation leadership of Lee Kuan Yew, through a judicious mixture of popular support and internal security legislation, established corporate controls over all political and economic activity. The creation of the PAP-managed National Trade Union Congress (NTUC) in 1961, followed by the elimination of alternative labour organizations through the Employment Act (1967) and the Amendment of Industrial Relations Act (1968), together with the creation of the National Wages Council (NWC) in 1971, created, in the euphemism of the World Bank, 'harmonious industrial labor relations' (Soon and Tan 1993, p. 34). Burgeoning administrative control, the judicial intimidation of the opposition and the creation of a regulatory machinery of statutory boards governing economic development, pensions, public housing and public utilities effectively imbricated Singaporeans in an 'administrative state' (Chan 1976).

In *Malaysia* an evolving state-driven corporatism reflected an 'unequal alliance between the elites of the Malay and non-Malay (mainly Chinese) communities' (Crouch 1993, p. 136). In practice government has taken the form of a theoretically multi-communal *Barisan Nasional* (National Front) coalition, which in practice is dominated by the Malay-based United Malay National Organization (UMNO) party. While political power has become effectively vested in Malay hands, the Chinese community, which constitutes more than 30 per cent of the population, remains economically powerful. In the aftermath of interethnic riots in 1969, UMNO introduced a series of economic plans to increase the indigenous Malay or *bumiputera* participation in the economic life of the country. In order to facilitate this, particularly during the abrasive leadership of Mahathir Mohamad between 1981 and 2003, the government strategy has been one of increasing centralization that has curbed federal autonomy, reduced the feudal influence of the Sultans, curbed the judiciary and vested power in the party rather than in parliament or bureaucracy.

Developing state autonomy emerged more erratically in *Thailand*. From at least the 1930s, when it experienced the first third world military coup, a military-backed bureaucratic polity shaped Thailand's political and economic development. Under a succession of military leaders beginning with Marshal Phibun in 1938, the Thai military not only assumed responsibility for the integrity of the Thai nation and the extirpation of the communist threat, but also oversaw economic development. Unlike South Korea, however, Thailand experienced difficulty in consolidating a coalition of military, bureaucratic and business interests for developmental purposes. The periodic recourse to the military coup served the purpose of breaking factional gridlock. Thailand witnessed 17 coups from 1932 to 1991 and government has tended to oscillate between periods of autocratic rule interspersed by short-lived and unstable constitutional coalitions in 1973–76, 1988–91 and more recently since the most recent failed coup in 1991.

Indonesian development after 1965 also occurred under military auspices. In 1949, a military–bureaucratic elite, which established a ruling estate 'free of control by parties or other non-bureaucratic forces' (Robison 1996, p. 68) occupied the socioeconomic vacuum left by the departing Dutch. After a brief and confused period of multi-party democracy, this estate evolved into Sukarno's guided democracy from 1957 to 1965. Informed by a heady mixture of charisma, socialism and economic nationalism, the government after 1958 embarked upon an orgy of nationalization and import substituting industrialization. Under the rubric, 'Guided Economy', the government established a regime of import monopolies, confiscated foreign assets and ran them as state-owned enterprises.

Military adventures including the Confrontation (*Konfrontasi*) with Malaysia (1963–66) led to increased external borrowing. The result was economic and political chaos. With the instauration of the New Order of General (subsequently President) Suharto, who ruled between 1965 and 1966, the army, as in Thailand, came to occupy a dual function (*dwifungsi*) as both a military and a sociopolitical force. Its political bureaucratic wing dominated the constituent assembly whilst President Suharto occupied the role of paternal guardian of the Republic. Under the slogan, 'unity through diversity' the New Order regime used the state ideology of *pancasila* to remove political opposition and incorporate bureaucracy, Chinese business interests and labour into a developmental coalition.

All the states considered here established between 1950 and the early 1960s single-party or military-backed regimes that removed political opposition, maintained a docile and pliant labour force and established the communist threat as an external 'other' against which popular unity and a nation-building ideology could be mobilized. The creation of popular unity through state-controlled media and education also served the purpose of progressive incorporation and mobilization for economic development and export-led growth.

The achievements of this praetorian or single party-led development were variable, but remarkable. In South Korea, the World Bank maintained that, 'despite unfavourable initial conditions', real GNP growth 'tripled in every decade since 1962' (Kim and Leipziger 1993, p. ix). In the World Bank's opinion the 'benefits of growth have been distributed widely' and occasioned a sharp reduction in the incidence of absolute poverty. This 'was only possible in an environment in which the state saw economic development as its primary responsibility' (ibid.). Indeed, commentators argued that Taiwan and Korea 'stand out from virtually all other countries of Eastern Europe and the Third World for having reduced the income gap with Northwest European and North American core [economies] between 1980 and 1988' (Wade 1992, p. 277). Thus Taiwan's gross national product (GNP) grew at an annualized average rate of 8.8 per cent between 1952 and 1992. As a consequence real per capita GNP increased from about $100 in 1952 to $10 000 by 1992. By 1992, 'the Republic of China [Taiwan] was the fourteenth largest trading country in the world' (ibid.) with exports of $81.5 billion and imports of $72 billion. Similarly resource-challenged post-colonial Singapore 'transformed itself from a . . . maritime center into a dynamic, industrialized economy' with real GDP growth averaging 8.2 per cent between 1960 and 1990 (Soon and Tan 1993, p. xi). Moreover, since 1990, growth has continued to average over 8 per cent per annum (Abeysinghe, Ng and Tan 1994, p. 11). By contrast, the resource-rich Southeast Asian economies grew less spectacularly despite sharing autocracies not dissimilar to those of Northeast Asia.

Differences notwithstanding, growth in all these 'High Performing Asian Economies', as the World Bank described them in 1993, contrasted profoundly with other Northeast and Southeast Asian states that failed to develop a foreign direct investment-friendly, manufacturing export-oriented, developmental coalition. The post-war experience of both communist East and Southeast Asia, the former US colony of the Philippines and the former British one of Burma/Myanmar, provided salutary examples of tried and failed alternative developmental models. In particular, the experiences of both Maoist China and the Philippines over the period 1950–86 demonstrated an interesting contrast to the strategies pursued in Northeast and Southeast Asian HPAEs.

During the early 1950s, the Chinese Communist Party (CCP) undertook a massive process of institutional transfer which laid down 'a vast lattice work of Soviet derived political and economic institutions' (White 1993, p. 4). Mao and his supporters subsequently adjusted this Soviet model of developmentalism to Chinese needs. This Maoist paradigm of development, which began with the convulsive 'Great Leap Forward' in 1958 and culminated in the social, economic and political anarchy of the Cultural Revolution (1966–76) left an ultimately tragic developmental legacy of famine, chaos and a somewhat more devolved pattern of local autonomy than characterized the centralized Soviet model.

It was, in fact, in order to restore some measure of political and economic credibility that the post-Maoist reformers under the pragmatic guidance of the paramount leader Deng Xiaoping embarked upon a course of economic reform after 1978. The strategy of market Stalinism, which has continued into the present, unleashed a process of unprecedented and rapid economic change in post-revolutionary China. This process has required the redefinition of the state's role in the economy in ways which by the 1990s brought the CCP leadership, somewhat reluctantly, closer to the 'state capitalist model' pioneered in Japan, to the extent that it disengages the state from direct economic control and increases the market accountability of productive enterprises while retaining 'the integument of socialist political ideas and institutions. This project of market socialism thus involves significant change in the developmental aspect of the state, but not in its political aspect' (Yoshihara 1994b, chap. 2).

The Marcos dictatorship, which replaced the traditional Filipino oligarchy with a mixed bunch of cronies extending from 1972 to 1986, saw a continuation and concentration of the pattern of government predation. Overseas borrowing financed economic programmes, but much of the finance ended up in the pockets of Marcos and his associates. Philippine financial institutions like the Philippine National Bank (PNB) and the Philippine Development Bank (PDB) lost 'economic rationality almost completely' during the era of martial law. By the 1980s, Marcos used the two institutions to 'dispense favours' and meet the financial needs of his wide base of supporters throughout the country (ibid.). When clients defaulted on their loans, the government transferred their debt to the public sector. Sources of commercial lending to the Marcos kleptocracy dried up and, by the early 1980s, the Philippines became increasingly dependent on the IMF and the World Bank. This, however, did little to improve fiscal accountability. By 1983, the Philippines was defaulting on debt repayment and, in a deepening economic crisis brought about by corruption and mismanagement, the Philippine GDP fell by 6 per cent in 1984 and 4.3 per cent in 1985. By the time 'people power' swept Marcos away in 1986, non-performing assets accounted for more than 90 per cent of the PDB's portfolio. Thus the Philippines, a founding member of the ASEAN grouping and characterized, like Thailand and Indonesia, by the rule of strong men represents a case of a state squandering its developmental opportunities (Hutchison 1997, p. 79).

Consequently, when the ASEAN *commentariat* or the World Bank subsequently elaborated on the success of a purportedly ASEAN way in economic development, the Philippines was conveniently dropped from the success story. Yet what clearly emerges from this genealogy of the preconditions for East Asian growth is the irrelevance of regional organizations to the economic take-off. In fact, the formal institutions that regionalism requires would have undermined the mobilization capacity that the developmental state demanded to be effective. Instead, it was the access provided by the post-World War II Bretton Woods liberal trading order, the General Agreement on Tariffs and Trade (GATT) and, more particularly, the openness of the US economy to which the various Asian dragon and tiger states were aligned during the Cold War that proved crucial to their rapid, export-fuelled, growth between 1960 and 1990.

BIG GOVERNMENT LEADERSHIP AND EXPORT-LED GROWTH

A central feature of successful, rather than ineffective or failed, state-led development, then, was the prioritization of state planning by a highly trained technocratic elite. The state controlled all aspects of the developmental process. Illustrating this in his National Day speech of 1996, Singapore Prime Minister Goh Chok Tong compared the People's Action Party government to 'a Board of Trustees and myself as its elected Chairman. We are responsible . . . like a publicly-listed company'. The state in this model is a corporation and the states discussed here have at various times described themselves as 'incorporated'. The state technocrats frame successive plans for four, five or even nine years and establish targets or quotas to be reached by designated industries or sectors of the workforce. The plan ultimately succeeds, moreover, through the generation of export-led growth.

However, although all the states discussed possess 'big leaders' and have developed elite cadres of state technocrats, it is possible to distinguish between those states, like Japan, Taiwan and South Korea, which combined technocratic planning with internal market governing and the capacity to develop industrial winners with those, primarily Southeast Asian and later developing states, which have unsteadily combined a mixture of technocratic guidance with resource dependence and foreign direct investment to achieve export-led growth.

In this practice, the Northeast and Southeast Asian experiences of bureaucratic guidance contrast dramatically. In South Korea, it was during the era of Park Chung Hee's authoritarian rule that government moved decisively away from a policy of import substitution towards export-led growth. During Park's regime Korea's economic priority was to expand manufactured exports (Song 1990, p. 120). Park adopted a 'variant of authoritarian capitalism, in which enterprises were privately owned but the management was shared between the government and the owners'. The Economic Planning Board (EPB), together with the Ministry of Commerce and Industry (MCI) and the Ministry of Finance (MOF), assumed central responsibility for planning industrial policy. In order to promote development, in the course of the 1970s, the EPB contributed 33 per cent of government direct investment towards infrastructure projects. Government promoted imports of capital and intermediate goods required by exporters and provided macroeconomic stability by restricting currency trading, maintaining an undervalued *won* and managing the banking sector in a manner that allocated capital to fund industrial and export expansion (Rhee 1994, p. 66; Patrick 1994, p. 330).

Throughout the 1960s and early 1970s, exports, not profitability, constituted the yardstick of industrial performance and established the foundations of subsequent financial moral hazard (Amsden 1989, p. 18). Moreover, since the government favoured economies of scale in production, marketing and technology acquisition, it rewarded size with better access to credit (Kim and Leipziger 1993, p. 3). As the EPB performed the Korean equivalent of MITI but more so, it particularly came to favour private, family-run conglomerates (*chaebol*) that resembled pre-war Japanese *zaibatsu* (meaning financial clique, which refers to the powerful family groups that industrialized Japan). It was the presidential decision in 1973 to reduce support for labour intensive, export-oriented light industry in footwear and textiles and promote instead the Heavy and Chemical Industry Plan (HCIP) that particularly facilitated this characteristic form of South Korean business conglomeration (Rhee 1994, p. 77; Kim and Leipziger, 1993, p. 18). Apart from a cheap and generally compliant labour market, Korea possessed no evident comparative heavy industrial advantage. Significantly, the programme evinced 'big leadership' by the state technocracy (ibid., p. 20).

Analogous big leadership characterized the development of both the automobile and electronics industries after 1974. In 1974, the EPB outlined an industry-specific plan for automobiles, identifying Hyundai, Kia and Daewoo as primary producers (Wade 1990, p. 310). Domestic sales were used to subsidize exports. As the World Bank observed, Korea's economic success in the 1970s and the late 1980s reflected 'Korea's bureaucracy and planning apparatus, the unique relationship between business and government [and] . . . the pragmatism . . . of policy formulation and implementation' (Kim and Leipziger 1993, p. 28).

Taiwan's development illustrates a similar capacity for detailed planning, control of access to the domestic market and export-oriented growth. As in Korea, government initiated the shift to export-led growth, and the super-technocrats of the Economic Stabilization Board (ESB), which was established in 1958, played the major role. In 1960, the government introduced a Nineteen Point Programme for Economic and Financial Reform together with a new four-year plan (1961–64) providing incentives for businesses that produced and marketed for export. In order to guide development the frequently updated Statute for the Encouragement of Investment (1960) coordinated investment by foreign nationals, overseas Chinese and local investors (Haggard 1990, p. 96). Like their South Korean counterparts, the ESB played a role 'much like that of good, traditional, Confucian advisors' (ibid., p. 27). Not only did they manage macroeconomic policy and the exchange rate in a manner that promoted exports, they engineered a mutually supportive combination of state and private enterprise.

In addition to coordinating the private sector, the government significantly extended the range of state-owned enterprises. 'The turn to world markets was thus coupled with anticipatory actions aimed at deepening Taiwan's base in intermediate and capital intensive industries' (ibid., p. 96). The international de-recognition of Taiwan as the legal government of China in 1971, followed by the oil shock of 1973, the slowing of GNP growth to 1.2 per cent and inflation rising to 47 per cent prompted the government to assert economic leadership even more forcefully during the 1970s. In this context, the state technocracy proactively developed high technology, opening the Hsinchu Science and Industry Park in the late 1970s. By 1990, Taiwan had developed the biggest pool of chip design talent in Asia outside Japan. Personal computers, peripherals and add-ons in consequence came to constitute a major component of Taiwan's exports, rising from zero to 6.9 per cent between 1980 and 1987. By the end of the Cold War virtually every major electronics multinational had opened a venture in Taiwan and firms like Acer became global names in the sphere of personal computers.

A notable feature of Taiwan's technocratic governance has been its ability both to influence indigenous business through its network of connections (*guanxi*) with the ruling KMT and yet to remain relatively autonomous from business pressure. This together with the lack of an organized labour movement and the relatively equitable distribution of the wealth created by growth has facilitated the technocratic capacity to adapt the economy to changing market conditions. This capacity to oversee the direction of Taiwanese development was again evident in the late 1980s as the success of the Taiwanese economy led to external pressure for market and financial liberalization and the revaluation of its currency. The technocracy moved proactively to restructure the economy by moving labour-intensive manufacturing and textile industries offshore. Taiwan's demand for a source of cheap labour fortuitously coincided with Deng Xiaoping's decision to open special economic zones in Guangdong and Fujian on the Chinese mainland. By 1989, Taiwan's direct overseas investment had increased to $6.95 billion or 4.6 per cent of GNP, and many small businesses relocated labour-intensive textile and shoe-making operations to mainland China.

The technocracy, then, in both South Korea and Taiwan has historically promoted export-led growth through an outward-oriented economic policy while at the same time maintaining trade barriers in key sectors. A closely supervised and highly regulated financial sector kept inflation low and the currency cheap, which in turn promoted export-led growth. This technocratic *dirigisme* contrasts significantly with the pattern of development in Southeast Asia. Whilst Taiwan and South Korea closely followed the Japanese path of flying geese ascending the economic and technological ladder, development in the city state of Singapore and the Southeast Asian states of Thailand, Malaysia and Indonesia, while favouring state planning, differed profoundly in the method of achieving growth. Partly because they developed later (after 1965) than either South Korea and Taiwan and partly because, with the exception of Singapore, they lacked the technocratic rigour of the Northeast Asian bureaucracies, these states relied far more upon foreign direct investment and multinational enterprises (MNEs) to generate economic impetus.

Export-oriented growth stimulated by the importation of foreign MNEs accounted for Singapore's rapid economic recovery after its humiliating expulsion from the Malaysian Federation in 1965. Successful FDI-financed growth, nevertheless, required 'institutional reforms that concentrated economic decision making and expanded the economic instruments in the hands of the government' (ibid., p. 113). In particular the technocratic guidance of the planners at the Economic Development Board (EDB) played a central role in attracting MNEs to the city state (see Huff 1994, p. 330; Schein 1996, chap. 1). Unlike the Northeast Asian states, it was foreign direct investment rather than state-funded conglomerates that facilitated Singapore's growth strategy.

An unforeseen consequence of this policy was that it restricted the opportunity for local merchant entrepreneurs, or indigenous, state-linked conglomerates to develop in Singapore. Instead, the government participated in business activity through a variety of statutory boards and state-owned enterprises. After 1973, the EDB moved its investment promotion efforts away from labour-intensive manufacturing industries and sought to upgrade and restructure the economy. Singapore's attraction to MNEs henceforth depended, not upon cheap labour, but, as former Deputy Premier Goh Keng Swee observed, 'a supply of efficient engineers and technicians' (*Sunday Times* (Singapore), 21 April 1991).

Singapore's success in upgrading, not only its manufacturing base, but also its service sector in the course of the 1980s, together with its increasingly tight labour market and emerging role as a global city dependent on an open trading environment, constituted the background to the 1991 Strategic Economic Plan (SEP). The SEP encouraged private and public sector investment abroad primarily in the ASEAN region, but also in China and India. In order to minimize entrepreneurial risk, government statutory boards piloted an 'external wing' of investment. The PAP's proactive choice of industrialization as a developmental strategy, the EDB's pioneering of Singapore as a low-cost base for foreign MNEs, investment in human capital and infrastructure, management and control of labour and maintenance of a stable macroeconomic environment through prudent monetary policy provided the environment for this industrial policy to work.

Unlike Singapore, the developing economies of Southeast Asia moved less certainly towards a policy of foreign direct investment and export-led growth. Thailand, Malaysia and Indonesia possess large rural and resource-rich hinterlands that facilitated their pre-war emergence as primary product economies. Decolonization and the political instability that engulfed Southeast Asia from 1950 to 1975 adversely affected investment and development. These Southeast Asian states, moreover, adopted economic nationalist and import-substituting strategies in order to acquire investment capital in the early 1960s and 1970s, much less successfully than in Northeast Asia. Indeed, it was only when they shifted to policies that favoured foreign multinational investment and export-led growth in the course of the 1980s that these later developing economies achieved rapid growth.

In the Malaysian case, communal violence inspired by relatively high unemployment amongst the *bumiputeras* and a growing concentration of private enterprise in the hands of the Chinese community contributed to a major socioeconomic re-think and the implementation of the New Economic Policy (NEP) in 1971. The NEP plan aimed to achieve growth with equity, eradicating poverty and redressing the economic imbalance between the predominantly urban Chinese and the Malay rural poor. The NEP thus began

an era of state activism in resource allocation primarily through public enterprise trusts like Perbadanan Nasional Bhd (Pernas) in order to promote a *bumiputera* interest in commerce and industry (Gomez 1994, p. 3). The NEP
established affirmative action employment quotas to reflect the ethnic composition of the population and sought to achieve a 30 per cent *bumiputera* stake
in Malaysian industry by 1991.

The new strategy also sought to promote export oriented growth through
export incentives, tax breaks and indirect subsidies to pioneer industries in
Export Processing Zones (EPZ). These incentives combined with the availability of low-cost, semi-skilled female workers attracted the first wave of
Japanese, South Korean and Taiwanese foreign investment. By 1980, 70 per
cent of Malaysia's manufactured exports originated from foreign-owned firms
located in the new EPZs. Foreign investment in labour absorptive semi- and
low-skilled light industrial production resulted in Malaysia becoming the
world's leading producer of semiconductor devices by 1978 (Jesudason 1990,
p. 174).

The discovery of substantial reserves of oil and natural gas offshore from
Sabah and Sarawak and in Eastern peninsula Malaysia further boosted
economic growth. Buoyed by these resources and revenue derived from the
1980 oil price rise, Mahathir Mohamad, the new ultra Malay Prime Minister,
launched a 'Look East' policy and a state-led programme of heavy industrialization under the auspices of the Heavy Industries Corporation of Malaysia
(HICOM). Mahathir and the UMNO elite looked somewhat contradictorily
towards Japan both as a model of the state-led industrialization and as a source
of FDI. In the period up to 1985, state-run enterprises constituted the vanguard
of state-led industrialization policy. This 'Malaysia Incorporated' strategy
sought to achieve Mahathir's twin nationalist policy objectives: economic
restructuring and accelerating industrialization, combined with the social and
political goal 'of redistributing national income to help the Malays who were
the group least active in the industrial sector' (Bowie 1994, p. 177). The
HICOM-sponsored national car, the Proton Saga, symbolized this policy.

In order to remedy the detrimental effects of industrial restructuring and
the inefficiency of public enterprises that saw a worrying escalation of
foreign debt, Mahathir and his Finance Minister, Daim Zainuddin, embarked
on a programme of privatization and a relaxing of the *bumiputera* affirmative
action provisions. In 1990, Mahathir announced a new National Development
Policy (NDP) to replace the NEP. The NDP set an annual growth rate of 7 per
cent per annum to achieve a fully developed Malaysia by 2020. To secure
growth targets the government relaxed the rules governing foreign investment. Liberalization and the search for FDI fortuitously coincided with
endaka, the strengthening *yen*, and encouraged a wave of Japanese and
Taiwanese investment. Japanese FDI, in particular, had the greatest impact on

Malaysian industrialization (Ali 1994, p. 105). Between 1986 and 1991 alone, Japanese investment exceeded $2 billion.

By 1995, unemployment had disappeared and UMNO had negotiated the developmental process relatively successfully, although by the mid-1990s a significant income gap had appeared between the urban centres and the rural hinterland and between the wealthier peninsula states of Johore, Malacca and Selangor and the less developed, but resource-rich, states of Terengganu, Kelantan and the West Malaysian states of Sarawak and Sabah. Nevertheless, the evolving capacity of UMNO technocrats to sustain both growth and infra-structural development and guarantee political stability has attracted foreign investment to Malaysia. This, combined with legal restrictions on trade union activity, a docile and compliant labour force, low inflation and competitive wages, 'rated highly in the decision of Japanese companies to locate in the country' after 1985 (Denker 1994, p. 54).

Malaysia's relatively successful pursuit of MNE-led growth contrasts with the more challenging experiences of both Thailand and Indonesia. In Thailand, a military-backed bureaucratic polity moved from a post-1945 period of economic nationalism to a policy of import substitution after 1971 that favoured capital-intensive manufactures such as automobiles and discrimi-nated against both labour-intensive agriculture and labour-intensive manufac-tures. The strong import-substituting strategy had a marked effect on the profile of the Thai economy with protected heavy industry contributing 42.6 per cent of value added to the GDP by 1979. However, this industrial policy, in contrast with the Northeast Asian and Singaporean experience, absorbed a comparatively small proportion of the labour force. Thus, while industry's share of GDP increased steadily from about one-quarter in 1970 to one-third by 1988, this industrial transformation was not accompanied by a comparable shift in employment. Indeed, by 1988, 'nearly 70 per cent of the labour force was still in agriculture, producing 17 per cent of GDP' (Salleh and Meyanathan 1993, p. 6).

The import substitution policy, exacerbated by the impact of the second oil shock after 1979, distorted Thailand's pattern of industrialization and culmi-nated in a slump in growth and a ballooning current account deficit in the early 1980s. To remedy this the authoritarian leadership of General Prem and the technocrats at the Board of Investment (BOI) organized the post-1981 export promotion drive. The government established export-processing zones, streamlined customs procedures, abolished unnecessary regulations to expe-dite export shipments and substantially reduced tariffs on capital goods, auto-mobile imports and computers (ibid., p. 141). This policy dramatically affected growth. Direct foreign investment played a major role in the export boom period (1985–95) as firms from the Northeast Asian HPAE's moved labour-intensive manufacturing to the Bangkok region. Between 1980 and

1988, direct foreign investment more than tripled. By 1993, more than half of Thailand's total exports were manufactures, mostly established directly by foreign investors or in the form of joint ventures. In particular, Japanese producers increasingly selected Thailand as a key offshore production base in their global network of export-oriented manufacturing, especially automobiles. By the early 1980s, moreover, a number of the larger Thai firms, supported by the leading commercial banks, had developed into large, vertically integrated, business conglomerates like Saha Union, Shinawatra, Dusit Thani and Charon Phokphand. In the course of the 1980s and early 1990s these conglomerates were expanding operations into Indochina and Southern China.

A noteworthy feature of Thailand's development across the period 1955–95 was its macroeconomic stability. The strength of Thai macroeconomic policy and the relative openness of the economy in the 1980s facilitated Bangkok's development as a regional financial and related services centre. To comply with the Uruguay round of the GATT, the government deregulated the banking sector in the course of the 1990s. Consequently, financial services were considerably more evolved in Bangkok than in Taipei or Seoul, though they both lacked maturity and facilitated a climate where short-term loans funded long-term developments premised on a steady exchange rate between the *baht* and the dollar and a rising property market. At the same time, technocratic initiatives undertaken by the BOI and various line ministries to promote industry 'have not been important in explaining Thailand's economic success' prior to 1997 (Christensen, Dollar, Siamwalla and Vichyanond, 1993, p. 7). Thai industrial policy significantly deviated from the Northeast Asian norm. Technocrats were not guided by a strategy of picking winners and instead succumbed to patronage and rent seeking, but never to the same extent as the Philippines with which it is often (favourably) contrasted (Laothamatas 1992, chap. 1).

The Republic of Indonesia encountered analogous but structurally more embedded problems with patronage and rent seeking. Like Malaysia, Indonesia was 'born with a classic colonial economy based on plantation estates producing for export' (Power 1994, p. 246). Its development, however, has been more troubled. After the 1965 coup and counter-coup, the New Order government moved quickly to introduce market-minded reforms. It had to. Per capita income actually fell by 15 per cent between 1958 and 1965. Inflation accelerated to 1000 per cent, foreign borrowing had risen to $2 billion and interest repayments on debt exceeded export earnings (Schwarz 1994, p. 52). The re-scheduling of the debt enabled the Indonesian government to aquire financial resources. Under the guidance of US-trained economists like Widjojo Nitisastro, the New Order cut spending, loosened trade barriers and overhauled investment laws. The technocrats removed most domestic price controls, returned some nationalized enterprises to private ownership and passed a 'balanced budget' law in 1967 prohibiting budget financing through foreign borrowing or money creation. By 1969, this fiscal policy had reduced inflation to a manageable 20 per cent.

The economy recovered surprisingly quickly from the Old Order's economic utopianism, recording double-digit growth for the first time in 1968 (Hill 1994, p. 61). With the economy stabilized, the government focus shifted to long-term developmental planning. The windfall tax revenues afforded by the Oil Petroleum Exporting Countries' (OPEC)-inspired oil price rises of 1973 and 1979 offered further scope for planning and a reversal of market-oriented policies. Indeed, the patrimonial ethic of the New Order advocated cooperative (*gotong royong*) capitalism rather than the individualist 'free fight' variety (ibid., p. 66; see also Taubert 1991, p. 132). The wealth attracted by increased oil revenues thus facilitated New Order control that permeated both economy and society by the early 1990s (Vatikiotis 1993, p. 109).

The evolving corporatism of the New Order entailed links between the centres of military bureaucratic power and domestic corporate conglomerates (Robison 1990, p. 104). Despite official commitment to indigenous (*pribumi*) entrepreneurs, the corporate giants that emerged after 1975 were Chinese, with close ties to the army in general and President Suharto in particular. Thus Liem Sioe Liong's Salim group, with interests in 'everything from cement to noodles', dates from Liem's relationship with Suharto in 1950s Semarang (*Forbes Magazine*, 13 February 1995). Significantly many of Salim's ventures involved at least one of Suharto's children and the group was deeply embedded in Suharto's 'patrimonial network' (Schwarz 1994, p. 113). Indeed, prior to 1998, Suharto's children owned the only indigenous conglomerates of substance. Second son Bambang's Bimantara group and eldest daughter Tutut's Citra Lamtoro Gung group were on a par with the Chinese conglomerates in terms of size and capitalization. As one analyst observed, 'the business careers of Suharto's children highlight the fundamental importance of clientelistic connections as the key to gaining access to state generated rent taking opportunities and thence to commercial success' (quoted in Power 1994, p. 254).

The decline in oil revenues in the course of the 1980s and the subsequent decision by the National Planning Agency *Bappenas* to open Indonesia to FDI, as in Malaysia and Thailand, coincided with the appreciation of the Northeast Asian currencies and facilitated an influx of foreign investment capital (Hill 1994, p. 70; see also Battacharya and Pangetsu 1993, p. 31). Japan, in particular, had, since the birth of the New Order, taken a keen interest in Indonesian primary resources. The rapid growth in manufacturing, moreover, has structurally changed the economy, but in a significantly different way from the other HPAEs. Unlike those economies, natural resource-based products still formed over 30 per cent of Indonesia's manufactured exports in 1991 (Hill 1994, p. 83; Battacharya and Pangetsu 1993, p. 31).

Indonesia, thus, moved to labour-intensive export-led growth at a much later stage than other East Asian countries. Indonesian economic development, then, oscillated between periods of state intervention and economic nationalism and periods of reluctant deregulation. The results of New Order development, consequently, were mixed, but nevertheless significantly more productive than strategies pursued either in the Philippines, or in Maoist–Leninist-inspired Southeast Asia prior to 1995.

CULTURAL CAPITAL AND POLITICAL AND ECONOMIC DEVELOPMENT

The emergence of the East Asian high performing economies in the course of the 1980s led some observers, primarily from Southeast Asia, to speculate on the extent to which shared Asian values of a Hindu, Buddhist, Islamic and Confucian provenance informed this seemingly irrepressible East Asian economic vitality, and gave it a distinctive quality that constituted the basis for further integration. In this view, Asian values that privilege the family, not the individual, group conformity and consensus, not self-interested materialism, deference to rational leadership, not the free articulation of interest and an emphasis on saving and deferred gratification, and not hedonistic self-indulgence, constituted a distinctively development-friendly Asian ethic. In the course of the 1990s this understanding of Asian values was somewhat misleadingly described as an ASEAN way in political and economic governance. Southeast Asian scholar-bureaucrats like Noordin Sopiee and Kishore Mahbubani subsequently portrayed these distinctive values as the basis both for deeper Southeast Asian and for wider East Asian economic integration.

This perspective, sometimes termed 'the Singapore school of development', overlooked the fact that the shared social values that might have facilitated the developmental state's technocratic guidance might not serve the purposes of broader cooperation at an inter-state level. Hence, at the state level, the Asian value of thrift sustained high rates of domestic savings across the Asian NIEs that checked both consumption and inflation. In South Korea, domestic savings enabled the government in the period after 1971 to defray some of the costs of the heavy industrialization programme. In Taiwan, domestic savings facilitated state-planned industrial expansion. In Singapore, Hong Kong and Malaysia, the state enforced savings schemes in the shape of Provident Funds. In 1990 the Central Provident Fund (CPF) scheme in Singapore accounted for 30.1 per cent of gross national savings. The high level of CPF contributions constituted an important part of Singapore's macroeconomic policy, both facilitating the accumulation of extensive foreign reserves and influencing 'the avenues of consumption and savings as well as to exert enormous social, political and economic control' (Huff 1994, p. 347; see also Asher 1993, p. 158).

Nevertheless, such policies by no means facilitated either domestic or regional consumption or the move to any form of an integrated market. The same is true of other shared Asian values. Consequently, alongside thrift, the Asian emphasis on the family and filial piety has also powerfully influenced both state practice and the provision of public goods in the form of welfare and education. The patriarchal understanding that underpins Asian political culture powerfully legitimates paternal guidance by an elite male technocracy. At the same time the stability of the Asian family and the emphasis on filial piety keeps welfare costs low. Domestic saving schemes and the reliance of old and young dependants on the extended family have enabled Singapore, South Korea, Taiwan, Hong Kong and, to a lesser extent, Malaysia to defray a minimum of public expenditure on social security.

At the same time the government recognizes that the Asian value of rewarding virtue reflected an improved economic performance. Consequently, the Northeast Asian states, Hong Kong and Singapore have stressed universal education and educational achievement which reinforces the stability of the Confucianized family. One of the most striking features of Japan, Taiwan, South Korea, Singapore and Hong Kong has been the emphasis on raising the educational standards of the whole population rather than an elite. Indeed, the ability of the strong states of Asia to draw upon these traditional societal resources stood, it seemed in 1996, in stark contrast to the regional exemplar of western values, Australia, whose individualist ethic and a Keynesian infatuation with state-sponsored welfarism to generate social equality have produced one of the highest divorce rates and lowest savings rates in the OECD.

At the same time, in educational terms the achievement of the more Confucianized cultures of Taiwan, Singapore and South Korea also stood out from the less advanced Southeast Asian states. While Thailand, Malaysia, the Philippines and Indonesia have certainly invested in primary education, the failure to 'upgrade' the skills of the workforce, together with the relative weakness of state planning, has occasioned doubts about the ability of these states to move up the technological ladder. In other words, there was evident unevenness in the regional application of purportedly shared values. Moreover, these values which undoubtedly proved helpful in creating a development-friendly political culture at state level, became highly problematic when transformed into norms to facilitate greater regional integration. For the rhetoric of shared ASEAN moral understandings actually reinforced internal resilience rather than the external integration necessary to generate an East Asian common market.

THE OVERSEAS CHINESE AND ERSATZ CAPITALISM IN SOUTHEAST ASIA

In this context of the economic impact of Asian values, the Japanese econo-mist Kunio Yoshihara has further argued that it is Confucianism particularly that accounts for substantial differences in the structure and development of the Southeast and Northeast Asian economies. Any survey of the political economy of Southeast Asia reveals the reliance on overseas, primarily Northeast Asian, finance and technology for development, together with the disproportionate role played by Chinese conglomerates across the region and increasingly in Southern China. Indeed, the scale of Chinese economic success presents an unresolved political problem for the new Southeast Asian ruling elites engaged in the seemingly endless task of 'nation building'.

Evidently, the economic success of the approximately 20 million overseas Chinese and more particularly the increasingly visible Chinese conglomerates 'is out of proportion to their numbers in the ASEAN countries' (Redding 1993, p. 57). This social fact has prompted speculation about the cultural basis of such entrepreneurial flair, its peculiar character and the extent to which it constitutes the basis of an interdependent regional economic system (Yoshihara 1988; McVey 1992; Mackie 1995). A number of commentators emphasized the role cultural values, notably the Confucian ethic of relation-ships, and the Chinese cultural practices of *guanxi, xinyong* (mutual trust) and filial piety, have played in facilitating the emergence of Chinese regional commercial dominance. This Confucian ethic is sometimes compared disad-vantageously with the comparatively 'weak' work ethic of both Southeast Asian indigenes and Australians (Yoshihara 1995, p. 77). The 'hard' Confucian culture of the overseas Chinese and their minority status lends credence to the further claim that their conglomerates constitute, in Harry Sender's words, an emerging 'supra national' regional network 'stitched together by capital flows, joint ventures, marriage, political expediency, and a common culture and business ethic' (quoted in Mackie 1995, p. 36).

However, although Chinese conglomerates constitute an important element in the political economy of Southeast Asia, they by no means represent 'a controlling one' (ibid.). Moreover, the historic particularity of conglomerate evolution in Southeast Asia cannot be ignored. The contingencies that shaped conglomerate development explain the central features of Chinese entrepre-neurial practice. Indigenous suspicion of Chinese capitalism and its 'pariah' status, which affected the standing of the Chinese in the Philippines before Marcos and continues to inflect attitudes to Chinese enterprise in modern Malaysia and Indonesia, necessitated a recourse to networks of affiliation based on family, clan and language group as the basis of trust. Political isolation forged a Chinese economic network and fostered a common cosmopolitan outlook.

The peculiar socioeconomic conditions that shaped the diversified Chinese conglomerate structure together with the poor quality of Southeast Asian government intervention further determined the distinctly ersatz character of Southeast Asian capitalism. Insecure Chinese entrepreneurs concentrate either on financial and banking services or on property, tourism, communications and distribution enterprises that are regional, potentially global and increasingly independent of their domestic base.

While openness to foreign investment together with the role played by Chinese conglomerates has distinguished the Southeast Asian economies, it is noticeable that, with the exception of Singapore, planning has been less effective and sometimes, as in the case of Indonesia in the period before 1965, or the Philippines across the period, disastrous. In fact, development across Pacific Asia by 1996 had left a legacy of political uncertainty and growing economic difficulty. In particular, the negative costs of political and economic cronyism and changes in the global trading order confronted the developmental technocracies with challenges that did not respond easily to planned solutions.

THE DOWNSIDE OF THE MIRACLE

Plan rational development has not been without cost. Politically, development required the often violent suppression of labour organizations and political opposition, not to mention minority groups in places as diverse as Timor, Irian Jaya, Sarawak, Sabah and Northeast Thailand and amongst Taiwanese aboriginals and Japanese *burakumen*. Big leadership in Northeast Asia also generated its own economic and fiscal difficulties, whilst in Southeast Asia the absence of the necessary skills to move up the technological ladder, coupled with burgeoning disparities between a relatively wealthy urban and bureaucratic elite and a poor urban underclass and rural hinterland, increasingly threatened socioeconomic cohesion. Let us then briefly examine the economic costs of development and the attendant political difficulties that in the course of time state-led development engendered and which constituted the preconditions not for continual growth but for economic meltdown.

Even where industrial policy has generally been highly effective in generating growth, as in South Korea, the costs were not negligible. Financing the *chaebol* heavy industrialization programme between 1973 and 1981 meant government contracted a large foreign debt which continues to haunt South Korea. By 1980, Park's bureaucratically engineered growth had generated a current account deficit that represented 9 per cent of GNP and a worrying external debt burden estimated at 49 per cent of GNP (*Economist*, 3 June 1995, p. 17). The period 1979–80 witnessed both 'the disorder of political institutions, of policy networks between the state and social groups and of the financial system' and 'the ineffective implementation of economic stabilization policy measures' (Rhee 1994, p. 146). It was in these difficult circumstances that the military coup staged by General Chun Doo Hwan in May 1980 re-established authoritarian controls. Chun's economic reforms significantly altered relations between government and big business and engendered conflict within the bureaucracy between economic liberals and conservatives.

The main big business interest association, the Federation of Korean Industries (FKI), openly criticized the EPB's liberalization programme. These tensions continued into the regimes of Roh Tae Woo (1987–92) and were further exacerbated during Kim Young Sam's (1992–97) presidency. In fact, the Kim government's decision to speed liberalization and business de-concentration in the seventh Five Year Plan (1992–97) had the unintended consequence of exposing the network of graft and corruption that permeated government, bureaucracy and *chaebol* links. The indictment for treason of former Presidents Chun and Roh, in 1996, revealed the extent to which the more compliant *chaebol* went to promote 'the government business nexus' that produced 'one of the world's fastest growing economies' (*Far Eastern Economic Review*, 30 November 1995, p. 6). Continuing state intervention in the finance sector and the consequent weakness of the stock market and the record external debt of $70 billion announced in 1995 further illustrated the conflict between *chaebol* expansion and bureaucratically determined financial policy. Korean banks operated as 'handmaidens', serving government industrial policy (*Far Eastern Economic Review*, 14 September 1995; Patrick 1994, p. 360).

In the post-Cold War era, however, the United States became less amenable to the trade deficit of between $4 and $9 billion per annum it had contracted with South Korea since the mid-1980s. The increasing readiness of the United States to respond bilaterally to markets closed to American goods further exacerbated the problem of South Korea's underdeveloped financial sector and the domestic protection accorded to South Korean conglomerates. Although Taiwan's economic and political development proceeded more smoothly than South Korea's, it too faced similar problems in deregulating fiscal controls and opening the domestic market to foreign competition.

In Southeast Asia the problems generated by growth were different, but even more acute. State planning in mainland Southeast Asia lacked Northeast Asian rigour. In Thailand, despite the achievement of almost double-digit growth between 1985 and 1995, both industry and wealth remained worryingly concentrated. The failure to develop effective regional light industry, especially in the poor Northeast, and the urban nightmare that constitutes commuter travel in Bangkok are enduring testament to the failure of Thai planning. Industrialization, moreover, failed to absorb the pool of underemployed urban and rural labour. Although labour remains cheap, docile and mobile, it came under pressure from even lower-cost neighbouring countries such as Vietnam and Southern China as those countries opened their economies to FDI in the course of the 1990s. Fiscal policy loosened disturbingly in the course of the 1990s. At the same time indifference to a consumption and credit boom allowed inflation to rise above 5 per cent and the current account deficit to exceed 8 per cent of GDP by 1995. In the same year external debt rose by 33 per cent (World Bank 1996; *Australian*, 20 March 1996).

Like other ASEAN economies, Thailand was moving from a position of dependency on cheap labour to dependence on capital goods and more advanced technology. Here again government planning has been ineffective. The state provides only six years of compulsory education, so that Thailand encounters difficulty promoting workers into higher value-added technologies. This limits Thai industrial exports to 'processed primary products, garments, textiles and other labour intensive products' (Yoshihara 1988, p. 117). Thailand, consequently, remains economically dependent on foreign companies. When Thai wages increase, 'Thailand cannot develop new industrial exports and thus upgrade the composition of its industrial products' (ibid.). Clearly, the Thai attempt to plan development has not been as successful as its Northeast Asian counterparts'. During the corrupt administration of Banharn (1995–96), moreover, even the previously sound technocratic management of the Bank of Thailand was subject to damaging political manipulation. As the 1985–95 boom ended, the Thai economy had acquired a worrying combination of a trade deficit amounting to 8 per cent of GDP and foreign debt corresponding to 46 per cent of GDP. This occasioned the departure of a series of finance ministers from 1996 to 1997 and the 'meltdown' of the inflated Thai stock market (*Far Eastern Economic Review*, 15 August 1996, p. 40; *Economist*, 24 August 1996, p. 58).

Malaysia similarly faced skill shortages, while FDI-provided employment has failed to develop links with domestic manufacturers. Japanese multinationals do not transfer technology. Even in joint ventures like the Proton Saga, Mitsubishi shipped ready assembled engines from Japan (Jomo 1994, p. 280). Such practices, combined with an acute shortage of skilled manpower, constrains Malaysia's capacity to move up the industrial ladder to higher value added technologies (*Far Eastern Economic Review*, 31 August 1995). Indeed, Malaysia's success in courting Japanese investment aid proved ultimately self-defeating. Malaysia, like Thailand, South Korea and Taiwan, runs a growing trade deficit with Japan. In 1991, Japan accounted for 15.9 per cent of Malaysia's exports but 26.1 per cent of imports.

Furthermore, the growth through borrowing and foreign investment strategy pursued since 1985 created a burgeoning foreign debt, whilst the rise in imports to sustain rapid growth pushed Malaysia's current account into deficit.

In 1994, the deficit stood at $4 billion or about 7.7 per cent of GDP and rose to 8.3 per cent of GDP in 1995 (*Business Times*, 10 March 1995). This together with external debt amounting to 39 per cent of GDP exposed the Malaysian *ringgit*, like the Thai *baht*, to speculative pressure.

These factors, together with growing inflation, high interest rates and the murky relationship between UMNO politicians and indigenous business groups, gave credence to the view that Malaysian-style capitalists were 'paper entrepreneurs' relentlessly pursuing 'opportunities for acquisitions, mergers, restructurings and leveraged buy-outs' at the expense of developing indige-nous manufacturing and technology (Yoshihara 1988, p. 4). The 40-year development process, moreover, has increasingly marginalized the smaller indigenous Chinese entrepreneurs, while the big Malaysian Chinese trading conglomerates, like Quek Leng Chan's Hong Leong Group, the Robert Kuok Group and Vincent Tan's Inter-Pacific, cultivated close links with key figures in the UMNO elite and functioned as their 'business proxies' (Gomez 1994, pp. 37–9). Such arrangements ensure that the UMNO elite's business activity occurs 'outside the purview of the party' (ibid., p. 43). Control and account-ability constituted crucial issues, therefore, for the continued management of Malaysia Incorporated. Thus, although the UMNO party state astutely manip-ulated domestic and foreign investment after 1985, the shadier aspects of this strategy generated a disturbing air of insubstantiality indicated by the growth of imports, mounting foreign debt and rising inflation.

The problem of crony capitalism, the widening gap between the business and military bureaucratic elite and the masses, and the disparity between urban worker and rural peasant, manifested itself most acutely, however, in Indonesia prior to 1997. While the GDP per capita of Jakarta had grown to $1145 by 1995, that of peripheral, but oil-rich, Aceh province was less than $500 per capita (*Australian*, 17 August 1995). The growing perception of a widening income gap between rich and poor and the absence of an efficient legal framework to deal with labour and property disputes prompted an inter-mittent recourse to urban and rural *jaquerie* (peasant revolt). Only military intervention suppressed Labour riots and wildcat strikes at Tanjung Priok (Jakarta) in 1984 and in Medan, Sumatra, in April 1994.

Exasperation with Chinese business ownership reflected a wider resent-ment of the close ties between Chinese conglomerates and the Suharto regime. Deregulation of the economy, moreover, served only the interests of the Chinese conglomerates and increased their popular opprobrium. The percep-tion of Chinese business dominance allied to a burgeoning income gap prompted contradictory demands for both greater economic liberalization and greater government intervention. The role played by Suharto's children in indigenous conglomerates linked to Chinese conglomerates further compli-cated any attempt to introduce an Indonesian version of an NEP. At the same time, the liberalization of financial services after 1986 was a case of 'too much too fast' (Schwarz 1994, p. 74). The rapid flow of money into the Indonesian banking system after 1989 led to a rise in lending, especially by state banks, and a growth in money supply. It also led to inflation. Property speculation and an overheating economy required the Ministry of Finance to raise interest rates to 30 per cent in 1991. The state banks were adrift on a pool of bad debt, estimated at $85.88 billion in 1995 (*Far Eastern Economic Review*, 18 May 1995).

Financial scandal, together with the government practice of running budget deficits, further eroded confidence in an increasingly unstable financial sector. More disturbing still was the level of foreign debt which by 1995 had risen to $100 billion. As a consequence, although the Indonesian government attempted to manage development through import substitution followed by export-led growth and bureaucratic planning, the strategy was significantly less effective than elsewhere in Southeast Asia.

THE CONTRADICTIONS IN THE POLITICAL ECONOMY OF THE EAST ASIAN REGION

Industrial policy, long-term planning and control of access to domestic markets represented crucial aspects of the developmental model that Japan exported to its former colonies of South Korea and Taiwan. In South Korea's version of this strategy, the technocracy directed and encouraged the formation of large conglomerates. In Taiwan, by contrast, the super-technocratic agency created by the ruling KMT in the 1950s planned joint ventures with multinationals like Philips, promoted indigenous small to medium-sized enterprises and developed one of the largest state-owned sectors in the economically developed world. Both states favoured successive five-year plans and technocratic supervision and intervention to 'pick the industrial winners' that would secure future GDP growth. In order to promote domestic industries and develop indigenous technology, the Northeast Asian states protected key manufacturing sectors, directed bank and government credit to favoured domestic champions and set limits to foreign direct investment. Manufacturing in Northeast Asia, nevertheless, depended upon Japan for high technological inputs and both South Korea and Taiwan accumulated trade deficits with Japan while achieving trade surpluses with their primary markets in North America and Europe.

In this regional context, small city states, like Singapore and Hong Kong, functioned as *entrepôt* hubs for multinational corporations, international banks and the rapidly developing financial services sector. Yet, whilst the administration of colonial Hong Kong until 1997 promoted a *laisser faire* culture of entrepreneurialism, Singapore favoured technocratically guided development that constantly upgraded infrastructural resources and, through the activity of the Economic Development Board, developed a variety of state-owned enterprises that ranged from media and press holdings to utilities, housing, banks and airlines.

Significantly, Japan's rapid export-oriented growth, followed by the emergence of these 'dragon' economies, occasioned mounting trade surpluses with the developed economies of Europe and the United States. Burgeoning trade deficits, in turn, prompted the United States in particular to press the East Asian NIEs both to open their domestic markets and to deregulate their currencies. The negotiation of the Plaza Hotel Agreement (1985) and the Louvre Accord (1987) created conditions for the globalization of financial markets and the rapid appreciation of the Taiwanese dollar, the Korean *won* and the Japanese *yen*. This appreciation fuelled a liquidity, stock market and property bubble in Tokyo, Seoul, Taipei, Hong Kong and Singapore. It also increased the cost of domestic manufacturing. Consequently, in order to reduce domestic labour costs, Hong Kong and Taiwanese businessmen, Singapore statutory boards, Korean *chaebol* and Japanese *sogoshosha* (large trading companies) scrambled to relocate lower value added manufacturing offshore.

Southeast Asia and, subsequently, China as it opened Special Economic Zones (SEZs) along the Chinese littoral from Qingdao to Guangdong, together with Vietnam after it joined ASEAN in 1995, became major destinations for Northeast Asian investment. Indeed, it was the boom decade 1985–95, fuelled by the strong *yen*, that gave rise to the misguided notion of a uniform East Asian economic miracle with shared developmental values. During the period 1986–92, 50 per cent of foreign direct investment in Southeast Asia came from the NIEs to the North (World Bank 1994, p. 43). Meanwhile, Japanese investment in the Southeast Asian economies of Thailand, Malaysia and Indonesia increased at over 100 per cent per annum between 1986 and 1988, growing from $270 million per annum at the start of the 1980s to $1.5 billion per annum by 1987. Even after the Japanese economy entered its long recession in 1990, investment in Southeast Asia and China continued to grow at double-digit rates between 1990 and 1996.

Moreover, the interest expressed by ASEAN in promoting free trade through the creation of an ASEAN Free Trade Area and the growing influence of APEC in promoting open regional trade, particularly after 1992, further facilitated foreign investment. Consequently, foreign-domiciled company investment constituted the characteristic mode of development in Southeast Asia. In 1994, the Pacific Economic Cooperation Council (PECC), a high-profile cheerleader for regional integration through trade, found that the list of regional multinational groups developing borderless manufacturing structures to serve the fast growing consumer markets of the Asia–Pacific region 'was growing at dizzying speed' (Pacific Economic Cooperation Council 1994). It was uncritically assumed that the 'massive offshore move' by Japanese industry, together with foreign direct investment from the US and Europe, would contribute to the inflow of liquidity into the first decade of the twenty-first century (Lim 1995, p. 38).

Interestingly, growth in Southeast Asia exploited the competitive advantage in regional political stability, the supply of cheap and compliant labour and a relative openness to trade and foreign investment. However, the World Bank noted, in 1992, that 'selective intervention on Korean lines' could not work in Southeast Asia 'because of weaker administrative and institutional structures, less clear economic objectives and skill limitations' (MacIntyre 1994, p. 262). As Japanese economist Kunio Yoshihara observed, economic growth in Southeast Asia was technologyless (Yoshihara 1988, pp. 125–6). Merely an available pool of cheap, domestic labour servicing semi-skilled manufacturing for overseas domiciled multinationals, services in sectors like tourism, and opportunities in property, retail and commodities drove short and longer-term investment.

Furthermore, Southeast Asian economies were also dependent on the role of 'overseas' (*huaqiao*) Chinese business networks (Redding 1993, p. 57). While a bamboo network of diversified Chinese conglomerates dominated commercial activity in Thailand, Malaysia, Indonesia and Singapore, in both Malaysia and Indonesia they were effectively excluded from political influence. Insecure Chinese entrepreneurs, like Lim Sioe Liong's Salim group in Indonesia or the Kuok group in Malaysia, concentrated on financial and banking services or on property, tourism, communications and the distribution of goods: enterprises, in other words, that are regional and potentially independent of the local polity.

Directly or indirectly, therefore, the Japanese model of state-directed, export-led growth has profoundly affected the political economy of Pacific Asia. The attempt to follow the Japanese example has given the East Asian region certain economic commonalities. All the HPAEs have established state technocracies with varying degrees of autonomy from domestic and external pressure. These bureaucracies devise developmental targets and outline successive four- or five-year plans in which to achieve them. Such plans have often involved strategically calculated shifts from import-substituting industrialization to export-led growth. State technocracies, with varying degrees of success, select and develop manufacturing 'winners'. An important precondition for subsequent growth has in all cases been a docile and compliant labour force and restrained domestic consumption.

Further, all the HPAEs have fostered, directly or indirectly, high rates of saving to facilitate domestic investment and share a penchant for universal education at least to secondary school level. With the exception of the city states of Hong Kong and Singapore, the HPAEs maintain considerable levels of tariff and non-tariff protection both in agriculture and in key areas of manufacturing. Apart from Malaysia, all the HPAEs have facilitated programmes to reduce population growth and have effectively curtailed the number of young people entering the workforce. All the HPAEs have pursued export-led growth in order to sustain consistent economic expansion over a long period. Again, with the exception of anomalous Hong Kong, all the HPAEs have increasingly favoured corporatist mechanisms that draw business associations into technocratic planning in order to sustain future growth as the economy matures (Campos 1991, pp. 21–3). Consequently, government encourages domestic consumers, small businessmen, state technocrats and conglomerates to consider themselves members of a team running, as Singapore's Prime Minister explains, 'the next lap of development together' (Government of Singapore 1991, p. 13).

Nevertheless, there are a number of substantial differences within the individual economies surveyed, and between the broadly different regional patterns of development, both in Northeast and Southeast Asia and between the city states, that render the notion of a monolithic developmental model and the flying geese analogy unsustainable. Whilst Northeast Asia has followed a strategy of bureaucratically planned growth through the development of domestic manufacturing or joint ventures and succeeded in generating internationally competitive industries, Southeast Asia, together with China's Special Economic Zones after 1978 and Vietnam after it joined ASEAN in 1995, relied, almost completely, upon technologyless growth and the vagaries of foreign direct investment. Conversely, Southeast Asian macroeconomic planning, as a consequence of its higher degree of deregulation, generated a more open investment climate, whilst Northeast Asia treated both banks and stock exchanges as 'handmaidens' or 'bureaucratic stewards' of government policy (Patrick 1994, p. 364). Indeed, the opacity and immaturity of financial and banking services in Northeast Asia have facilitated a worrying escalation of non-performing bank loans on real estate in Taipei, Seoul and Tokyo. In Taiwan this has left the property sector highly 'distorted' and the Japanese banking sector cruelly exposed to asset deflation, insolvent *jusen* (housing loan companies) and up to $170 billion bad debt (*Far Eastern Economic Review*, 8 June 1995).

It would be inaccurate, though, to assume that the relatively deregulated financial markets of Southeast Asia constitute an alternative or more efficient Asian capitalism, as the *Economist* maintained in 1995 ('Asia's competing capitalisms', 1995). Southeast Asian deregulation and the foreign investment it made possible certainly opened these later developing HPAEs to Japanese and NIE investment on an unprecedented scale. Northeast Asian conglomerates and small and medium-sized enterprises came, particularly after 1985, to use Malaysia, Thailand and Indonesia as low-cost manufacturing bases for low-level technology, assembly and subsequent export in a relationship of evolving dependency. Moreover, the more attractive investment climate in Southeast Asia has by no means expunged the fiscal predation facilitated by government–business collusion in maintaining opaque property and financial practices. In fact, the early 1990s witnessed across developing urban Pacific Asia from Jakarta to Shanghai and Seoul a 'massive overbuilding' of real estate and office space. Low planning standards and equity funding not subject to accountable financial institutions created the prospect of a 'colossal crunch' in Pacific Asian real estate values (*Asian Wall Street Journal*, 24–5 November 1995). By 1995, the avid pursuit of FDI and short-term foreign loans and the opaque boundary between private and public sector debt, coupled with growing current account deficits, exposed Thailand, Indonesia, South Korea, Malaysia and Indonesia to a debt crisis (*Fortune Magazine*, 6 March 1995).

A yet more enduring problem for future Pacific Asian development lay, however, in the distinctive pattern of trade between Japan, the NIEs of South Korea, Taiwan, Singapore and Hong Kong, the ASEAN economies of Thailand, Malaysia and Indonesia and the large and relatively open United States market, that accounts for the impressive export-induced growth of Pacific Asia, which is, however, unlikely to be sustained long into the twenty-first century. The large-scale relocation of labour-intensive export-oriented manufacturing to low-cost, FDI-seeking countries in Southeast Asia enabled Japan and the NIEs to divert, via these third countries, their growing trade surpluses with the United States. At the same time, Japanese *keiretsu* were notably reluctant to transfer high value-added technology offshore. Consequently, whilst all the HPAEs ran trade surpluses with the United States, they equally maintained trade deficits with Japan, deficits that were increasingly exacerbated by the rising cost of the *yen*. By 1996, the following trade pattern existed: Japan ran trade surpluses with the US, the Asian NIEs and ASEAN countries, while the Asian NIEs and ASEAN countries maintained trade surpluses with the US but deficits with Japan. By 1995, the trade flows between Pacific Asia and the US accounted for 32.5 per cent of total US trade (Rodner 1995, p. 403). This prompted demands both from the US Senate and the European Union for reform of the international trade order to address the impermeable nature of the Japanese market, the tariff and non-tariff mechanisms deployed by the HPAEs and the trade imbalances they continued to generate. In other words, by the mid-1990s, the external trading environment that facilitated Pacific Asian export-led growth was undergoing unpredictable but fundamental change, the consequences of which are the subject of the next chapter.

4. The contradictions in the political economy of East Asian regionalism

Given the character of the Asian developmental state that we described in the previous chapter, the requirement after 1996 to demonstrate increasing evidence of market opening under the provisions of the post-GATT World Trade Organization (WTO) obviously posed a significant challenge to the structure of these recently developed and developing economies and the pattern of trade that sustained them. In the mid-1990s it seemed the trading order would either move rapidly toward what Kenichi Ohmae somewhat optimistically termed a 'borderless world' or, alternatively, adopt a practice of managed or strategic trade grounded either in bilateral *quid pro quo* agreements or regionally based, protectionist trading blocs (Ohmae 1991).

It was in this context of the strategic management of Pacific Asian and intra-Asian trade that Asian scholar-bureaucrats in a variety of Track Two fora began to explore the possibilities of interregional trade, and economic and technological cooperation. It should, however, be observed that, prior to the opening of negotiations for an ASEAN Free Trade Area (AFTA) that began in 1992, ASEAN as a regional economic grouping had developed little subregional economic cooperation. This would seem somewhat surprising given the rhetoric of the grouping and its admirers and that Chapter 3 Article 4 of the Treaty of Amity and Cooperation (1976) explicitly required 'active cooperation in the economic, social, technical scientific and administrative fields', while in the Joint Communiqué that accompanied the treaty the various ASEAN heads of government had called for 'cooperative action towards establishing ASEAN large-scale industrial projects as well as preferential trading agreements'.

Even so, it was not until 1989 that some ASEAN states sought to establish cross-border economic growth zones. For example, Singapore, Johore in Malaysia and Battam in Indonesia formed a regional growth triangle in 1989. This was followed in 1991 by a northern growth triangle embracing Northern Sumatra, Southern Thailand and Northern Malaysia. These growth zones relied upon foreign direct investment (FDI) from Northeast Asia and, with the onset of financial crisis in 1997, appeared stillborn. In other words, growth zones notwithstanding, the ASEAN economies were not only export-oriented, but competed between themselves both for FDI and as low-cost manufacturing bases for Northeast Asian, European or North American multinational corporations. As a consequence, unlike economically developed and increasingly economically integrated regions like the European Union (EU) where intra-European trade, amongst the core economies, accounted for over 70 per cent of EU gross domestic product (GDP) by the mid-1990s, intra-ASEAN trade represented a mere 20 per cent of ASEAN GDP at the time of AFTA's formation. As Fred Herschede observed in 1991, 'by far the most significant aspect of ASEAN trade is the importance of the industrialized countries', which between 1975 and 1989 accounted for 54 per cent of ASEAN imports and 57 per cent of total exports (Herschede 1991, pp. 181–2). Over the same period intra-ASEAN imports averaged 18.6 per cent and exports 20 per cent of total trade.

So, according to a number of commentators, despite the rhetoric of ASEAN economic cooperation, 'the bound tariff levels of the ASEAN countries are among the very highest in the world'. Moreover, 'to bring themselves into line with the more open economies [of the Asia–Pacific] region the South-East Asians (with the exception of Singapore) would have to bear very high initial adjustment costs' (MacIntyre 1997, p. 239). This was a cost which, as we shall see, the ASEAN states were not prepared to pay. A familiar ASEAN pattern, once again, appears where a theoretical commitment to cooperation intimating eventual regional integration obscures an actual practice of inter-ASEAN state competition for the overseas investment dollar, reinforced by highly protected access to domestic markets.

Given that ASEAN experienced difficulty establishing minimal sub-regional cooperation in growth zones, let alone reducing highly protected manufacturing and agricultural sectors through AFTA, it is not surprising that economically maturer states in the Asia–Pacific looked to alternative multilateral arrangements to facilitate integration. Consequently, in an attempt to address the increasingly vexed issue of Asia–Pacific trade, it was Australia, with the evident support of the Japanese Ministry for Trade and Industry (MITI) (*Australian*, 4 January 1996) that inaugurated a process of Asia–Pacific Economic Cooperation (APEC) in 1989. This loose grouping of initially 15 Asia–Pacific economies included Australia, New Zealand, the United States, Canada, Hong Kong, Taiwan, South Korea, Japan, China and the then ASEAN six. As an intergovernmental forum, APEC evolved from earlier non-governmental arrangements, notably the Pacific Economic Cooperation Council (PECC), that in the course of the 1980s established confidence in broader intergovernmental cooperation. APEC was notable, given the previous history of Asia–Pacific economic agreements, for its rapid development into an annual summit of Pacific Asian leaders (Kahler 1992, chap. 2).

By the first APEC summit held in Seattle in November 1993, membership had expanded to 17 countries, including Mexico and Papua New Guinea, and offered the seductive prospect of increasingly free Pacific Asian trade through an apparently oxymoronic commitment to a process of 'open regionalism'. At the Bogor summit in 1994, the group had expanded to 18 countries, including Chile, and accepted the report of its Eminent Persons Group proposing a framework for what the American delegation termed 'steadily increasing liberalization' (*Straits Times*, 1 October 1994). The Bogor Declaration of 15 November 1994 committed APEC members 'to adopt the long term goal of free and open trade and investment in the Asia–Pacific'. Industrialized countries were to achieve this goal by 2010 and developing countries by 2020 ('Apec economic leaders' declaration of common resolve' 1994). Bogor, it seemed, presaged a new era of Pacific Asian growth premised on a regional commitment to the principle of free trade that would both erode trade imbalances and create a broad range of economic and political interdependencies.

Despite these auspicious beginnings, however, it soon appeared that APEC members interpreted their commitment to free trade in very different ways. In particular, Pacific Asian countries embraced a distinctively Asian understanding of both free trade and trade agreements. Expounding this Asian way at Bogor in 1994, President Suharto explained, 'consensus must be broad and flexible, decisions should be made collectively and there can be no quick or delayed implementation' (*Straits Times*, 17 November 1994). Such a gradualist and voluntarist approach to free trade contrasted diametrically with the growing desire of the various branches of American government and its business lobby for a strict rule-based approach to Pacific Asian trade with sanctions for non-compliance (*Far Eastern Economic Review*, 30 November 1995, p. 14).

While the region's diplomatic and 'epistemic' community saw in APEC the prospect of a structured, coherent, multilateral, organizational basis for regional economic and political development, in practice this was not to be the case. Already in 1990, President Bush had inaugurated the North American Free Trade Area (NAFTA) as an alternative to Pacific Asian cooperation. NAFTA intimated a potential 'fortress America' antithetical to Pacific Asian exports (Eden and Molot 1993, p. 219). Moreover, increasingly abrasive exchanges with China over issues of human rights and trade surpluses and with Japan over its reluctance to open its automobile market indicated growing trade friction rather than cooperation. Reflecting this, the Office of the United States Trade Representative decided in May 1995 to impose 100 per cent duties on 13 Japanese car models. South Korea and Japan's attempt in the course of 1995 to 'water down' APEC's commitment to regional free trade by excluding agriculture from the deal only exacerbated mounting US frustration with APEC (see *Australian*, 1 October and 25 October 1995). Although at the subsequent Osaka summit in November 1995 APEC announced a timetable for trade liberalization to begin in 1997, its flexibility and absence of penalties for non-compliance left APEC with 'an agreement that is not enforceable or even binding' (*Far Eastern Economic Review*, 30 November 1995, p. 14). Subsequently, the US Senate called in November 1995 for a 'cooling off' period before entering into further trade agreements with the Pacific Asian states. US concern towards both APEC and the Asian reluctance to open markets remained undiminished throughout the Asian crisis and surfaced again when Asian economic growth resumed after 2002.

Interestingly, mounting US disenchantment with APEC had its Asian corollary in demands for a pan-Asian economic nationalism, which somewhat unfortunately mirrored the Greater East Asian Co-prosperity Sphere briefly inaugurated by Japan in 1942. Asian nationalists like Mahathir Mohamad and Shintaro Ishihara somewhat bizarrely questioned the value of a continued US economic presence in Pacific Asia. In 1990, Mahathir proposed as an alternative to APEC and NAFTA, an East Asian Economic Caucus (EAEC) comprising ASEAN, South Korea, Japan, Taiwan, China and Hong Kong. In 1993, Mahathir declined to attend the APEC summit in Seattle and appended an annex to the Bogor Declaration of 1994 dissenting from its provisions. 'East Asian countries,' he declared, 'should have their own forum' (*Straits Times*, 17 November 1994). Although in 1993 the ASEAN Annual Ministerial Meeting agreed that the EAEC might form a grouping within APEC (*Straits Times*, 30 August 1993) and represent a building bloc to a multilateral trading order, it could only do so realistically, as the Malaysian Minister of Trade, Rafidah Aziz, explained, if APEC was 'under no obligation to achieve free trade' (*Straits Times*, 25 April 1995; *Australian*, 8 November 1995). While a number of ASEAN states, notably Singapore and Indonesia, expressed reservations about the utility of a pan-Asian economic grouping, they, together with the other ASEAN states, nevertheless agreed to form an ASEAN Free Trade Area (AFTA) committing member states to reduce tariffs on almost all items of intra-ASEAN trade to 5 per cent by 2003 (*Economist*, 16 December 1995, p. 69). Such an arrangement represented a potential Southeast Asian insurance policy 'should the EC and NAFTA at some future date decide to block ASEAN products' (Emmerson and Simon 1993, p. 31; see also Goldsmith 1994, pp. 55–75).

Hence, prior to the financial meltdown, Pacific Asian governments between 1950 and 1996 effectively exploited the embedded liberalism of the post-Bretton Woods international trade regime. In so doing, the more efficiently organized and coherently planned Northeast Asian economies succeeded in both managing trade and picking industrial winners. Latterly, and less coherently, the core Southeast Asian economies, followed by China and Vietnam, also sought export-led growth through a haphazard exploitation of natural resources, cheap labour and FDI. This planned growth and bureaucratic mobilization of both capital and labour in a favourable external environment sustained impressive growth over long periods. Yet, as more sceptical studies by Alwyn Young and Paul Krugman demonstrated (Young 1992, 1995; Krugman 1994), the high growth achieved by the so-called High Performing Asian Economies (HPAEs) could be explained by an effective mobilization of inputs like the rise in participation rates, transfer of labour from agriculture to higher value-added work, investment in machinery and the education of the workforce (Young 1995, pp. 673–5). In other words, the most effective HPAEs efficiently mobilized resources. They did not, however, achieve a 'miracle' in total factor productivity. Moreover, in the process of mobilizing capital, South Korea, Thailand, Malaysia and particularly Indonesia accumulated disturbingly high levels of external debt, together with burgeoning current account deficits, rendering the latter three currencies, by the mid-1990s, highly susceptible to international financial speculation (*Fortune Magazine*, 6 March 1995).

Finally, the long-term effects of the growth strategies pursued by the HPAEs had the unintended consequence of mounting the Pelion of trade surpluses with the open United States market upon the Ossa of protected domestic markets, thereby destabilizing international currencies in an era of globally traded derivatives, and adding unnecessarily to the debt burden of weaker HPAEs, while simultaneously threatening deflation in Japan. Meanwhile, the attempt to manage trade engendered countervailing American and European responses that made the emerging multilateral framework of Asia–Pacific Economic Cooperation less conducive to management and more fractious than during the era of benign American hegemony. The international ramifications of this emerging pattern were to be interestingly transformed by the financial crisis and ASEAN's response to it, which we shall explore next.

THE IRRELEVANCE OF THE ASEAN WAY TO THE EVOLVING ECONOMIC STRUCTURE OF THE ASIA–PACIFIC

One of the more fashionable nostrums underpinning thinking about the globalizing political economy and the evolving world order assumed that the territorial state no longer constituted the key unit either for political analysis or for political action in a post-modernizing world shaped by transnational factors beyond its sovereign territorial grasp. Increasingly, it was alleged, supranational regional groupings represented the building blocs of a new, interdependent, market-friendly, open regional trading order. In fact, its oxymoronic terminology connoted the incoherence at the heart of East Asian regionalism.

The unforeseen impact on regional arrangements of exchange rate deregulation and derivative trading through internetted stock exchanges that never slept, exposed how illusory the link was (and remains) between a ponderous, bureaucratic regionalism and the virtual world of global finance. Whilst the prophets of regionalism attended primarily to the role of conglomerates and transnational corporations in the fashionably borderless world trading order, relatively little attention was paid to the political and economic consequences of currency convertibility and the role of speculative investment in the Asian miracle post-1985.

Those enamoured of the region at the expense of the state envisaged trading arrangements like APEC and polymorphous economic and security arrangements like ASEAN, together with the economic and security arrangements it spawned, like the ARF, AFTA and ASEAN Plus Three as the necessary mechanisms for building what many of its analyst/admirers considered to be a new, multilateral, regional order. Retrospectively, it now appears that such regional arrangements were essentially Cold War products which concealed local differences by uniting against the real or imagined external threat of Communism. With the demise of Communism, the emergence of market-Leninism in an irredentist China and the inability of Japan to project political as opposed to economic power, a great deal was expected from regional consensus-building mechanisms like APEC and an expanded ASEAN. Much was made of an 'Asian way' facilitating what former Malaysian Deputy Premier, Anwar Ibrahim, termed an 'Asian Renaissance' (Ibrahim 1996) constituting the ideological foundations of a new Asian order appropriate for the eagerly anticipated 'Pacific Century'.

Part of the problem here was that some of the more enthusiastic proponents of the Asian way also doubled as academic analysts. These scholar-bureaucrats from Canberra to Tokyo considered Asian values of face-saving and face-giving cooperation, consensus, hierarchy, harmony and balance to be the ideological template for a new pan-Asian economic and political order (see for example Sopiee 1992). Western democracies might, with reservations, join the new dispensation; however, they would have to accept that the Asia–Pacific was a 'two-way street' (Mahbubani 1995a, p. 107). Regional agreements on trade, like the APEC-brokered Bogor Declaration (1994), which appeared to presage a new era of economic and political interdependency, assumed shared Asian values in their provision for regional economic development. APEC agreements were neither enforceable nor binding. Nevertheless, this *modus operandi* was enthusiastically embraced by western academics in second track diplomatic gatherings (see Ramesh 1997, p. 268).

Equally insubstantial and even more grandiose in its regionalist pretensions was the rapid expansion of ASEAN. This sole indigenous regional grouping of any note received growing international respect in the post-Cold War era. After

1991, European, North and South American and Australasian diplomats, bureaucrats and academics scrambled to attend its dialogue groups, workshops and multi-level fora. Its many admirers claimed its excursions into multilateralism through arrangements like the ASEAN Free Trade Area and the ASEAN Regional Forum provided the foundations for the new regionalism.

Ultimately, though, in the manner of political delusion, the ASEAN way represented the triumph of appearance over reality. The promotion of non-confrontational Asian values and the emphasis on good interpersonal relations between ageing gerontocrats merely established a mechanism for evading the threats posed by unresolved border disputes, ethnic and religious tensions, environmental problems, arms race benchmarking and dubious fiscal and trading practices across the region. Yet attempts to reform ASEAN and APEC procedures in the direction of openness and rule-governed accountability were, as we have shown, rebuffed. This reluctance continued after the meltdown of regional economies in 1997. Thus, at the July 1998 ASEAN ministers' and dialogue partners' meeting in Manila, the more autocratic members of the regional grouping (Myanmar, Singapore, Malaysia) and the grouping's largest and most unstable member, Indonesia, rejected the call by more democratically accountable member states (Thailand and the Philippines) to abandon the Panglossian faith in non-interference and interpersonal ties in favour of a more proactive 'flexible engagement' in matters of common political, economic and environmental concern ('ASEAN: the game goes on', 1998, p. 57; *Straits Times*, 5 July 1998). In view of the systemic inability of regional arrangements to address either long-standing territorial disputes or the fiscal, environmental and political consequences of rapid growth followed by vertiginous recession, receding Asian economies were thrown back on the resources, not of regional institutions, but of what were once assumed to be strong states. Let us then briefly examine the state of the states in littoral Pacific Asia as the meltdown wound back their double-digit growth, emptied their treasuries and drove their stock markets remorselessly south.

CAN TIGERS CHANGE THEIR STRIPES? STRATEGIC IMPLICATIONS OF THE FINANCIAL MELTDOWN

The impact of the financial meltdown that began in Thailand in July 1997 had a traumatic impact on the economic, social and political arrangements of those East Asian states that modernized in the course of the Cold War through their alliances with and access to the United States and its market. Yet whilst the causes of the crisis have been widely advertised and its economic consequences extensively prognosticated, much less attention has been given to the economic implications of the crisis at both regional and state level. Indeed, amidst the regular reports between 1997 and 2002 of collapsing *chaebol*, gangster-dominated *keiretsu* and Japanese banks with more illiquidity than Manhattan during the prohibition, it was a curious fact that the dominant orthodoxy in the study of political development and international relations still considered East Asian miracle growth and the 'open regional' order it promoted the basis for the borderless world of a 'post-modern' multilateral dispensation. What, we might wonder, happened to the uniquely Asian values that sustained the Asian model and what impact has the spectre of financial meltdown still haunting the political elites of the Asia–Pacific had upon the domestic and foreign relations of the states of the Pacific littoral? Does it entail an increased emphasis on Asian bonding and 'multi-level regionalism' that the promotion of ASEAN Plus Three seems to intimate or something far more uncertain, state-driven and unstable (see Higgott 1998, p. 6)?

MYTH MAKING IN PACIFIC ASIA: THE STRENGTH OF ASIAN POLITICAL AND ECONOMIC 'GOVERNANCE'

One of the more interesting consequences of the revelation that the East Asian miracle was about as authentic as the Turin Shroud was the exposure of the myth of the strength of the Asian developmental state. The myth, widely promulgated before 1997, maintained that state-managed politics facilitated state-managed growth, equitably distributing the results of that growth, emphasizing family values, inducing high savings rates and investment in universal education. The conjunction of these beneficent factors thereby produced utility-maximizing citizens and engendered a virtuous circle of productivity. Even as late as 1997, western newspaper editors and re-invented social democrats from Canberra to Islington and the Washington Beltway favourably contrasted the East Asian virtues of bureaucratic guidance and community values with the Anglo-American alternative of casino capitalism, egoistic individualism and the short-termism of private banks and fund managers. Indeed, the strategic capitalism of East Asia both shaped Will Hutton's fulmination concerning *The State We're In*, and formed the backdrop to what, other than vacuity, informed the 'Third Way' (Hutton 1995, pp. 268–77; Giddens 1998, pp. 153–8). Significantly, those commentators most entranced by the apparent success of the Asian model initially considered the traumatic downturn that began in July 1997 only a blip. They further contended that the crisis was essentially a financial panic induced by western financiers and hedge funds who either took flight or exploited the speculative possibilities afforded by the first premonitory signs of East Asian monetary instability (see, inter alia, Grenville 1998; Krugman 1999, pp. 142–5; Radelet and Sachs 1997, pp. 52–3).[1]

The problem with this view is that it overpromoted the strengths of Asian structures of governance. The apparently autonomous Asian state and the corporatist developmental coalitions it endorsed were really much weaker than Asian adherents and western enthusiasts thought. For, prior to the crisis, those of a more sceptical disposition, like Brian Reading, had described the alarming fiscal deficiencies that informed East Asian state-led development (Reading 1992, chap. 20). The Japanese iron triangle of business, bureaucracy and a single dominant party, replicated with more authoritarian overtones in South Korea and Taiwan, showed a disturbing propensity to rigidity, inflexibility and political sclerosis. Somewhat differently, in Southeast Asia, Kunio Yoshihara and E.T. Gomez had identified an ersatz form of capitalism based on short-term loans, cheap labour, low-value manufacturing, property speculation and tourism (Gomez 1994; Yoshihara 1988).

Uncritical acceptance of the virtues of the opaque relationship between state-owned or influenced banks and state-owned or influenced conglomerates facilitated the accumulation of debt to equity in the 'private sector'. The actual character of the developmental model meant that private sector business was inextricably entwined with public sector technocrats and politicians. Moreover, the easily available credit of the boom decade, 1985–95, left Asia–Pacific countries sitting on a property bubble that extended from Tokyo to Jakarta. Interestingly, and perhaps as a consequence of easily available credit, the miracle states of the Pacific Rim never developed either a corporate or a government bond market, leaving capital little option but flight at the first indication of financial difficulty (Tsang 1998; *Financial Times*, 12 August 1998). In other words, outside of colonial Hong Kong prior to 1997, one of the devices long established in the west to hedge states and corporations against the consequences of an economic downturn had not occurred to the technocrats who determined the long-term growth strategies of the Asian miracle economies.

Futhermore, the close relationship between bureaucrats and business that increasingly characterized East Asian long-termism rendered conglomerates from Fuyo and Mitsubishi in Japan, Kia in South Korea, Charoen Phopkand in Thailand, Renong in Malaysia or the family cartels of the Suhartos in Indonesia unaccountable either to shareholders or to normal practices of accounting and, in the absence of any effective hedging instruments, vulnerable to capital flight. They were necessarily exposed when global markets began to question the premises of endless growth based on the mobilization of inputs and the risk involved in investing in such opaque and overexposed arrangements.

This notwithstanding, a number of East Asian governments, their social scientists and their western academic acolytes, argued that manipulative hedge funds promoted the currency crisis that induced the flight of hot money from Pacific Asia. They further contended that the International Monetary Fund (IMF) policies, designed to rescue the ailing tiger economies, merely intensified the currency crisis. Exploiting academically fashionable notions of Orientalism, these claims ultimately served to deflect attention from the structural and economic weaknesses of the Asian model in both its Southeast and Northeast Asian guises. For, somewhat problematically for the hedge fund speculation thesis, it was local traders, residents and banks that triggered the initial panic on Asian bourses by moving funds offshore (*Financial Times*, 6 October 1998). Moreover, despite its limitations, if the IMF had not played the role of lender of last resort, the financial panic and ensuing economic chaos across Pacific Asia would undoubtedly have been even more far-reaching in its social consequences. The fact that it was not immediately apparent whether the rapid meltdown constituted a banking crisis requiring lower interest rates, or an exchange rate crisis requiring higher ones evidently complicated the IMF's task ('Prognosis dismal for Asian flu', 1998; Park 2001, pp. 112–15). Nevertheless, to the extent that the IMF exhibited incompetence, it was through its propensity to promote 'moral hazard' by providing money to unreformed and unaccountable state bureaucracies, notably in Indonesia, and reimbursing losses incurred by overexposed overseas investment banks and incontinent hedge funds.

Retrospectively, it is evident that the spectacular economic growth of the East Asian Pacific Rim after 1960 benefited from the embedded liberalism of the Cold War trading order and the comparative advantage enjoyed by those states that signed up to it during the Cold War. The economic and geo-political consequences of the shift in that order after 1990 eventually exposed the bureaucratic and structural rigidity of the Asian model. In other words, the inadequacy of Asian financial practice, coupled with an uncritical belief in its own self-serving ideology, explains why investors both within and outside the Asia–Pacific took flight after July 1997. Paradoxically, what were once perceived as the strengths of Asian governance, in particular the synergy between government banks and business, soon came to represent its structural defects. The systemic limitations of an economic and political culture founded on *gotong royong* (cooperative) capitalism, *guanxi* (relationships) and *xinyong* (mutual trust), explained its ultimate failure. In the emerging virtual world of hot money and the electronic herd, Asian governments and conglomerates from Japan to Indonesia found it difficult to adjust to the practices of legal and political accountability that would attract the infusion of liquidity that, after 1998, they desperately needed. Let us then briefly inspect the etiology of the crisis and its impact on the region and regional arrangements like ASEAN.

EAST ASIA DISINCORPORATED: THE JAPAN THAT SAID VERY LITTLE

In the first stage of the bursting of the East Asia bubble it was widely assumed that, although the Japanese economy had slowed down, there was little likelihood of the world's second-largest economy being seriously undermined by a little local difficulty in South Korea and Southeast Asia. This clearly underestimated the manner in which Japan functioned in the Pacific Asian economy. Since the 1960s, Japan had been the major investor in labour-intensive offshore manufacturing, initially in Northeast Asia, then in Thailand, Malaysia and Indonesia, and latterly in China and Vietnam. Japan also represented the market for Pacific Asian raw materials and low value added, or unfinished manufactures. As the Japanese economy first stagnated and then slumped, it became evident not only that Japanese banks were exposed to a raft of bad or doubtful domestic property loans estimated to exceed $100 billion in 1998,[2] but also that their *keiretsu*-linked trading arms, the *sogoshosha*, were exposed to non-performing loans across Pacific Asia, particularly in Indonesia. Multinational *keiretsu* like Fuyo, which include Nissan, Fuji Bank and Canon, faced bankruptcy.

Continuing high savings rates, low domestic consumption and, latterly, deflation meant that overloaded Japanese conglomerates could not be the engine to extricate its putative greater Eastern Asian co-prosperity sphere from deepening recession. By 1998, it was evident that the flailing, as opposed to the flying, geese model had cost Japan not only its economic leadership but also whatever moral authority it exercised in the Southeast Asian region. The replacement of the once youthful and dynamic Ryutorao Hashimoto, the man who was to break the mould of Japanese politics when first appointed Prime Minister in 1995, by the unprepossessing Keizo Obuchi indicated that, since the Japanese property bubble burst in 1990, the otiose governing Liberal Democratic Party (LDP) had developed neither the capacity to correct its regional financial failings or reform itself nor the cronyist relationship that obtained between government, bureaucracy and business. International markets greeted Obuchi's new team, that included the already tried and failed former Prime Minister, Kiichi Miyazawa, with a notable lack of enthusiasm by selling off the *yen*, which subsequently plummeted to new depths against the dollar.

Moreover, despite eventually securing a massive bailout package of 60 000 billion *yen* in a desperate effort to rescue the Japanese banking sector, the LDP lacked the political will to impose the necessary strict disclosure rules that might ensure present and future financial transparency ('Obuchi's big bailout', 1998). As Martin Wolf observed in 1998, LDP policy towards the banking sector 'is a shambles; few believe the official figures on non-performing loans . . . and the opposition and much of the public fear the government's sole desire is to bail out banks without confronting the incompetence and fraud that lay behind the disaster . . . make believe and dark suspicion is a recipe for dangerous drift' (Wolf 1998c). The appointment of a new and even more dynamic leadership in the shape of Junichiro Koizumi, yet another politician intended to break the mould of Japanese governance, did little to address the sense of drift and stagnation in the Japanese economy prior to 2002.

THE FEARFUL SYMMETRY OF THE 'TIGER' STATES

As Japan became politically and economically calcified, those economies that sought to emulate the Japanese model of development, yet remained paradoxically dependent upon access to the Japanese market, Japanese investment or higher technology, confronted an increasingly uncertain future. Kenneth Courtis, chief economist at Deutsche Bank, Tokyo, observed in 1998 that, 'if Japan continues to contract then the other countries in the region have no hope of turning their economies around' (quoted in *Australian Financial Review*, 10 August 1998). The inability of government and bureaucracy to reform the banking sector in Japan made such a scenario increasingly plausible.[3] Indeed, the formerly strong states of the Asia–Pacific littoral, irrespective of their purported transition to democracy, shared a fearful symmetry of bureaucratic overload, bad loans, illiquidity and evolving political fragility and instability. At the peak of the crisis, Jean-Michel Severino of the World Bank calculated that \$115 billion in FDI fled Malaysia, South Korea, Thailand, Indonesia and the Philippines. In effect, the equivalent of 18 per cent of GDP vanished from the Asia–Pacific region between July 1997 and 1998 (Wolf 1998a). Significantly, Japan was the major creditor of the ailing tiger economies and directed 40 per cent of its exports to Pacific Asia (Wolf 1998b). Between 15 and 25 per cent of the exports of the meltdown economies went to deflating Japan. Over the same period, regional trade plummeted by 50 per cent. As regional trade accounted for almost a quarter of the total trade of these export-oriented economies, lower consumer demand in each receding tiger affected the export performance of its neighbours.

Ironically, what seemed like a virtuous Asian circle of high savings and state-engineered growth ultimately turned out vicious. This engendered a variety of political and social problems at both state and regional level (*Jakarta Post*, 22 June 1998). South Korea had to endure the 'national shame' of a \$58 billion IMF bailout package, a 6 per cent contraction in GDP, a liquidity crunch, high interest rates and, with unemployment rising to 10 per cent of the workforce, mounting labour unrest. Significantly, the constitutional transition from Kim Young Sam to Kim Dae Jung in December 1997 did little to address

South Korea's failed corporatist, conglomerate-based economic and political model. Despite the amalgamation of a few banks, the South Korean financial sector remains opaque. Even with mounting losses and labour unrest, *chaebol*, such as Hyundai, continue to cast their monolithic footprint over the economy and resist foreign access to ownership of domestic companies.

Irrespective of political moves to constitutional, as opposed to military, rule, the Korean economy and Korean politics remain mired in a culture of illiberalism that views the state as a paternalistic guardian and resents the intrusion of foreign goods into the domestic market or foreign takeovers of indigenous economic champions. Notwithstanding IMF blandishments to open the South Korean market, both Microsoft and Ford abandoned attempts in 1998 to take over failed South Korean software and motor manufacturers, complaining of political and bureaucratic interference that rendered their bids unsustainable (*Financial Times*, 7 September 1998). Given the continued appeal of corporatism to the national psyche, structural reform in South Korea was minimal. Even after the shift to a new generation of leaders between 2001 and 2004, South Korea's bureaucracy and powerful trades unions continue to frustrate market access to all but the largest international conglomerates.

If the state of the state in Northeast Asia looked grim, the prospects were even bleaker in Southeast Asia. Thailand, which triggered the crisis in July 1997, when the Bank of Thailand ineptly tried to maintain the *baht* peg to the dollar, received an IMF rescue package of $18 billion. The unavoidable restructuring of the economy witnessed the bankruptcy of financial institutions, manufacturing decline, rising interest rates and unemployment rates, and a liquidity crunch. Although Chuan Leekpai's Democrat-led coalition government tried to implement elements of the IMF package in the course of 1998, the continuing opacity concerning the extent of private and public sector debt, combined with laws to restrict foreign ownership of Thai property and businesses, deterred the foreign investment necessary to generate recovery. In Thailand, as in South Korea, democratic leaders showed little evidence of making any more than cosmetic adjustments to a political, financial and business culture inured to cronyist clientilism. By 1999, Chuan's unstable six-party coalition had not only failed to implement radical economic reform, it had also exposed itself to charges of widespread corruption (*Financial Times*, 16 September 1998). General elections in 2000 saw the replacement of a weak, Democrat-led coalition by Thaksin Shinawatra's Chart Thai Party. The rule, however, of a single party reflecting the interests of Thailand's largest conglomerate did little to address the issue of transparency in Thai business–government relations.

Similar practices have long characterized the New Economic Policy that the United Malay National Organization (UMNO) dominated National Front coalition government carefully nurtured in Malaysia after interethnic riots in

May 1969. Significantly, Malaysia avoided the IMF in 1998, although the private sector was 'tied up with debts'. By the second quarter of 1998, Malaysia possessed one of the world's highest ratios of debt to GDP output (*Straits Times*, 2 July 1998) and non-performing loans had risen to between 25 and 30 per cent of all loans (Economist Intelligence Unit 1998a, p. 29). By early 1999, Malaysian banks faced write-offs equivalent to 20 per cent of GDP (*Straits Times*, 2 July 1998). Malaysia, then, suffered from the same systemic weakness that afflicted all the tiger economies: non-performing loans on speculative property investments; conglomerates seeking court protection from creditors (*Asian Wall Street Journal*, 8 July 1998); shaky local banks, like Sime Darby and Bank Bumiputera (*Asian Wall Street Journal*, 4 July 1998); and a collapsing currency.

Moreover, the questionable policy, promulgated by Prime Minister Mahathir Mohamad's finance minister, Daim Zainuddin in August 1998, of reducing interest rates in order to allay recession merely facilitated capital flight to Singapore. The subsequent decision to reimpose currency controls not only led to the resignation of the director of Bank Negara, the Malaysian central bank, it also had the deleterious effect of terminating western investment and the infusion of liquidity necessary to revive growth. Further attempts to stimulate the economy through subsidies to struggling indigenous conglomerates like Renong and Mirzan Mahathir's *Konsortium Perkapalan* reflected the enduring charms of cronyism. Mahathir's petulant attacks on western finance capital, the removal of his more market-friendly deputy, Anwar Ibrahim, for alleged sexual misconduct amounting to treason, together with restrictions on 'negative' reports (*Sunday Times*, Singapore, 19 July 1998) turned an economic crisis into a political crisis amongst the formerly unified Malay governing elite and facilitated the emergence of a politically attractive Malay/Islamist alternative in the shape of *Parti Islam Se-Malaysia* (PAS).

If Malaysia was in a state of denial during the economic crisis, Indonesia's state was one of economic and political fragmentation. Triggered by the *baht* crisis, the meltdown of the *rupiah* in August 1997 exposed a 'vast overhang of unhedged short-term private sector debt' conservatively estimated at $80 billion (Economist Intelligence Unit 1998b, p. 27). The collapse of the financial sector and various Chinese and Suharto family-linked conglomerates followed. The economic crisis undermined the authority of President Suharto's New Order and, following riots and student demonstrations in May 1998, the ageing president resigned in favour of his ineffectual Vice President, B.J. Habibie.

Indonesia was, China and the Philippines apart, both the largest, the croniest and least bureaucratically competent of the emerging Asian economies. The flight of capital, the failure of Indonesian banks and the collapse of Indonesian business necessitated an IMF bailout package of close to $50 billion. In July 1998, then Finance Minister Bambang Subianto conservatively calculated that GDP would contract by 12 per cent, and inflation rise by 60 per cent. At that time, the government required 95 trillion *rupiah* per annum merely to service its debt repayments. Throughout Pacific Asia economic dislocation caused rising unemployment, along with rising interest rates. The Asian emphasis upon family values, moreover, meant that there was no safety net for those who fell into poverty. Nowhere was the absence of welfare provision more acutely felt than in Indonesia.

The spectre of half the 220 million population falling below the poverty line with no imminent prospect of economic recovery raised the political and economic stakes. The replacement of Suharto by his protégé Habibie did little to legitimate or stabilize the post-Suharto order. The suggestion that Indonesians should fast two days a week to overcome food shortages symbolized the bankruptcy of Habibie's political style. The period between the resignation of Suharto in May and the convening of a special session of the People's Consultative Assembly in November 1998 to agree on the process for a presidential election in 1999, subsequently followed by the introduction of a new constitution that provided for both direct presidential and parliamentary elections in 2004, witnessed both a largely successful *perjuangan democrasi* (fight for democracy) and a proliferation of political parties that strikingly resembled the *aliran* (political streams) of unstable post-independence Indonesia (1950–57).

By 2004, Megawati Sukarnoputri's faction of the *Partai Demokrasi Indonesia* (Democratic Party of Indonesia) (PDI), the *Partai Demokrasi Indonesia Perjuangan* (Democratic Party of Indonesia of Struggle) (PDI–P) sought, increasingly unsuccessfully, to revive the nationalist legacy of her father. Abdurrahman Wahid's *Nadhlatul Ulama* (Council of Islamic Scholars), Indonesia's largest Islamic organization that had previously shunned politics for 14 years, established a political party, the *Partai Kebangkitan Bangsa* (National Awakening Party) (PKB) in June 1998, representing both the rural Islamic *pesantren* (villages with Islamic schools) tradition and a moderate civil Islam. Meanwhile Amien Rais' *Partai Amanat Nasional* (National Mandate Party) (PAN) reflected an inchoate, reformist, modernizing Islam represented in the pre-Sukarno era by *Masjumi* (a contraction of *Majlis Sjuro Muslimin Indonesia* (Consultative Council of Indonesian Muslims) founded in 1949 and loosely aligned to Sukarno, which combined progressive and conservative Islamic elements). It is to this constituency and a broader middle-class concern for order, stability and a conservative consensus that Habibie and subsequently Akbar Tanjung also appealed through *Golkar*, the official New Order party of government,[4] that survived the transition and retained its extensive organizational base. Indeed, at the 2004 election, *Golkar* achieved the majority of votes to the new parliament, *Dewan*

Perwakilan Rakyat (People's Representative Assembly) (DPR), although its candidate for the presidency, General Wiranto, failed to make the second round. Historically, these various political streams have shown little capacity for compromise. Moreover, the fact that the successful candidate in the second round of the Presidential election in September 2004, General Susilo Bambang Yudhoyono, commands only a small base in the DPR, combined with the failure of former Presidents Wahid (1999–2001) and Megawati (2001–2004) to revive the economy or address the climate of cronyism and corruption, has rendered the transition to democracy worryingly disjointed.

Political uncertainty and economic turmoil, however, exercise little appeal for the *Tentara Nasional Indonesia* (Indonesian Armed Forces) (TNI) that remains ideologically wedded, if not to its dual function (*dwifungsi*) as the source of order and guarantor of the Indonesian state, at least to a role in preserving the integrity of the archipelagic empire. Since the events of May 1998, and more particularly since its questionable role in the militia-inspired extra-judicial killing that preceded East Timorese independence in September 1999, the army has kept a low profile in Indonesian politics. The TNI is also internally divided between nationalist (*merah putih*) and Islamic (*hijau*) factions and it is unlikely that either faction could accept the uncertainty of multi-partism, or independence for troublesome provinces like Aceh and Irian Jaya.

Significantly, the role of army factions both in the riots of 13–20 May 1998 and during the special session of the national assembly in November 1998 illustrated both the contradictory forces at work within the army and the uncertain status of the Indonesian Chinese, the traditional scapegoats for political and economic breakdown. The flight of Chinese capital from Indonesia in the course of 1998 and its somewhat reluctant return after 2002, together with the rise of militant Islam in the shape of the *Partai Keadilan Sejahtera* (Prosperous Justice Party) (PKS) that achieved 8 per cent of the national vote in 2004, *Jemaah Islamiyah* (Islamic Organization) (JI) and the *Front Pembela Islamiah* (Islamic Defenders Front) (FPI), added a volatile ethno-religious dimension to the apparently shared Asian values of ASEAN and the ARF.

ECONOMIC DOWNTURN, CHINESE PARIAHS AND THE EMERGENCE OF GREATER CHINA

As the depth and severity of the economic crisis engulfing the export-oriented economies of Indonesia and Malaysia intensified, long-suppressed ethnic and religious tensions became increasingly visible. Significantly, the severity of the 1997–98 economic downturn once again raised questions about the role of the overseas Chinese in the economies of Malaysia and Indonesia in general and the status of Singapore as an island of Chinese 'sojourners' in what Lee Kuan Yew termed a 'sea of Malay peoples'. Why, we might wonder, did the economic meltdown so dramatically undermine the consensus that had officially characterized the region's most significant regional grouping, ASEAN, and its core economies Indonesia, Singapore and Malaysia? And what are the prospects for regional stability, premised as it is on continued economic growth, and driven by the official ASEAN ideology of bonding, good interpersonal relations and non-interference in the internal affairs of member states?

The inter-ASEAN difficulties that emerged after 1997 between Singapore and its neighbours must be cast against a backdrop of the growing popular appeal of a revived Islamic identity to Malay and Indonesian political reformers and the increasingly hostile perception of economically influential, but 'non-indigenous' Chinese minorities. Ethnic and religious suspicion, coupled with economic turmoil and the local predilection for conspiracy theory and a plot mentality, makes for a heady regional brew. The re-emergence of long-suppressed communal and religious tensions, coupled with the emergence of China as a regional economic and political force, has additional implications for both regional institutions and economic recovery in Southeast Asia.

A notable feature of economic growth in Southeast Asia in the boom decades after 1969 was, as we have observed, both its curiously technology-less character and the disproportionately influential role played by Chinese business. In Indonesia, although the Chinese represent less than 4 per cent of the population, Chinese conglomerates accounted for two-thirds of Indonesia's private, urban economy. They dominated the distribution network for food and other essentials (see *Straits Times*, 18 July 1998; Wibisono 1995) and controlled 80 per cent of the assets of the top 300 conglomerates. In Malaysia, the numerically much larger Chinese population similarly occupied a disproportionately influential role in commercial life. Here the big Malay–Chinese conglomerates, such as Hong Leong and the Robert Kuok groups, cultivated close ties with key figures in the ruling, ethnically Malay, UMNO elite, ensuring that elite business activity occurred beyond the realm of public scrutiny or comment (Gomez 1994).

This distinctive and opaque relationship between Chinese business and an ethnically dissimilar political elite reflected the contingent historical legacy that marked the emergence of the new states of Southeast Asia after 1945. Both the post-colonial Malaysian and Indonesian states deliberately evolved an official distinction between indigenous and non-indigenous subjects (*bumiputera* and *non-bumiputera* in *Bahasa Melayu* or *bumi* and *non-bumi* in *Bahasa Indonesia*). While who precisely constituted the *bumi* remained vague, the prime function of the category was to exclude the Chinese.

The paradox of being economically powerful but politically impotent seemed unimportant when the regional economy boomed. If things went wrong, however, the wealthy Chinese *towkay* (businessman) stood out as an obvious target for the politically and economically disaffected. And things, of course, went spectacularly wrong. The tendency to scapegoat the Chinese community had evident domestic and regional implications. In Malaysia, since his political emergence as a Malay 'ultra' in the aftermath of the 1969 riots, Prime Minister Mahathir promoted a eugenic vision, outlined in *The Malay Dilemma* (Mahathir, 1970). This emphasized the need to forge a modern, dynamic *bumiputera* identity for a new Malaysia Incorporated. A notable feature of Mahathir and the UMNO-controlled press's rhetoric in dealing with the 1998 crisis was to stress the dangers of communalism, the need for Malay unity and to blame either western speculators, Jews or Chinese Singapore for bad faith in their financial and commercial dealings with Malaysia. As Mahathir's handling of the economic crisis turned into a political one, Islamic groups supporting deposed Deputy Prime Minister Anwar Ibrahim and demanding *reformasi* by no means presaged a new political pluralism. Significantly, the Chinese minority that accounts for over 37 per cent of the population remains politically isolated. Indeed, the inability of the Malay elite to adopt credible structural reforms to address the crisis has continuing implications for ASEAN, Singapore–Malay relations and Chinese business groups in Malaysia, that are yet to be addressed by the new Mahathir-lite Malaysian Prime Minister Abdullah Badawi (2003–).

More disturbingly still, in Indonesia, the Chinese community, already traumatized by the events in May 1998 in which organized groups of *primam* (hooligans) systematically murdered, raped and pillaged their way across the Chinese districts of Glodok, West Jakarta and Solo, East Java, constitute the obvious scapegoat for economic failure. The continuing political uncertainty that induces permanent fear of further racial unrest and undermines the ability of Chinese business to function in Indonesia, casts doubt on the capacity for Indonesia to recover economically and adds a new and disturbing ethnic component to regional dynamics. Despite the centrality of Chinese traders to Indonesian food distribution, Habibie and his successors, Wahid and Megawati, did little to allay the anxiety of those who fled the country. Their place, Habibie insouciantly observed in July 1998, could be 'taken over by others' (quoted in *Straits Times*, 20 July 1998).

Although both military and civilian politicians hold the Chinese conglomerates largely responsible for Indonesia's difficulties, the plight of the overseas Chinese did not go unremarked elsewhere in the region. In July 1998, the Chinese foreign ministry expressed 'concern and sympathy for the ethnic Chinese people' assaulted in the May riots (*Jakarta Post*, 15 July 1998; *Financial Times*, 4 August 1998). Meanwhile, China's sole remaining rebellious province, Taiwan, suspended rice shipments to Indonesia in August 1998 in order to demonstrate its concern at the Indonesian government's indifference to the plight of the Indonesian Chinese (*Financial Times*, 21 August 1998).

Ethnic tension, the rise of militant Islam (which will be discussed in a later chapter) coupled with economic decline and the contentious role played by overseas Chinese networks in developing Southeast Asia's ersatz form of capitalism, has weakened, rather than strengthened regional consensus. Economic collapse and the re-emergence of old religious and ethnic cleavages in the cultural mosaic that constitutes the ASEAN locale have only revealed that organization's incapacity to address these difficulties. Two fault lines have appeared in the arrangement that to many observers both prior to 1997 and, more surprisingly, since 2001, offers the basis for a secure and economically prosperous Pacific Asia (see, inter alia, Naisbett 1995, pp. 252ff).

Firstly, ASEAN's more autocratically disposed members considered the grouping's central tenet of non-interference to be 'misunderstood' and are unwilling to abandon it. Meanwhile representatives of the more democratically accountable ASEAN countries, like the Thai Foreign Minister Surin Pitsuwan maintained that the crisis required the amendment of the non-interference doctrine. He argued in 1998 that the organization should adopt 'flexible engagement on issues that have a negative bearing on others in the region' (quoted in *Jakarta Post*, 13 July 1998). Across this emerging ideological divide runs a less widely advertised cultural cleavage, which isolates the overseas Chinese, whose home base in Southeast Asia is Singapore, from an increasingly Islamically conscious cultural area. Despite a shared regard for the ASEAN ideology of non-interference established in its Treaty of Amity and Cooperation (1975), both Singapore's, and to a lesser extent Thailand's and the Philippines', relations with both Malaysia and Indonesia have cooled dramatically since the inception of the crisis. Lee Kuan Yew's accurate, but undiplomatic, observation, that Suharto's decision to appoint B.J. Habibie to the vice-presidency, (prior to his assumption of the Presidency in May 1998) would 'disturb' financial markets did little to enhance the good interpersonal relations between regional leaders that ostensibly constituted the capstone of ASEAN style diplomacy. The subsequent failure of Singapore to disburse $3 billion in trade credit guarantees promised in April 1998, because Indonesian officials refused to abide by Singapore ministry of trade and industry conditions, prompted Habibie to describe the city state as a mere 'dot on the map', indifferent to a 'friend in need' (quoted in *Financial Times*, 21 August 1998).

Secondly, at the same time, a number of recession-related factors frayed the always volatile relations between Singapore and Malaysia. Malaysian officials criticized Singapore banks for aiding capital flight out of Malaysia. Adverse Singaporean comment on Malaysian crime levels in the neighbouring city across the causeway of Johore Bahru, together with the decision to move passport control for the city state along the Singapore–Malaysia railway without sufficiently consulting the Malaysian government further provoked Malaysian ire in the course of 1998. Continuing disagreement about treaties guaranteeing Singapore's water supply into the twenty-first century, and the Malaysian government's requirement that all exports leave the country from Port Klang after 1998, further exacerbated the omnipresent anxiety of Singapore's ruling elite.

Furthermore, the banks and state-owned enterprises of the cybernetic technocratic machine that organizes every aspect of Singaporean life are directly or indirectly affected by insolvency in the Malay and Indonesian economies. Thus, when Malaysia arbitrarily decided to reimpose currency and stock exchange controls in September 1998, Singapore banks had to clear billions of *ringgit* in transactions made in its foreign exchange market. As one local economist observed, 'in the process of taking control' of its currency, 'the biggest casualty ... [was] Singapore' (quoted in *Financial Times*, 19 September 1998). Yet Singapore's ruling People's Action Party's (PAP) neurocratic propensity to advertise publicly its concerns over the policies responsible for regional recession, environmental decay and the rise of radical Islam only served to fuel interregional irritation between 1998 and the Bali bombing of October 2002.

One intriguing feature of the meltdown was that, while Chinese minorities were being persecuted, China itself began to emerge ever more clearly as the dominant player in Asia. As the Japanese economy stalled and the *yen* fell, it took the rest of Asia's currencies and economies down with it, in the process exacerbating lingering ethnic, religious and border tensions across littoral Pacific Asia and exposing the weakness of the 'strong state' and the vacuity of the ASEAN way as a method for promoting regional harmony. Yet Japan's fiscal loss of face has notably facilitated the recuperation of China's international image. Unlike Japan, China played 'the politics of the Asian crisis brilliantly' ('Weakness is strength in policy scapegoating', 1998). In June 1998, former President Jiang Zemin significantly contrasted China's stoic refusal to devalue the *yuan* with Japan's fiscal and monetary selfishness. Such stoicism enabled China to extract political capital from the crisis both by restoring its hitherto frayed relations with the United States and by presenting itself as both hero and victim of the currency crisis: hero, because of its monetary rectitude, and victim, because Chinese exports briefly lost some of their competitive advantage against the *yen*-linked tiger economies. With the erosion of Japanese economic leadership and its increasing inability to shape the political destiny of the region, China is evidently seeking to reassert its traditional hegemony in both Northeast and Southeast Asia. China's criticism of the Indonesian government's handling of the May 1998 riots in the Chinese enclave of Glodok in Jakarta exemplified its emerging regional presence.

However, despite enhancing its international cachet, the Chinese model merely replicates, and on a massive scale, the defects of the late-developing state (Lardy 1998).[5] Its banking sector sits on a massive amount of bad or non-performing loans, its *soi-disant* private sector is effectively run either by regional state collectives or by the PLA (People's Liberation Army) and is dependent on good links with the party bureaucracy in Beijing. In other words, cronyism, nepotism and corruption were as rife in the People's Republic as they were elsewhere in Southeast Asia in the late 1990s. Moreover, only because its currency was not fully convertible and, after 1995, was devalued at a significant discount to the greenback, did China prove impervious to the meltdown.

ASIA REDIVIVA OR DEAD TIGERS BOUNCING?

What in early 1997 appeared to many regional enthusiasts as the basis for a pan-Asian regional order premised upon communitarian values modified by bureaucratically determined but market-oriented economic goals increasingly resembled, at the millennium, a ramshackle collocation of states whose commonalities were the negative ones of high debt, bureaucratic mismanagement and a systemic inability to adopt meaningful market-oriented reforms. Pacific Asia consequently seemed destined to become a zone of worrying uncertainty dependent upon the US security presence and continuing favourable access to the US domestic market. Indeed, we can perhaps generate two interesting conclusions from the events in Pacific Asia in the last decade of the twentieth century. First is the importance of the market-oriented state to the process of globalization. Significantly, it was those East Asian states with the most flexible and efficient bureaucracies, Singapore and Taiwan, that most effectively weathered the financial storm. Second, it became increasingly evident in the aftermath of the meltdown that issues of political economy were ineluctably woven into security problems in an era where increased global interconnectedness by no means assured global integration. The most salient feature of the financial crisis was the manner in which it reawakened dormant nationalisms and ethnic and religious tensions, which after 2001 eschewed a potential for transnationalization and which, as we shall show in the next chapter, rendered regional political and economic arrangements increasingly impotent.

At the time of the crisis, the meltdown evoked little enthusiasm for greater regional cooperation. Rather, it exposed the shallowness of regional integration. Between 1997 and 1998, East Asian states pursued their own national interests and a recourse to a Darwinian survival of the fittest appeared the only shared regional value. Somewhat curiously, the uncertain recovery in East Asia between 1999 and 2000, halted by another externally induced recession from 2001 to 2003, followed by renewed growth towards the end of 2003, revived the desire for closer integration premised on a revised version of the ASEAN formula. It reflected, it seemed, 'a shared perception of the need to do something collectively to counter the vulnerability to outside influence' (Ravenhill 2002, p. 175). The initial spur to this renewed enthusiasm for some version of a more functionally integrated East Asian regional way was the temporary recovery of 1999–2000. In the course of the first quarter of 1999, Japan awoke briefly from its decade-long recessive slumber, Asian economies started posting pre-crisis growth rates, trade balances swung back into surplus and the recession looked like something the formerly High Performing Asian Economies might shrug off. This uncertain recovery in Northeast Asia in the period 1999–2000 was, however, followed by a global recession, beginning with the US tech wreck, and exacerbated by the economic impact of 11 September 2001, the US-led war on terrorism and its negative impact on investment sentiment.

This notwithstanding, by the end of 2003, China, which had grown throughout the financial crisis, was booming, Japan's economy had ceased deflating and growth rates and current accounts had moved dramatically into the black from Seoul to Jakarta. Such was the apparent transformation in the economic fortunes of East Asia that James F. Hoge Jr could once more identify a 'global power shift in the making' as the Chinese and Indian economies powered a regional boom and 'the Southeast Asian "tigers" have recovered from the 1997 financial crisis and resumed their march forward' (Hoge 2004, pp. 2–3). Analogously, *Le Monde Diplomatique* recognized 'a global power shift in the making' (*Le Monde Diplomatique*, 12 November 2004).

Something curious happened, therefore, both economically and politically, between 1999 and 2003 that, despite the continuing absence of any significant regional economic integration, occasioned the belief that this was indeed taking place and mechanisms like an expanded ASEAN Plus Three had made it possible. Had the regional crisis and its causes been resolved? If it had, had the structure of the developmental state and the pattern of regional development fundamentally altered? Finally, was, as the editor of *Foreign Affairs* intimated, 'Asia's rise . . . just beginning' (yet again)? Let us first review the contesting accounts of what went wrong with the Asian model and then consider the character of the uncertain revival since 2003 and what it entails for the relative distribution of economic power in East Asia and the role of ASEAN, AFTA or an expanded ASEAN Plus Three within it.

WHAT WENT WRONG?

The crisis, which began with what Paul Krugman describes as an outbreak of 'bahtulism' in Thailand in June 1997, spawned two essentially contested explanations of what happened. On the one hand, the market-unfriendly school led by Mahathir Mohamad and abetted by an otherwise unsympathetic bunch of supporters that ranged, at different times, from Paul Krugman to Jeffrey Sachs and President Suharto, maintained that the crisis was a product of the deregulated nature of global capitalism. Having opened their capital markets to global trade in the course of the 1990s, the new boys on the international currency trading block, South Korea, Malaysia, Thailand, Indonesia and even financially streetwise Singapore and Hong Kong were the innocent victims of a brutal mugging by a gang of spivish Hedge Funds and futures traders from New York, Chicago and London. From this perspective there was little wrong with the Asian developmental state that a few lessons in central banking and sovereign bond floating would not fix.

The alternative, and, until recently, more widely accepted, hypothesis maintained that it was the structural features of the Asian economic model that had been the sufficient cause of meltdown. In this view current account deficits, a speculative property boom, short-term borrowing to fund long-term investment, poor banking and financial regulation, that ran the spectrum from inept and opaque to fraudulent and corrupt, constituted a fundamental systemic fault. In 1997, the world markets severely punished this systemic weakness. By mid-1998, the currency contagion had left the region in turmoil and with little to show for its much-vaunted developmental path, apart from a profusion of underpatronized high rise hotels, office blocks and golf courses.

Such academic disagreement had important political and economic ramifications. What caused the crisis affected how state, regional and international organizations like ASEAN or the IMF dealt with its consequences, and will continue to have an influence on how organs such as ASEAN Plus Three will seek to devise policies and institutions to address future contingencies. If Dr Mahathir's diagnosis was correct, the prescription is a bit of rest and recuperation behind a wall of currency controls until the market returns to reason (Mohamad 1999, p. 7). In this view, the cure lies not in the reform of the Asian model but in the building of a new global and regional financial architecture, the central props of which would be the Tolbin tax upon the world's richest economies combined with regional financial structures like the Chiang Mai initiative of May 2000 to establish an Asian Monetary Fund.

The IMF diagnosis, by contrast, requires a rigorous examination of the body politic, the excision of the cancer of corruption entailed in too close business–government links, and the oxygen of rule-governed transparency supplied through a machinery of public accountability, at both state and regional level. This ultimately implies a political as well as economic makeover rendering the rule of strong men and single parties accountable to the constitutional rule of law in domestic politics or binding treaty obligations in the international arena. Let us then briefly examine the apparent easing of the economic crisis in 1999–2000 and consider its ramifications for future economic and political developments around the Asia–Pacific.

SCENARIO 1: ASIA'S 'MIRACULOUS' RECOVERY

By the second quarter of 1999, currencies had stabilized and growth evanescently returned to the region. Even the region's weakest economy, Indonesia, displayed some signs of life whilst the most successful Asian bounce-back economies witnessed growth of over 5 per cent between 1999 and 2000. Regional stock markets surged ahead, and in the case of Singapore and Taiwan briefly surpassed pre-crisis levels. Business confidence in Japan rose after a decade in the economic doldrums, while South Korea's banks posted $500 million in profits in fiscal 1999 (compared with losses of $600 billion the previous year) and the economy achieved growth of 6 per cent.

From the perspective of both Mahathir and Paul Krugman, the basis of the recovery could be attributed to the reimposition of monetary stability. With the exception of the Hong Kong dollar and the Chinese *yuan*, all the regional currencies traded on the international currency market were devalued as a consequence of hedge fund speculation and capital flight. Once the speculative dust settled and illiquid conglomerates and banks rehydrated courtesy of the IMF, these economies reverted to their classic growth path. Thus, from Japan through South Korea to the Malay peninsular, imports declined and exports grew because of their increasing affordability. Malaysia, Thailand, South Korea and Indonesia, which all witnessed growing trade deficits in the period 1993–97, saw this pattern reversed in the fiscal year 1998–99. At the same time budgets were balanced and investor confidence, at least temporarily, was restored.

From this monetary perspective, alteration to East Asian economic fundamentals were unnecessary. Here the Malaysian case seemed particularly salutary. In September 1998, Mahathir sacked his market-friendly deputy, Anwar Ibrahim, and imposed both currency controls and restrictions on the movement of foreign investment funds from the Kuala Lumpur Stock Exchange (KLSE). To a chorus of international disapproval that included, inter alia, Amnesty International, Presidents Habibie and Estrada of Indonesia and the Philippines, respectively, the *Business Times* (Singapore), the *Economist* as well as US Vice-President Al Gore, Malaysia's National Economic Action Council used state-imposed currency stability to address foreign debt without recourse to the IMF. Malaysia looked East for liquidity.[6] Japanese loans through the Miyazawa Fund together with judicious raids on the state pension fund provided the capital necessary to refloat faultering UMNO-linked conglomerates.

Meanwhile, to restructure Malaysia's indebted financial sector in August 1999, the Malaysian Central Bank combined 58 banks and finance companies into six financial groups. Interestingly, this compulsory restructuring only reinforced the corporatist links between party and business, for the terms upon which banks were amalgamated depended not upon their bottom line but on their ties to politically favoured UMNO patrons.[7] Fuelled by a cheap currency and external demand for Malaysian electronics, the Malaysian economy rebounded strongly in the second quarter of 1999. Moreover, when investment restrictions in Malaysia were lifted in September, foreign investors seemed happy to remain. Malaysia's exceptionalism, then, did not see it reduced to a regional pariah. In fact, Mahathir maintained that those economies that had recourse to the IMF received the wrong treatment. For, alongside receiving a necessary infusion of liquidity, Thailand, South Korea and Indonesia had to accept strictures on interest rate and debt restructuring, making the recession and its political consequences far worse in those countries than it need have been. If little else, the Malaysian case demonstrated that, structural weakness notwithstanding, the developmental model could survive the challenges of globalization with only superficial modifications. From the Malaysian perspective, forcefully advocated by Mahathir and from 2001 supported by Japan, what Asia needed was its own monetary fund and closer integration through the mechanism of an enhanced ASEAN trading area incorporating China, South Korea and Japan.

SCENARIO 2: ASIA INC. RATIONALIZED, NOT REFORMED

Those who criticized the financial structures of the Asian developmental state argued by contrast that, although these states evinced signs of recovery from the very deep recession of 1997–98, structural problems continued to haunt the region's economies. In this view the initial panic was justified because of the undisclosed debt, cronyism, unaccountability and corruption that pervaded the Asian model from Japan to Jakarta (see Kawaui, Newfarmer and Schmukler 2001, pp. 5–10). From this viewpoint, the brief regional 'bounce back' in 1999–2000 was unsustainable and obscured the need for further financial and political reform.

Interestingly, this understanding seemed to be confirmed when the US boom of the late 1990s stalled, tech stocks plummeted and the market for the reviving Asian economies entered recession between 2001 and 2003. Friedrich Wu, chief economist with the Development Bank of Singapore, argued correctly in 1999 that 'Asian stock markets [were] running ahead of fundamentals' (*Business Times*, 9 July 1999). Short-term currency depreciations gave countries like Thailand and Indonesia a renewed, but brief, lease of life as low-cost manufacturing centres, but the neglect of thorough supply-side reforms in areas like education, training and financial regulation were notable only for their absence from these countries' reform policies. Radical economic restructuring required the destruction of the 'crony capitalist' relationships that existed between business and government. Nevertheless, despite the shock administered by the meltdown, and the strictures of the IMF, there was little sense in which local business cultures and practices were fundamentally altered.

Despite a 1999 survey by Harvard University's Center for International Development, which showed how 'Asia's spectacular growth over the past several decades' had been able to hide 'a host of inefficiencies' (Seivers and Wei, 1999), advocates of a distinctive Asian way of development prior to 1997, and the proponents of closer regional integration after 1999, continued to practise the informal deal making, preferential loans and *guanxi* networks that they maintained constituted the lubricant of future Asian growth. Thus, in Thailand, the inadequacy of bankruptcy provisions permitted technically insolvent businesses to continue trading, while the courts were unable to enforce foreclosure, and indebted companies refused to repay loans. 'Across the country companies [in 1999 were] challenging banks to convert bad debts to long-term loans. That way they [got] breathing room to rebuild without having to restructure their operations' (*Newsweek*, 12 July 1999). The net effect was that the level of bad debt and non-performing loans held by banks in Thailand actually increased between 1999 and 2001.

Thailand was by no means the only country to resist root and branch over-haul of the financial system in the first decade of the new millennium. In Indonesia, the most financially and politically challenged economy in the Asia–Pacific at the millennium, IMF loans had an uncanny knack of ending up in the accounts of banks linked to the party of former President Habibie, or subsequently, between 1999 and 2000, of former President Wahid's personal masseur ('The Bank Bali scandal', 1999). The Indonesian Bank Restructuring Agency (IBRA), established in 1998 to overhaul insolvent banks and clean up corporate loans, failed to establish its independence from business and political pressure. By 2000, the agency was evidently colluding with failed banks and businesses in administering assets valued at $60 billion (Murphy 2000). Scandals involving the failure to sell Bank Bali to Standard Chartered Bank in 1999 and the sale of the two largest Indonesian auto-makers, Astra and Indomobil, further dented investor confidence in the transparency of the restructuring process (*Asia Wall Street Journal*, 13 June 2002).

The uncertainty of the Indonesian legal process compounded foreign investor anxiety. The Jakarta Commercial Court's decision to declare Canada's Manulife Financial Corp bankrupt in June 2002 (*Asia Wall Street Journal*, 12

June 2002) and British insurer Prudential Life's local unit bankrupt in April 2004, together with the Central Jakarta District Court's decision to fine BFI finance, a company jointly owned by Chase Manhattan Bank and Royal Bank of Scotland, $23 million in the same month, reinforced the view that foreign investors could not rely upon the Indonesian judicial system to apply contract law or protect legal rights (*Jakarta Post*, 27 April 2004; *Australian Financial Review*, 10 July 2002; *Australian Financial Review*, 16 April 2004). By the end of 2003, foreign investment in Indonesia had declined to a trickle and its major foreign donors (Japan, Australia and the US) warned that widespread corruption, legal uncertainty and the failure of the successive governments of Wahid and Megawati to overhaul the country's foreign investment climate 'could spark increased poverty, political instability and violence' (*Australian Financial Review*, 13 December 2003). By 2004, Indonesia faced growing difficulty in servicing its debt repayments to the IMF (*Australian Financial Review*, 17 August 2004).

Meanwhile, in South Korea, reform-minded President Kim Dae Jung was compelled to institute an investigation into the country's five main *chaebols* for extending illegal preferential loans to their subsidiary companies. Additionally, the bureaucratic restrictions placed on western banks or companies taking over ailing South Korean banks or conglomerates raised continuing doubts about South Korea Incorporated's commitment to reform. The government's attempt to rehydrate the economy through domestic consumption by offering tax concessions to credit card holders saw a dramatic increase in household debt between 1999 and 2003 that required the launch of a 'bad bank' by 2004 to cater for the 3.9 million credit card loans that were in arrears ('Hangover cure', 2004). The fact that the government also permitted ailing conglomerates like Hyundai and Daewoo to sustain debt levels exceeding $50 billion and debt/equity ratios over 350 per cent indicates that, whatever else it is, the latest South Korean model is not driven by market considerations (*Financial Times*, 1 September 1999). By June 2002, the *Financial Times* pronounced that Hyundai and the Korean *chaebols'* 'glory days' were over, yet they continued to exercise a damaging grip on the economy (*Financial Times*, 29 June 2002).

More interestingly still, with the end of the US decade-long, hi-tech-led, boom in 2001, the more market-oriented and financially developed East Asian states of Singapore, Taiwan and the Special Administrative Region of Hong Kong entered a deeper recession between 2001and 2002 than they experienced during the Asian financial crisis itself. Further, the East Asian propensity for concealing bad news, such as the outbreak of the SARS virus that swept through the coastal province of Guang Zhou, before reaching Hong Kong and much of Southeast Asia in the course of 2002, only reinforced the impression that opacity remained a central characteristic of the Asian way in business and development.[8] In other words, the Asian model *circa* 2003 was at best rationalized rather than reformed.

HAZY PROSPECTS FOR THE REINVENTED ASIAN MODEL

Interestingly, then, whether we diagnose the causes of the Asian crisis from the perspective of Mahathir or of the IMF, we can show that, apart from some judicious financial tinkering, the basic lineaments of the Asian model, ASEAN's largely ineffectual role within it and its export-oriented character, were not substantially altered after 1998. The question remains: does this failure to reform matter?

Clearly, the Asian model had somewhat more resilience than it seemed initially in 1997. However, the export dependency of the region, while masking structural faults, has also created new problems. Historically, the pattern of Asia–Pacific trade has been unbalanced. Japan has traditionally protected its domestic markets and exported high value-added technology. During the 1980s, Japan transferred labour-intensive manufacturing offshore to Thailand, Indonesia or Malaysia. The market for this manufacturing was the United States and, to a lesser extent, Europe. Indeed the strength of the US economy prior to 2000, the openness of its market and its continuing appetite for consumption led-growth, fuelled by very low interest rates after 2002, together with the rise of China and India as important regional growth engines, were integral to East Asia's somewhat disjointed recovery after 2002. The unexpectedly high demand in the US market single-handedly revived the flagging electronic industries on which Thai, Malaysian and Indonesian growth depended between 2000 and 2001.

Yet, as a consequence of this hesitant revival, Asian currencies strengthened, along with their trade surpluses. Japan achieved a trade surplus of $118 billion by the end of March 1999. To sustain this, the Japanese Central Bank intervened in the foreign exchange markets to keep the value of the *yen* low. Other countries, like Singapore and, more recently, China, similarly intervened in the money markets. However, the Office of the US Trade Representative increasingly began to question whether 'manipulating currencies' facilitated long-term prosperity (quoted in *International Herald Tribune*, 10–11 July 1999). The US economy incurred record trade deficits with Asia during 1999–2000, and the US current account moved from a deficit of $117 billion in 1996 to one of $291 billion in 1999, and 'from a modest to a sizeable [budget] deficit' (Wolf 2004).

Fundamentally, when the US economy stalled with the bursting of the hi-tech stock bubble in the course of 2000 and went into a shallow recession after

11 September 2001, it exposed the continuing dependency of Asian export-oriented growth upon US consumption and a strong dollar. The US recession of 2001–03 had an immediate impact upon the previously reviving economies of Northeast and Southeast Asia, which plunged into recession as well.

Equally significant, as a result of the meltdown and its aftermath, Japan lost its regional economic influence. Japanese banks were the first to panic about Asian contagion in 1997 and their *sogoshoshas* have, ever since, been notably reluctant to return to Southeast Asia (see Japan Bank for International Cooperation 1999, p. 21; *Australian Financial Review*, 1 June 1999). Mahathir's infatuation with a 'Look East policy' notwithstanding, Southeast Asian economies became increasingly dependent on American, Australian and European sources for new foreign direct investment and upon demand from the China market for natural resources to sustain their patchy recovery.

Meltdown and recession have altered dramatically the international perception of Southeast Asia. Prior to the crisis, it was plausible to speak of shared developmental commonalities such as export-oriented growth dependent on Japanese foreign direct investment, technocratic planning, single-party rule and a governed labour and domestic market. Since 1997, the strategies adopted to deal with the meltdown, particularly in Southeast Asia, have created distinctive differences in the region's political economies. Hence, whilst Singapore reformed its banks and Thailand and then Indonesia invited the IMF to sort out their finances, Malaysia, in September 1998, imposed currency controls and prohibited the repatriation of foreign funds invested on the Kuala Lumpur Stock Exchange.[9] Furthermore, whilst Thailand moved tentatively to open its government as well as its domestic market, Malaysia witnessed acrimonious factionalism, and Indonesia imploded both politically and economically.

Outside the ASEAN core, the new members of the group struggle or compete amongst themselves for an evaporating pool of foreign investment. Consequently, the Philippines has continued its long post-colonial experience of political and economic malaise. Unlike other export-oriented economies in the region, the Philippines' only successful export is people, East Asia's *gastarbeiters*. In spite of this, unemployment is at record highs and the *peso* hovers at record lows. Foreign investment plunged 82 per cent in 2003, while the country's debt soared to 120 per cent of GDP. Corruption, combined with the government's inability to collect income tax, has contributed to a growing budget deficit that stands at 4.2 per cent of GDP, a level that currently exceeds that of Argentina when its debt crisis struck (see *Asia Wall Street Journal*, 30 June 2004; *Australian World Wide Special Report*, 19 July 2004; *Far Eastern Economic Review*, 30 September 2004). Elsewhere, Cambodia, Laos and Myanmar remain anchored amongst the globe's poorest countries, whilst Vietnam, ASEAN's most successful newcomer, has successfully attracted foreign direct investment and achieved export oriented growth of 7.4 per cent per annum over the last decade at the expense of more expensive low-cost manufacturing countries in the region, such as Indonesia. In other words, ASEAN both economically and politically seems to be developing in different directions. Indeed, during the later 1990s, one of the few areas which Bill Clinton and Mahathir seemed to agree upon was the irrelevance of much-vaunted open regional fora like APEC.

Despite the shock to regionalism and its much-vaunted architecture after 1997, together with evidence that Southeast Asia was responding uncertainly at best to the post-crisis environment in the new millennium, commentators as diverse as the *Economist, Foreign Affairs* and the usual scholar–bureaucratic *commentariat* once again announced a global power shift to the East. It is not difficult to identify the source of the latest burst of pan-Asian enthusiasm. It follows from the rapid and continuing growth of China since it opened up its special economic zones to foreign investment, together with the less remarked emergence of India as a centre for hi-tech computer software and program-ming and as an outsourcing destination, notably call centres, for globalizing conglomerates.

Whilst India's recent growth has been impressive, China's has been stag-gering, with its economy growing, albeit from a very low, cultural revolution-induced base, at over 8 per cent per annum for 25 years. More importantly, its unfathomable pool of cheap and compliant labour, which appears irresistible to foreign investors, has fuelled supercharged manufacturing growth since 2000. By 2003, the OECD reported that, of \$62 billion in global foreign direct investment, China accounted for \$52 billion (*Jakarta Post*, 29 June 2004). China's heavy industries, power, steel and petrochemical, evince an insatiable demand for resources, consuming 31 per cent of the world's coal, 30 per cent of its iron ore, 40 per cent of its cement and 17 per cent of its oil by 2003 (*Australian Financial Review*, 27 April 2004). Its demand for automobiles, industrial parks and apartments and its emergence as the globe's low-cost manufacturing base for everything from baseball caps and footwear to computers and televisions almost single-handedly revived growth across Northeast Asia after 2002.

Paradoxically, though, while the rise of China has been the salvation of the high-technology economies of Japan, South Korea and Taiwan, it has simulta-neously sucked investment out of the technologyless economies of Southeast Asia. As a result, Japan's apparently accidental recovery in the last quarter of 2003 remains heavily dependent upon foreign demand. Indeed, its achieve-ment of 3 per cent growth in 2003–04, after a dozen years of stagnation, was attributable to its exports to China, with which it has developed a burgeoning trade surplus. Stephen Roach of Morgan Stanley maintained that the China market accounted for more than 73 per cent of Japan's growth after 2002

(*Australian Financial Review*, 8 March and 12 December 2004). China had a similarly salutary impact on the other Northeast Asian economies, accounting for 75 per cent of South Korea's reviving growth by 2003, and was even to blame for the Taiwanese economy overheating by the second quarter of 2004 as growth exceeded 5 per cent after being negative between 2000 and 2002.

However, growth in China, while reviving Northeast Asia, has not been an undiluted blessing either domestically or for the wider regional and global economy. By the first quarter of 2004, the Chinese economy too was in danger of overheating. By some estimates, growth was heading towards 13 per cent, fixed asset investment had risen by 43 per cent and car sales 50 per cent between 2002 and 2004 (*Australian Financial Review*, 27 April 2004; *Australian*, 30 April 2004; *Weekend Australian*, 1–2 May 2004). In order to address the wave of speculative investment, bad loans and state-owned and subsidized but unproductive heavy industries and the emerging property bubble, the central government, through its control of the four major banks, introduced 'forceful measures' in April 2004 to curb inflation (running at 8 per cent per year), credit and loan-fuelled investment. In spite of this, China's banks, like their Southeast Asian counterparts before 1997, sit on non-performing loans estimated at $500 billion (*Australian Financial Review*, 10 March 2004). Even in 1998, the *Economist* considered China to possess 'the worst banking system in Asia' (*Economist*, 2 May 1998). As elsewhere in East Asia, China failed to develop a modern bond market and the government-owned banks have absorbed non-performing loans primarily generated by the inefficient state sector (Preiss 2004, p. 2). Worryingly, the failing state sector absorbs most of the available credit, yet accounts for less than 40 per cent of China's production, 'a horrible misallocation of resources' (Chang 2004). In order to sustain its 'third world financial system' the government, therefore, keeps the currency undervalued and depends on its export trade to conceal bad debt (Green and He 2004, p. 2).

Rising inflation and its burgeoning trade surplus with the US render this strategy, in the long term, unsustainable. As Jack Redman of Ernst & Young observed in March 2004, 'in every market we've ever been in, there's never been a sustained recovery until the market has opened up to foreigners to buy bad debt'. Yet as 'historical experience shows communism does not do soft landings' (quoted in *Australian Financial Review*, 30 April 2004). China, like the ersatz economies of Southeast Asia prior to 1997, has effectively replaced a short-term with a long-term fiscal problem, while the growing income disparity between the rural provinces and the booming littoral means that the officially communist state sustains one of the highest income gaps between rich and poor and between town and country in the developing world. Moreover, if the Chinese economy slows down in the course of the next decade, it will dramatically affect the accidental recovery elsewhere in East Asia.

The rise of China after 1998, and its attraction for foreign investors, has already affected growth negatively in Southeast Asia, whose low-tech manufacturing industries depend upon foreign direct investment. In zero sum terms, ASEAN's deteriorating FDI attractiveness directly reflects the rapid growth of the Chinese 'titan'. In 2003, ASEAN attracted only 16 per cent of Asian FDI, compared with China's 66 per cent. This is the exact reverse of the position in 1990 (*Australian Financial Review*, 26 April 2004). By 2004, Chinese and, to a lesser extent, Vietnamese competition had devastated the Indonesian and Filipino garment and footwear industries. Global brands like Nike and Gap increasingly source China and Vietnam for new supplies where 'wages are lower and productivity higher' (*Australian Financial Review*, 31 March 2004). Moreover, as a new World Trade Organization negotiated multi-fibre agreement comes into force in 2005, China could move from a 17 per cent to a 45 per cent share of the global garment wear industry within five years. It already dominates the global footwear industry.

As the IMF explained, somewhat euphemistically, 'countries whose factor endowments are similar to China's and which . . . compete with it in world markets will need to undertake sizable adjustments and display flexibility in product and labour markets' (International Monetary Fund 2003, p. 63). Yet flexibility has not been a feature of the ASEAN way in economics. Facing a profound shift in regional economic dynamics, the Southeast Asian economies seem either individually or collectively impotent. In democratizing Indonesia an opaque judiciary and corrupt semi-autonomous regions, whose authority has grown with reform since 1999, actively deter investment, whilst an inept Jakarta administration struggles to repay its international debt. Similarly, recent elections in the Philippines have done nothing to inspire business confidence and the Arroyo government struggles to reform its inutile constitution while staving off fiscal crisis. Elsewhere, although economic growth has returned to Malaysia and Thailand, both they and the Singaporean economy remain exposed to consumer and investor confidence in the US.

Nor has the creation of an ASEAN Free Trade Area, which officially came into existence in 2002, done much to boost regional economic integration. Although the six long-standing members (Thailand, Brunei, the Philippines, Singapore, Malaysia and Indonesia) agreed to reduce tariffs on one another's goods to a maximum 5 per cent, non-tariff barriers and excise duties remain in place. More particularly, where manufacturing industries might benefit from economies of scale and an integrated internal market, ASEAN governments remain stubbornly protectionist. Thus Malaysia insists on protecting the state-owned car maker, Proton, oblivious to the fact that patriotic Malays increasingly prefer to pay an extra 110 000 *ringgit* for a Toyota or a Honda that actually starts (see *Financial Times*, 2 January 2004; *Economist*, 8 May and 31 July 2004; Madani 2001). The Philippines protects its ailing petro-chemical industry, whilst rice, the region's staple, is excluded from the pact altogether. Rather worryingly, from a market opening perspective, the Indonesian, Philippine and Malaysian economies possess 'very small, mostly negative cross industry scale effects'. Ironically, perhaps, any integration advantages that exist between the Singaporean, Malaysian, Indonesian and Philippine economies actually predate the formation of ASEAN (ibid., p. 3). The fact that ASEAN as a putative economic community has had minimal impact on regional integration receives further confirmation from the ASEAN secretariat's home page devoted to trade. It observes that 'while trade with traditional industrial markets remained robust, [the] share of intra-ASEAN trade remained low with intra ASEAN exports constituting 22.75 per cent in 2001. The share was 21.4 per cent in 1993 when AFTA was formed' (ASEAN Secretariat 2005, p. 2).

All of this indicates that the extent to which the ASEAN economies have grown since 2002 has been as a result of the Association's diminishing role as a low-cost base for manufacturing goods assembled in Southeast Asia for export to the US and Europe. Although trade with the booming China market rose by 18 per cent in 2002 this reflected China's insatiable demand for the region's raw materials. ASEAN, unlike Northeast Asia, has had little success in exporting higher value-added products to China. Despite the post-financial crisis enthusiasm for deeper regional integration elaborated in the Japanese call for an ASEAN Plus Three summit in 2004, and the Declaration of ASEAN Concord in 2003 that envisaged the realization of economic integration by 2020, there is little to sustain its vision of a 'stable, prosperous and highly competitive ASEAN region in which there is a free flow of goods, services [and] investment' (ASEAN Secretariat 2004). Indeed, in those areas where a relatively free flow of goods occurs, it appears that lower-cost bases for manufacturing, such as Vietnam, take investment from more expensive regional 'partners' like the Philippines and Indonesia.

Given the mounting evidence that regional economic cooperation within both AFTA and ASEAN Plus Three is more theoretical than real, it is not surprising to find that the region's more pragmatic economies conclude bilateral free trade agreements instead. As John Ravenhill observed, the conclusion of the Japan–Singapore Economic Partnership Agreement in January 2003 constituted a 'dramatic . . . turn in East Asia to preferential trade'(Ravenhill 2002, p. 181). The conclusion of bilateral trade deals between Singapore and New Zealand and Singapore and Australia as well as between Thailand and Australia followed. Bilateralism has altered both the direction and the pattern of trade in the region and illustrates that ASEAN's most developed countries, Thailand and Singapore, are concentrating on their own markets and 'depriving ASEAN of its best integrators in the process' (*Economist*, 31 July 2004). Meanwhile, the aspiration of ASEAN to negotiate a free trade arrangement with China and putatively with Australia remains, as with all things ASEAN, essentially an aspiration. First mooted in 2000 as a building bloc to regional 'self-reliance and stability', the free trade agreement stalled as the more marketized states in the region increasingly act autonomously of AFTA and explore preferential trade deals both within and beyond the region (see ASEAN–China Expert Group 2001, p. 91).

THE STATE THEY'RE IN

By 2003, there appeared premonitory signs of East Asian economic rejuvenation with only cosmetic changes to the developmental model. With a number of its core components punctured by the crisis of 1997, however, the direction in which the Asian model moves can no longer be as smoothly interdependent or as export-oriented as it was in the growth era. Southeast Asia, in particular, is less dependent on Northeast Asian investment and increasingly reliant upon western foreign direct investment. Here, moreover, it has come into conflict with the rise of China and its far greater attraction to investors and fund managers. The rise of China and to a lesser extent India, together with the dominance of Japan in high-technology and its aversion for technology transfer leaves ASEAN between an investment-friendly rock and a technology-free hard place.

The recourse to different strategies by ASEAN members in the face of the post-financial crisis economic realities presages not greater integration in Southeast Asia but growing economic and political fragmentation. This was manifest at the ASEAN foreign ministers meeting in Jakarta in June 2004. Thus, whilst Indonesia sought to engender some greater regional coherence, the meeting manifested concern about the proposal for an East Asian summit that would give enhanced credibility to an enlarged East Asian community composed of ASEAN plus the Northeast Asian 'Three': China, Japan and South Korea. By contrast, both Singapore and Malaysia view China's market as a source of regional regeneration and cautiously welcome the prospect of deeper regional integration. Other members of the grouping, meanwhile, notably Indonesia, but also Vietnam and the Philippines, evince concern at China's potential for exerting regional economic and, eventually, political, hegemony. Somewhat differently and ambivalently, Japan, which formally proposed an East Asian summit in December 2003, welcomes the export opportunities offered by the China market while at the same time anxiously observing the thrall that China increasingly exercises over Southeast Asia.

In terms of its political economy, therefore, ASEAN has operated only perfunctorily as an economic grouping. Paradoxically, whilst economic deals within and outside the region occur on a bilateral basis that undermines the notion of an integrated economic community, state interested *realpolitik* in Asia plays through the multilateral facades of arrangements like APEC, AFTA and ASEAN Plus Three. Ironically, the failure to develop rule-governed procedures during the good times has left Asia–Pacific regional economic arrangements weak, unstable and increasingly vulnerable to the machinations of the global marketplace.

In this globalized context, any attempt to broaden economic regional integration through mechanisms such as ASEAN Plus Three has to take into account that economic growth in Asia has become more dependent on US consumption since the financial crisis. In fact East Asian high savings and budget surpluses post-1998, together with central bank interventions in the foreign exchange markets, support both the US current account deficit and the greenback. In the final analysis, governments across the Pacific littoral and particularly in China seek to bring the Asian labour pool into efficient employment by encouraging both inward direct investment and exports. For growth, East Asia requires accommodating markets and willing inward investors. The US is the most accommodating market and the most willing inward investor. In a Faustian bargain, that ultimately belies any attempt to exclude the US from regional economic arrangements, the Asian economies necessarily finance the US twin deficits as a form of collateral against the direct investments they receive from multinational conglomerates. The US is Asia's consumer of first and last resort (see Dooley, Folkerts-Landau and Garber 2004). Consequently, the notion of shared Asian developmental commonalities has attenuated along with the myth of any shared cooperative approaches to economic development. The ASEAN multilateral approach to regional security and economic development premised upon internal resilience looks, as a result, increasingly forlorn.

From this brief tour of the Asian meltdown and its aftermath it is plausible to conclude that the once unfashionable territorial state is far from irrelevant in an era of globalization. However, the state that adapted most effectively to the opportunities afforded by the revolutionary internationalization of financial markets was not the strong, bureaucratically driven Asian developmental version in either its Northeast or Southeast Asian manifestations. As Philip Cerny observed, 'globalization as a political phenomenon basically means that the shaping of the playing field of politics itself is increasingly determined not within insulated units . . . globalization is a process of political structuration' (Cerny 1997, p. 253). By the early 1990s, the most effective competition states were those that enforced decisions which emerged from the world markets. From a comparative perspective, the long-term development programmes and strategic capitalism practised by the developmental states of Pacific Asia became dysfunctional in an emerging global financial market. Ironically, the close links between banks, business and governing elites which had facilitated the detailed planning necessary to sustain double-digit growth prior to 1996 became unsustainable in the integrated financial order that developed in the course of the 1990s.

In other words, prior to the era of currency convertibility and internationally traded derivatives, Asian plan rational states, with varying degrees of success, had assembled developmental coalitions of bureaucratically guided conglomerates and labour unions in collectively mobilized enterprise associations based on the model of Japan Incorporated. As global financial markets became increasingly integrated and hedge funds explored the possibilities of derivative and option trades, it emerged that the most successful state arrangements were those with flexible and open capital and labour markets that had most effectively marketized their bureaucracies (ibid., p. 266). In Pacific Asia, the only states to demonstrate the flexibility necessary to adapt to the new requirements of the changed international economic order are small, pragmatic, technocracies like Taiwan and Singapore.

The growing utility of flexible competition states and city regions based on the urban dynamism of, inter alia, Bangkok, Hong Kong, Seoul, Singapore, Shanghai, Sydney or Tokyo, to the internetted financial order further undermines the economic pertinence of bureaucratically overloaded, supranational regions. Clearly, regional arrangements are not halfway houses on the way to a new international order. Rather, they constitute obstructions to the free flow of capital and ideas and hinder the efficient performance and market transparency of the more marketized city regions. In Pacific Asia, a characteristic sclerosis over economic issues renders AFTA and APEC increasingly irrelevant to the political and economic forces that are recasting Pacific Asia.[10]

An additional casualty of the meltdown is the blind faith in the necessity of a democratic or democratizing end of history. In this context, it is significant that social science paradigms have consistently ignored the continuing appeal of traditional high cultural understandings adapted to the nation-building and modernizing needs of developmental coalitions in emerging markets during the decades of very rapid growth (see Gellner 1994). During the 1980s, state ideologists from Seoul to Jakarta devoted considerable resources not only to what Singapore's Economic Development Board termed planning 'the next lap of development', but also to engineering traditional, non-liberal values suitable to sustaining a technocratically driven modernity. The studied indifference of western economists and social scientists to the political ramifications of reinvented tradition facilitated a simplistic and economically determinist belief in the inexorable emergence of an interdependent, global democratic order.

The continuing neglect of the impact of recently reinvented Asian values upon the even more recent loss of national face reflects the analytic determination to present states and their members as rational economic calculators rather than products of distinctive and historically contingent political cultures. Significantly, the extent to which the limping tiger economies accepted the liberalizing conditions attached to IMF packages by no means implied the acceptance by state technocrats of an inexorable causal link between the market, liberal values and the polymorphous joys of civil society or the third way (Fukuyama 1992). In reality, the principal driver of change has been necessity. The exposure of Pacific Asian domestic markets to competition and their financial systems to western rules of disclosure has been imposed by the external discipline of the market. This economic *force majeure*, reluctantly endorsed by national elites, leaves a residue of resentment.

At the same time, while states like the Philippines, Thailand and Taiwan have democratized either in the course of the 1990s or, as in the Indonesian case, as a direct consequence of the financial crisis, the process has by no means facilitated the emergence of marketized competition states. Rather, it has exacerbated levels of government–business defalcation. More worryingly, those states that did not possess the capacity to liberalize sufficiently rapidly have found significant urban populations taking succour in some form of democratically endorsed, but market-unfriendly fundamentalism. In Indonesia, and a lesser extent Malaysia, the recently created, and politically insecure, middle classes find growing solace in the demands of a new generation of reformers who consider a revitalized Islamic moral programme central to the *reformasi* of failed developmental coalitions. As Benjamin Barber observed, the global order is disturbingly Janus-faced and offers the prospect of the vacuous blandishments of McWorld together with the anxious recourse to the primordialist certainties of Jihad (Barber 1996). Unfortunately, this emerging dialectic in Southeast Asia offers little immediate prospect of a happy synthetic resolution.

NOTES

1. The former Deputy Governor of the Reserve Bank of Australia, Stephen Grenville, American economist Jeffrey Sachs and, in somewhat more abrasive terms, Malaysian Prime Minister, Dr Mahathir Mohamad, made this point, as also did Paul Krugman in a somewhat backhanded compliment to Mahathir (see, inter alia, Grenville 1998; Krugman 1999, pp. 142–5). Yet, although hedge funds were roundly condemned for exploiting the currency crisis, it would seem that the more Asia exposed funds like the Tiger Fund and George Soros' Magnum fund all suffered substantial losses as a consequence of exposure to the *baht*, *ringgit*, *rupiah* and, most notably in October 1998, the *yen* (see *Financial Times*, 11 October 1998.

2. The *Asian Wall Street Journal* (20 July 1998) estimated that Japanese banks held $500 billion in bad loans and another $625 billion in doubtful loans.

3. A number of Japanese banks, notably the Long Term Credit Bank and the Nippon Credit Bank, both went into government receivership in 1998.

4. *Golkar* is a contraction of *Golongan Karya*, which in English is translated as Functional Group.
5. Lardy notes that 'loans due to crony conglomerates may be similar to those in Indonesia', p. 80.
6. Malaysia borrowed $5 billion from the Miyazawa Fund and $1 billion from the Exim Bank; Japan also sponsored the successful launch of a Malaysian government bond in May 1999.
7. Thus Hong Leong, a well-regulated financial group, but part of a conglomerate linked to Anwar, found itself threatened with a merger in a financial institution dominated by Bank Bumiputra, an indebted bank patronized by Daim Zainuddin.
8. The Thai and Chinese governments' reluctance to reveal an outbreak of Asian bird flu in November 2003 had implications not only for Thai agri-conglomerates like Charoen Pophkand, but also for their European business partners, like Tesco supermarkets in the UK. In January 2004, the European Union condemned the Thai government for its 'non-transparency' (*Age,* Melbourne, 28 January 2004).
9. The move froze approximately $10 billion in foreign emerging market funds in Malaysia and left $2 billion of shares in limbo on the Singapore CLOB (Central Limit Order Book). It also led to Malaysia being removed from the Morgan Stanley Capital International Index and the International Finance Corporation Index.
10. This was most recently exemplified at the Kuala Lumpur meeting of APEC which, as the *Financial Times* observed, functioned as 'a showcase for . . . divisions' amongst the member states (*Financial Times*, 19 November 1998).

5. A delusion transformed: ASEAN and East Asian regionalism

In the late 1980s, Barry Buzan maintained that Southeast Asia constituted a 'security complex'. By this he understood that the region appeared both divided and balanced between the communist states of Indochina and the non-communist states represented by ASEAN. According to Buzan this bipolar structure looked 'stable' and was 'likely to define the internal dynamics of the Southeast Asian security complex for the foreseeable future' (Buzan 1988, pp. 1–16). Writing in 1997, Khong Yuen Foong somewhat captiously observed that the 'shelf life' of Buzan's theory 'was approximately a year' (Khong 1997, p. 318). Buzan's 'affection for realism', Khong contended, had led him to privilege 'enmity over amity'. Buzan's penchant for realism, it seemed, had caused him to misapprehend the 'process that turned out to be more enduring and relevant for the 1990s and beyond', namely, the 'transformation of intra-ASEAN security relations from enmity, fear, and rivalry to amity, trust, and cooperation' (ibid.).

Unfortunately for Khong the shelf life of his own fashionably multilateral-ist view of the ASEAN way was even shorter than Buzan's. For 1997, the year when Khong's observations appeared, also witnessed an unprecedented Asian financial crisis that devastated the tiger economies of Southeast Asia. In the process, ASEAN leaders engaged in unseemly public displays of mutual suspicion, rivalry and denunciations of their putative partners. The Association itself, meanwhile, stood impotent in the face of both financial meltdown and the growing internal discord that accompanied it.

Khong, of course, was no more guilty of misreading Southeast Asia's prospects than any number of scholars who had, since 1990, commended ASEAN as a 'weighty and influential player in the international system' (Dorsch and Mols 1998, p. 168). More intriguingly, however, Khong's uncritical endorsement of the ASEAN way in international relations led him to speculate further whether ASEAN's seemingly consensus-driven approach 'might have relevance for other non-ASEAN states in Southeast Asia' (Khong 1997, p. 320). Other commentators equally impressed with ASEAN's unique diplomatic style and convinced that the 'economic rise of Southeast Asia' along with the rest of the Pacific littoral had 'proven itself a sound developmental model' (Nesadurai 1996, p. 51) had already begun to consider that ASEAN might fashion a wider East Asian order. Thus, for Bobrow, Chan and Reich, the 'activism of the ASEAN members' had already been 'amply demonstrated in their domestic, regional, and international initiatives'; this entailed a growing, 'unwillingness to leave it to others to construct the Asian or international order for them' (Bobrow, Chan and Reich, 1996, p. 27). Even more outspokenly, Helen Nesadurai declared that the years of spectacular economic growth had 'given the East Asian states a degree of confidence' that had 'led a number of their leaders to question the validity and suitability of US norms in the economic as well as the social and political spheres' (Nesadurai 1996, p. 51).

Certainly, the official articulation of claims for the broader relevance of the ASEAN way began almost as soon as the Cold War ended. The ASEAN Regional Forum (ARF), for example, sought explicitly to export the virtues of ASEAN's non-confrontational diplomacy into the general Pacific arena, in particular by providing a cooperative link between Northeast and Southeast Asia (Simon 1998, pp. 204–9). The prevailing scholar–bureaucratic assumption was that ASEAN itself would be comfortably nested at the centre of a web of transnational institutions like APEC and AFTA, benignly spreading its harmonious, inclusive and economically effective practices across the region. ASEAN, it was held, would be the cornerstone of a new Asia–Pacific-wide regional management process in which the Association would function as the core of a network of multilateral institutions that would facilitate the regional cooperation and help build a new global community and sense of regional identity (see Almonte 1997, p. 80, 90; Abdullah 1992; Acharya 1993; Pupphavesa and Crewe 1994; Parreñas 1998; Kahler 1990; Harris 1994; Garnaut 1994; Thambipillai 1998).

However, ASEANs institutional ineffectiveness in the face of the 1997 economic crisis seemed to destroy the argument for its wider East Asian application, based as it was on the alleged success of the Association's distinctive practices. Yet this was not the case. For, strangely, in the post-crisis era, the evidence of political and economic failure that ostensibly negated assertions of both ASEAN's regional and wider Asian relevance was now either overlooked or used to sustain (rather than critique) the notion that ASEAN remained a force for fashioning an integrated East Asian region. Singapore Prime Minister Goh Chok Tong intimated as much in 1998, when he stated that the 'regional crisis does not spell the end of Asia's progress ... the reforms now being adopted in most countries will lay the foundations for a stronger and leaner Asia' (Goh 1998).

Predictably, this perspective was quickly adopted by academic commentators. It became the new orthodoxy amongst Aseanologists to assert that 'the dynamics of the crisis ... rather than debilitating ASEAN and APEC, may well remake them as effective regional organisations' (Ferguson 1999, pp.

4–5). How, we might wonder, was it possible to proceed from the claim that ASEAN before 1997 represented a successful model of economic and political development that would inexorably expand its institutional framework into the broader East Asian region, to the view that ASEAN's economic and political failure after 1997 equally validated the projection of its managerial way into the wider region? It is to inquire into the sources of this incoherence that is the principal aim of this chapter. The purpose is not only to demonstrate that positions advanced between pre- and post-crisis eras were inconsistent but also to show how and why it is that Aseanology's latest methodological fashion enables its analysts to move from proposition to contradiction without reflection. The lack of critical introspection and academic scepticism in this field, we shall show, indicates that regional delusion does not die easily, even in the face of empirical refutation.

EXPORTING RESPONSIBILITY: EXPLAINING THE CAUSES OF THE 1997 ECONOMIC CRISIS

In tracing the origins of the incoherence in regionalist thinking the natural place to begin is with an assessment of the political and scholarly reaction to the 1997 economic crisis. Evidently, for ASEAN enthusiasts, this unforeseen event represented the crucial discontinuity in recent Asia–Pacific international relations. Moving from the boundless optimism of the Pacific Century to fiscal basket case over the space of a few months obviously provided a great shock both to the system and to regional pride. The crisis undermined previous certainties, and left both regional politicians and academics desperately searching for explanations.

Moreover, the fact that the economic crisis had spread from Southeast Asia to ravage parts of Northeast Asia, most notably South Korea, induced feelings of collective humiliation across the Asia–Pacific. It was not simply that the once high-performing Asian economies like Thailand, Indonesia and South Korea required the assistance of the International Monetary Fund (IMF) and surrendered to externally imposed fiscal constraints in return for a financial rescue package. It was further compounded by the fact that western countries on the Asian periphery like Australia and New Zealand, along with the United States, escaped the effects of the financial contagion altogether. It was from the perception that East Asia had lost face by submitting the region to the tender mercies of essentially 'western' institutions like the IMF and World Bank that occasioned the felt need for a revived sense of regional solidarity. An evident willingness of some East Asian leaders and regional commentators to export responsibility for the crisis first announced this disposition (Lewis 1999, para. 1).

In particular, the IMF was accused of aggravating the crisis through its 'too sudden and too harsh' demands for economic re-structuring and financial reform (ibid.). It stood accused of lacking sensitivity to local feelings. In Indonesia, the Southeast Asian basket case par excellence, 'western financial institutions' were guilty of ethnocentrically misunderstanding Indonesian culture. Apparently, it was culturally insensitive to expect Indonesian leaders to acknowledge their economic mistakes and to be seen to be subject to pressure from foreign institutions (Katzenstein 1999, p. 19). In Peter Katzenstein's view: 'The IMF's approach helped push General Suharto to tap into a deep strain of Javanese nationalism. The result were [*sic*] deadly anti-Chinese pogroms and the downfall of the regime' (ibid.).

While academic and media critics in both western and East Asian universities, Non-Governmental Organizations (NGO) and think tanks blamed the IMF for its insensitivity toward ASEAN styles of governance, the origin of the crisis itself was more generally ascribed to US-dominated global financial institutions that recklessly shifted hot money in and out of Asian growth funds (Harding 1998). Former Malaysian Prime Minister Mahathir Mohamad, a politician not averse to conspiracy theory, considered it expedient to find one at work in the crisis. He soon discovered that a cabal of primarily Jewish hedge fund managers and shady futures traders in New York, Chicago and London had manipulated Asian currency markets in order to profit from their wild fluctuations (Mohamad 1999, p. 7).

A bowdlerized version of this thesis found its way into the commentary of some regional academics who also deduced the hidden hand of the United States manipulating the crisis. Thus R. James Ferguson contended that the US had first facilitated 'an unregulated release of financial capitalism', subsequently followed by a cynical manipulation of the IMF that sought 'both . . . to limit the scale of the baling out and demanding a strongly interventionist role in return for aid' and ultimately compounded the disaster by its unwillingness 'to provide a strong leadership role for Asia–Pacific recovery' (Ferguson 1999, p. 19).

The attempt to blame the crisis on actors outside the region (see Gilpin 2003) inevitably perceived a western/Jewish conspiracy overtly or covertly corroding Asian economic growth and reputation. To sustain this assumption, both regional politicians and analysts alike veiled their accusations in vague and unverifiable terms. A *pot pourri* of unsubstantiated allegations about insouciant western institutions, coupled with a general angst about the pace and shape of global capitalism, adumbrated by the apparent insensitivity of both the IMF and the US government to Asian sensibilities, served the interests of regional governments. Shifting responsibility westward thus enabled the largely unaccountable East Asian political class to evade blame for their own culpability in causing the meltdown.

Likewise, western scholars and Asian scholar–bureaucrats also had a vested interest in reinforcing this developing climate of blame in order to conceal their own analytic failure to foresee the crisis. Nor was all this intellectual effort to export the burden of responsibility for the meltdown entirely free of hypocrisy. After all, the governments of Southeast Asia were hardly in a position to complain about the financial medicine prescribed by the global market that they were required to swallow after 1997. Before the crisis, ASEAN politicians and scholar–bureaucrats from Lee Kuan Yew to Kishore Mahbubani and Noordin Sopiee had triumphantly announced and enthusiastically promoted the virtue of a non-liberal Asian way of managing political and economic development.

Ironically, it was this widely advertised and atypically Asian synergy between government and business that facilitated the very cronyism and lack of accountability that initially precipitated regional financial crisis. At the same time, the ASEAN states had actively utilized the open and increasingly globalized, financial and trading arrangements that emerged at the end of the Cold War to attract the foreign direct investment that drove double-digit economic growth in the miracle years prior to 1997. Only a delusional complex built on a mixture of hubris and narcissism could assume that international financial institutions and mutual funds would agree that the remedy to the region's ills lay in the re-application of tried, and failed, Asian economic values.

The growing belief that the outside world had neglected Asia in its hour of need fed a burgeoning sense of resentment (see Higgott 1998). The image of a monolithic 'west' gloating over the plight of the once formidable but now ailing Asian tiger economies was never an accurate picture, but it provided a suitable balm for the hurt pride of politicians and regional commentators. It was this mood of damaged *amour propre* that spurred support for the idea of East Asian regionalism. Regionalism offered the seductive prospect of Asian solutions for Asian problems that would engender a sense of growing independence and inure regional economies against further externally induced shocks. The project further assumed the rejection of any further reliance on an unfeeling west and its equally insensitive institutions. As deputy Prime Minster of Thailand, Supachai Panitchpakdi explained in 2000: 'We cannot rely on the World Bank, Asian Development Bank, or International Monetary Fund . . . we must rely [instead] on regional cooperation' (quoted in *Nation*, Bangkok, 10 June 2000).

The years following the crisis therefore witnessed an upsurge in the rhetoric of pan-Asian renewal. Jusuf Wanandi, therefore, declared that ASEAN lacked 'the critical mass and influence needed to face the new and formidable challenges of globalization'. There was instead a 'need to revitalize multilateral institutions in the region' because only by 'the strengthening of this cooperation can the East Asian region have some influence globally' (Wanandi 1999a). In a similar vein, Singapore Ambassador-at-Large Tommy Koh argued that the economic crisis had 'stimulated a new sense of East Asian regionalism and brought the countries closer together' (quoted in *Financial Times*, 13 May 2001). It was the felt need to stimulate belief in a shared destiny and thereby engender greater East Asian resilience that spurred ASEAN to action. At the 6th ASEAN summit in Hanoi, in December 1998, its members announced:

> We shall move ASEAN onto a higher plane of regional cooperation in order to strengthen ASEAN's effectiveness in dealing with the challenges of growing inter-dependence within ASEAN and of its integration into the global economy. In doing so, we commit ourselves to intensifying our dialogue on current and emerging issues, further consolidating our unity in diversity, our cohesiveness and harmony. (Hanoi Declaration 1998, point 5)

In the months following the outbreak of the economic crisis ASEAN promoted a dialogue partnership with Northeast Asia through the new mechanism of an East Asian Summit (EAS). The first summit was held in December 1997 in Kuala Lumpur, where the leaders of ASEAN participated in discussions with their peers from China, Japan and South Korea. Subsequently, at ASEAN's Hanoi Summit, it was agreed to formalize these meetings into the arrangement now known as 'ASEAN Plus Three'.

This push for East Asian consolidation reinforced the perceived need for closer economic cooperation, which took the form of suggestions for trade liberalization, tariff reductions and the strengthening of AFTA (see Soesastro 2001, pp. 6–11). Perhaps the most novel idea was the Japanese proposal for an Asian Monetary Fund tailored to regional needs and more sensitive to regional vanity than the IMF (Johnstone 1999, p. 125). Carried away with this latest exercise in Asia bonding, some members even envisaged an Asian free trade area and monetary union (Soesastro 2001, pp. 7–9), while Jusuf Wanandi, impressed with the regional integration achieved by the European Union, raised the prospect that one day East Asia might also develop into 'a community' on similar lines (Wanandi 1999b).

Japanese Prime Minister Junichiro Koizumi gave official credence to this sentiment in a lecture in Singapore in January 2002. He maintained that East Asia should evolve into a 'community' that 'acts together and advances together'. Such an integrated East Asian 'whole [could] be greater than the sum of its parts', and he added that, while 'our pasts may be varied and divergent ... our futures can be united and supportive of each other' (quoted in Low 2002). Significantly, Koizumi's speech seemed to accept and welcome the idea that Southeast Asia's political destiny was intimately linked with that of Northeast Asia, and the Japanese Prime Minister further suggested that

ASEAN Plus Three should provide the institutional framework for forging a common East Asian destiny (ibid.).

South Korean President Kim Dae-jung kept up the post-crisis momentum for East Asian integration. At the Hanoi summit, he proposed the establishment of an 'East Asia Vision Group' that would report on ideas to deepen long-term cooperation among members of the ASEAN Plus Three grouping (East Asia Vision Group 2001). The promotion of East Asian cooperation thus became the principal justification for subsequent ASEAN Plus Three summits (Soesastro 2001, pp. 1–2).

Clearly, ASEAN Plus Three constitutes the most significant regional political reaction to have emerged from the aftermath of the crisis years. As Soesastro noted, ASEAN Plus Three had become the 'embryo of an East Asian regional organization' (ibid., p. 1), a view Japan's Koizumi subsequently reinforced. As its name intimated, moreover, the new arrangement represented the most promising mechanism to regenerate a moribund ASEAN. Moves towards a more developed sense of East Asian regionalism held out the prospect of a new, but nevertheless still seminal, role for the Association. As one of its enthusiasts, former Indonesian foreign minister Ali Alatas averred, ASEAN Plus Three, like the original rationale envisioned for the ARF, 'should, at least during the initial phase, continue to be ASEAN driven' (Alatas 2001, p. 4).

Perhaps the most distinctive feature of ASEAN Plus Three, however, was that it reflected an exclusive understanding of regionalism. Unlike inclusive trans-Pacific groupings like APEC or AFTA, ASEAN Plus Three was notably 'Asian' in composition, effectively drawing the boundaries of 'East Asia' in a way that ruled out those countries on the periphery. These countries were, implicitly, deemed 'external' to the region. Those most obviously ascribed outsider status were 'caucasian' states: the United States, Australia and New Zealand. In this respect, the arrangement bore more than a passing resemblance to the East Asian Economic Caucus (EAEC),[1] a grouping comprising the ASEAN states along with a number of Northeast Asian states such as Japan, Taiwan and Hong Kong, originally promulgated by Prime Minister Mahathir in the early 1990s to act as a counter-weight to US influence in APEC. EAEC never got off the ground, but it nevertheless expressed a widespread regional sentiment that wished to reject US hegemony in the Pacific together with the wider civilizational value-system it seemed to uphold and promote.

Later proponents of ASEAN Plus Three, of course, denied that the framework had any correspondence with Mahathir's earlier exclusionist regional vision (Wanandi 2000). Even so, in the sense that ASEAN Plus Three was born out of resentment arising from the perceived mistreatment of Asian sensibilities at the hands of western countries and their financial institutions, there is an obvious genealogy from EAEC to ASEAN Plus Three. In fact, Ali Alatas early acknowledged the lineage claiming that 'there has always been a strong political will to enhance mutually beneficial cooperation in East Asia. On the ASEAN side, a significant manifestation of this political will has been the early advocacy of Malaysia's Prime Minister, Dr Mahathir, for the establishment of an East Asian Economic Caucus' (Alatas 2001, p. 2). EAEC constituted the stillborn precursor for East Asian collaboration. Its subsequent mutation into ASEAN Plus Three represented for both regional officials and analysts alike the primary framework for both reinvigorating and, indeed, constructing the East Asian region. For Alatas, the 'ASEAN + 3 forum is an idea whose time has come' (ibid., p. 1).

CONSTRUCTING EAST ASIA

East Asia's entrenched scholar–bureaucracy welcomed the expanded regionalist thinking that came to dominate the diplomatic conversation among East Asia's capitals. They were, moreover, fortuitously supported by an apparently new and exciting methodology that both explained and endorsed the new momentum in East Asian affairs. Social constructivism, the current vogue in international relations methodology, maintains that discursive activity constructs our understanding of reality. In its application to international relations, constructivism emphasizes the centrality of ideational factors in the formation of state interests. Such an ontological premise was not in itself particularly original. In fact, philosophy post-Bishop Berkeley and the later Wittgenstein, psychoanalysis after Freud, and sociological inquiry since Herbert Mead, had all attempted, at various times, to analyse or deconstruct the factors that compose identities and create the context for languages of self-understanding and self-disclosure. Even within the somewhat theoretically light domain of international relations what amounted to a constructivist approach *avant la lettre* had been evident in the writings of Raymond Aron (Aron 1966, pp. 177–366) and in certain works by strategic theorists from the 1960s if not some years before (see Liddell Hart 1935; Mead 1951; Bauer 1952, 1954; Haimson 1953; Tomasic 1953; Weigley 1973; Fairbank 1974; Snyder 1977; Gray 1981).[2] In a late developing and nescient international relations theory, however, it arrived on the scholarly scene via the influential studies published by Alexander Wendt in the early 1990s (Wendt 1992a, pp. 391–425, 1992b, pp. 384–6, and 1999).[3]

According to Wendt, constructivism investigated 'how knowledgeable practices constitute subjects' (Wendt 1992a, p. 394). It sought to demonstrate, further, that it was the process of inter-activity with other agents in a social system that determined the understanding of the structure of that system. In his densely argued *Social Theory of International Politics* (1999), Wendt evinced that anarchy in the international system was a consequence of social processes and, therefore, not given by fixed, material conditions. From this premise, it necessarily follows that the place of norms in international relations – how they help construct the social identities of agents in the international system, and how this subsequently defines perceptions of the state and its interests – preoccupies constructivism's research programme.

The appeal of constructivism for many contemporary social scientists whether of a liberal–institutionalist or post-Marxist provenance, resides in its implicit transformative possibilities because the central tenet of constructivism holds that the continuing process of socialization can re-make identities and interests (see Legro 2000, p. 419–32). As Wendt explains, in his own inimitable way: 'the process by which egoists learn to cooperate is at the same time a process of reconstructing their interests in terms of shared commitments to social norms. Over time, this will tend to transform a positive interdependence of *outcomes* into a positive interdependence of *utilities* or collective interest organized around the norms question'. Thus the 'process of cooperating' will assist in 'reconstituting identities and interests in terms of new intersubjective understandings and commitments' (Wendt 1992a, p. 417).

What Wendt means is that, through the process of interactive communication and exchange, actors in the international system can free themselves from the debilitating effects of self-interested, competitive state relations. A felt need for interdependence and a common destiny (or fate) can over time transcend egotistical state identities and forge a group identity that will, in turn, fashion new norms that establish an alternative pattern of interests that has the potential to displace older, more restrictive identities. Central to the constructivist project, therefore, is the understanding that, once formed, norms assume their own dynamic, even if the actors that first gave them voice intended otherwise. Ultimately, norms re-define interests in a way that may eventually subsume individual state identities within wider collectives. Unsurprisingly, the geo-political discourse of medium powers and NGOs that seek to mould and shape distinctive regions from nations and states yields easily to the blandishments of constructivism.

All the above notwithstanding, a major criticism of Wendt's thesis focused upon the lack of hard data to support his theory (Copeland 2000, p. 209). For that reason it was both fortuitous and timely that the evolving debate over East Asian regionalism occurred at a time when constructivism's converts in Ivy League schools and regional institutes, armed with large grants and postgraduate scholarships, sought empirical validation for their treasured hypothesis. The later 1990s onward saw a proliferation of constructivist studies that examined the developmental norms shaping the Asia–Pacific region (see Acharya 2000, 2001; Busse 1999, pp. 39–60; Haacke 2003, pp. 57–87; Nabers 2003, pp. 113–36; Peou 2002, pp. 119–38). Examining the 'speech acts' of Asian leaders and picking over the 'interpretive schemes' that emerged from regional colloquies, analysts sought to validate methodologically that 'East Asia and Southeast Asia are beginning to emerge, through debates and controversies' (Hemmer and Katzenstein 2002, p. 610). ASEAN, naturally, played a crucial role in the process of 'region-wide community building and the formation of a collective identity' (Nabers 2003, p. 130). According to commentators, the process of pan-Asian socialization was such that 'the East Asian region is so closely connected in political, economic, social and ecological terms that it is impossible to consider one state's fate independently from another' (ibid., p. 132). For Katzenstein, *pace* Ali Alatas, 'Asian regionalism is an idea whose time has come' (Katzenstein 1999, p. 16).

DÉJÀ VU IN THE ASIA–PACIFIC

Despite the confidence with which regional analysts have endorsed constructivist developments in the Asia–Pacific, a number of theoretical and practical problems arise that might cause those not wedded to constructivism to ponder sceptically the evolving shape of East Asian international relations. Certainly, both Wendt's hypothesis and constructivist approaches in general have not been without their detractors. Critics have noted, for example, that constructivism ultimately entails a logical absurdity. If constitutive processes are all, then all phenomena collapse back into language. This robs constructivism itself of any meaning. As Copeland observes, if human agents were merely 'puppets of the ideational environment in which they find themselves' then 'each would exist simply as a socially conditioned "Me," without the free-willed "I" capable of resisting the socialization process' (Copeland 2000, p. 197). Such overdetermining conditioning would undermine any prospect of transforming the structure of the international system through human interaction – the very thing that most constructivists want to show is possible.

Somewhat differently, constructivism in international relations often demonstrates a limited understanding of its philosophical underpinnings whilst its attempts at theory testing are invariably superficial (Palen 2000, pp. 575–98; Sidel 2001, p. 162). Indeed, they often bear an uncomfortable resemblance to Jorge Luis Borges's fiction, *Tlön Uqbar Orbis Tertius*. For Borges, significantly a keen student of Berkeleyan idealism, the people of Tlön have constructed a world that is not a concurrence of objects in space, but a heterogeneous series of independent acts. Interestingly, the metaphysicians of Tlön, endlessly fascinated by system building, do not pursue truth or even an approximation of it. They are in pursuit of a 'kind of amazement' (Borges 1962, p. 25).[4]

Rather than the fantastic systems of Tlön, constructivist authors are instead in pursuit of positive norms – nice norms – assuming that the transformation of identities always promotes cooperation and is thus an innately benevolent process (Finnemore and Sikkink 2001, pp. 403–4). Hence, Muthiah Alagappa informs us that 'The ASEAN approach emphasizes principles, norms and rules as the key to regulate international interaction', privileging multilateral institutions designed 'to reduce the role of power' (Alagappa 2003, p. 77). This preferencing clearly discounts negative norms that may equally well explain international behaviour (see Jervis 1998, p. 974). Yet, as Jonathan Mercer has shown in an application of situational identity theory to international relations, cooperative behaviour among certain actors inevitably generates competitive behaviour against others (Mercer 1995, p. 251). Such an uncomfortable outcome of normative processes (clearly apparent in the ASEAN Plus Three approach to non-Asian states) tends to be overlooked by those who apply a constructivist ontology to international relations.

Such incoherence notwithstanding, let us accept the central constructivist premise that identities are capable of changing over time for the purposes of understanding developments in Asia–Pacific relations. Most social scientists would acknowledge that ideational factors condition social actors and that these factors are capable of change over time. This, after all, is how perceptions alter and progress occurs. What we can dispute in the context of East Asian regionalism, however, is whether, below the discursive level of speech acts and rhetorical exhortation to regional unity, constructivism explains the practice of Asia–Pacific international relations and whether, as it further contends, any genuine transformation is taking place in that practice. Do discursive practices in international relations, we might wonder, accurately forecast political change, or do they instead create the politically useful illusion of transformation?

It is a question that has obvious resonance in the Asia–Pacific because Southeast Asian regionalism in the post-Cold War period manifestly failed to fulfil its rhetorical promise. This earlier failure provides both an empirical and a rhetorical framework in which to assess current claims about the direction and intensity of East Asian regionalization. For it is evident that, in the period from 1990 to 1997, ASEAN's constant proclamation of regional harmony and stability and the machinery of regional consultation merely obscured the reality of a loose collection of competing states, briefly united (for a few decades) by their self-denying ordinance of non-interference in the internal affairs of member states and a shared opposition to Communism. During the 1980s, rapid economic growth spurred on by foreign direct investment had dampened the multifarious claims, rivalries and suspicions that perennially agitated its membership.

While ASEAN expanded its membership and attempted to export its managerial style to wider regional problems it achieved minimal institutional deepening before the 1997 economic crisis. Yet the consequences of the economic crisis revealed how little of substance there was to the rhetorical claims of harmony and cooperation as each of the major states in ASEAN looked abroad or to its own resources to survive the meltdown.

A properly value-neutral political scientist committed to empirically testing hypotheses would find in the Southeast Asian case between 1990 and 1998 the conspicuous failure of a regional project. Aware of the causes of that failure our putative scientist might be inclined to exercise a degree of scepticism towards new claims from the proponents of the previous failure to have engineered an even bolder scheme conceived on an East Asian scale. Instead, the current literature on East Asian regionalism endorses and repeats on a broader Asian canvas claims made by Southeast Asian autocrats and their scholar–bureaucracies in the 1990s, manifesting an uncritical propensity to conceive events in East Asia as essentially transformative in nature. Amitav Acharya, an eager proponent of both constructivism and an evolving ASEAN security community, exemplifies this approach, asserting that 'Asia is moving in the same trajectory of greater interdependence, institutionalization and political transformation as Europe did in the past centuries, and there can be reasonable hope that their pathways will converge more fully in the long-term future' (quoted in Lim 2003).

However, events from 1994 to 2004 indicate – from the Spratly Islands dispute between China and almost all the ASEAN states, which remains unresolved, to the very different post-meltdown political and economic experiences of North and Southeast states – that the current 'trajectory', far from propelling Asia towards European-style integration assumes a rather different 'pathway'. In fact, the appropriate comparative region is not the European Union, or even looser structures like the Organization for Security and Cooperation in Europe, but Africa and the Organization of African Unity (OAU). While Asian leaders, like their African counterparts, evince their 'unity' through repeated declarations of regional solidarity, ASEAN is in fact a fading institution. Like the OAU, only relative geographical propinquity and a sense of shared grievance that belies an underlying divergence of interest hold East Asian regionalism together. As we know, moreover, in the case of the OAU, this stretches the meaning of both 'Organization' and 'Unity' in highly tenuous ways.

If we probe further into the international relations of the Asia–Pacific we can discern a number of issues that challenge the constructivist representation of an East Asia transforming itself into a coherent region. Peter Katzenstein, one of constructivism's *illuminati*, maintains that regionalization charts a course towards more satisfactory forms of international cooperation, transcending inadequate national approaches while avoiding the pitfalls of more 'unworkable universal schemes' (Katzenstein 1995). The process of divining the agreed form and extent of international cooperation among disparate states sufficient to define a region is, of course, complex, and subject to continual negotiation and re-negotiation. This notwithstanding, the premise assumes that regions will eventually cohere into an accepted and acceptable form.

The notion of an 'East Asia', however, presents especially acute problems for this approach to overcome. If regions are essentially discursive creations formed by the interplay of language and politics, which in due course become acculturated within the thinking of governing elites and a wider public over time, then what constitutes East Asia is still inchoate. Consequently, while the idea of a 'Southeast Asia' emerged from the formation of a British theatre of operations in World War II – South East Asia Command – and is currently framed by membership of ASEAN, no such simple delineation frames East Asia (see Huxley 1996).

Indeed, 'Asia' has always been something of a movable feast. The term, together with sub-variant forms like East Asia, Southeast Asia, Farther India, Indochina and Northeast Asia, arose not from amongst those states integral to that 'region' but from political actors external to it, most notably during the period of European colonial expansion from the seventeenth century onwards (see Segal 1992, pp. 414–17; Osborne 1995, pp. 4–5). The term 'Asia', then, was an essentially European coinage that gave rise to misleadingly monolithic images of the Orient that still persist today (Jones 2001b). For, paradoxically, Asia as a distinct region is constituted, if at all, only through its geographic, ethnic and religious diversity.

Because of Asia's historically nebulous character, it is necessary to be cautious in interpreting the signs of its emergence into a coherent East Asian regional form. As John Ravenhill observes: 'Statements by East Asian political cal leaders at regional forums affirming such an identity and a new commonality of interests have to be read in the particular context in which they were made and not be assumed to translate automatically into new collaborative outcomes' (Ravenhill 2002, p. 175). Furthermore, not only are declarations of regional solidarity frequently made for demonstrative effect, they also conceal very different understandings of this putative region. Thus Japanese Prime Minister Junichiro Koizumi's call for an East Asian community envisaged the ASEAN Plus Three framework broadening to embrace countries like Australia and New Zealand and a wider free trade area (Low 2002). This vividly contrasts with Malaysia's push, supported by the People's Republic of China, for a more segregated and racially determined understanding of the region. In the latter view, as Rafidah Aziz, the Malaysian trade minister explained, non-Asiatic countries like Australia and New Zealand 'are [not part] of the region' (Asia Times Online, 8 March 2001, cited in Nabers 2003, p. 121).

Uncertainty over who or what constitutes the East Asian entity raises a further problem: can any arrangement so broadly and ambivalently conceived address the diverse economic and security problems confronting the Asia–Pacific? As we have seen, the main impetus for regional expansion sprang from the 1997 financial crisis, which inspired visions of pan-Asian cooperation strengthening regional economic resilience, and prompted ideas for an Asian Monetary Fund, the reduction of tariff barriers and free-trade agreements. Scrutiny of trans-Pacific economic and trade cooperation reveals, as the previous chapter indicates, that progress in this area has been negligible.

In sum, there are continuing differences over what form regional economic cooperation should take. Political entities like Hong Kong and the city state of Singapore favour trade liberalization, while others such as Malaysia prefer mutual technical and economic assistance aimed more at developing an economically defensible 'fortress Asia' (Ravenhill 2002, p. 178). Efforts within the ASEAN and APEC frameworks to reduce tariff barriers remain a commitment only in theory, the intention being to reduce tariffs to zero by 2015, while in practice numerous commodities are subject to a Temporary Exclusion List, a General Exception List and a Sensitive List (excluded permanently from any liberalization) (Soesastro 2001, pp. 3–6). Indonesia, Malaysia and Thailand continuously re-negotiate trade 'sensitive' items and extend their protection well beyond the next decade ('Par for the course', 1995).

Interestingly, the most recent exercise in ASEAN bonding, the 'Bali Concord 11', declared at the ninth ASEAN summit in October 2003, envisaged an ASEAN community built on the three pillars of political and security, economic and sociocultural cooperation. Significantly, the Concord merely reinforced and updated the Treaty of Amity and Cooperation of 1976 that had failed to integrate the region in the past. Clearly, the putative political community is founded on a principle of non-interference. Its economic integration, despite the introduction of 'new mechanisms', remains consensus-driven rather than rule-driven. What is more, the Concord does not foresee an integrated economic community emerging any time before 2020 (ASEAN Secretariat 2004). Even for slow-moving ASEAN, a decade and a half is a long time in international politics.

Ultimately, attempts to extend consensus-based community ideas for an Asia free trade area and an Asian Monetary Fund have fallen by the wayside for a similar lack of will. As Ravenhill again notes, the inconsistent character of the rhetorical attachment to inter-Asian trade deepening was exposed in 2001, when arch pan-Asianist, Prime Minister Mahathir, warned of the danger to Southeast Asian investment and economic growth posed by the increasing flow of imported goods from, and foreign direct investment into, China (Ravenhill 2002, p. 182). ASEAN's poor record of trade integration has, Ravenhill continued, 'been punctuated by some member states flouting even its modest demands' and provides 'little reason for confidence that rapid progress will be made' across the broader Asia–Pacific (ibid.).

In fact, economic integration, to the extent that it is taking place at all, occurs through the mechanism of bilateral free trade agreements between states both within and outside the 'community/region'. The US, Australia, China, Japan, Singapore and Thailand are all actively pursuing or signing bilateral trade agreements. Singapore early on signalled its frustration with the pace of trade liberalization in the ASEAN economic community by concluding a bilateral free trade agreement with New Zealand in January 2001, and Australia in 2003, which contradicted any ostensible commitment to regional solidarity (ibid., p. 181). China is examining closely free trade agreements with both the ASEAN grouping and Australia. As Greg Sheridan observed, with evident perplexity, none of 'the formal multilateral architecture of East Asia ... has had much effect on these matters' (Sheridan 2003).

If the attempt to deepen and extend inter-Asian trade possesses only rhetorical rather than real collective economic integration, how will a wider regional bloc cope with the even more difficult problems that afflict the security order in the Asia–Pacific? ASEAN has been unable to resolve underlying grievances and intramural tensions amongst its own membership, yet the presumption persists that the organization's machinery, inculcation of norms of good regional behaviour and diplomatic style can deal with the protracted security issues that trouble Northeast Asia. Yet the regional security architecture evinces little evidence of even addressing, let alone managing, complex and entrenched issues that, *inter alia*, include historically deep-seated Sino-Japanese cultural, economic and territorial rivalry, China's hegemonic claims over Taiwan and the South China Seas, North Korea and its dangerously unstable nuclear programme, as well as sensitive 'internal' matters concerning human rights, good governance, environmental degradation and transnational crime and terror organizations (for a survey of these problems see Friedberg 1993, pp. 261–85; Yahuda 1996, pp. 216–85; Roy 1994, pp. 149–68).

ASEAN's attempt to demonstrate its wider regional utility through the ARF was built on the illusion that the supposed success of the organization's conflict avoidance mechanisms could be applied across the Pacific. In practice, the ARF simply reflected ASEAN's preferred strategy of consensus diplomacy, which manages problems rather than solves them. Consequently, a variety of ARF-inspired workshops and ministerial dialogue sessions have made no impact on any security issue they have addressed (see Jones 1998, pp. 185–6). This has been evident since its earliest efforts to manage the evolving dispute over oil and gas reserves beneath the Spratly islands in the South China seas. Given that, Singapore, Laos and Cambodia apart, all the ASEAN states claimed some part of the seas, and China claimed the whole lot, it would appear to be both a conflict amenable to ASEAN-style management and at the same time an opportunity to induct China into the regional norms of responsible behaviour that the ARF sought to extend northwards.

The result was something of a disappointment. China ignored any attempt to establish an ASEAN-designed multilateral approach to the crisis. Indeed, China considered any attempt to address its claim multilaterally with suspicion. Instead, to the extent it negotiated at all, it was on a bilateral basis and at no time relinquishing its historic claim to treat the South China Sea as a greater Chinese lake. Some form of bilateral approach to the still unresolved dispute is, moreover, inevitable. Even when China's occupation of the aptly named Mischief Reef in March 1995 agitated regional sensibilities in general and Philippine ones in particular, the ASEAN members could not even formulate a consensus amongst themselves as a basis for any agreed multilateral approach to the disputed islands (see 'China's creeping assertiveness', 1995).

The poor performance of the ARF, like the failure of ASEAN regionalism in the wake of the 1997 economic crisis, should have been sufficient to confound future expectations that a broader multilateral arrangement would have any capacity to address the region's security dilemmas. Yet the illusion persists that the involvement of a triumvirate of regional powers, China, Japan and South Korea, guided, of course, by ASEAN diplomatic processes, will constitute a concert of Asia capable of regulating the region's affairs. Inherent in ASEAN initiatives dating from the 1971 ZOPFAN plan has been the aspiration to enhance regional integration free from great power interference. This aspiration, however, ignores the further and crucial strategic question of how this prospective concert can operate without the active participation of the United States. Given that the US is the major power in the Pacific any long-term effort to reduce the influence of 'outside' powers must mean excluding the US (Khoo and Smith 2002, pp. 77–8). Even here another incoherence appears, for a majority of the ASEAN states welcome, to various extents, the presence of a benign US hegemony across the Asia–Pacific both to mitigate the numerous inter-Asian security dilemmas and specifically to balance the potentially destabilizing rivalries of the region's major powers, namely Japan and an irredentist China. As one Southeast Asian diplomat observed in 2001: 'Basically our choice is between a hegemony in Washington or a hegemony in Beijing. We are still choosing the United States' (quoted in Pomfret 2001).

ASEAN's practical reliance on the US security umbrella, while rhetorically committing itself to schemes for enhanced regional resilience that ultimately imply a diminution in US regional power in Asia, is clearly contradictory. Yet at no time since its formation as a US proxy in the wake of the Guam doctrine have ASEAN politicians or scholars sought to address this contradiction adequately. More disturbingly, extending this incoherence to ASEAN Plus

Three by excluding the US from the broader Asian security arrangement risks disrupting the delicately calibrated understanding of balance in the Asia–Pacific. In the past, only Mahathir Mohamad, in conjunction with the odd Japanese ultra-nationalist like Shintaro Ishihara, was associated (outside the People's Republic of China) with promoting anti-Americanism as a basis for a pan-Asian identity (Mohamad and Ishihara 1995). Post-meltdown and post-September 11, however, this viewpoint has received growing scholarly endorsement, particularly from a Singapore school of constructivist security analysis. Promiscuously coupling Wendt's concern with multilateral norms and Mahathir's *ressentiment*, this emerging school has engendered the thesis that it is the United States that threatens the construction of a new and purposeful East Asian regional identity. Thus, Kwa and Tan somewhat solipsistically claiming to speak on behalf of 'we, the countries of Southeast Asia', represent the 'mood in East Asia' as one which increasingly resents American 'arrogance' and the 'evangelistic zeal of U.S. foreign policy makers to remake East Asia into an annex of Americana, or, failing that an authoritarian Other' (Kwa and Tan 2001, pp. 95–6). Likewise, Goh's constructivist analysis of the impact of American foreign policy upon Asia implies that the US is responsible for causing the war on terrorism that now confronts it (Goh 2003, pp. 77–97). Elsewhere, Acharya, rails against the evils of the US's post-September 11 doctrine of pre-emption (Acharya 2002a) and further contends that one of the major 'challenges' ASEAN faces is that of 'American unilateralism', which he believes 'demand [*sic*] a response from the Association', although we are not told quite what this response might entail (quoted in 'Challenges and prospects in the current international situation', 2003).

Intellectual consistency has rarely been a hallmark of the Singaporean scholar–bureaucracy and in a constructivism married to a fashionable academic anti-Americanism it has evidently found a useful ideological weapon to mask its failings. Precisely why 'American unilateralism' poses a 'challenge' to ASEAN and East Asia is, for example, never explained. Such inconsistency aside, they nonetheless imply that ASEAN in conjunction with a wider East Asian caucus should work to diminish a potential US hegemony in the Pacific, the logical implication of which is that ASEAN should actively collaborate with the emerging regional hegemon, China, to undermine US power.

Such a radical reversal of ASEAN's traditional perception of China seems immediately feasible only in the concrete encrusted towers of Southeast Asian academe. Nevertheless, such officially endorsed scholasticism only adds the Pelion of constructivist discourse to the Ossa of regional incoherence. For, in the end, the only properly constructive role ASEAN Plus Three can play in the increasingly complex security dilemma that faces the Asia–Pacific region is not to coopt China into an anti-US crusade, but to constrain its irredentist proclivities through diplomatic engagement (see Leifer 1995, p. 34). At most

ASEAN Plus Three can extend the ASEAN way, involving 'a commitment to carry on with consultations without any specific formula or modality for achieving a desired outcome' (Acharya 1997a, p. 329), to the wider Asia–Pacific. Yet the fulfilment of even this modest enterprise seems unlikely given the ARF's conduct towards the Spratly dispute and China's inflexible approach to the rebellious province of Taiwan and continuing claim to the Japanese-occupied Senkaku islands.

These cases should again induce a degree of scepticism amongst scholars when any loose collocation of states riven by ethnic differences, historic jealousies, territorial disputes and a litany of mutual antipathies claims, but fails to manifest, a capacity to manage regional problems. Instead, we find a pattern of failed scholarship reinforcing failed multilateral initiatives repeating itself. Central to this pattern is the seemingly intractable habit of mistaking process for progress. Analysts eagerly see in yet another ASEAN-inspired ministerial meeting, declaration of concord or adoption of unenforceable commitments to realize forms of low-level cooperation, irrefutable evidence of the transformative socialization processes that 'identify a compelling imperative for further institutionalization' (Nabers 2003, pp. 124–5). In other words, an interesting convergence of a questionable but scholarly appealing ideology combines with the felt need of regional elites to sustain the delusion of regional integration.

Ultimately, the process is self-fulfilling, but it raises a further question: if, as we have demonstrated, the construction of wider East Asian arrangements is rhetorical rather than real, what, we may ask, sustains the apparent desire amongst the ASEAN Plus Three states to indulge in illusory declarations of regional unity? From an academic perspective, as we have shown elsewhere, it is relatively easy to demonstrate how methodological fashion aided by major grant-giving institutions in hock to the latest orthodoxy sustains a pseudo-scholarship devoted to regionalization. This is an unstoppable bureaucratic process that continues despite events that ought to induce a reality check. But what do the states of the Asia–Pacific actually gain by inflating the rhetorical balloon of East Asian regionalism? It is to the resolution of this perplexity that we shall now proceed.

REVERSING THE DIALECTIC: THREE PLUS ASEAN

At face value, it seems strange that realist state actors in Northeast Asia consider it useful or desirable to support an institution like ASEAN Plus Three. Why should three major Asian powers wish to associate themselves with a grouping of weak states like ASEAN whose collective sum is much less than its constitutive parts? If there was any prospect that China, Japan and South Korea could form a concert of powers to manage economic and security relations in Northeast Asia, why would these countries require ASEAN?

Let us momentarily and constructively engage in a short international relations thought experiment. Imagine, for example, that a group of weak states in the Mediterranean – Spain, Portugal, Italy and Greece – had during the Cold War constituted an Associated Region of Southern Europe for economic and security purposes. Then consider Germany, France and the United Kingdom desperately trying to join such a union in the post-Cold War era. It sounds unlikely, yet this is exactly how the Northeast Asian states are acting in relation to ASEAN. As Amitav Acharya observed, ASEAN has recently witnessed 'so many suitors knocking on its door'. China, Japan and India are all queuing up to sign free-trade agreements with the Association. 'Why' is there 'so much wooing of an allegedly sunset organisation?' Acharya asks rhetorically (Acharya 2002b).

Two answers may be given. The first is that East Asian diplomatic solidarity comes at a discount. The price of commitment to regional cohesion is negligible. Forging trade agreements, or even signing up to the Treaty of Amity and Cooperation, is a cost-free exercise. The governing principle of non-interference embodied in the TAC is particularly appealing to Asia's Heinz 57 variety of authoritarian governments and semi-demi-semi democracies and thus has little difficulty attracting adherents who resent any external scrutiny of their internal affairs. Adhering to the precepts of the TAC, therefore, incurs no obligation other than to mind one's own business, something which a number of the states in the Asia–Pacific, from China to Myanmar, Laos and Vietnam, are only too happy to respect.

A second, and more interesting, answer that helps unravel the dynamic of state self-interest in the evolving East Asian enterprise appears if we reverse the dialectic. Aseanologists are by habit and training ASEANcentric. They assume that much East Asian diplomacy occurs through ASEAN's institutional machinery. Hence the presumption that, because ASEAN appears to have 'so many suitors', this indicates its continuing importance to the affairs of the Asia–Pacific. In fact, the very opposite is true. ASEAN Plus Three should really be viewed as 'Three Plus ASEAN'. By itself ASEAN has, since its meltdown in 1997, little relevance for Northeast Asia. But, in contrast, the economic development and international relations of Northeast Asia possess mounting significance for Southeast Asia.

For the states of Southeast Asia, the putative utility of exporting ASEAN way diplomatic initiatives through the ARF or ASEAN Plus Three resides in restricting the growing power differential between them and the states of Northeast Asia. In practice, however, the reverse is the case. Far from preventing Chinese and Japanese expansionism, ASEAN Plus Three provides an attractive vehicle for Northeast Asians to explore their regional ambitions and vie for influence in Southeast Asia. ASEAN itself is an empty vessel. It can be easily manoeuvred by external powers who, like Japan and China, use the rhetoric of regional solidarity to pursue their self-interested competition for regional hegemony.

Such an understanding, moreover, fits with the Cold War history of ASEAN. As the late Michael Leifer endeavoured to show in a number of books and articles, ASEAN functioned in the Cold War as a proxy for US and Chinese interests (see Leifer 1989, 1996). This was most evident in the resolution of the Cambodian crisis in the early 1990s. In addition, since the late 1970s, Japanese foreign policy thinking has consciously sought to increase its influence in Southeast Asia via ASEAN. In 1977, the then Japanese Prime Minister's eponymous 'Fukuda doctrine' declared Japan's commitment to 'cooperate in the development of Southeast Asia, under the ideal of equal partnership' (*East Asian Strategic Review*, 2003, p. 211). In practice, of course, the relationship was far from equal, as Japanese foreign direct investment poured into the fledgling economies of ASEAN. Furthermore, as trade friction developed between Japan and the US during the 1980s, the Japanese Ministry for Foreign Affairs and Defense steadily expanded the Fukuda doctrine (see Jones 1998, p. 190; Johnson 1996, pp. 23–9), seeking to diversify its foreign policy by increasing multilateral cooperation with the states of Southeast Asia, especially through trade and investment links, and subsequently, after 1992, extending collaboration in the broader diplomatic and security fields through the ARF (see Hughes 1996, pp. 229–50).

Commentators continue to debate the intent of Japanese foreign policy (see Inoguchi 1993). On the one hand, the emphasis on dialogue diplomacy with ASEAN could be interpreted as Japan attempting to position itself in the post-Cold War order as a potential counter-weight to American influence in the Pacific (Bobrow, Chan and Reich 1996, p. 5). On the other, it is equally plausible to contend that Japan's willingness to engage in ASEAN-sponsored multilateral forums was undertaken with the aim to improve its image in Asia by diluting the impression that it was the US lackey in the Pacific (Hara 1999, p. 529). Whatever tensions have emerged between the US and Japan since the end of the Cold War, it is clear that the alliance with the US remains the cornerstone of Japan's security (Segal 1989; Levin 1991, p. 237). Consequently, it can be argued that involvement in Southeast Asian multilateralism served primarily to assuage growing Japanese nationalism at home while advancing its internationalist credentials abroad, yet without ever seriously imperilling its crucial bilateral relationship with the US. So whether Japanese diplomacy after 1990 sought *de facto* leadership in the Asia–Pacific or reflected a more subtle repositioning, the power-political outcome was the same: Japanese diplomacy has not elevated ASEAN to a position of equality with the aim of building a broader East Asian identity, rather ASEAN serves and is subordinated to the ends of Japanese foreign policy.

At the same time that Japan was re-defining its role with regard to ASEAN, so too was the People's Republic of China. In other words, after 1990, Southeast Asia became the playing field for Northeast Asian power politics. Chinese foreign policy initially perceived ASEAN and its expansionary multi-lateral ventures like the ARF suspiciously, seeing behind them the hidden hand of the US attempting to contain China in its own hemisphere (Wang 1997, pp. 10–11). Such suspicions, moreover, were by no means groundless, given that the formation of the ARF reflected ASEAN's growing concern over China's post-1990 assertiveness. In particular, ASEAN worried about China's claim over the South China Sea and its attempts to enhance its naval power projection capabilities (see Valencia 1995) which, as Michael Yahuda stated, threatened to 'reach right into the heart of Southeast Asia' (Yahuda 1996, p. 271).

It was the post-economic crisis period after 1997, however, that sharpened Sino-Japanese rivalry over Southeast Asia. The economic crisis damaged Japan's economic credibility in Southeast Asia. Japanese financial institutions were quick to withdraw from the region after the currency turmoil struck, and slow to return. These circumstances offered China an opportunity to 'strengthen its influence over ASEAN members in order to challenge Japan's leadership in the region' (*East Asian Strategic Review*, 2003, p. 209). China's refusal to devalue its currency, the *renminbi*, which might have further exacerbated the Asian financial meltdown, gave it regional credibility. The refusal to devalue indicated China's responsible 'regional' economic leadership. The perception in Japan that China had increased its leverage in Southeast Asia through its response to the crisis, in turn, elicited a further response. This took the form of the New Miyazawa Initiative in 1998 that subsequently broadened into the Obuchi–ASEAN plan to provide large-scale financial assistance to facilitate economic recovery (see Ministry of Foreign Affairs 1998, 1999).

It is, therefore, in the context of this evolving Sino-Japanese competition for Southeast Asian influence that the ASEAN Plus Three project must be understood. It is essentially a forum where the major powers of Northeast Asia contest the economic (and, ergo, political) leadership of Southeast Asia. Indeed, Japanese policy makers have few illusions about this. They maintain that, without the participation of the United States and Australia, ASEAN Plus Three presents China with 'an ideal framework within which it can exercise its influence, making it easier for China to play a leading role in forming a free-trade area in East Asia' (*East Asian Strategic Review*, 2003, p. 210). Japan, in other words, does not consider China's participation in ASEAN Plus Three, and its negotiation of a regional free trade agreement with ASEAN, as cementing an East Asian identity, but rather as a mechanism to diminish Japanese influence in Southeast Asia. This, in turn, compels Japan to 'cooperate with ASEAN members' on investment, technology, human resources and security strategies because 'through such measures, Japan can match the growing influence of China in that region' (ibid., p. 213).

It is in this evolving competition between East Asia's historic great powers that statements like the Koizumi doctrine must be read. Prime Minister Koizumi envisages 'an expanded East Asian community' not as some idealistic attempt to forge an East Asian community but in order to balance China's bid for regional ascendancy. Official Japanese publications like the *East Asian Strategic Review* confirm the accuracy of this, observing: 'Using ASEAN as their stage, it appears that Japan and China are jockeying for a leadership role in East Asia' (*East Asian Strategic Review*, 2003, p. 213).

Of course, the theatre of ASEAN Plus Three is not open only to Chinese and Japanese actors. ASEAN connoisseurs can appreciate elsewhere dramatic posturing by minor characters in inter-ASEAN rivalry. This may be illustrated, for example, by Malaysia's proposal in mid-2002 to fund the establishment of an ASEAN Plus Three secretariat in Kuala Lumpur, much to the chagrin of other member states who tried to 'neutralize' the idea (Saiful and Mahavera 2002). However, it is in the machinations of Asia's two most significant powers that we see the operation of foreign policy imperatives coming to the fore. Accordingly, reversing the understanding of ASEAN Plus Three exposes the emptiness of constructivist assumptions of multilateral norm construction along with the fatuous notion of an emerging regional identity. It reveals, in its place, the naked pursuit of traditional, realist, state interests.

CONSTRUCTIVIST UTOPIANISM AND THE POLITICS OF FAITH

If ASEAN Plus Three is thus exposed as a front concealing very conventional forms of inter-state diplomacy then we can move closer to resolving the final question: why have many analysts abandoned an empirical assessment of regional reality in favour of upholding the notion of East Asian transformation into an attractive multilateral norm-enhancing enterprise?

On reflection, there may be an uncomplicated answer. As we have noted, the recent study of East Asia reflects an enthusiasm for a constructivist explanation of regional relations. This is because, despite its failure to say anything insightful or interesting about the region, it places the official view of Southeast Asian political elites in a satisfyingly self-fulfilling methodological framework. For the notion that ideational factors modify perceptions of material self-interest and sustain an open-ended transformative process is inherently unfalsifiable (see Copeland 2000, p. 208). Wendt, somewhat predictably, maintains that the 'transformation of identity and interest' is 'incremental and slow' (Wendt 1992a, p. 418). Consequently, all speech acts and any other foreign policy initiative can be treated as evidence of remorseless transition. Constructivist commentators on Asian regionalism, like Acharya, *pace* Wendt, also perceive the process of international change in terms of 'incremental interactions and socialization' (Acharya 1999b, p. 5). By a selective use of data, he identifies a global 'trend towards intrusive regionalism' resulting in the 'development and mutual observance' (Acharya 1999c, p. 23) of universalized norms that in East Asia's case is leading to 'greater interdependence, institutionalism and political transformation' (quoted in Lim 2003). Similarly, Stuart Harris finds that the 'contribution of multilateralism in the Asia–Pacific has been to alter the environment within which interactions take place and, in encouraging cognitive learning about the way the world works to change or reinforce how Asian states want to pursue their interest and reshape their national objectives' (Harris 1999, p. 7).

Hence impediments like terrorism, war or economic crisis that occasion purely self-interested national responses and repudiate the constructivist case are airily dismissed as minor details delaying but by no means stopping the inexorable process of transformation. Constructivists appear to treat evidence of the continued pursuit of state interest as a temporary phase soon to be overcome. Eventually, inter-state rivalries will mutate into an appreciation of interdependent regional interests. Given these historicist assumptions, constructivism considers itself released from the need for scepticism (see Popper 1959, pp. 64–71). We can see this by the way in which the constructivist idiom replaces the requirement to question ruling assumptions with the accumulation of data on policy and procedures that demonstrate the 'institutionalisation of the ASEAN + 3 process' (see 'Regions in transition', 2000, p. 2). Interestingly, the thickly descriptive, and often meaningless, discussion of technical and bureaucratic processes that characterized the scholarship of ASEAN before 1997 has, post-1997, been transferred to the wider Pacific arena to sustain the delusion of an emerging East Asian region (see Ferguson 1999, pp. 4–19; Harris 1999 pp. 2–18; Haacke 2003, pp. 57–87; Katzenstein 1999, pp. 2–24; Nabers 2003, pp. 113–36).

Analysts of the Asia–Pacific are evidently reluctant to abandon a predestined understanding of international affairs to which they have formed, implicitly or explicitly, an ideological and emotional attachment. Observers have noted that attempts to account scientifically for the modernization process often carry a value-laden, or what Yahuda has termed a 'redemptionist' (Yahuda 1996, p. 282), baggage that sees history as an inexorable movement towards a capitalist, democratic and thymotically self-regarding End of History (see Jones 1998, p. 164). In international relations this baggage further entails a liberal/internationalist predilection towards both the desirability and the inevitability of transcending the state as the primary unit in the international system. Regionalization, from this perspective, appears to be the first stage in the process towards a properly interdependent international system. Accordingly, foreign policy should facilitate the transformation[5] because regionalism, as Acharya explains, is 'an important tool for promoting a range of positive values' throughout the international system (Acharya 1999c, p. 24).

Ultimately, this orthodoxy is, itself, a deeply normative construct and an example of what Michael Oakeshott would have recognized as 'the politics of faith' (Oakeshott 1996, pp. 45–67). In Oakeshott's conception, the politics of faith sustains an intellectual scheme utterly resistant to scepticism. The problem for the politics of faith, however, is that a belief in infallibility invariably, as Jonathan Clark notes, 'fails to yield predictability' (Clark 2003, p. 54). So, when regionalization falters in Southeast Asia as a result of ASEAN failing to live up to its promise, the object of affection is not subject to critical scrutiny, but instead broadened to an East Asian canvas in order to maintain the faith. Consequently, much of what passes for scholarly analysis of contemporary East Asian affairs is not value-neutral but accumulates information to affirm the faith. Hence commentators passionately declare that regional interdependency in the Asia–Pacific represents a 'basic truth', asserting that it 'is not in doubt that the process will foster the identity of an East Asian community' (Nabers 2003, p. 133). Statements of future resolve support this belief structure. They are acts of faith, not scholarly scepticism. Thus, in order to consolidate Asia–Pacific regionalism, we are told that 'new visions of regional governance will need to be developed to bypass blockages in solving transboundary problems, in moving towards effective preventive diplomacy, and in moderating triangular patterns of "great power" competition' (Ferguson 1999, p. 19). For proof that this worldly regional utopia is about to be realized, we need look no further than 'regional multilateral dialogues' which have 'probably led to learning' in the economic and security fields, and give 'grounds for believing it has made important contributions in both directions' (Harris 1999, p. 8).

By piling assertion upon incoherence, regional commentary avoids confronting internal dissonance, never pausing to question whether ASEAN's flawed Southeast Asian project renders its wider applicability to East Asia suspect. Faith coupled with discourse enables commentators to overlook the manner in which the 1997 economic crisis undermined ASEAN's regionalist pretensions and instead maintain, very oddly, that 'ASEAN is not as weak as it may seem' because, despite the consequences of economic crisis, it 'demonstrated a high degree of commitment to its institutional principles' (Ferguson 1999, p. 15), thereby making 'an important contribution to the normative environment of the region by reinforcing the fundamental principles of international society' (Narine 1998, pp. 33–47, quoted in Ferguson 1999, p. 15). The problem is that the only 'institutional principle' to which ASEAN adheres is that of non-interference. For this reason, the only 'fundamental principle of international society' it has reinforced is a realist commitment, not to the region, but to the sovereign inviolability of the nation-state.

There may be a final level of understanding that reconciles the idealistic, faith-based character of much scholarship on Pacific affairs with the essentially realist practice of inter-state diplomacy that actually regulates regional relations. This further understanding brings us as close to explaining the delusional basis of East Asian academic discourse as it may be possible to achieve.

If we examine the history of the Asia–Pacific over the *longue durée* of the twentieth century, it becomes evident that the rhetoric of East Asian regionalism has presented itself in many guises, waxing and waning over the decades. Arguably, imperial Japan's attempt to impose its notion of an East Asian Co-Prosperity Sphere in the 1930s and 1940s constituted the first coherent regionalist enterprise. Later regionalist schemes revealed themselves in the South-East Asia Treaty Organization (SEATO) and then in ASEAN's attempts to establish regional neutrality through ZOPFAN in the 1970s. Later, in the 1980s and 1990s, economic cooperation was regarded as the principal agent of a regionalist dynamic, with APEC depicted as the harbinger of an East Asian community (see Bhagwati 1996; Wanandi 1996). As Asia entered the post-Cold War era, bilateral and trilateral growth areas in Northeast and Southeast Asia proliferated, together with the assertion of shared 'Asian values' constituting a cultural commonality across the Pacific. Indeed, the formation of the ARF intimated the culmination of the vaunted 'ASEAN way'. Now, in the post-economic crisis environment, we have ASEAN Plus Three and visionary promises of future East Asian integration.

However, all these initiatives have consistently foundered on the rocks of global power politics and national interest. The Japanese imperium turned out to be the East Asian Co-Poverty Sphere, and other powers in the international system (as well as most Asians themselves) rejected it. ASEAN's various schemes to promote regional resilience, consensus and harmony have, likewise, failed to resolve intense bilateral antipathies, often of an ethno-religious nature. The absence of any deepening of inter-Asian trade relations and, after 1997, evidence of economic mismanagement, rendered the ASEAN way illusory (Harland 1993, pp. 8–16). Similarly, as Gilbert Rozman has shown in Northeast Asia, the attempt to sustain regional growth in the early 1990s through practical economic and developmental initiatives between China, Japan, South Korea and Russia were 'flawed' by 'narrow local or national self-interest'. Rozman concluded: 'Impulsive regionalism flailed against entrenched nationalism, distorted reform programs, unbalanced decentralization, conflicting ideals for the future division of labor, and untrusting personal relations' (Rozman 1998, p. 3).

What we have, then, is the continual re-imagining of the regionalist project in ever more fanciful forms, but – Japan's failed attempt to forcibly incorporate an East Asian sphere during World War II notwithstanding – nothing concrete ever appears (Ravenhill 2002, p. 193). Yet, rather than examine why this is the case, regional commentary instead seems transfixed by the latest incarnation into which a discursive Asian vision has metamorphosed. In this regard, the regionalist rhetoric emanating from the Asian scholar–bureaucracy and their adherents in European, American and Australasian universities reflects an anxious need to sustain the regional fiction that guarantees official patronage as Asian governments and grant-disbursing agencies remain wedded to the vision (see Copeland 2000, p. 212). Consequently, predictive success is not the criterion by which the regionalist scholocracy necessarily judges itself. Whether East Asia ever attains the status of a fully integrated 'community' is almost beside the point. In the transformative discourse of constructivism one has a methodology designed to evade empirically evaluating assumptions. The conclusion we come to is that what has changed in the East Asian firmament is not the underlying dynamics of regional relations, but merely the discourse by which regional analysts have sought to maintain the faith in the transformation of the Asia–Pacific into a fashionably seductive, but ultimately delusional, East Asian community.

NOTES

1. EAEC was originally rendered by the Malaysians as the East Asian Economic Grouping (EACG).
2. Constructivist forms of approach were prominent in studies of what has become known as strategic culture that emerged in the late 1970s with works like Jack Snyder (1977), *The Soviet Strategic Culture: Implications for Limited Nuclear Options*, Santa Monica: RAND; and Colin Gray (1981), 'National style in strategy', *International Security*, 6 (2). This literature could itself trace its origins back to the early 1950s in works that tried to use 'culture' to dissect Soviet understandings of the world (see for example Mead, 1951; Bauer 1952, 1954; Haimson 1953, Tomasic 1953). In addition, such approaches can also be seen in the 'way of warfare' school of military history and strategy that have an even older lineage in the works of Liddell Hart (1935), Weigley (1973) and Fairbank (1974).
3. Even Wendt, it should be noted, is pre-dated in contemporary international relations by Nicholas G. Onuf (1989), *A World of Our Making: Rules and Rule in Social Theory and International Relations*, Berkeley: University of California Press.
4. Ultimately, pervading constructivism is the subjective idealism of Bishop Berkeley's *Principles of Human Knowledge* (1710). The idea that *esse est percipe* and that the world we perceive is a world of ideas has inspired writers from Dean Swift to Flann O'Brien and Borges. Only recently has it unconsciously appealed to political theorists of an activist hue (see John Gray, 1995, 'Notes toward a definition of the political thought of Tlon', in *Enlightenment's Wake*, London: Routledge) and now, limping along in political theory's wake, to those who purport to practise international relations theory.
5. One of the exemplars of this line of thought was the French political theorist and civil servant, Alexandre Kojève (see Lilla 2001, pp. 113–16).

6. Constructing and deconstructing regions: Australia's engagement with 'Asia'

In the last chapter we saw how constructivist commentators have consistently recast their view of events in the Asia–Pacific region in order to sustain a delusion. To a certain extent, this endeavour represented an abstruse scholastic exercise. Yet, if we examine the case of Australian foreign relations between 1983 and 1996, we discover one of the few examples where a constructivist project, *avant la lettre*, was formally adopted as a foreign policy goal. For, unlike the conduct of foreign policy elsewhere in East Asia, where an active pursuit of the national interest belied their pan-Asian rhetoric, the prospect of imminent regionalism so captivated an Australian *classa politica* that it conceived Australia's destiny as intimately tied to its integration into an evolving East Asian monolith.

The felt need to integrate a culturally European state into a geographically Asian continent grew out of the more unstable consequences of the globalization of the world economy, in particular its capacity to exacerbate concerns about national identity and project them into the international arena. In the course of the 1980s, what former Prime Minister Paul Keating termed the 'new regionalism' absorbed both the policy elite in Canberra and their journalistic and academic adherents and became an imperative of foreign policy (Keating 1996). According to this line of thinking, the closing of the Cold War in Asia afforded the potential for a new multilateral order in which Australia, as a middle power, could play an enhanced role. For the Labor governments that ruled Australia successively between 1983 and 1996, this constituted a unique window of opportunity. During the 1990s, this generated in both academic, media and political discourse a preoccupation with the national character and the constitutional order that would befit Australian enmeshment with Asia. To accomplish this objective, the Labor administrations set an explicit course in the 1990s to re-orient the Australian psyche towards its ineluctable Asian absorption.

The Australian case is therefore compelling, not least because the evolution of this engagement policy raises some perplexing questions. Why did a policy elite assume that the process of globalization would ineluctably promote the formation of regional blocs? Why did policy makers become so preoccupied with this idea that they felt it necessitated the reconstruction of the national identity? And what consequences for Australia followed from the shattering of the new regionalism by the Asian economic crisis of 1997 and the serious ethnic and religious instability in Southeast Asia, further exacerbated by transnational terrorism post-2001, that followed in its wake? The attempt to re-define Australia as an Asian state is also instructive from the perspective of international relations theory, given that when policy makers launched this project they did not have access to a theory of constructivism. In other words, the attempt to re-position Australia within Asia pre-dated the constructivist approach to international relations. In a paradoxical conjunction of influences, the Australian policy of engagement reached its apogee at exactly the time when the constructivist theory, that fed off foreign relations practice, asserted its presence in the groves of academe in the mid-1990s, and yet just before the policy itself was to receive a brutal mugging by economic and political reality.

What the Australian case demonstrates is the distorting impact that ideological enthusiasm can have on foreign policy practice and, more particularly, the power of a delusion once it attains the status of official orthodoxy. Although the advent to power in 1996 of a conservative administration under Prime Minister John Howard saw a gradual retreat from the more fundamentalist tenets of engagement, the orthodoxy has proved hard to dislodge, its believers clinging tenaciously to its nostrums, despite their demonstrable refutation by events after 1997. The new era in foreign relations ushered in after 11 September 2001 revealed the more egregious effects of this legacy, exposing a culture of denial about the state of insecurity in Southeast Asia. The delusional nature of the engagement orthodoxy meant that it had lost the ability to test its ruling assumptions. The result was a failure to confront the truth that dare not speak its name: that there had never existed a monolithic Asia in which to integrate a putatively multicultural, post-modern Australian republic.

A DELUSION IS BORN

To investigate how the ideology of engagement with a significantly amorphous Asian entity took hold of the Australian consciousness requires us to recount, not only how official policy developed during the 1980s and 1990s, but also how it demanded a Manichean interpretation of the evolution of Australia's foreign relations post-1942. The policy elite that felt it necessary to fashion an Australian identity commensurate with integration into an Asian region sought to build that identity upon a re-fashioned past. The reconstruction of the national identity that came to dominate public discourse in the 1980s and 1990s required a radical revision of recent Australian history, that traced 'the "modern" era of Australian politics' (Warhurst 1992, p. 502) to 1972 and the arrival in Canberra of Australian Labor Party (ALP) Prime Minister Edward Gough Whitlam, after 23 years of unbroken rule by the conservative Liberal–Country coalition.

From the mid-1980s onwards, reaching its zenith during the premiership of Paul Keating (1993–96), a media, academic and policy elite attempted to 'reconstruct' Australia's past in a way that providentially anticipated its deeper integration in Asia in the forthcoming 'Pacific Century'. A political consensus gradually emerged that held that it was only with the dawn of the Whitlam era that Australia embarked on a truly independent course in world affairs. It contended that, in foreign policy, in trade and defence, the Whitlam 'watershed' severed outmoded ties to Britain and the United States, setting the nation on a liberating voyage of self-discovery and national destiny. This view, that by the late 1980s assumed the status of a consensus, explicitly sought to contrast the mould-breaking Whitlam era with the conservative Australian self-understanding that preceded it and which required, if not complete excision, at least radical surgery.

Prior to 1972, the prevailing international image of Australia, Gareth Evans and Bruce Grant contended, was of a 'brash' yet 'anxious' Anglo-Celtic people deposited on an isolated continent by a feckless British Empire (Evans and Grant 1995, p. 15). Alienated by distance from Europe, Australia nevertheless relied on foreign guardians throughout its short history. First Britain, and then, as Empire receded, the US protected the immature Australian entity from external threats. In effect, so it was argued, outsiders in the shape of Britain and the US framed Australia's self-image. Consequently, Australia possessed neither an authentic foreign policy nor a national interest and, to the extent that it had a national identity at all, it was a mixture of post-colonial servility and resentment.

An anti-imperialism that rejected traditional attachments to the mother-country, the monarchy and the Anglo-Saxon world in general constituted a significant theme in Australian social commentary after federation. After World War II, this theme became increasingly prominent. Poets like A.D. Hope lamented 'a vast parasite robber state/where second hand Europeans pullulate/timidly on the edge of alien shores' (Hope 1972, p. 13). Others like A.A. Phillips articulated the central motif of elite *ressentiment*, namely, the 'cultural cringe' towards everything English that haunted the Australian intelligentsia like a 'minatory ghost' (Phillips 1958, p. 94). Even conservative commentators like Geoffrey Blainey assumed by the 1960s that the 'tyranny of distance' separating Australia from the United Kingdom left 'the Antipodes . . . drifting, though where they were drifting no-one knew' (Blainey 1968, p.

335). More worryingly still, 'pioneering Republicans' (O'Brien 2000) like Donald Horne considered Australia a weak and exposed 'orphan of the Pacific' (Horne 1972, p. 229).

To end its orphan status, an established, but dependent, identity would have to be replaced by one ideologically tailored to the demands of what Whitlam and his successors in the ALP deemed necessary for a mature Australia to enmesh itself in the wider Asian community. In order to pursue this felt need, the emerging elite view sought to caricature the recent Australian past, particularly the period dominated by the premiership of Sir Robert Menzies and his Liberal successors between 1949 and 1972, as a servile monoculture. The project of re-defining Australian identity therefore combined an endorsement of the *soi disant* Whitlamite revolution in foreign affairs after 1972 and the deliberate distortion of the achievements of the Menzies era.

Thus this chapter will first delineate this exercise in identity reconstruction, which grew out of the revisionist critique of Australian foreign policy priorities during the 1960s. We will then show how official policy internalized this critique and evaluate its impact on Australian efforts to negotiate a new and emancipated relationship with East Asia generally and ASEAN in particular. The analysis will further demonstrate that this policy was flawed from the outset because the re-description of the pre-1972 era, and the planned future it required, both distorted the historical record and failed as a strategy. In effect, this policy was built on a delusion that, *pace* Phillips, would become the true minatory ghost that haunted a policy and academic elite.

PRE-MODERN AUSTRALIA: A NATION WITHOUT A NATIONAL IDENTITY?

So what exactly was the nature of Australian identity in the Menzies era? Less than 50 years ago there was no question that the core values of Australian self-belief stemmed from the connection with Britain and the imperial tradition. 'The British tie,' according to the Commonwealth journal, *The Round Table*, 'was and is very precious to Australians. They are loyal to the throne: they are conscious of the British origins of their parliamentary and legal systems . . . they share in the cultural traditions of the British Isles' ('An Australian view', 1960, p. 348). Although overt reliance on the United Kingdom as the ultimate guarantor of the country's security had diminished after 1942, this role had been transferred to the United States (Brown 1977, p. 27). Australia naturally embraced the ANZUS (Australia, New Zealand, United States) Treaty in 1951 and later in 1954 the South-East Asian Treaty Organization (SEATO). In the early years of the Cold War, Australia was a committed and optimistic member of an Anglo-Saxon liberal–democratic world (see Huntingdon 1996, chap. 7).

Australia's foreign and defence policies reflected this sense of purpose, being robustly Anglocentric and anti-communist: a guardian of 'Western ideals in South East Asia' ('On being Australian in 1959', 1959, p. 26). The premise of Australia's alliance system was that, by supporting British and American attempts to stabilize Asia and fend off communist challenges in the region, Australia would enhance its own security. It was this rationale that led Australia to contribute directly to the military effort in Korea and to assist Britain in the Malayan Emergency between 1948 and 1960 and the *Konfrontasi* with Indonesia between 1963 and 1966. The definitive expression of this policy was Australia's decision, in April 1965, to contribute military forces in support of the American military intervention in South Vietnam. Involvement in Vietnam ensured a continuing US commitment to the security of the region and strengthened the probability that the Americans would come to Australia's aid if it should be threatened directly (*Australian*, 5 April 1968; Gelber 1968, pp. 25–34).

By the late 1960s, however, the stagnation of the American campaign in South Vietnam made the precise security benefits that Australia was meant to derive from its alliance increasingly questionable. Analysts began to wonder whether 'adherence to some of the more rigid and militant aspects of American foreign policy' was really in Australia's wider interests (Millar 1968, p. 124; see also Miller 1969, pp. 77–80). Moreover, President Richard Nixon's enunciation of the Guam Doctrine in 1969, which required states in the region to provide for their own protection, appeared to undermine the basis of Australia's security policy in the post-World War II era (Miller 1970, p. 297).

Growing concern over the wisdom of Australia's involvement in Indochina eventually broadened into a full-scale revisionist critique of Australia's traditional foreign relations (Albinski 1970, pp. 207–9). The dénouement in Vietnam afforded the opportunity for an increasingly prominent group of politicians, journalists and academics, generally linked to the left of the ALP, to articulate a radical alternative for Australia. Rejecting the Anglocentric terms of their immediate post-war Asian engagement, critics argued for a more regionally sensitized and nationalistic role for Australia in world affairs. The focus of revisionist ire, inevitably, was the legacy of Sir Robert Menzies, whose long tenure as Prime Minister from 1949 to 1966 dominated the Australian political landscape.

Revisionist critics maintained that the determined anti-communist stance adopted by Menzies had inhibited the expression of a coherent and distinctive set of national interests. As critics observed sourly, 'most Australians still adhere to some version or other' of the traditional 'creed', which demanded that 'we must be prepared to have a permanent protector, strong enough and willing to save us' (Chiddick and Teichmann 1977, p. 87). This 'dependency' on external guarantors was demeaning because it tended 'to make paternal-ists of those *above*', breeding 'arrogance, ignorance and superiority', and 'servility in those *below*' (Pettman 1983, p. 2). Crystalizing this view, Donald Horne considered Menzies the chief architect of this obsequiousness in foreign affairs. In *The Lucky Country*, Horne mocked Menzies for locking Australia into 'obsolete and irrelevant ideologies and values' (Horne 1964, p. 211).

Domestically, the impact of this external dependency was to sustain a reac-tionary political culture that was racist in its treatment of non-British immi-grants and aboriginal peoples. However, the unspoken fear reinforcing this claustrophobic Anglophilia was of 'Asia'. This geographical fact prompted an obsessive 'need to keep Asians out and to strengthen . . . [Australia's] own ties with white peoples' (Miller 1970, p. 279). Thus the Menzies era had created a land that was backward-looking and reluctant to change. Menzies' heirs as leaders of the Liberal–Country coalition, Harold Holt, John Gorton and William McMahon, though seen as less in thrall to imperial nostalgia (Cairns 1972, p. 124), nevertheless retained Menzies' policies, which continued to lend Australia the 'period-piece aroma of his own now-bygone regime' (Burns 1970, p. 151).

Conservative Anglocentrism, critics asserted, fatally undermined Australian foreign policy because 'throughout the whole time span our under-lying strategy was preservation of the status quo' (Chiddick and Teichmann 1977, p. 87). For Bruce Grant, writing in 1968, 'by constantly seeing ourselves in the mirrors of London or Washington, we have come to believe that our contribution to world affairs must be insignificant' (Grant 1968, p. 264). Worse still, the practical result was disaster, placing Australia on the losing side of nearly every external engagement from the Suez crisis to Vietnam (Foster 1983, pp. 480–81).

In other words, Australian foreign policy was not just based on a faulty set of assumptions, it actually reflected a society that was politically and morally retarded. In Grant's view, the impoverishment of the national self-image stemmed from the failure to attain 'cultural identity'. Australia was prevented from playing a mature role in international affairs because 'we do not know what our national interests are' (Grant 1972, p. 2). According to Chiddick and Teichmann, the problem was 'that we do not really feel ourself [*sic*] a nation, nor do we possess a distinct culture. Even our history might be regarded as a derivation or a continuation, in a foreign place, of someone else's history' (Chiddick and Teichmann 1977, p. 85). The revisionist mission, therefore, sought to end this adherence to a failed cultural legacy that had engendered a false consciousness and thwarted the emergence of a modern nation.

RECONSTRUCTING THE NATION

The solution to the problem of identity was for Australia to 'acquire some kind of organic separateness' from its English-speaking allies (Chiddick and Teichmann 1977, p. 85). Australia in the 1970s had to transform the way Australians thought about themselves. This, in turn, would lead to a natural re-ordering of foreign and defence priorities. An independent identity would enable Australians to liberate their foreign policy to 'take a more initiating and creative role in defending and promoting the national interest' (Grant 1970, p. 61).

To win over a sceptical population, however, a new ideology needed not merely to expose outmoded practices, but also to offer a plan rational model that enlightened the Australian people to their destiny. In other words, revisionism required a vision and a prophet. Having come to power after the *longue durée* of the Menzies period, Gough Whitlam, Labor Prime Minister from 1972 to 1975, considered himself peculiarly suited to this task. His government claimed a mandate to address a range of problems, which pro-government supporters argued had 'lain dormant or been suppressed under a policy of secrecy and inadequate development of information resources, research and public discussion' (Ironmonger 1973, p. 225). The desire for a complete overhaul of the Australian body politic applied as much to domestic as to foreign policy: 'Australia has to do a great deal of catching up. The Liberal–Country administration has thus, through its inactivity . . . provided the new Labor Government with an extensive policy vacuum to fill' (Ironmonger 1973, p. 255).

To fill the vacuum, Whitlam sought to corporatize further Australian industry and sever cultural links with Britain. The reform programme abolished the honours system for federal government representatives, reduced the right of appeal to the House of Lords in Britain, and changed the national anthem from 'God Save the Queen' to 'Advance Australia Fair' (see MacLeod 1974, p. 291). The government ended automatic rights of entry for British subjects and eased immigration procedures to permit a broader settler intake from non-European countries (see Price 1975, pp. 369–77). This, it was asserted, represented the 'final destruction of White Australia' (ibid., p. 377), and removed the stain of 'racial discrimination from immigration procedures' (Evans and Grant 1995, p. 27). As result, the number of migrants from Northeast and Southeast Asia increased to the point that, by 1980, Asians numbered 30 per cent of new arrivals (*Yearbook Australia 1982*, 1982, p. 111).

The desire to transform Australia's identity was most apparent in foreign policy. The image of a progressive and uniquely Australian ideology required self-reliance in defence, greater independence from the United States, and eventual cultural, economic and political integration with the developing states of the Asia–Pacific. The new government immediately renounced the policy of 'forward defence' that had been the cornerstone of Australian security for the previous 30 years. Whitlamite revisionism now asserted that this posture was both flawed and at odds with the conciliatory, internationalist image that the government wished to cultivate. In particular, Australia's vexed involvement in Vietnam was seen as 'the most dramatic example of how we were drawn into a situation precisely defined by our policy of "forward defence" ' (Grant 1972, p. xiv). Consequently, Australia withdrew its forces from South Vietnam and ended assistance to the regimes in Saigon and Phnom Penh. By endorsing a new accommodation with neighbouring states it was felt that Australia could 'shrug off some of its old attitudes of dependence and find a unique place for itself' in a region previously considered 'alien and even hostile' (ibid.).

The Whitlam government initiated its new look foreign policy by publicly questioning the centrality of Australia's alliance with America and excoriating continuing US involvement in Indochina (see O'Neill 1973, p. 31; 'Bash a yank a day', 1973). As a reformed international citizen, Australia took a more active interest in the United Nations, siding regularly with the Non-Aligned Movement, taking positions against apartheid in South Africa and white rule in Rhodesia. Whitlam pursued a policy of demilitarization in the Indian Ocean and the South Pacific by ratifying the Nuclear Non-Proliferation Treaty and opposing French atomic testing in the region.

Principally, this new and more accommodating attitude would allow Australia to re-negotiate its relationships with its Asian neighbours and, in particular, this entailed reversing a quarter-century of overt anti-Communism and conciliating the more authoritarian members in the international system in general. Australia formally recognized North Vietnam, North Korea and the People's Republic of China (de-recognizing Taiwan in the process). The new policy also involved official toleration of North Vietnam's invasion of South Vietnam in 1974 and, most controversially, diplomatic complicity in the Indonesian invasion of East Timor in 1975 (Way 2000, pp. 337, 486). Just for good measure, in August 1974, Australia recognized the *de jure* incorporation of the Baltic states into the Soviet Union, the only democratic western state ever to do so (O'Brien 1980, p. 15).

Underlying this radical foreign policy agenda was the implicit theme of re-casting Australian identity more broadly. Revisionist sympathizers justified these often contentious foreign policy shifts on the grounds that they drama-tized 'the need for new departures' that would 'assist Australians in the process of self-identification as a people belonging to a young, vigorous and wealthy country with a big future ahead of it' (MacLeod 1974, p. 291) This was a premise that provided an intriguing precursor to the constructivist debates that were to find an explicit echo in Australian foreign policy 20 years later. Certainly, after one year in office, Whitlam's judgment on his own record was clear:

> We are no long a cipher or a satellite in world affairs. We are no longer stamped with the taint of racism. We are no longer a colonial power. We are no longer out of step with the world's progressive and enlightened movements towards freedom, disarmament and co-operation. We are no longer enthralled to bogies and obsessions in our relations with China or the great powers. (Whitlam 1973b)

THE MYTH OF WHITLAM'S FOREIGN POLICY

From the late 1970s onward, Whitlamite self-congratulation elevated itself into an officially promoted orthodoxy. Whitlam was deemed to have single-handedly shifted the focus of Australian foreign policy away from its 'hitherto strict ideological–military orientation' (Nathan 1991, p. 336) to 'one based on more enduring ties such as trade, aid programmes, regional cooperation, and the development of a network of cultural contacts and agreements' (Theervit 1979, p. 6). In 1979, Alan Renouf, Head of the Department of Foreign Affairs, declared that Whitlam had been a 'good advertisement for Australia' because he had recognized that 'Australia should not have sought so diligently to tie herself to the United States' (Renouf 1979, pp. 25, 531). A year later, James Walter, in his largely uncritical biography, *The Leader*, claimed that Whitlam had 'prompted recognition that our traditional ties back to the western hemisphere countries no longer could be counted as more important than relations with the countries around us' (Walter 1980, p. 122).

By the 1990s, this adulation found its way into international relations textbooks, which held that, after 23 years of reactionary conservatism, 'the Whitlam period in office provided a watershed' (Evans and Grant 1995, p. 26) that 'divided the prolonged obeisance of Menzies to the idea of imperial unity . . . from the emergence of the kind of Australian foreign policy that we now take for granted' (ibid.). Whitlam's period in office, from 1972 to 1975, therefore, represented the symbolic beginning of a new Australian independence and maturity in world affairs. Policy analysts inured to the revisionist orthodoxy looked back nostalgically on the early 1970s, when the 'Whitlam Government dramatically revitalized the Australian political landscape, both externally and internally' by shattering 'the pattern of Australian politics and Cold War thinking about foreign policy in Australia' (ibid., p. 26–7).

The difficulty is that such acclaim fails to stand up to serious historical scrutiny. For the idea that the mould of Australian foreign policy was broken

during the Whitlam watershed and that external relations became more sensitized to regional sensibilities is deeply flawed.

Australia's military involvement in Vietnam was, undoubtedly, a low point
in the country's foreign policy. In hindsight, it is easy to see the defects in
containment thinking with its monolithic view of Communism. But, equally,
it is also easy to use the example of Vietnam to portray Menzies and his
successors as out of step with the times and promote a simplistic view of that
period. The whole basis of Australia's external relations, which Menzies
understood very well, was that the country's core democratic value system
conferred responsibilities on the country to make hard choices and take action
to support allies and, thereby, uphold the national interest. This was Cold War
reality. States were compelled to take sides. Non-alignment for Australia was
never a credible option. This understanding, working logically from first principles about where the national interested resided in the Cold War, dictated the
policy of forward defence. As Shane Paltridge, the Defence Minister, stated:
'by virtue [of Australia's] location on the periphery of Asia, [we] can make a
unique contribution to the policies aimed at the security and stability of South-
East Asia' (Paltridge 1966, p. 23).

The Australian government throughout the 1950s and 1960s, thus,
perceived regional responsibility in terms of seeking 'the support of at least
the United States and the United Kingdom for promoting cooperative arrangements with South-East Asian countries for collective security purposes in this
area and for the defence and security of Australia' (ibid., p. 23). The integral
part Australian forces played in stabilizing Southeast Asia and the rest of Asia
with the commitment of forces to South Korea (1950–53), during the Malayan
Emergency, and the period of Confrontation with Indonesia, established a
solid record of achievement for forward defence. Many of Australia's Asian
neighbours, notably Malaysia and Singapore, endorsed Australian intervention, often requesting the retention of an Australian military presence in their
countries. Even Australia's intervention in Vietnam was applauded by all the
non-communist states in Southeast Asia.

Yet revisionists regarded 'forward defence' as the most pernicious aspect of
the national torpor. For Whitlam, the Cold War stance adopted by Menzies
concealed implicit racism. The premise of forward defence, Whitlam
complained, was that 'its focus was fear of communism; and because these
fears in turn focused so sharply on China and the Chinese version of communism, they were rooted in racism. Racism was the common denominator of a
whole range of foreign policies of the Menzies era' (Whitlam 1985, p. 26).
From such tainted well-springs, foreign policy failure resulted, permitting
those like Bruce Grant to pronounce that the damaging 'commitment to
Vietnam has been the most dramatic example of how we were drawn into a
situation precisely defined by our policy of "forward defence" ' (Grant 1972,

p. 45). This, in the view of those like Labor politician J.F. Cairns, constituted irrefutable proof that Australia had incurred the animosity of Asian peoples (cited in Hughes 1967, p. 181).

However, the belief that Australia's foreign and defence policy during the Menzies period antagonized Asian countries is superficial. It underestimates Cold War imperatives by negating the communist threat to Southeast Asia; it discounts those non-communist states in Asia that welcomed Australia's military involvement in the region; and it selectively focuses on the abortive military commitment in Vietnam to suggest the failure of forward defence. That Australia earned the displeasure of China and North Vietnam as a result of its forward defence posture, according to Whitlam, condemned the strategy as racist. Yet, if one accepts this view, the preservation of good relations with every country in Asia represents the only objective of Australian diplomacy.

Thus, it was by distorting Cold War reality that Whitlamite foreign policy defined itself. For Whitlam, his arrival in office terminated the 'xenophobic' policy of forward defence (Whitlam 1985, p. 153). Undoubtedly the growing complexity of regional geo-politics following Nixon's visit to China in 1972 and the disillusion that followed the American withdrawal from Vietnam facilitated both Whitlam's denunciation of forward defence and the articulation of his vision for Australia in the world. Even so, Whitlam's 'watershed' left a peculiar political legacy of ambiguous internationalism.

Firstly, the metaphor of a 'watershed' obscures the extent to which Australian foreign relations had changed well before 1972. By the late 1960s, it was already apparent that economic links to the UK were no longer crucial to Australian growth ('Australia and EEC', 1961, pp. 43–6). The prospective loss of trading preferences due to Britain's entry into the European Economic Community (EEC) helped widen Australia's economic horizons, raising awareness for export diversification and improved efficiency (ibid., pp. 47–9; Bruns 1971, pp. 527–31). In particular, Menzies recognized the growing importance of Northeast Asian markets for Australia's economic development (see Prest and Perkins 1962, p. 24). By the late 1950s, Japan had become Australia's second-largest trading partner, a fact given formal recognition by the Japan–Australia Trade Agreement of 1957 and by a second treaty in 1971 ('Britain in Europe', 1962). The need to adapt to new economic realities was already reflected in amendments to immigration policy. Nearly all the discriminatory elements in Australian immigration procedures had been removed before Whitlam came to power.

Just as significantly, well before the end of the 1960s, the Liberal government saw that Australia would have to recast its foreign policy in the light of changing British and American commitments to Southeast Asia ('Asia without British power', 1968, p. 352). Foreign Minister Paul Hasluck acknowledged in

August 1967 that 'Up to date our foreign policy has been based on certain assumptions regarding British foreign policy. To the extent to which British foreign policy changes, so we will have to change the assumptions on which our own policy rests' (Hasluck 1967). Indeed, the 1972 Australian Defence Review White Paper explicitly announced a move towards greater self-defence reliance (Department of Defence 1972, p. 27).

Secondly, in contrast to the widely held view that the Whitlam administration ended military involvement in South Vietnam, the withdrawal of forces had actually begun on 22 April 1970 and was largely completed before Whitlam took office (O'Neill 1973, p. 30). Moreover, while Whitlam formally recognized the People's Republic of China (PRC), the previous government had systematically moderated its position towards the PRC, making gradual moves toward official recognition (see Mediansky and Palfreeman 1988, pp. 24–5; Greenwood and Harpur 1963, p. 96). In this context, as Hedley Bull observed in 1975, Whitlam's government had 'accelerated these changes and dramatized them', thereby giving the appearance of making a radical break with the past simply because it had been out of office for two decades and was 'less encumbered by its own past policies' (Bull 1975, p. 31).

Whitlam's foreign policy, Bull continued, tended to mistake 'posture to the neglect of substance' (ibid., p. 34). Whitlam was preoccupied with a progressive image of Australia rather than fashioning policies that were 'prudent and morally sound' (ibid.). Indeed, if one looks past the idea of the watershed, the record of Whitlamite foreign policy reveals a remarkable degree of failure. The truth is that Whitlam's supposedly more independent stance masked an incoherent policy that was ultimately detrimental to Australian interests.

One of the first examples of inconsistency was that, on assuming office, Whitlam and his cabinet denounced the resumption of the US bombing of North Vietnam and publicly downgraded ANZUS. Whitlam belatedly, however, recognized the value of the alliance with the US and subsequently devoted months of diplomacy to assuaging American irritation (MacLeod 1974, pp. 289–93). Similar contradictions appeared in the Whitlam government's anti-nuclear stance. Australia ratified the Non-Proliferation Treaty in January 1973 and strongly criticized French nuclear testing in the Pacific. The government also promoted schemes for regional demilitarization and protested at the Anglo-American plan to build a base on the Indian Ocean Island of Diego Garcia. Yet, at the same time, the government overlooked Chinese atmospheric nuclear tests in June 1973 and continued to permit the presence of American military installations on Australian soil, which included communications with the nuclear-armed US Navy submarine fleet.

More problematically from the perspective of engagement, far from re-orienting Australia towards Asia, Whitlam's policy betrayed an immaturity that often incurred the mistrust and, sometimes, outright contempt of Asian allies. For example, despite declaring that Australia had a 'vital interest in Japanese policies and the way in which Japan conducts its foreign affairs' (Whitlam 1973b, p. 8), Whitlam proceeded to treat Japan, by now Australia's biggest trading partner, with indifference and suspicion (MacLeod 1974, p. 294). The main effect of this was to limit foreign investment and damage prospects for economic growth (Bruns 1971, pp. 397–401).

Most notably, inconsistency characterized Whitlam's dealings with Southeast Asia. While asserting that the region should be treated with 'patience, tact and diplomacy' (Whitlam 1985, p. 6), Whitlam nevertheless managed to alienate most countries in Southeast Asia. Singapore's Lee Kuan Yew considered Whitlam a 'sham white Afro-Asian' whose 'new look foreign policy' Lee considered entirely bogus ('Thoughts of chairman Lee', 2000). Lee regarded Whitlam's idealistic view of regional security conditions with suspicion (Harries 1975, p. 1091). As a long-time admirer of Mao's 'scholarly refinement' (Whitlam 1985, p. 59), Whitlam's evident enthusiasm for China invariably alarmed Australia's near neighbours, most clearly Indonesia – the state which Whitlam had done most to conciliate (Whitlam 1985; MacLeod 1974, p. 292). Consequently, Southeast Asian states summarily rejected Whitlam's proposal for a regional cooperative bloc excluding the United States and the Soviet Union, recognizing that it would be Chinese influence that would predominate in such a forum. Elsewhere, Whitlam's overtures to the New Order regime in Jakarta served only to undermine Australia's previously excellent relations with Malaysia.

A curious feature of Whitlam's foreign policy, which became ingrained in post-Whitlamite engagement practice, was a propensity to be both internationalist and defensively nationalist at the same time. Britain's entry into the EEC in 1972 enabled Whitlam and successive Labor governments to promote a mood of self-absorbed republicanism expressed after 1983 in assaults upon the monarchy. Ultimately, however, rhetoric rather than substantive change characterized Whitlam's foreign policy revisionism. The basic constituents of Australia's external policies remained intact: the American alliance continued to be central to Australian security; Japan, the United States and western Europe remained Australia's main trading partners; and its Asian neighbours still perceived Australia as part of the western world (Harries 1975, p. 1096; MacLeod 1974, p. 292).

THE GOSPEL ACCORDING TO GOUGH

In retrospect, the image of the Whitlam revolution lay not in any actual achievement in foreign relations, but in its intimation of a new regional and international identity for Australia. In fact, Whitlam's status as an agent of progress had to do, not with his foreign policy, but with the manner of his removal from office by the Governor-General, John Kerr in 1975, and the importance this event assumed in socialist–republican iconography. His sacking defined the fault line in Australian politics for the next generation, permitting the image of Whitlam's rule as mould-breaking to flourish. Whitlam's watershed in the direction of Australian foreign policy is thus a myth manufactured in hindsight by those with a political interest in portraying his demise as a constitutional crisis fought between progressive modernizers and conservative reactionaries. What counted was not the substance of Whitlam's foreign policy but the representation of his political legacy.

Consequently, Bob Hawke's government (1983–91) explicitly articulated the doctrine of Asian 'enmeshment', especially in the economic field. In this spirit, the Department of Foreign Affairs and Trade (DFAT) sponsored the Asia–Pacific Economic Cooperation forum to facilitate regional trade (McDougall 1989, p. 170; Cotton 1990, pp. 171–2). It was Paul Keating, however, who assumed Whitlam's mantle as a radical mould-breaker in foreign affairs, seeking to integrate Australia in the then booming Southeast Asia. For Keating, Whitlam 'had given new hope and international standing to Australia's foreign policy' (Keating 2000, p. 10). During the 1990s, DFAT placed the Asia–Pacific at the heart of its policy planning. Foreign Minister Gareth Evans developed a notable taste for the non-binding consensual practices of the 'ASEAN way', which, he maintained, provided a refreshing contrast to the formalized, regulatory approaches to diplomacy (see Cheeseman 1996, pp. 79–81).

ALP foreign policy between 1986 and 1996 emphasized multilateralism achieved through the economic incentive of Asian engagement. In Keating's assessment engagement possessed three key ingredients. First was the promotion of a zone of Asia–Pacific economic cooperation premised on the informal spirit of Asian cooperation manifest in the Bogor Declaration of 1994. Second, it was held that this approach would draw potentially recalcitrant regimes, notably China, into rational discourse through the benefits of trade. Echoing Whitlam, Keating maintained that China needed understanding from the west. It had to be 'encouraged' rather than 'contained' (Keating 2000, pp. 59–60). Finally, the cornerstone of Keating's foreign policy was the relationship with Indonesia. In Keating's opinion he succeeded in forging a 'warm and deep' commitment with Australia's 'nearest and largest neighbour' (ibid., p. 126).

Keating's diplomacy towards Indonesia reflected a close personal regard for President Suharto, the sultanist ruler of the vast archipelago. This warm relationship resulted in the Timor Gap Zone Cooperation Treaty of 1989 and reached a pinnacle with a secretly negotiated security agreement in 1995. Keating's official biographer, John Edwards, claimed that this represented one of his 'best moves . . . cutting through timid conventional concerns [like the genocidal incorporation of East Timor] to change the way in which Indonesia and Australia thought about each other' (Edwards 1996, p. 535). This curious policy of building close ties with Indonesia while at the same time promoting regional integration and dialogue with ASEAN only served to confuse ASEAN leaders who considered Australia's cultivation of Suharto and dismissal of Malaysia's Mahathir as 'recalcitrant' at the Seattle meeting of APEC in 1992 indicative of a failure to grasp the etiquette of good regional citizenship. Despite numerous sycophantic forays by Keating and Evans, ASEAN steadfastly refused to welcome Australia to its meetings and summits as a dialogue partner. This rebuff constituted a source of anxiety to the Australian *commentariat*. Nevertheless, it earned Keating's Asia policy the stamp of approval of Whitlam, who claimed that Keating had been 'the only Prime Minister other than I to have shown a consistent and constructive attitude [to Asia]' (Whitlam 1997, p. 49).

The trouble for Keating's promulgation of the Whitlam orthodoxy was that it appealed only to a narrow, though influential, political, academic and media elite inured to the prospect of re-orienting Australia's foreign policy towards a seemingly monolithic Asia. The vast majority of the Australian public, conversely, remained indifferent to the Asian destiny prepared for them. To convert a sceptical public therefore required the academic and media construction – and promotion – of a benign, prosperous and coherent Asian region with which Australia had no alternative but integration. More specifically it required changing the public perception of Indonesia and Southeast Asia more generally (see Taylor 1999).

Having established this construct of a stable and prosperous region to the North, it obviously constituted Australia's logical destiny to enmesh itself in a web of ASEAN-determined relationships. As ASEAN expanded to embrace Vietnam, Cambodia, Laos and Myanmar after 1992, the Australian media promoted this strategy relentlessly. By 1995, the foreign editor of the *Australian*, Greg Sheridan, maintained portentously that 'A revolution is sweeping across Australia. The nation is changing fundamentally and irreversibly . . . This revolution is occurring within the Australian psyche and also within Australia's material circumstances . . . it is the transformation of the spirit and body. I speak of the Asianization of Australian life' (Sheridan 1995, p. 3).

To secure the revolution, moreover, required a politicization of both Australian academe and senior policy advisors working in the federal bureaucracy. According to the *Australian Financial Review*, with the appointment of Ashton Calvert, a Keating admirer, as Secretary of DFAT the

Asian enmeshment strategy exerted a 'total stranglehold in the corridors of power' (*Australian Financial Review*, 16–17 October 1999). The government disbursed generous grants in Asia–Pacific studies intended to lend academic credibility to this political agenda. The former diplomat and chairman of the Asian Studies Council, Stephen FitzGerald, demonstrated its ideological character, declaring that Asia should become a 'commitment of the heart and mind', requiring an 'Asia-literate', 'honey-coloured' society because 'the whole fabric of Australia's external connections had shifted' (FitzGerald 1997, pp. 62–4). This scholar-bureaucratic and media *commentariat* became so convinced of this prospect that it mistook its own preferences for objectivity and thus lost the capacity to question its underlying assumptions. It became, instead, an article of faith.

The general election of March 1996, however, showed amongst other things the inability of this elite ideology to capture the hearts and minds of the Australian masses, who rejected Keating's grand vision in favour of the unprepossessing pragmatism of John Howard, the conservative leader of the Liberal party. Of course, this need only have been a temporary setback on the road to a new regional order, but, in mid-1997, the Asian economic miracle that was supposed to constitute the material base for Asianization proved to be no such thing, thereby exposing the fallacy at the heart of the engagement orthodoxy.

The regional financial crisis and its political consequences, especially the turmoil it created in Indonesia, thus removed the props that sustained the policy of Asian enmeshment. Australia escaped the crisis precisely because it was not closely integrated into a regional trading system premised upon export-oriented growth. Australian business had largely ignored the government's exhortations about its Asian destiny. Australian direct investment in the East Asian region never rose beyond 6 per cent of the accumulated stock of overseas investment. Even in 1996, at the height of the 'Asian miracle', Britain, the US, Japan and Germany remained the major foreign investors in Australia. This situation had not changed significantly over the previous three decades (*Australian*, 27–8 January 1996).

Above all, the fallout from the Asian economic meltdown exposed the delusions that had since 1972 informed an evolving foreign policy orthodoxy. For, problematically, the revisionist orthodoxy was built upon a *non sequitur*, namely, that a nation cannot 'possess a distinct culture' if it is 'regarded as a derivation' (Chiddick and Teichmann 1977, p. 85). Yet all nations are ultimately derivative of something. In Australia's case this derivation is clearly European and Anglo-Celtic. As A.W. Martin observed: 'the hackneyed allegation that Menzies "grovelled" to the British and to the monarchy is shallow and anachronistic in the extreme. He had a reasoned understanding of what he and the majority of an almost exclusively Anglo-community instinctively felt:

that they were British' (Martin 1993, p. 429). Of course, times and the population mix have changed since the 1950s. But this does not mean that national self-understandings can be abandoned and replaced by an identity tailored to an elite's regional aspirations. In their eagerness to transcend an apparently irrelevant Anglo-centric identity the leading exponents of 'new regionalism' contrived an incoherent ideology appropriate for what they mistakenly assumed would be the new multilateral order of the 'Pacific Century' (see Bell 1996, pp. 3–9).

DENIAL'S LEGACY

In security terms the collapse of the regional economy revealed the ultimate shallowness of the revisionist construct. The dissolution of the Suharto regime in Jakarta, accompanied by widespread instability in the Indonesian archipelago, culminating in Australia leading a United Nations peacekeeping mission to restore order in East Timor in September 1999, disclosed the folly of seeking security within a supposedly monolithic Asia. In this respect, the idea of a Whitlamite revolution in foreign affairs and the abrogation of the forward defence concept after 1972 appear more like an aberration rather than a watershed. Nevertheless, despite the decline of the Whitlam orthodoxy after 1997, it left a legacy of denial about the character of Southeast Asian stability that proved even more deleterious to Australian interests.

Orthodoxies are not dispelled easily even in the face of evidence to the contrary. Instead, they mutate in an effort to sustain the orthodoxy's main precepts. The tenacity of the regionalist orthodoxy lies in a convergence of an economic policy with an intellectual passion. The coming 'Pacific Century', as we have shown, mesmerized economic and political commentators. The vision of regional integration also coincided with the dominance in the intellectual realm of constructivist theory that enthralled Australian departments of international relations in the course of the 1990s.

Constructivism, as an explanatory tool, emerged from various post-structural debates going back to the 1960s. It claimed to discern the privileged assumptions that upheld dominant, and therefore repressive, systems of power, and knowledge. Constructivists broadly agreed with the post-Whitlamite policy elite that identities were constructs that could be easily manipulated and replaced. In foreign policy terms, constructivist analysts contended that only a pathological fear of the non-western Other and a preoccupation with a narrowly defined national interest prevented Australia's seamless integration with the wider region. Australian constructivism, therefore, maintained that covert or overt racial prejudice underpinned foreign policy and consequently 'perceived Australia as being under constant threat from Asia' (Campbell

1989, p. 26). According to David Campbell: 'Explicit fears of foreign invasion were constructed on these racist fears' (ibid.). Nebulous fears, it was asserted, buttressed the sense of threat to white Australian identity, thus fuelling resistance to non-white immigration and maintaining a generalized aversion to ideas of multiculturalism (ibid., pp. 27–30).

More precisely, fear permeated Australian attitudes towards Indonesia, which were bound up with 'phobic narratives' (Morris 1998, p. 246) that sustained images of threat from an 'arc of instability' to the north (see, for example, Dibb 2001, p. 830). Such images, it was asserted, tacitly encouraged the view that Australia was always in imminent danger of being overwhelmed by its northern neighbours (Philpott 2001, pp. 371–88; see also Broinowski 1992; Quilty 1998). Attitudes to Indonesia always stressed the 'unrelenting production of difference as the defining characteristic of Australian–Indonesian relations' (Philpott 2001, p. 378), thereby preventing the development of intimate relations between the two countries and, more generally, erecting barriers to Australia's integration into the East Asian region.

The fact that 90 per cent of Indonesia's 200 million people practise Islam further reinforced Australian cultural prejudices. In the constructivist idiom, 'the west' developed a unique predilection for defining itself against an enemy constructed in terms of its cultural or ideological difference. After 1990, the west replaced the communist Other with the threat of Islam (Karram 2000, p. 17). 'Islamophobia', it was held, reflected an Orientalism that constructed images of Islam as 'incomprehensible, irrational, extremist, threatening' (Esposito 1995, p. 231), which inevitably contributed to the stereotyping of Muslims as 'fundamentalists and fanatics' (Slisli 2001, p. 45). For constructivism the foreign policy process exemplified 'practices of differentiation or modes of exclusion'. The production of threats presented through a 'discourse of danger' maintained the national identity (Campbell 1998, p. 68). The 'Other' represented a construct for domestic consumption, built to sustain an Anglo-Celtic Australian identity. As one commentator argued, the 'enemy is not "out there" ', instead ' "we" are it' (Brian Massumi, quoted in Philpott 2001, p. 376). In this view of foreign policy, then, there are no material threats, only dangerous discourses. Threats frame Australian national security perceptions 'because the character of Indonesia is narrated in . . . negative terms' (Philpott 2001, p. 386).

This academic orthodoxy ultimately maintained that Indonesia or Southeast Asia more broadly could only be construed as a threat by committing that most opprobrious of intellectual crimes, namely, racism. Moreover, if all threats are imagined – the sick fantasy of paranoid white males – the very idea of self-defence becomes problematic. And, for some commentators, this was indeed the case. Australian defence planning was a white Australian cultural conceit to maintain the image of an external threat. Therefore even a prudential concern to protect Australia from attack was deemed to be 'arguably irrational' (Cheeseman 1999b, p. 281).

This conjunction of multilateralist policy towards Asia with the dominance of constructivism in academia formed an edifice of denial that permeated academe, the media and political debate. This effectively excluded alternative viewpoints. To maintain that Indonesia, for example, might constitute a potential security problem for Australia was to commit Orientalism in the first degree. To observe that the majority of Australians did not greet the prospect of Asian engagement with unalloyed pleasure invoked the prospect of denunciation as a fellow traveller with racially motivated anti-immigration extremists (see Makinda 2001, p. 319). To consider that Australia should adhere to its traditions of liberal democracy and open debate when confronted by criticisms from geriatric Southeast Asian autocrats was, in the words of one critic of the elite consensus, to be tagged with the deplorable label of 'rightwing' or worse, 'conservative' (James 2002). This intolerant elite culture of the 1990s maintained the regionalist orthodoxy by disciplining opinion and punishing dissent through a mixture of *ad hominem* slurs and the rhetoric of silence.

As a result, most scholarship and media commentary in Australia prior to 2002 disconnected itself from any objective understanding of regional realities. In this respect, the ideology of Asianization eroded effective area studies, most notably of Indonesia, as well as the wider Southeast Asian region. The belief that one need only analyse 'discourses' rather than empirical evidence attenuated the space for sceptical assessment of regional affairs. It also promoted an academic culture of self-loathing where Australian scholars promoted a multicultural guilt complex at home, while tolerating authoritarian regimes in the rest of Asia and, in the process, uncritically endorsing the delusions promulgated by ASEAN and its scholar–bureaucracy. In practical terms, this edifice of denial revealed itself in a propensity to misread events. The dismal record of predictive ineptitude manifested itself initially in the over-optimistic assessments of Asia's growth and recovery prospects, which systematically ignored the underlying fragility of the economies of East and Southeast Asia. Even in November 1997, for instance, the former foreign editor of the *Australian* blithely announced that the 'overall outlook, despite all you have heard, remains good for sustained high economic growth throughout East Asia' (Sheridan 1997).

Those in denial also maintained throughout the 1990s that Southeast Asia continued to play host to 'domestic tranquillity and regional order' (Acharya 1997b, p. 310) rather than burgeoning ethno-religious terror. Ever since 1997, ASEAN had been in crisis, along with the meltdown in the regional economy, but analysts continued to maintain that the Asia–Pacific would become the dominant regime in the global economy into which there would be no choice but to integrate. This in turn fed the inability to determine threats to Australian national security. So complete was the edifice of denial that the Australian policy, media and academic complex found itself incapable of appreciating the political instability brought about by the economic meltdown. The extent of this edifice only became apparent in the rubble of the Kuta Beach resort in Bali on 12 October 2002, when bombs ripped through a series of nightclubs, killing over 200 people, nearly half of them Australians.

As Australian commentators maintained their unwarranted faith in the coming Pacific Century, *Jemaah Islamiyah* and its regional affiliates, like *Abu Sayyaf, Hizb-ut Tahrir* and *Kumpulan Mujahideen Malaysia*, all franchises of the al-Qaeda transnational Islamist terror network, were busily establishing closer operational linkages across Southeast Asia (International Crisis Group 2002, p. 9). ASEAN, meanwhile, obliviously maintained its doctrine of non-interference in the internal affairs of member states and advertised the utility of shared Asian values in maintaining regional serenity. The Australian intelligence and academic communities happily reinforced ASEAN's delusion. Throughout the years leading up to the Bali bombing, DFAT insisted that Australia's interests were best served by admission to the colloquies of 'ASEAN Plus Three' and the other empty paraphernalia of ASEAN multilateralism. Equally disturbingly, in the course of the 1990s, an ASEAN-induced miasma overcame the Office of National Assessment (ONA), the intelligence analysis arm of the government, whenever it peered north of the Timor Gap.

Whitlamite revisionism, the Sovietology of Southeast Asian studies, and academic constructivism so dominated regional analysis that it deferred to the sensibilities of Southeast Asian governments, which in the years before Bali had a vested interest in understating internal instability. Australian commentary uncritically accepted the views expressed by scholar-bureaucrats in ASEAN-sponsored institutes of regional affairs, believing that they were listening to the authentic voice of the 'Other'. For example, Jusuf Wanandi of the Centre for Strategic and International Studies (CSIS) in Jakarta argued, pre-Bali, that: 'Attention to such groups as the Laskar Jihad has been overblown. They are rather noisy groups, but small and marginal' (Wanandi 2002d, p. 142). Such views found their answering echo in Australian analytic comment on Indonesia, with those like Alan Dupont declaring only a few weeks before the Bali bombing that the 'tendency is still to overplay the [terror] threat' (quoted in *Far Eastern Economic Review*, 2 October 2002).

After Bali, Jusuf Wanandi changed his mind, declaring, somewhat belatedly, that 'it has become crystal clear that global terrorism is present in Indonesia' and that the nation had 'been in denial too long' (Wanandi 2002b). Yet, even as the odd Indonesian analyst acknowledged the scale of the Islamist terror network in the aftermath of the Bali bombing, Australia's *commentariat* remained steadfastly in denial. Initially, Australian analysts dismissed the notion of transnational involvement in the attack as irrelevant, until the Indonesian authorities formally declared the attack the work of al-Qaeda-linked extremists (Firdaus 2002). In the days following the bombing, allegations that senior al-Qaeda and *Jemaah Islamiyah* operatives travelled to Australia and established the lineaments of a network in the country ('Al-Qaeda boss reported to have visited Australia', 2002) led the Australian Security Intelligence Organization (ASIO) to raid the homes of suspects, some of whom were Indonesian nationals.[1]

Although the raids were conducted peacefully, this did not prevent a media and academic outcry that such acts were likely to damage Australia's relations with Indonesia. Australian National University professor and former ONA analyst, Greg Fealy, considered that the raids put 'Australia firmly in the Western camp' which 'is not necessarily in our longer term interests if we're trying to maintain a harmonious relationship with Muslim countries' (quoted in 'ASIO raids vs Australian Indonesian relations', 2002). In the wake of the ASIO raids, the Shadow Trade Minister, Craig Emerson, attacked Prime Minister John Howard for being 'anti-Asian' (quoted in 'Indonesia issues warning over ASIO raids', 2002). In the strange world of the Australian scholar–bureaucracy acts of preventative internal security were perceived as evidence of ingrained cultural prejudice.

REALISM REINVENTED

The legacy of denial revealed by the economic meltdown and confirmed by the Bali bombing exposed the myth of engagement with a supposed regional monolith. In its original manifestation under Whitlam, the myth assumed that the long conservative rule of Menzies and his successors had created a nation without national interests. A post-Whitlamite elite in media and academe argued that Australia did not 'possess a distinct culture' because the country's self-identity was 'a derivation or a continuation, in a foreign place, of someone else's history'. To build an authentically Australian identity, it was subsequently declared, somewhat incoherently, Australia's future had to be tied to an Asian destiny. This, it was held, would free Australia from the false consciousness of its colonial past and facilitate the identification of the nation's true interests.

Ironically, the multilateralism that sustained the Asian engagement myth proved untenable precisely because it explicitly sought to divorce itself from Australia's historical, cultural and, indeed, democratic identity. For, the moment that this myth came under pressure following the Asian financial crisis and the Bali bombing, it was those most enthralled by regional engagement that proved least capable of identifying Australia's real interests.

One of the more remarkable features of the Howard government's foreign policy since 1997 has been the absence of mythology. As a sceptical conservative, Howard eschewed the notion of an independent Australia pursuing multiculturalism at home and multilateral engagement abroad. Interestingly, as an admirer of Menzies, Howard has returned Australian foreign policy, despite the media brickbats hurled at him by a generation of what one Liberal MP described as 'doddering daiquiri drinking diplomats', to its pre-revisionist, pragmatic, roots. In the Menzies era, Australia's core value system assumed the responsibility to make choices and take action to support allies. A similar realism has informed Howard's approach since the Asian financial crisis and has become clearer since the Bali bombing. In particular, the government has questioned whether Asia can be addressed as a uniform community that must be somehow 'engaged'. Predictably, this has only served to reinforce the delusions of those most attached to the engagement myth. Defending the received orthodoxy, Richard Woolcott, the former ambassador to Indonesia under Whitlam, argued that the government had created confusion about Australia's 'real approach to the region' by 'sending out the wrong message to Asian countries' (Woolcott 2003, p. 287). The 'perception', he declared, had been allowed 'to grow that the government has stepped back from decades of bipartisan support for constructive Asian engagement' (ibid., p. 292). Likewise, Alison Broinowski prognosticated that 'our slavish subservience as allies is the very reason that Australia's drift away from involvement with Asian countries, and towards regional pariahdom continues' (Broinowski 2003, p. 28).

Unmoved by criticism from media, academe and former diplomats at home and ASEAN-way scholar-bureaucrats abroad, Howard's foreign policy has shown little interest in ASEAN diplomacy or its putative mutation into ASEAN Plus Three to embrace China, South Korea and Japan. Instead, the government has concentrated on bilateral ties reinforced by close links to the US to secure regional security and promote economic growth. For Howard's critics the mere fact that his government deals with Asian countries primarily on a bilateral basis is indicative of his 'rejection' of Asia. As we have noted in a previous chapter, the politics of faith fix an image of the world in the mind that ignores or misinterprets discrepant evidence. Consequently, Howard's antagonists are invariably interested only in information that confirms what they already believe, while the reality of any given situation may be quite different. The truth is, *contra* Broinowski, that Australia is actually far more involved in Asian affairs than it was in the pre-Howard era. The key difference is that this involvement is not conducted according to the delusive ASEAN way.

To play down ASEAN, however, by no means entails ignoring Southeast Asia, the political integrity of which, as it did in the 1960s, remains crucial to Australian security. In this context, Australia has been the only country in the region to contribute seriously to Southeast Asian stability. Australia gave generously to the IMF bailout package that financially salvaged the region in 1997/98. With UN approval, Australia played the leading role in stabilizing East Timor at a time when ASEAN looked on impotently. More recently, effective low-key cooperation between the Australian Federal Police and the Indonesian police has disrupted, although by no means destroyed, the *Jemaah Islamiyah* terrorist group, while ASEAN merely demonstrates its marginality to the threat that networked transnational terrorism poses.

Beyond Southeast Asia, Australia has also played a crucial role in stabilizing the fragile island states of the Southwest Pacific, most notably in July 2003, by sending a team of 2000 military and police officers to the Solomon Islands in order to rebuild the systems of government after the islands had been ravaged by civil strife and economic mismanagement (Dinnen 2004, pp. 90–91). In the wider Pacific arena, Australian pragmatism plays well in South Korea and Japan. Prime Minister Howard's visit in July 2002 to Seoul and Tokyo solidified strong bilateral relations, a shared vision of the region's security dilemmas and extended an already well established and mutually beneficial trading relationship. A similar uncomplicated approach to China helped secure a $25 billion liquefied natural gas contract in 2003 in the teeth of strong international competition. Indeed, the careful cultivation of ties with the current generation of Chinese leaders culminated in Howard's visit to Beijing in August 2003 that reinforced relations with a country that has rapidly developed since 1997 into Australia's third trading partner. Australia's resource-rich continent complements well the needs of a rapidly industrializing, but resource-poor, Chinese economy.

In other words, rather than conducting foreign policy according to the tenets of a fashionable pan-Asian orthodoxy, Howard has applied instead a sceptical and measured realism in keeping with Australia's economic and political interests. Against the abstract rational planners of the ideology of Asian engagement, Howard prefers to revert to a traditional and pragmatic Australian foreign policy stance. Rather than fantasizing about Australia's role as a middle power shaping a new 'Pacific Century', the current emphasis is on the pursuit of bilateral ties. Instead of chasing the mirage of an integrated Asian economic community, Australian foreign policy would rather balance the variety of developed, developing, unstable, weak, and not so weak states that comprise Pacific Asia with the need to maintain close relationships with traditional and powerful friends, most obviously the United States.

Against the regional propensity to manage and gloss over flashpoints, rather than solve them, the Howard government has also reinvigorated the concept of forward defence for the globalized transnational politics of the new century. Such a posture is not without difficulty, given the current uncertain geopolitical environment and the relative size of Australia's armed forces. Now that Southeast Asia and the wider Pacific increasingly resembles a darkling plain where ignorant armies clash by night, the defence of Australia faces the possibility of both military and financial overstretch. To avoid this requires the strategic calculation of what Australian security needs to cope with the fallout from the slow-motion disintegration of ASEAN and the failing states of the Pacific Island Forum. This entails a basic change in an entrenched foreign policy mentality to acknowledge the fact that Australia is not dealing with a dynamic Southeast Asia but a disparate set of weak states, of which the weakest and most fissiparous is clearly Indonesia.

Forward defence, now, as opposed to the Cold War version, might necessitate the deployment of Australian forces without significant support from larger allies. The threats themselves, particularly those emanating from failing post-colonial states, previously held together largely by the superglue of Cold War balance, are more diffuse. They range from the conventional need to secure a balance between states in the wider Asia–Pacific to the asymmetric tactics preferred by transnational terror and crime groups that have proliferated rapidly since the 1990s. What we know of these latter phenomena is that they derive from weak states, like Indonesia, the Philippines, Myanmar and Cambodia; that they are not necessarily rationally deterrable in the conventionally accepted sense, and that they are adept at using the openness and speed of the global economy for the purposes of raising finance, drugs, arms and people trafficking, and coordinating attacks on population centres and critical infrastructure. One suspects that combating the al-Qaeda-linked network of regional groupings that are prepared to countenance mass casualty attacks requires sophisticated intelligence cooperation with those elements of the state elites in Southeast Asia that also feel challenged by the threat, along with a flexible and highly trained army with a rapid reaction capability.

The return to a pragmatic realism under John Howard's administration represented a dramatic reversal of the prevailing rationalist orthodoxy of the Keating–Evans era. Despite the carping of a media and academic elite, the unspectacular pursuit of bilateral relations in Asia, combined with the maintenance of close links with the United States, has proved highly successful.

Howard, therefore, has followed a consistently realist policy towards both the region and the wider world since he assumed office. This policy has emphasized the role of the state, rather than multilateral fora or international and regional arrangements like the UN, ASEAN or AFTA, as the crucial actor in international affairs. This has been evident from the Asian financial crisis, where Australia contributed directly to the financial relief of its ailing tiger neighbours, through its realistic pursuit of bilateral approaches both to the regional war on terror and to trade through its negotiation of free trade agreements with the US, Singapore and Thailand, down to its contribution of military and infrastructural aid to the relief of the stricken Indonesian province of Aceh following the tsunami disaster of December 2004.

Nor does this pragmatic pursuit of the national interest apply only to Howard's Asia policy. Howard is equally realistic in his dealing with the US, whose continued presence in the region as a necessary stabilizer has been secured with a minimal contribution to the American-led coalition stabilization force in Iraq. It is also evident in Howard's dealings with Europe and its petulant anti-Americanism.

The achievements of Howard's consistent and understated bilateral focus contrasts dramatically with the meretricious foreign policy posturing of the Keating–Evans era which was long on rhetoric but short on substance. Much admired by their academic *apparatchiks* in think tanks and international relations departments, this policy sought to portray Australia as an autonomous middle power pursuing a fashionable multilateral policy of regional enmeshment with a dynamic East Asia abroad while cultivating a multicultural republic at home. From this perspective, still dear to the ALP, Asia constitutes a monolith which Australia must embrace even if it means abandoning the US alliance. It receives an answering echo from the more out-of-touch Asian authoritarians like current Singapore Prime Minister Lee Hsien Loong, who warned Howard about 'neglecting Asia' in February 2005. Howard's policy, however, is balanced and realistic. As he stated in Singapore in 2005, while he recognized that Australia's dominant interests in the years ahead will be found in the region, Australia relates not to a monolith but 'to a large number of countries that make up the aggregate' called Asia. Moreover, the true value of Australia's relations with Southeast and East Asian states, Howard maintained, is to be found in the substance of its associations with individual countries rather than in 'the symbolism or the architecture' (quoted in Callick 2005).

Such realism is refreshing after the multilateral pretension and delusional thinking that has so often clouded Australia's approach to the diverse assortment of states that constitutes Australia's neighbourhood. The numerous problems evident in Southeast Asia undoubtedly present Australia with manifold challenges. However, the counter-orthodox revisionism of the Howard era foreign policy means that at least Australia can now recognize that it has a burgeoning security dilemma on its hands, rather than a multicultural guilt complex.

NOTE

1. Most of those questioned were Australian citizens, although this did not prevent Imron Cotan, Indonesia's Acting Ambassador to Australia, from threatening that the ASIO raids would jeopardize the investigation into the Bali bombing ('Indonesian ambassador warns Bali probe "at risk" ', 2002).

7. Political illiberalism and the war on terrorism in Southeast Asia: the problems of the surveillance state

Ultimately, the most graphic confirmation of the state of delusion that gripped official and academic commentary on Southeast Asia, and the tragic effects it could have, was exposed in the aftermath of the Bali nightclub bombings of October 2002, which killed 202 people. The attack demonstrated the existence of active Islamist terror cells in Southeast Asia. Following the terrorist attacks on New York and Washington on 11 September 2001 some Southeast Asian governments moved to detain a number of suspected Islamist extremists ('Alien arrests bid to flush out "sleepers" ', 2002; Ahmed 2002a). Curiously, though, until the Bali bombings, official and academic opinion continued to neglect or discount the extent to which an Islamic terror network had taken root across the region. Such oversight appears even more surprising given the often intrusive intelligence structures that exist in many Southeast Asian states. Why was it that they so manifestly failed to discern the evolving threat?

The short answer is that the security structures in most Southeast Asian states had, in effect, imbibed the regional delusion, promoted by ASEAN, which proclaimed endless harmony and stability among its membership. Consequently, the state intelligence agencies of ASEAN became overwhelmingly concerned with policing political stability within their own borders, while paying only minimal attention to the growth of transnational threats. This, in turn, influenced much academic and media commentary upon the region that was, as we have seen, often overdetermined by official rhetoric that played down sources of internal instability within the states of the region. As a result, there was little awareness of the threat posed by Islamism. Thus, prior to the Bali bombings, regional intelligence and security cooperation, despite official rhetoric, was often poor (Wanandi 2002a, 184–9; Desker and Ramakrishnan 2002, pp. 161–76). In particular, there was a conspicuous ignorance of the growing links between the most pervasive militant Islamic group in Southeast Asia, *Jemaah Islamiyah* (Islamic Organization) (JI), and the globalizing jihadist pretensions of Osama bin Laden's al-Qaeda global terrorist franchising agency (see Fisk 1993).[1]

Before governments in the region were alerted to the threat of radical Islam after the attacks on the United States and Bali, scholars of Southeast Asia, as we have indicated in earlier chapters, painted a distinctly rosy picture of regional developments. In contrast to what appeared to be the escalating number of ethnic wars elsewhere in the world, Southeast Asia enjoyed, in the view of its *commentariat*, both impressive economic growth rates and unprecedented levels of political stability. The ASEAN states, it was maintained, were in the process of forging their own distinctive developmental path, untainted by the tremors of communal conflict. During this period of apparently unstoppable growth and regional optimism western commentators upon Southeast Asia neither challenged nor problematized the claims made for regional harmony by official declarations. Instead, they attended to the local particularities that contributed to the region's 'economic miracle' and successful multilateral diplomatic practices that had transformed ASEAN in the 1990s into a 'hub of confidence building activities and preventive diplomacy' (Almonte 1997, p. 80).

Again, as this study has sought to demonstrate, the more prosaic reality was that, for 20 years, economic growth and the rhetoric of regional harmony had obscured the underlying tectonics of Southeast Asian politics. Vociferous official pronouncements by Southeast Asian governments extolling the virtues of regional governance over the previous two decades created an academic orthodoxy that captured intellectual opinion about the region. This orthodoxy not only glossed over the intensity of bilateral tensions that existed between many Southeast Asian states, which festered largely unresolved since the achievement of independence, but also disguised the extent to which a network of Islamic extremism had taken root amongst the ASEAN nations by the early 1990s; that is, a decade before the world awoke to the 'war on terrorism'.

How, therefore, may we explain the strange neglect of Southeast Asia as a theatre of instability and terrorism before 2002? The question is all the more compelling given that most ASEAN states possess degrees of authoritarian government where nearly all forms of unofficial political activity are subject to heavy restriction and surveillance. These political conditions have given rise to large and sometimes pervasive domestic intelligence structures. Such systems of governance, one might assume, should be acutely sensitive to any potential subversive challenges. This gives rise to a series of puzzling questions. Why were these states apparently taken by surprise by the growth of a militant Islamic threat that had developed in their own backyards? Did the inattention to this threat, we might ask, reflect the nature of the authoritarian structures that prevail in the region and which ASEAN, through its foundational Treaty of Amity and Cooperation, reinforced in the Bali Concord of 2002, effectively sustains? Further, given the capacity for *post hoc* overreaction, does Islamic extremism constitute a serious and continuing threat to the economic and political stability of the region?

It is these questions relating to the failure of the intelligence structures to identify threats to national and regional security that this chapter explores. In order to do this, we shall postulate two supplementary questions about how illiberal regimes and shared non-western values in Southeast Asia might have affected the awareness of an evolving threat. First, did Southeast Asian illiberalism and the ASEAN way contribute to a complacent belief in regional harmony that facilitated a fallacious understanding of the region's purported security community? Or, alternatively, could it be that the region's political elites, to varying degrees, were 'somewhat' aware of the growing threat via their extensive intelligence systems but, driven by authoritarian imperatives, believed it expedient to conceal its character from wider public scrutiny, with fatal political consequences? The response to these questions will subsequently enable us to assess the current ASEAN response to the 'war on terrorism' and to discern whether Southeast Asia's elites are likely to move to improve the quality of their intelligence and threat analysis in future, or whether they will, instead, extend the instruments of illiberal rule, further curtailing civil and political space under the convenient rubric of combating terrorism.

THE ROOTS OF DELUSION: A CASE OF COMPLACENCY?

To address the first of these questions: did ASEAN's rhetoric during the so-called miracle years 1986–96 lull its members into a complacent belief in the idea of regional stability? Did this so blind its membership that the various state intelligence bureaucracies also became blind to the growth of the danger? There is some evidence to support this proposition. As we saw in previous chapters, for much of the 1990s, the leaders of Singapore, Indonesia, the Philippines, Thailand and Malaysia – the founding members of ASEAN – congratulated themselves on their developmental formula (see Mahbubani 1995a, pp. 105–10, 1995b; Zakaria 1994, pp. 109–13). ASEAN's distinctive brand of diplomacy, conducted through informal mechanisms of good interpersonal relations, had, so it was argued, generated rapid economic growth while sustaining regional stability amongst its members.

As we noted earlier, for its many international admirers this represented a uniquely Asian way in international diplomacy, not to be discounted or modified in favour of 'western' preoccupations with rule-based governance (Kausikan 1993, p. 34; Mahbubani 1994a, 1994b; Mohamad and Ishihara 1995). Yet so well entrenched was its style of consensus diplomacy that

ASEAN demonstrated little capacity to react to the economic crisis of 1997. Commentators continued to extol regional resilience, claiming that ASEAN would overcome any short-term setbacks and would 'emerge victorious' (Koh 1998; 'ASEAN makes bold moves for recovery', 1998). As a consequence, the Association failed to take any meaningful action to deal with either the economic or the political fallout from the crisis, maintained a studied indifference to the growing Balkanization of Indonesia and conspicuously ignored the plight of East Timor. The mounting levels of regional instability failed to stir any desire to reform its foundational Treaty of Amity and Cooperation (1976) that held rigidly to the doctrine of non-interference in the internal politics of member states as the basis for regional cooperation.

If the attachment to the ASEAN way seemed complacent prior to 2001, its maintenance in the wake of the war on terror and the exposure of an apparently hitherto unsuspected Islamist terror network spanning Southern Mindanao, Malaysia, Singapore and Indonesia seemed to reflect a remarkable degree of laxity. In the three years leading up to the 11 September 2001 attacks in the US, it was evident to those not in thrall to Aseanology, which was still deluding itself that the region was one of domestic tranquillity and regional order, that a strain of militant Islam deployed as an all-embracing ideological programme of social and political change, or Islamism as it will be referred to in this chapter, was on the rise in Southeast Asia. In Indonesia, for example, a younger generation of educated radicals inspired by the Mujahideen's resistance to the Soviet occupation of Afghanistan challenged the largely apolitical, moderate Islam of Abdurrahman Wahid's *Nahdlatul Ulama* government, which fitfully ruled the vast archipelago between 1999 and 2001. Ironically, these Islamist groups, like *Laskar Jihad* (Jihad Troopers),[2] the *Majlis Mujahideen Indonesia* (MMI) (Mujahideen Council of Indonesia) and the *Front Pembela Islamiya* (FPI) (Islamic Defender's Front), only came to prominence during Wahid's ineffective presidency (Wilson 2001: 'Is there an Al-Qaeda connection in Indonesia?', 2002). Elsewhere in federal Malaysia, the *Parti Islam Se-Malaysia* (PAS), which forms the main opposition to the ruling United Malay National Organization (UMNO)-dominated *Barisan Nasional* (National Front) coalition, began to impose *Sharia*-style discipline in the states of Kelantan and Terengganu, where it held power at provincial level ('Terror investigations strain Malaysian politics', 2002).

Arguably, the failure of the ASEAN governing elites and their scholar–bureaucracy ensconced in regional institutes of defence and strategic studies (along with their western academic adherents) to attach any significance to the growth of Islamic radicalism in the region resided in the fact that, until 1997, the region seemed, superficially at least, set to maintain its impressive economic performance. We noted earlier in this book how both journalistic and scholarly commentators became mesmerized by the 'spectacularly successful' (Krasner 1996, p. 123) economic growth in the region, which convinced observers that economic success had been founded on regional stability premised on the evolution of 'shared norms' of diplomatic behaviour in ASEAN that had been 'operationalised into a framework of regional inter-action' based on 'a high degree of discreetness, informality, pragmatism, expe-diency and non-confrontational bargaining styles' (Acharya 1997a, p. 329). The ASEAN model was seen, therefore, to offer 'the prospect of long-term stable peace in the region' (Chalmers 1996, p. 53). As we now know, this was but the first step in the suspension of intellectual judgement leading to regional delusion. The official orthodoxy further maintained that Islam in Southeast Asia – unlike its Middle Eastern equivalent – was capital-friendly and well disposed both to economic modernization and to regional multilateralism. For those commentators absorbed by the prospect of Indonesian democratization after 1998, this benign 'civil' Islam offered the possibility of a tolerant and pluralist Islamized democracy (see Hefner 2000, chap. 1).

After the meltdown of 1997, however, the region mutated into a theatre of economic uncertainty and rising instability, revealing the fact that the forces of globalization had volatized traditional interethnic rivalries. It is these forces that gave impetus to the formation of an increasingly fundamentalist Islamic identity politics (Barber 1996, chap. 19). One product of these forces that emerged from the economic meltdown has been a jihadist *ressentiment* fuelled, ironically, by the very forces of globalization it seeks to deny. This Islamism exploits the opportunities arising from the modern industrial state and the interconnectedness of an increasingly internetted global trading system, in order to engineer an apocalyptic confrontation with the forces of modernity (see Roy 2000, p. 156).

Thus, although moderate, civil Islam represented the norm in regional poli-tics, since the end of the Gulf War in 1991 and the Islamist liberation of Afghanistan in the course of the 1990s, the appeal of a Middle Eastern, anti-western, anti-democratic Islamism had been on the rise, most evidently in Malaysia and Indonesia. Its appeal has been sustained by the economic melt-down post-1997 that has generated a disturbingly vicious downward economic and political cycle. The middle and lower-middle-class urban salaried workers who might have anticipated material gains in terms of job opportunities and an improving lifestyle were cruelly disappointed by the uncertain and unpre-dictable actions of globalized 'super [financial] markets' after 1997 (Freidman 2001, chap. 1). Hence the burgeoning appeal of the non-liberal anti-democra-tic scriptural certitude that informs the *salafist* revivalism in the thought and practice of groups like the *Laskar Jihad* and the FPI. As the appeal and public profile of such groups grew, moreover, the possibility for foreign direct invest-ment diminished, further accelerating the appeal of the chiliastic certainties promulgated by these same groups.

Officially, ASEAN maintained that little had changed in the fabric of the regional order, despite the ravages of the economic crisis after 1997 and the rising Muslim separatist violence in Mindanao in the Philippines and around the Indonesian periphery. Only after 11 September and the revelation of a sustained level of Islamist cooperation stretching from Solo in Java, through Singapore, Malaysia and extending to the Southern Philippines – and ultimately Kabul – was the surface of regional harmony pulled back to reveal a practice of suspicion and non-cooperation between ASEAN governments and their intelligence services. This contrasted alarmingly with the illicit, transnational, often sophisticated, networks of collaboration developed by Islamist organizations dedicated to recasting entirely what they view as the failed *jahiliyya* (pagan and ignorant) states of Southeast Asia.

The obsession with economic growth had in effect blinded the region's governing elites to the fact that a new generation of Malay and Indonesian middle-class radicals, alienated from the process of post-colonial nation building in Southeast Asia, had turned instead to a purified Islam of *Wahhabist* origins learnt from a variety of sources: either in Afghan or Philippine training camps, Middle Eastern universities, at western mosques or via the world wide web. At the same time these radicals ostensibly pursued the passive, bourgeois professions that would, to all outward appearances, sustain both GDP growth and political stability in their respective domiciles ('The Pakistan connection', 2002). It is this apparent conformity that provides an explanation as to how both western analysts and the intelligence services of the states of Southeast Asia were deceived. In this respect, it can be suggested that ASEAN's preoccupation with surface harmony inhibited any attempt to comprehend the underlying motivations of growing Islamic rage. This, in turn, it can be maintained, led to delusion. It was, very much in the mould of the Sovietology of Southeast Asian studies outlined in Chapter 1, a failure to probe beyond the surface impression of outward regional stability.

The disturbing lack of cooperation between the ASEAN members' military and security services has long been obfuscated by academic and media obeisance to a shared regional vision. This vision held out the seductive prospect of constructing a shared identity that in terms of regional defence might evolve into a collective security community (Acharya 1991, p. 176). In fact this was always an illusion. Indeed, previous chapters have shown that this official and academic discourse effectively disguised the fact that ASEAN operates essentially as a realist concert of powers (Leifer 1999, p. 25). The foundational *raison d'être* of ASEAN was not, as commentators often assumed, to develop into some regional community that surmounted the state and overcame previous antagonisms (Snitwongse 1995, p. 519). Instead, it lay in two simple goals: a pact to stop the spread of Communism in Southeast Asia after 1967, and a plan to devise a diplomatic framework 'to lock Indonesia into a structure of multilateral partnership and constraint that would be seen as a rejection of hegemonic pretensions' (Leifer 1989, p. 13). Through these means, Southeast Asian regimes could simultaneously consolidate themselves internally while pursuing economic growth (ibid., p. 4).

This official ideology of non-interference enshrined the external conduct of member states in terms of a 'realist' appreciation of national interests, while internally pursuing state consolidation. In security and political terms, this meant that countries such as Singapore and Malaysia developed into illiberal states, in part by dramatically extending the remit of internal security legislation, dating from colonial times, into the post-colonial era. Throughout the region, Southeast Asian states evolved extensive mechanisms for the surveillance of the civilian population, conducted via the internal security apparatus and the bureaucratic machinery, as in Singapore, or, in the case of Indonesia, through the development of regional military commands, in which considerable powers to control the civil populace were, and despite democratization after 1998 remain, invested. Since the inception of the Indonesian Republic through resistance to Dutch colonial rule in December 1949, the Indonesian armed forces – *Tentara Nasional Indonesia* (TNI) – have always perceived their role to serve a dual function. This embraces the conventional roles of an armed force within an ideological mission to preserve national integrity. During the 'New Order' of President and former General Suharto, who ruled from 1966 to 1998, the state's evolving corporatism afforded the military a central role in coordinating internal security, especially in the peripheral regions of Papua, West Irian and East Timor. Although moves towards democracy continued slowly under Abdurrahman Wahid, Megawati Sukarnoputri and former General and current President Susilo Bambang Yudhyono, the role of regional military commands has by no means been abrogated or subjected to civilian control. Indeed, the TNI's 'Crisis Team on East Timor', led by General Zacky Anwar Makarim, coordinated the 30 pro-Indonesian militias responsible for the population displacement and widespread carnage that accompanied the East Timor independence process in September 1999 (Kingsbury 2001, p. 114). Thus the official rhetoric within ASEAN of maintaining a spirit of friendly cooperation on regional affairs belied the actual practice of the member states themselves, which policed their societies, in their own distinctively opaque, unaccountable and frequently repressive ways.[3]

Yet, for all their preoccupation with internal security and the harsh punishment meted out to internal dissidents, Southeast Asian states failed to recognize, let alone counter, the emergence of an antagonistic, politically sophisticated Islamic radicalism operating within and across internal borders. Meanwhile, the largest state in the regional grouping, Indonesia, tolerated the presence of self-styled Islamic radical clerics like Sheikh Abu Bakar Bashir,[4] a radical teacher who operates a boarding school in Sukoharjo in central Java and is the leading figure in the pan-Islamist MMI based in Jakarta as well as the spiritual *emir* of both the *Kumpulan Mujahideen Malaysia* (Union of Malaysian Mujahideen/Jihad Fighters) (KMM) and *Jemaah Islamiyah*,[5] that by 2000 was operating across Southeast Asia. The Indonesian government's subsequent ambivalence to radical Islamism in its midst heightened inter-ASEAN friction. By 2002, Malaysian and Singaporean diplomats openly criticized Indonesia as the 'weakest link' in the fight against regional terrorism (Chandrasekaran 2002).[6] Despite protestations from successive Indonesian governments that they considered the threat serious after the Bali nightclub bombings of October 2002, the fact that Bashir and his supporters continued to operate openly after the JI-linked attacks on the Marriott Hotel (August 2003) and the Australian embassy (November 2004) in Jakarta indicated a lack of political resolve.[7]

Paradoxically, then, not only did the ideology of ASEAN harmony after 1990 serve as a rhetorical cloak to disguise the realist structure of this concert of insecure new states, even the supposedly hard-headed authoritarian regimes that composed the concert, with their fearsome array of internal security instruments, seemed strangely incapable of identifying militant Islamic activity within their societies and across the region. Why, we may ask, was this the case?

A CASE OF AUTHORITARIAN IMPERATIVES?

Officially induced complacency about regional security provides one level of analysis to explain why Southeast Asian regimes were taken by surprise by the extent of a militant Islamic threat. An alternative way of looking at the problem might be to postulate that governments were, to some extent, aware of the dangers, but for reasons of political expediency could not admit or comprehend the nature of the threat, especially the extent to which local radical Islamic groups had established connections with the umbrella organization of Osama bin Laden's al-Qaeda (commonly translated as 'the Base') movement.[8] To assess this proposition, one needs, first, to examine how far al-Qaeda had a foothold in Southeast Asia prior to 2001, and second, to what extent this was known to governments in the region.

It is now increasingly evident that the incomplete nation building among the ASEAN states had failed to dissolve ethnic and religious attachments. This left a number of disaffected Muslim minorities who found themselves unreconciled to post-independence regimes that promulgated secularist ruling ideologies or maintained official ethnocratic arrangements or non-Muslim religious dominance. Separatist Islamic insurgencies have thus been a feature of the political landscape in Southeast Asia for nearly 50 years and have, as a result, received desultory academic attention over the years (see Tan 2000b; Chalk 2001).

In line with ASEAN's governing precept of non-interference, the assumption among the political elites of Southeast Asia was that unresolved Islamic challenges were purely internal matters, to be dealt with by individual states. Consequently, member states approached their local Islamic difficulties in their own ways – harshly or benignly as they saw fit. The Philippines handled its separatist Muslims in Mindanao through a mixture of military offensives, moving Catholic migrants into Muslim areas and reaching political compromises with more tractable Muslim factions. Indonesia similarly engaged in policies of *transmigrasi* (transmigration) coupled with military repression. The Achenese independence movement, the *Gerakanan Aceh Merdeka* (GAM) (Free Aceh Movement), has been suppressed by the central government in Jakarta on the grounds that this separatist group in Aceh province promoted a strict interpretation of Islam in order to disrupt the official New Order (1966–98) creed of *pancasila*.[9] Burma, meanwhile, has dealt with its Muslim Rohingya minority who inhabit the Arakan region by refusing citizenship and the favoured regional strategy of population displacement (Human Rights Watch 2000). Only in Thailand did the government attempt, in a limited way, to deal with Muslim minority concerns by addressing issues of language, religion and culture. Yet, even here, a younger generation of radicals motivated by what Lieutenant General Kitti Rattanachaya considers 'hatred and bitterness against the injustice that prevails in the South' have resorted to violence in order to revive the Pattani United Liberation Organization's (PULO) long-standing claim to independence (quoted in *Straits Times*, 28 January 1998; see also Tan 1998, pp. 46–53).

The belief that Islamic separatist movements were purely internal affairs also led to the assumption that these insurgencies were particular to, and, therefore, containable within, each member state. Even so, well before the Bali bombings of 2002, a conspicuous feature of this violent separatism was that it paid no heed to the ASEAN injunction to confine its activity within state boundaries. Traditionally, Moro separatists have looked for support to sympathisers in Southern Thailand and the more Islamic states of Northeast Malaysia, where the leader of the renegade popular Moro National Liberation Front (MNLF) leader, Nur Misuari, was arrested in December 2001. Furthermore, the growing appeal and increasing technological ease of operating transnationally through globalized networks to undermine the infidel notion of the secular nation state (Simon and Benjamin 2000) constitutes the critical ideological link between militant Islam in Southeast Asia and the franchising terror operations of the al-Qaeda network. The notion of a *darul Islam* (sphere of faith) that transcends national boundaries, and the call to *jihad* (holy war) to achieve it, has long been promoted by radical critics of failed post-colonial states in the Middle East. In Southeast Asia, evidence of this phenomenon has only in relatively recent times come to the fore, despite the fact that it now seems clear that Islamic cells had been organizing in the region since the early 1990s, and reach back to the *Darul Islam* movement that emanated from Indonesia at the end of the colonial era and which resisted the secular nation-building ideologies of the post-colonial new states of the region in the 1950s (Bonner and Mydans 2002). How, we might next consider, did this transnational network evolve?

THE DUAL SOURCES OF THE NETWORK

Piecing together the available source material reveals an insight into the origins, growth and direction of Southeast Asian groups like JI and their deepening relationship with al-Qaeda that the states of ASEAN failed to recognize, let alone address. The roots of the JI group can be traced to the 1970s and two geographically separate ethno-religious struggles in the Philippines and Indonesia. Guerrilla groups orchestrating these distinct struggles were eventually combined under the auspices of al-Qaeda and the globalized franchising opportunities it exploited, from the early 1990s as the movement emerged as an entity of concern.[10] By tracing the evolution and growth of Islamist sentiment in Southeast Asia we can identify two specific geographical sources of what has become a sophisticated network of de-territorialized, transnational movements dedicated to undermining, not just individual states in the region, but the imagined community of Southeast Asia.

The Philippine Connection

The first branch of the network emerged in the Philippines from the separatist struggle of the Muslim Moro in Mindanao. Sustained Moro resistance dates from the 1950s but became increasingly networked globally in the course of the 1970s with the emergence of the Moro Islamic Liberation Front (MILF) and later *Abu Sayyaf* (Father of the Sword), a violent splinter group, which broke away from the Moro National Liberation Front (MNLF) in 1991 (State Department 2002a).[11]

From the late 1980s, both MILF and *Abu Sayyaf* received support from al-Qaeda. As early as 1988, Mohammed Jamal Khalifa, bin Laden's brother-in-law, had set up a number of businesses that supplied financial and logistical support to *Abu Sayyaf* and MILF (*Manila Times*, 1 November 2002). Khalifa established front organizations like E.T., Dizon Travel – a business active in shipping goods between the Philippines, Malaysia, Netherlands and Saudi Arabia – as well as Dizon and Dizon Realty, and non-governmental organizations and charities to launder money, such as the International Islamic Relief Organization (IIRO) (*Guardian*, 23 September 2001). Through these organizations Khalifa established further links with Libya and the Algerian *Groupement Islamique Armé* (Armed Islamic Group) (GIA) in Algeria. Khalifa's philanthropy also enabled *Abu Sayyaf* personnel to study at Islamic universities in Pakistan. Khalifa left Manila in 1995 and later renounced his association with al-Qaeda (Thayer 2005, p. 87).

The revenues from such enterprises sustained training centres like camp Abubakar in Mindanao in the Southern Philippines (Dalangin 2003). Until it was overrun by the Philippine army in 2001, the camp provided instruction in munitions handling and assassination skills and, by the mid-1990s, regularly brought in Mujahideen expertise from Pakistan, Afghanistan and Algeria to train local Islamists (Hidalgo 2000). For example, Philippine police documents from the Directorate for Intelligence state that in 1998 Osama bin Laden sent a Sudanese colonel, Ahmad al-Gamen, to Mindanao to train MILF members in explosives and commando techniques (Republic of Philippines 1999, p. 2).[12] Indeed, camp Abubakar maintained strong international linkages and was internally sub-divided into Algerian, Palestinian and other sections. According to the police file, 'The MILF is known to be maintaining Camps Hodeibia and Palestine inside the Camp Abubakar complex for the training of mujahideen volunteers from other countries handled by Afghan veterans believed to be supported by bin Laden' (ibid., pp. 1–2). Former counter-terrorism task force head of the Philippine National Police, Senior Superintendent Rodolfo Mendoza corroborated this in an interview with Cable News Network (CNN), observing that 'There were foreign nationals like French Algerians, Egyptians, and Pakistanis who were trained by Filipinos inside Camp Abubakar' (quoted in Ressa 2002).

By 1998 and 1999, while camp Abubakar remained in operation, bin Laden himself facilitated links between the Algerian GIA and the MILF's leader Salamat Hashim (Republic of Philippines 1999, pp. 1–2). Thus the Philippine Directorate of Intelligence maintained: 'Sometime last mid-Februrary 1999 Osama bin Laden reportedly contacted separately MILF chairman Salamat and the Algerian leader Hassan Hattab. Bin Laden reportedly sought the assistance of Salamat in establishing new camps in Mindanao and instructed Hattab to start operations in his areas respectively [*sic*].' (Ibid.).[13]

Prior to this development, in 1991, Khalifa had also established close ties with Abdulrajak Janjalani, the founder of *Abu Sayyaf*, who in turn had links to Ramzi Yousef who had a coterie of Filipina girlfriends and, like most middle-class *salafist* jihadis, liked to party ('Dancing girls and romance on road to terrorist attacks', 2002; *Washington Times*, 18 October 2002). Yousef, who shared the Islamist international terrorist propensity to multiple identities, trav-elled on a variety of passports and planned the first World Trade Center bomb-ing in 1993 ('The Baluch connection', 2003). His putative uncle, also a Baluchi Sunni, Khalid Sheikh Mohammed, was number three in the al-Qaeda hierarchy and featured in later JI operations ('Top al-Qaeda suspect captured', 2002).

Before his arrest in 1995, Yousef had, according to press reports, planned to assassinate the Pope and was in the process of organizing 'operation Bojinka' to blow up a dozen planes over the Pacific en route to Los Angeles ('Al Qaeda planned to kill Pope', 2002; Kremmer, 2003). By 1995, Osama bin Laden's own imprimatur on these Philippine extremist groups could be detected, not least in the fact that the loose, protoplasmic framework served as the model for *Abu Sayyaf*. The arrest and interrogation in Pakistan in March 1995 of Abdul Karim Murad, who had operated under Ramzi Yousef's guid-ance, further substantiated the bin Laden connection ('The Baluch connec-tion', 2003).

The Indonesian Connection

Over the same time period that inspired al-Qaeda to develop links with the Philippine Moros, a second strand of regional Islamic militancy took shape, this time in Indonesia. This took the form of radical groups like the paramili-tary organization *Komando Jihad* (Holy War Command). While linked by some analysts to the post-1966 New Order Indonesian government's attempt to destabilize moderate Islamic opposition (Jenkins 2002; Asia Watch 1989, pp. 76–85), *Komando Jihad* nevertheless drew upon a colonial era of Islamist thinking of the *Darul Islam* movement dating from the 1950s. It was this movement's pursuit of an Islamic Indonesian state at the inception of the Republic which established the ideological foundations for later develop-ments. A central figure in *Komando Jihad* was Sheikh Abu Bakar Bashir, who, together with Abdullah Sungkar, established the al-Mukmin boarding school at Pondok in Solo, Central Java ('Hambali plotted terror campaign', 2003). This school became the basis for what the analyst Sydney Jones termed the 'Ngruki Network' which spread *Darul Islam*'s teaching throughout the region (International Crisis Group 2003).

Arrested in 1978 for their links to *Komando Jihad*, Bashir and Sungkar eventually escaped to Malaysia in 1985 where, together with Abu Jibril, they established a school, hospital and small Islamic community in Selangor. It was here that Nurjaman Riduan Isamuddin, also known as Hambali, another Javanese linked to Bashir, came in the early 1990s, after fighting with the Mujahideen in Afghanistan ('Hambali: SE Asia's most wanted', 2002). By 1999, Hambali had also become a leading figure on al-Qaeda's Military Command Council (*Christian Science Monitor*, 30 April 2002).

It was in the course of the 1980s that Bashir and Hambali established the lineaments of the KMM, which constituted the basis of one of the four regional groupings known as '*mantiqi*' of *Jemaah Islamiyah* (Barton 2002). In Malaysia, there was also an evolving linkage between al-Qaeda and KMM through Yazid Sufaat, a former Malaysian army officer, who, by the 1990s, had business interests in companies in Kuala Lumpur such as Green Laboratories and Infocus Technologies ('Tentacles of terror', 2002; Jones and Smith 2002). In January 2000, Sufaat hosted the Pentagon highjackers Khalid Al-Midhar and Nawaq Alhamzi ('Bush backs independent 9–11 Probe', 2002; 'The FBI's hijacker list', 2001). Later, in October 2000, he met Zacarias Moussaoui, subsequently tried in the US for his role in the 11 September attacks, in the same condominium. At this meeting he provided Moussaoui with funds and documents to enter the US as an Infocus Technologies 'marketing consultant'. Also in October 2000, Fathur Raman al Ghozi, another key al-Qaeda figure in Southeast Asia, instructed Sufaat to purchase the ammonium nitrate subsequently used in the Bali nightclub bombings of 2002.[14] Al Ghozi had formerly attended Bashir's school in Solo, majoring in explosives. He also possessed ties to MILF and had made at least two trips to Afghanistan to further his studies (*Christian Science Monitor*, 12 February 2002).

In the same period, the Malaysian connection extended its reach into Singapore via mosques across the causeway in Johore Baru. Mas Selamat Kastari oversaw the Singapore link whilst Ibrahim Maidin coordinated the JI cell in the city-state. Ibrahim Maidin had spent three weeks training in Afghanistan in 1993, and had in 1999 written to Osama bin Laden and Mullah Omar, the head of the Taliban in Afghanistan, seeking spiritual and ideological guidance (*Straits Times*, 10 January 2003). From the early 1990s, he held religious classes in Singapore which doubled as a recruitment centre for the JI cells he established there (Rahim 2003).

The collapse of Suharto's secular nationalist New Order regime in 1998 further facilitated the extension of regional and international connections. By the end of 1998, Bashir, Hambali and Abu Jibril had returned from Malaysia to Solo and Jakarta, where they established the *Majlis Mujahidin Indonesia* (Council of Indonesian Islamic Fighters) (MMI) and activated JI (Office of Public Affairs 2003). Through these organizations they encouraged links among Islamic radicals in Indonesia, the Philippines and Singapore. Contacts with Khalid Sheikh Mohammed, who regularly visited the Philippines, together with Hambali's significant position on the Military Command Council of al-Qaeda, advanced the integration of regional strategy and ideological guidance with a wider, transnational Islamist agenda. In December 2000, Hambali organized attacks on Christian churches across Java, the most widespread terror assault in Indonesian history, and which bore the al-Qaeda signature of multiple coordinated targets ('The Bali bomber's network of terror', 2003). Also involved in Hambali's Indonesian military operations were those like Mukhlas, who operated under the name of Ali Gufron, and Imam Samudra and Amrozi bin Nurhasyim, all of whom were implicated in the bombing of a church in Batam in January 2000. Subsequently, they formed the cell responsible for planning and executing the Bali bombing (Mydans 2003).

THE BALI BOMBINGS AND BEYOND

Both JI's ambitions and the al-Mukmin school's somewhat unorthodox curricula activities, were only exposed by the discovery of JI's video plan to attack western embassies in Singapore. Somewhat fortuitously, an American soldier stumbled upon the video in the rubble of al-Qaeda's headquarters in Kabul following the US-led attack on Afghanistan ('Al Qaeda plot to bomb US ships foiled by MI6', 2002). It also emerged that the Changi naval base and several other installations in Singapore, including the main civilian airport, were also on JI's target list ('PM reveals plan to crash jet into Changi', 2002). As a result, al Ghozi was arrested in Manila in January 2002.

In February 2003, Singapore's Internal Security Department (ISD) revealed that it had found e-mails and letters linking Maidin, the leader of the Singapore JI operation, with Mullah Omar, Mohammed Atta and Osama bin Laden in Kabul (Rahim 2003). These contacts date from 1999. Informing the strategic thinking of the Singapore plot was a sophisticated attempt to damage the increasingly fraught bilateral relations with Malaysia, with the aim of creating conflict between the two neighbours and, thereby, further destabilizing the region ('Sweeping Asian terror alliance uncovered', 2002; 'Opening remarks by Prime Minister Goh Chok Tong', 2002).

Mohammed Mansoor Jabarah, a 19-year-old Kuwaiti with Canadian citizenship, who had met bin Laden on at least four occasions, provided the finance for the operation and its link to al-Qaeda (Baker 2002a). Jabarah escaped to Malaysia in December 2001. Subsequently, Khalid Sheikh Mohammed sent Jabarah to organize new missions with Hambali. In January 2002, Jabarah met Hambali, and Omar al Faruq, leader of the Indonesian branch of JI ('Confessions of an al-Qaeda terrorist', 2002), in Southern Thailand. Here they agreed to hit soft targets such as the Kuta Beach resort in Bali ('A deadly connection', 2002). Jabarah made available $150 000 for the Bali operation. Hambali delegated the planning and execution of this mission to Mukhlas ('Four Corners: the Bali confessions', 2003). This complex web of transnational interconnections culminated in the devastating Bali attack and afforded the final proof of the danger that a transantional Southeast Asian terror network posed.

In piecing together the evolving relationship between al-Qaeda and various Islamic groupings in Southeast Asia, such as JI, since 1989, it is particularly hard to understand or explain why regional intelligence and police services exhibited such a marked degree of complacency about the nature and extent of the threat. Jabarah, for example, was detained in March 2002 and Faruq was arrested in August 2002. An American Federal Bureau of Investigation (FBI) report derived from their interrogations was made available to Australian and regional intelligence agencies in August 2002 (Wilkinson 2002).

Interestingly, even, after the Bali attack, Australian police and intelligence, like their ASEAN counterparts, officially denied any connection between JI and al-Qaeda. In January 2003, Australian police sources maintained that 'there is nothing concrete to link al-Qaeda to the [Bali] bombings' (*Australian*, 25–6 January 2003). In this Australia, still notionally attached to the doctrine of regional engagement, followed the Indonesian and wider ASEAN illusion of regional order. Eventually, in February, the Australian government officially, but somewhat obscurely, admitted that 'until the events of October 12' JI was 'an unknown quantity' (*Australian*, 15–16 February 2003).

In many ways, the scale of the intelligence failure across the region reflected a wider intergovernmental complacency towards the spread of Islamic extremism prior to the Bali bombing, which consistently underestimated the nature and extent of the threat. As we noted in the previous chapter, scholar-bureaucrats in regional centres of strategic and international studies played down the threat of militant groups (Wanandi 2002c, p. 142). The neglect of the growth of the terror network in Southeast Asia is all the more surprising given the availability of evidence on JI well before the assault on Bali. Like intelligence failures of the past, the facts were available but analysts failed to connect them. Indeed, concern at al-Qaeda's penetration of Southeast Asia, and the absence of regional response, led the Commander in Chief of US forces in the Pacific, Admiral Dennis Blair, to take the unusual step, in March 2002, of publicly naming Indonesia, Malaysia, the Philippines, Singapore and Thailand as countries where al-Qaeda enjoyed a measure of local support (State Department 2002b). The FBI's well-founded suspicion that, as al-Qaeda was chased out of its former Afghan sanctuary, it would seek refuge within the filigree of Southeast Asian states and form the Islamist *internationale*'s second front, prompted this warning (Tan 2002).

It was not entirely surprising that al-Qaeda's regional franchise, JI, would find both sympathy and covert support in some of the ASEAN countries, most notably the geographically extensive and porous archipelagos of Indonesia and the Philippines, which afforded suitably remote bases for training camps. Nor, perhaps, is it unexpected that states with Muslim populations or with long land frontiers would also find themselves the object of al-Qaeda's interest.

Thus, for example, countries like Malaysia and Thailand, which are not considered terrorist safe-havens, find themselves useful conduits for al-Qaeda funds, arms and personnel (Harnden 2002; Smith 2005, chap. 11).[15] These countries, nevertheless, have, since 2002, been increasingly active in arresting a number of nationals with suspected links to the organization (see Ahmed 2002a; 'Alien arrests bid to flush out "sleepers" ', 2002).

However, it was the arrest of 15 members of *Jemaah Islamiyah* in Singapore (Nathan 2002), the tiny city-state, known for its tight immigration controls and heavily restricted public sphere, that most graphically exemplified the scale of al-Qaeda's penetration of Southeast Asia. Of all the countries in the region that one would expect Islamic terrorists to find least accommodating, it would be Singapore. Yet, according to investigators, members of *Jemaah Islamiyah* had infiltrated Singapore as long ago as 1993.

According to official news reports, however, Singapore authorities argued that they already 'had a handle on the problem from the beginning' and would have dealt with the matter 'without US assistance' (Star 2002). However, this raises the curious question that, if local intelligence services did indeed have knowledge of the problem, why did regional governments not act years earlier, given that an apparently decade-long threat had been brewing in ASEAN's midst?

In June 2002, in a conference speech, then Senior Minister Lee Kuan Yew clarified how Singapore had garnered knowledge of the threat posed by Islamic terrorists. In the tense atmosphere after 11 September 2001, Lee claimed that the country's domestic intelligence service, the ISD, placed a Singaporean of Pakistani descent, Muhammad Aslam Yar Ali Khan, under surveillance after receiving a tip-off from a local Muslim that he and his associates had links to al-Qaeda. Aslam departed suddenly for Afghanistan on 4 October 2001 and a 'foreign intelligence agency' later reported he had been detained by the Northern Alliance on 29 November. The authorities decided to arrest Aslam's *Jemaah Islamiyah* associates in early December, before news of his detention in Afghanistan caused them to flee Singapore. It was following the interrogation of the 'detained terrorists' that the Singapore security services discovered that Islamic extremists had been 'building up since the early 1990s' (Lee Kuan Yew 2002).

It is clear from Lee Kuan Yew's account that the extent of the Singapore authorities' 'handle on the problem' was limited only to events post-11 September. Before that date, the country's intelligence services, widely acknowledged to be the most efficient in the region, had little idea of how far Islamic terrorist cells had infiltrated this most tightly controlled of Southeast Asian societies. Lee's speech was notable for his candid admission: 'What came as a shock was that [the] heightened [Islamic] religiosity facilitated Muslim terror groups linked to al-Qaeda to recruit Singapore Muslims into their network' (Lee 2002). In contrast, the Malaysian state appears to have been more sensitive to such threats arising from the growing electoral challenge from the Islamically based PAS opposition. In August 2001, one month before the attacks on the United States, the Malaysian police detained ten people under the Internal Security Act (ISA), including Nik Aldi Nik Aziz, the son of the PAS leader, who were accused of belonging to the KMM (Human Rights Watch 2002, p. 5).

What emerges from this picture is that there were varying degrees of understanding of the threat posed by Islamic militancy prior to 2001. While it might be sensible to assume that the region's intelligence services were conscious of the growth of Islamic radicalism both in their own countries and in Southeast Asia as a whole, what clearly took them by surprise was how far these seemingly disparate Islamic groups were both interconnected within Southeast Asia and plugged into the al-Qaeda-sponsored Islamist network. To this degree, Southeast Asian states were probably no more or less aware of the ever-expanding tentacles of al-Qaeda prior to 11 September than other intelligence agencies elsewhere, including the United States, Australia and Europe, but with a key difference: the post-colonial states in Southeast Asia devoted considerable efforts to crushing any sign of internal political dissent. The question remains: how was it possible for the powerful internal security structures in these countries to miss an expanding terror network in their already heavily policed domestic polities? This failure was most apparent in Singapore, the rich, ethnically diverse, but Chinese-dominated city-state. The Singapore government, moreover, is fixated with the notion of 'total defence', which aims to sensitize the population at all levels to the need to retain vigilance. Let us, therefore, briefly examine the ideological precepts underpinning total defence, because this reveals the official mindset behind intelligence failure both in Singapore and across the wider ASEAN region. This is because Singapore's small size and state capacity to administer all aspects of social and political life offers an ASEAN ideal of internal resilience to which other ASEAN states, because of their size and less efficient mechanisms of social control, can only aspire.

THE IMPLICATIONS OF ILLIBERAL HYPERVIGILANCE FOR NATIONAL SECURITY

According to official Singapore Ministry of Defence statements, total defence functions as the 'cornerstone of Singapore's defence policy' (Ministry of Defence, 2001a), embracing not only military defence, but also economic defence to maintain a strong economy 'that will not break down under threat of war', and civil defence to ensure the continuing functioning of society in times of national emergency. Interestingly, the total defence concept encompasses the intangible factors of 'social defence', to ensure that 'our people work together in harmony' (Ministry of Defence, 2001b), along with 'psychological defence' which aims to secure the 'individual citizen's commitment to the nation and the confidence in the future of our country' (Ministry of Defence, 2001a).

The government devotes much energy to inculcating the values of total defence, particularly through national education programmes, along with state-managed media flows and endless campaigns that reinforce the idea of 'One Nation, One People, One Singapore'.[16] Total defence demands not only political stability at home, but also the formal political commitment to the state on the part of the individual citizen. The logical accompaniment of the total defence concept is a large domestic counter-intelligence organization, the ISD, credited by most Singaporeans with an almost limitless capacity for surveillance.

The state licenses all forms of public activity, which has brought it as close to a surveillance state as one can find in the industrialized world. To this extent, the creation of an atmosphere of hypervigilance is one that the government has deliberately fostered as an instrument of social and political control (see George 2000). The paradoxical question is how, in a society in which hypervigilance is imbued, did the authorities manage to overlook the growth of a potentially subversive Islamist network? This paradox can be resolved by examining the conditions that gave rise to the practice of hypervigilance in the first place.

The obsession with total defence reflects the ruling People's Action Party's (PAP) more general preoccupation with 'total administration' to ensure the mobilization of the population towards national goals. To further this objective, government agencies, including the Internal Security Department, extensively monitor all aspects of the public space, including the Internet, media outlets and voluntary groups, while formally controlling all local education and university institutions (see Worthington 2001, pp. 490–519; Gomez 2000, 2002). Consequently, the precepts of total defence compound the *kiasu* (scared to lose) mentality nurtured by the ruling PAP over four decades of uninterrupted rule (Kurlantzick 2000, pp. 72–3). The result has been to instil within the media, academe and across the public sector an uncritical propensity to follow state directives, an inability to move or think beyond self-censoring boundaries (Gomez 2000). Collectively, such an illiberal style of governance has all but neutered civil society, thus closing down avenues of independent thought and analysis that might have identified emerging threats to regional security.

In Singapore the ruling ideology was actually termed 'Shared Values' and arose from the government's National Ideology project of 1988. The aim was to 'sculpt a Singaporean identity by incorporating the relevant parts of our various cultural heritages and values' which 'Singaporeans of all races and faiths could subscribe to and live by' ('Shared values', 2001). The ideology, officially adopted in 1993, stipulated five 'shared values': nation before community and society above self; the family as the basic unit of society; community support and respect for the individual; consensus not conflict; and racial and religious harmony (ibid.).

Shared values promoted total defence by claiming that the National Ideology 'would also help safeguard against undesirable values permeating from more developed countries which may be detrimental to our social fabric' (ibid.). Singapore president Wee Kim Wee, in January 1989, under- lined the target of the National Ideology, when he claimed that Singapore's status as a 'cosmopolitan city' had left it 'exposed to alien lifestyles and values', which particularly affected the younger generation. He added that 'Traditional Asian ideas of morality, duty and society' were 'giving way to a more Westernized, individualistic and self-centred outlook on life' (ibid.). As a consequence of such anti-western attitudes, the state's internal security apparatus became attuned to thinking that the principal threat to national security came, not from a dangerous Islamist terror network, but from an insidious form of western democracy. Those that the state trailed, denounced and punished with large fines were, more often than not, harmless, non- violent liberal democrats such as Chee Soon Juan, or veteran opposition figures like J.B. Jeyeretnam, with limited and largely inconsequential constituencies (see Chee 2001).

By accentuating the dangers of western-style democracy, the government machinery ignored problems of a religious and communal nature and presented a façade of interracial harmony. The formal commitment to racial harmony effectively masked feelings of religious or racial grievance, rather than providing outlets for legitimate expression. It was thus assumed that 'the different communities' were 'living harmoniously together' ('The five shared values', 2001). In this way, the security apparatus ignored the increasingly alienated Malay–Islamic minority community, which constitutes 15 per cent of the population. The Singapore government's own single-minded pursuit of secular developmental goals had merely exacerbated Malay disadvantage and political marginalization (Rahim 1998, pp. 242–3). Over the years such alien- ation succeeded in radicalizing a younger generation of Malays who, unlike their elders, rejected the official process of depoliticized cooption that denies them an effective political voice (see, for example, 'Malay MPs call for "care- ful approach" to tudung issue', 2001; Latif, 2002).

The ruling PAP further aggravated the problem by treating young Malay democratic activists, like those who ran the *Fateha.com* website, who sought to debate government policy, as indistinguishable from those prepared to advance their cause by violent means. So, when *Fateha's* (Fateha means 'The Key' in English) founder, Zulfikar Mohamad Shariff, observed that both Singapore's foreign policy alignment towards the US and its domestic education policy that prevents Muslim girls from wearing head scarves at school offended Muslim feelings, the government reacted with characteristic lack of proportion ('Ex-Fateha chief gets out of headscarf debate', 2001). Defence Minister Teo Chee Hean declared such views a 'slow poisoning' calculated to turn Singapore into a new Afghanistan ('Fateha pol', 2002; 'Muslims here reject Fateha chief's remarks', 2002). After a week of denunciation in the state-owned media, Zulfikar quit Fateha in late January 2002. Subsequently, he and his family quit the city state for more tolerant, but more decadent Australia. In this light we can see that the practice of total defence has had a perverse impact on considerations of national security, repressing the problem of minority alienation, rather than addressing it politically.[17]

The further paradox is that adherence to a rigid total defence mentality actually intensified Singapore's security dilemmas rather than solving them. Total defence was no defence. What Singapore and states in the wider regional grouping required were mechanisms that enhanced attachments to the state and its institutions through an open and active civil society that might criticize government policy, but through the capacity to articulate difference actually fosters an evolving political bond of allegiance. Such strategies, however, do not appeal to the administrative state's elite, or to state elites elsewhere in ASEAN.

THE DELUSION OF 'SHARED' VALUES

In effect, what the Singapore experience reveals is how the wider region became susceptible to delusion. It has been noted in a number of instances throughout this book that one of the central precepts that originally united ASEAN from the late 1960s onward was a shared resistance by its members to the threat of Communism. However, the receding communist threat from the late 1980s, robbed the Association of the prop that underpinned its authoritarian pact of non-interference. To fill the void, an ideology of 'shared' non-western values arose to take its place. ASEAN's official philosophy, post-Cold War, promoting the vision that Confucianism and Islam harmoniously blended into the shared values of the ASEAN way to economic growth and political stability, reflected and complemented Singapore's understanding of 'shared values'. The security practice of the other ASEAN states, although somewhat less total than Singapore's surveillance state, displayed a similar concern throughout the 1990s with counteracting the corrosive influence of western liberalism, rather than radical Islam. In other words, ASEAN states bought their own Asia bonding rhetoric, despite the growing evidence after the financial meltdown of 1997 that Southeast Asia was an increasingly problematic economic and political neighbourhood (Holland 2000). The overall impact of this ASEAN-wide promotion of internal resilience and externally shared norms has been political and institutional incoherence. State security agencies disregarded the evolving problem of Islamist/ethno-separatist discontent in the wider region, despite the existence of draconian internal security legislation. In fact the norm of non-interference and the practice of internal resilience undermined any wider capacity to perceive a regional threat because member states encouraged their security agencies to ignore criminal or terrorist activity outside their borders.

One of the enduring features of this official ASEAN incoherence is that member states are compelled in public to maintain outward harmony in deference to the concept of shared regional values, while in reality ignoring and repressing clashes of interest between them. As a consequence, obtaining unity on specific measures has proved difficult to achieve. This leads to an official practice for grand public relations gestures that give the appearance of action, but which lack substance. Since 1990, the Association has held meetings and summits on an annual or biennial basis and established the ASEAN Regional Forum to promote its 'shared' vision further afield. Rarely does any concrete plan of action or a practical and measured ASEAN response eventuate, be it towards the 'war on terror', or indeed anything else.

To the extent that ASEAN showed any cognizance of the growing threat, its efforts were characteristically minimalist and largely declaratory. Before the Bali attack ASEAN established a number of discussion forums to look into the issue of extremism in the region. The Association also held a number of ministerial meetings in 2002 on the state of the terrorist threat in Southeast Asia. These meetings were mainly notable for their rhetorical aspirations and at best only provided for low-level logistical support (see Ahmed 2002b). At the ASEAN summit of November 2001, Southeast Asia's leaders only just managed to agree to a condemnation of the 11 September attacks upon the United States, but avoided any mention of military interdiction in Afghanistan, which both Malaysia and Indonesia opposed (Head 2001). Even after the discovery of the militant Islamic penetration of their societies, ASEAN members generally treated the revelations as an opportunity to disclaim any responsibility for the growing security crisis in the region via the far more conspicuous, if unofficial, shared ASEAN value of condemning the failings of their ostensible partners (see 'The plot thickens, but mostly outside Singapore', 2002; 'The trail to Kuala Lumpur', 2002).

Eventually, in May 2002, ASEAN ministers somewhat belatedly met in Kuala Lumpur to consider the threat of terrorism. Subsequently, the two-day ASEAN ministers meeting adopted what was described as a 'slew of measures to face up to the threat of regional terrorism'. On closer examination the 'slew' revealed itself to be little more than non-specific aspirations to establish 'contact points' for the exchange of information and various forms of low-level logistical support. Indonesia subsequently hosted a series of workshops on international terrorism (Ahmed 2002b).

Significantly, in May 2002, and in their subsequent July Joint Communiqué of the 35th ASEAN Ministerial Meeting on 'Responding to Challenges: Securing a Better Future', the Association could not agree upon a definition of terrorism (Ahmed 2002c). Instead, the organization declared that 'defining terrorism is not crucial, fighting it is' (ibid.). The Association's deputy secretary-general, Datuk Mokhtar Selat, contended that terrorism is 'like you have a car. You don't define what is a car, but how the car moves. The focus is not on definition, the focus is on how we work together' (quoted in ibid.). Notwithstanding the fact that most people can distinguish a car from, for example, a durian (a popular Southeast Asian tropical fruit),[18] this definitional imprecision reinforced the view that ASEAN's understanding of the character of the threat and how to respond to it lacked focus. Despite a subsequent ARF agreement to freeze terrorists' financial assets, ASEAN could not agree a collective strategy towards transnational crime and terror. Consequently, individual member states were effectively left to their own devices in dealing with the evolving Islamist threat.

The Association remained hamstrung in dealing with the Southeast Asian terror network as a result of its commitment to the principle of non-interference at both the ideological and the ministerial level. As a consequence, some ASEAN states, along with regional commentary more generally, continued to exhibit a degree of ambivalence toward the global interconnectedness of radical Islam (see Djalal 2003). For example, the Indonesian authorities, despite mounting evidence to the contrary, continue to discount any clear link between regional Islamism and al-Qaeda. Interestingly, the 35-page indictment of the alleged nightclub bomber, Amrozi, failed even to mention his membership of JI ('Bali opens terror trial in blast fatal to 200', 2002) whilst the indictment of Bashir in April 2003 for treason made no mention of his links with al-Qaeda (Munro 2002). Significantly, successive Indonesian governments failed between 2002 and 2005 to prosecute effectively the *emir* of regional terror, who retains a significant support base in Indonesia.

Meanwhile, in early 2003 the Thai government threatened to prosecute any foreign journalist who alleged that senior al-Qaeda operatives like Hambali had ever met in the Muslim-populated south of the country to coordinate attacks across the region, despite well-informed reports that this was indeed the case (Baker 2002b; 'Into the heart of darkness' 2002). Several months later, Thai police arrested Hambali in Ayodhya, Thailand. Facing evidence of mounting Muslim disaffection and JI activity in Southern Thailand, the Thai

Prime Minister reversed his previous stance of denial and vigorously prosecuted any manifestation of Islamic dissent in the South. This culminated in the massacre of several hundred Muslims in Pattani in April 2004. Later the same year, as Prime Minister Thaksin's autocratic tactics drove dissident Muslims down the extremist path (Kurlantzick 2005), the Thai government accused the Malaysian government of affording terrorists sanctuary and support from the North Malaysian and Islamically purist PAS-governed state of Kelatan. This in turn prompted denials from Malaysia and a deterioration in bilateral relations (*Star*, 22 December 2004).[19] The Thai–Malay experience of prosecuting transnational terrorism does not suggest that ASEAN states have evolved particularly sophisticated cooperative strategies for addressing the phenomenon since 2002.

Indeed, the predilection for member states unilaterally to go their own way in the war against terrorism, while remaining suspicious of their regional partners, has not improved threat assessment within and among Southeast Asian states and does not intimate a developing security community. Instead, between 2003 and 2005, after Bali and other JI-inspired attacks in the region, ASEAN members essentially reinforced standard operating procedures. Singapore once again exemplified this tendency, the discovery of Islamic sleeper cells merely intensifying the retreat into the artificial cocoon of total defence (see Latif 2001). Discussion of the city-state's security situation and the appropriate response remains off-limits (Henson 2002).[20] Worryingly, the continuation of the strategy of state-directed threat assessment will succeed only in driving out objective analysis in a way that harms rather than furthers the national, or the wider regional, interest.

Significantly, such international cooperation that has occurred since 11 September has taken place outside ASEAN's remit, either by bilateral and trilateral agreements between individual states or with outside powers. In May 2002, for example, Indonesia, Malaysia and the Philippines entered into a trilateral agreement officially billed as an 'anti-terrorism pact'. The terms of the agreement obliged its members to exchange information on a wide variety of illicit activities, ranging from money laundering and piracy to the theft of marine resources and marine pollution. These items could not be said necessarily to fall under the rubric of 'anti-terrorism'. Additionally, they provoked suspicion that the pact was merely a covert vehicle for advancing various territorial claims in the South China Sea and elsewhere, not least against other ASEAN members. Moreover, the terminological vagueness in which various forms of unlawful activity were couched led to predictions that the agreement would increase political disputes. Indeed, Singaporean commentators speculated that the provisions on money laundering would simply enable some member states to pursue local tycoons who moved funds out of their domicile countries through Singapore's banking system (Lee Kim Chew 2002).

The most significant international collaboration against militant Islamic terrorist groups, however, has involved bilateral approaches with actors outside the region. In practice this has meant with either US or Australian assistance in terms of intelligence sharing and more direct practical assistance. Ironically, extending from 2002 to 2005, the most effective collaboration occurred between the Australian Federal Police and the Indonesian police in the investigation of the Bali attack. This illustrated what could be attained through concerted action (see 'Minister for Foreign Affairs, Alexander Downer', 2002; 'Bali bombing – Australian and Indonesian police', 2003). Meanwhile, in the Philippines, the United States provided military advisors and equipment to improve the Philippine army's effort against Muslim insurgents, particularly against the *Abu Sayyaf* group (State Department 2002a).

The growing level of US support for regional governments raises concern in some quarters that countries with poor human rights records will be accorded both respectability and aid through their willingness to endorse the American-led war on terrorism. This applies particularly to countries like Indonesia, which the United States Congress banned from all military collaboration following the organized ransacking of East Timor in 1999 by Indonesian Army-backed militias. In the wake of the Bali and subsequent Jakarta bombings of the Marriott Hotel in 2003 and Australian Embassy in 2004, the largely ineffectual presidency of Megawati Sukarnoputri (2000–2004) received US aid to improve the training of Indonesian police and customs officials ('Al-Qaeda in Southeast Asia', 2002). The democratic election of the more congenial US-educated figure of Susilo Bambang Yudhyono to the Indonesian presidency in 2004 prompted Congress to rescind the ban on military cooperation, and the US army once more resumed training programmes for the TNI in 2005 (*Australian*, 28 February 2005).

No-strings aid discourages any reform of institutions, such as the military, that are guilty of human rights abuses. The US moderates criticism of states in the region with poor human rights records provided they support the effort to curb global terror.[21] Human rights organizations in 2002 predicted that Jakarta would use its 'Hate-Sowing Articles' in the Indonesian Criminal Code to suppress separatist unrest in areas like Aceh, whilst militant, but nationalist, Islamist groups like *Laskar Jihad*, the MMI and the FPI promote their brand of fundamentalism with relative impunity (Amnesty International 2002a, pp. 1–2). Events between 2003 and 2005 confirmed these fears. In 2003, after the collapse of autonomy negotiations for the Sumatran province of Aceh with GAM, the Indonesian government imposed martial law across the province. At the same time, Jakarta tolerates radical Islamist proselytizing both in Aceh and across the archipelago by groups like *Laskar Jihad,* and its mutation *Lascar Mujahideen*, and the FPI. Elsewhere, former Malaysian Prime Minister Mahathir exploited the post-11 September *mentalité* to justify the detention of

PAS supporters under the ISA (Amnesty International 2002b, p. 1; Human Rights Watch 2002, pp. 2–5). Furthermore, the fact that cyberspace has emerged as a new theatre in the war against terror only encourages governments in both Malaysia and Singapore to regulate the net as a medium for civil society (Rodan 2002). Indeed, the fact that certain Southeast Asian regimes use the war on terror to suppress relatively innocuous political dissent at home has become a notable feature of the ASEAN response to the transnational threat.

ASEAN'S FUTURE: FORWARD TO THE PAST

During the 1980s and 1990s, a peculiar intellectual salient appeared in the study of Southeast Asian international relations. It maintained that ASEAN's official philosophy had successfully accommodated the rise of Islam. This led to an incoherent interpretation of the character of regional Islam. On the one hand, Islamic virtues were considered part of the region's shared culture which could assist economic development. On the other, the official philosophy held that Islam's 'traditional values' served as a prophylactic protecting the region from the intrusion of the more unsavoury aspects of modernity embodied in western notions of liberal-democracy and human rights. Simultaneously, regional scholarship, sometimes abetted by US political science models, considered the moderate, syncretic Islam practised in Southeast Asia a harbinger of democratization and a politically pluralist Muslim consciousness (see Hefner 2000). Among western analysts, ASEAN scholar-bureaucrats and the region's intelligence services alike, this created an edifice of mutually supporting indifference towards the spread of an Islamic challenge to the legitimacy of the Southeast Asian states themselves.

Thus, for most of the 1990s, writing about ASEAN by its own *commentariat* maintained a positive political image rather than offering detached analysis of regional problems. Even though the presence of radical Islamism was both observable and, to some extent, known to the political elites of Southeast Asia, ASEAN's rhetorical adherence to 'shared values' inhibited the identification of both the nature and the spread of an Islamic terror network. As the extent of al-Qaeda's penetration of the region in the wake of 11 September graphically illustrated, it is the avowed intention of al-Qaeda-linked groups like *Jemaah Islamiyah* to destroy the precarious work of post-colonial nation building in Southeast Asia, and replace it with an Islamic arrangement, a *Darul Islam Nusantara* (Southeast Asian homeland), encompassing Southern Thailand, Malaysia, Mindanao, Singapore and the Indonesian archipelago. Such groups are motivated, not by shared Asian values, but, as Lee Kuan Yew now admits, a 'shared ideology of universal jihad' (Lee 2002). Given the protoplasmic character of al-Qaeda, the threat remains pervasive. Al-Qaeda's plans for regional control envisage Southeast Asia divided into four areas or *mantiqis* for operational purposes: *mantiqi* 1, covering Malaysia, Singapore and Southern Thailand; *mantiqi* 2, most of Indonesia; *mantiqi* 3, Eastern Malaysia and Indonesia including Sulawesi, Borneo, Brunei and the Southern Philippines (the *mantiqi* that can perhaps be seen to be the most active in its international links); and *mantiqi* 4, Irian Jaya and Australia ('Twisted ties to terrorist network', 2002).

What, then, is the kind of response necessary by the states in the region and/or ASEAN collectively? Quite clearly, increased surveillance of the ISD variety is part of the problem, not the solution. As has been indicated, hyper-vigilance does not of itself yield increased conditions of safety and well-being, but, on the contrary, tends to undermine the fabric of national security. Ideally, what is needed at the state level is the development of mechanisms that enhance community attachments to the political order and its democratizing institutions that would improve independent analysis of threats to national security as well as opening avenues to address politically motivated grievances within and across borders. Yet the original members of ASEAN neglected the opportunity to develop such communal attachments during the 1990s – a time of growth and expansion when economic development could have facilitated liberalizing decompression. Instead, the years of economic growth were marked by an extension of state surveillance and the contraction of civil and political space in Singapore and Malaysia. Even in those regional states like the Philippines, Thailand and Indonesia that underwent some form of democratization over this period, it has not engendered tolerance or political accommodation of minority grievances.

Finally, regarding the role of ASEAN, the widely dissipated ideas promulgated by both local and western analysts concerning the region's alleged strategic cultural commonalities, a shared ASEAN way and a multilateral 'imagined' security community, have only obscured any substantive regional institutional development. Ironically, it is precisely now, in the wake of a threat that is able to operate transnationally, that ASEAN could conceivably give substance to its claims for harmony and cooperation. Strategically, this would require intelligence sharing and police collaboration and the capacity, first outlined after 1997, by former Thai foreign minister Surin Pitsuwan, for a pan-ASEAN agency to interfere in cases of state breakdown, like East Timor in 1999, as opposed to the standard ASEAN practice of rigid adherence to the principle of non-interference, rather than risk losing face. The downside of any potential increase in cooperation, of course, is that it might only reinforce stagnant regional authoritarianism. This might be avoided if increased security cooperation were combined with a pan-ASEAN campaign to win hearts and minds by advancing civic attachments. Given the entrenched structures of governance in Southeast Asia and the strategic culture of the ASEAN way, together with the external environment engendered by the war on terrorism, this is an unlikely prospect. For the foreseeable future, expectations of meaningful cooperation in the security realm, let alone real democratization, remain limited, with negative consequences for effective threat identification and the enhancement of national security objectives.

NOTES

1. The misapprehension of al-Qaeda's threat potential before 11 September 2001 was clearly evident. For example, writing in 1993, it was Robert Fisk's opinion that the 'Saudi businessman who recruited mujahideen now used them for large-scale building projects in Sudan' and was thus putting his army 'on the road to peace' (Fisk 1993).

2. *Laskar Jihad Ahlus Sunnah wal Jammah* (www.laskarjihad.or.id). The *Laskar Jihad* homepage informs readers that 'Jihad as a holy ibadah for Muslims is the only answer to the . . . many oppressions borne by the Muslims in different areas of this country.' Visitors to the website will be greeted with a professional-looking header featuring a picture of a bullet with the accompanying exhortation: 'Victory or Martyrdom in Ambon'. Ambon is the capital of the Maluka Islands where *Laskar Jihad* has been helping to sponsor the murderous communal feud between Christians and Muslims in these once peaceful territories, also known as the Spice Islands. This conflict has claimed an estimated 5000 lives since 1998.

3. Researching internal security issues in Southeast Asian states is notoriously difficult. As a topic for intellectual inquiry it simply does not exist in these countries. Hence material has to be pieced together from disparate sources, including journalistic reports and other unofficial information. It hardly needs to be stated that those in the region who might evince an interest in such matters will not only be denied access to any records, but would likely find themselves the object of attention from the intelligence services. There are few other scholarly studies in the area, apart from Desmond Ball's research into signals intelligence (see Ball 1995, 1998).

4. Abu Bakar Bashir is also known to operate under the pseudonym of Abdus Samad.

5. Bashir was also involved with the protean fundamentalist group *Komando Jihad*, a shadowy outfit seemingly manufactured in 1977 by elements within Indonesian army intelligence in order to discredit the Muslim-based political party, *Partai Persatuan Pembangunan* (PPP) (United Development Party), which posed a serious electoral threat to President Suharto's secular *Golkar* party. The conspiracy was the alleged brainchild of General Ali Moertopo, Suharto's right-hand man, and devised from within the Jakarta-based Center for International and Strategic Studies, which functioned as a front group for the intelligence services. The intention was covertly to encourage Islamic militants to wage a violent campaign for the creation of an Islamic state in a way that would reflect badly on the PPP. It is still not clear whether the *Komando Jihad* was a conspiracy that got out of hand or a pretext for a more general round-up of opponents of the regime (see Asia Watch 1989, pp. 76–85).

6. This comment was attributed to a Malaysian official.

7. Abu Bakar Bashir was summoned for questioning by the Indonesian authorities in late January 2002, in order, according to National Police spokesman Inspector General Saleh Saaf, 'to clarify accusations that he is linked to the Kumpulan Mujahidin Malaysis militants', adding that the 'police do not yet have any evidence that indicates connections between Ba'asyir and the al-Qaeda network' (quoted in 'Jakarta takes terrorist link claims seriously', 2002).

8. The term 'al-Qaeda' may also be interpreted in other ways to mean 'the foundation', 'the ideology' or any number of other related ideas.

9. *Pancasila* means 'five principles' and comprises the belief in one God, justice, national unity, guided democracy and social justice.

10. Whether it is appropriate to say that al-Qaeda existed in the 1980s is debatable. It is not certain when the grouping actually came into being, though 1989 is often stated as the year of its formation. The origins of the movement appear to reside in the Maktab al-Khidmat lil-Mujahideen (or MaK for short) founded in Afghanistan in 1980 by Abdullah Azzam. MaK's literal translation into English is the College that Serves the Arab Warriors, but is often rendered simply as the Afghan Service Bureau. MaK's function was to recruit Arab fighters to support the struggle against the Soviet occupation of Afghanistan and it is the MaK that was to form the nucleus of ideas about transnational jihad. In this respect, al-Qaeda's origins reside in the later evolution of the MaK. There is even evidence to suggest that 'al-Qaeda' is not a self-given name, but was the name of a file found on Osama bin Laden's personal computer listing members and contacts within the MaK. The appendage 'al-Qaeda' thus appears to have been coined by the US authorities as a convenient short-hand to describe the loose, if rather complex, arrangements of a network based on MaK's membership (for further information, see 'Al-Qaeda's origins and links 2003'; 'Blowback', 2001; Bazi 2001; Conesa 2002; Symons 2003; Gunaratna 2004).

11. The US State Department's *Patterns of Global Terrorism 2002* formally lists the Abu Sayyaf Group as having broken away from the MNLF in the early 1990s under Abdurajak Abubakar Janjalani, although this is questioned by other analysts who argue that it evolved somewhat more independently, based on the Tauseg ethnic group (State Department 2002a; for a more concerted examination of the general development of Moro separatism, see Gowing 1974; Che Man 1990, chap. 1).

12. A document compiled by the Philippine Directorate of Intelligence, marked D1, and classi-fied as secret, referred to MILF's links with al-Qaeda and MaK, stating that: 'A certain Zine el Abiddin Abou Zoubaida of Maktab al Khidmat has been in contact with 2 prominent personalities of the MILF', Zoubaida being a Saudi on the leadership council of al-Qaeda (Republic of Philippines 1999).

13. The Philippine police report concluded that 'Bin Laden and Khalifa are channelling funds to support the MILF through its various Islamic NGOs. The MILF on the other hand provided training venues for other Islamic extremists in their stronghold areas' (Republic of Philippines 1999, pp. 1–2).

14. In March 2003, Malaysian police found the rest of the four tons of explosive in a plantation near Muar, Malaysia (see Fineman and Drogin 2002).

15. For example, it was reported in mid-2002 that the plan for the 11 September attacks origi-nated in a meeting in Kuala Lumpur in January 2000 convened by Ramzi Binalshibh, a Yemeni al-Qaeda activist. It was alleged that the participants at the meeting agreed to attack US naval targets in the Yemen, and US cities, with hijacked aircraft. It was claimed that Binalshibh was identified from photographs taken by Malaysian intelligence at the request of the CIA while he was attending the Kuala Lumpur meeting (see Harnden 2003; Smith 2005, chap. 11).

16. A patriotic slogan developed by the Psychological Defence Unit of the Ministry of Defence (see David 1994, p. 59).

17. For an illustration of this belief, see 'Fateha break up shows extremism not supported', 2001).

18. This of course would not apply to those affected by post-modern theories where the free-floating nature of the signifier in the process of signification would mean that any distinc-tion between car and durian would be an arbitrary act of power (see, in this context, Barthes 1977, pp. 142ff).

19. Subsequently, the Malaysian police detained Chae Kumae Kuteh, who travelled on a Saudi Arabian passport. The Thai authorities wished to extradite Kuteh for his alleged role in lead-ing the Mujahideen Islam Pattani (*Asia Wall Street Journal*, 28–30 January 2005).

20. This was signalled during one of the government's periodic attempts to show that it is 'loosening up' by allowing members of parliament to speak more freely. However, the

state-controlled *Straits Times* newspaper relayed the limits of the MPs' – and, ergo, public –
room for debate by stating that 'matters of critical national importance, such as security'
were 'not for negotiation' (Henson, 2002).

21. It was noted, for example, that during a meeting of the Asia–Pacific Economic Cooperation
(APEC) forum that President George Bush made no mention of human rights issues (see
Human Rights Watch 2002, p. 1).

Conclusion: it's no fun at the A.S.E.A.N.

One of the more surreal rituals on the contemporary diplomatic circuit must be the obligatory karaoke evening that follows the annual ASEAN meetings with its various dialogue partners. Former US Secretary of State, Colin Powell, has twice attended this event. In July 2001 at the 34th ASEAN Ministerial Meeting in Hanoi, Powell, dressed as a cowboy, crooned 'El Paso' and expired in the chaste embrace administered by former Japanese foreign minister, Mikiko Tanaka, fetchingly dressed as a Vietnamese peasant ('Ministers let their hair down', 2001). In late June 2004, at the 37th ASEAN Ministerial Meeting, Powell gave further proof of his karaoke skill, this time offering a version of 'Y.M.C.A.'. In retrospect, Powell's rendition of the Village People's late 1970s camp classic may be construed as an ironic diplomatic commentary upon ASEAN's karaoke version of a diplomatic community, and the edifice of official and academic delusion that sustains it.

Before 1997, with the regional economic miracle in full swing, ASEAN's self-confidence and self-regard reached a peak, buoyed by articles in the international and regional media that announced the Pacific Century and encouraged the young and ambitious to 'Go East young man' (Mahbubani 1994a, pp. 6–7). By 2004, however, as Powell's song suggests, ASEAN was more of 'a place you can go/I said, young man, when you are short on your dough'.[1]

ASEAN, might, indeed, possess everything for Track 2 diplomacy junkies to enjoy, and offers plenty of opportunities 'to hang out with all the boys'. In the five star Southeast Asian locations where these encounters take place, you can, generally 'do whatever you feel'. But ASEAN diplomats might usefully ponder the question asked by the Village People: 'Young man, what exactly do you want to be?' For, in truth, despite the usual proclamations of its regional significance as an evolving security community, ASEAN since the financial crisis does not seem to know either its purpose or its role.

As delegates shuffled through security gates to attend the 2004 ASEAN ministers' meeting in Jakarta, an atmosphere that ASEAN was 'down and out with the blues' hung over the conference reinforced by a cloud of smog blown over from burning rainforests in Sumatra. Observing no incoherence between 'the haze' (on which ASEAN has a less than effective trans-boundary agreement) and the intrusive security arrangements, the delegates exchanged conventional pieties about the growing maturity and confidence of the

Association in matters of regional harmony and stability. Official statements announced the organization's intention to establish a regional security and economic community, enhance maritime safety and bolster provisions against terrorism.

The European Union commissioner for external relations Chris Patten, attending the ASEAN Regional Forum (ARF) session of the meeting, even sought a more passionate multilateral embrace between two regional organizations that were, he claimed, 'more than the sum of their parts'. The embrace, however, was somewhat perfunctory as proposals for an ASEAN–Europe Meeting (ASEM) later that year stalled over the issue of Myanmar's attendance, with the European Union insisting that the regime in Yangon (Rangoon) with its egregious human rights record should not be permitted to participate, while ASEAN members were equally adamant that the Europeans should not 'impose conditionalities' (Jayakumar 2004).

Differences over Myanmar notwithstanding, the ARF, through its informal dialogue mechanisms and confidence-building measures, remains (its aficionados maintain) the region's premier security forum (ibid.). This claim appeared to be given credence at the meeting, which witnessed the accession of Pakistan, Japan and Russia to ASEAN's foundational Treaty of Amity and Cooperation (TAC). On the surface, it would seem that, despite the instability caused in Southeast Asia by the continuing war on terror and the enduring weakness of the Southeast Asian economies since the financial meltdown, ASEAN and the ARF continue to be central to the security and stability of the region.

In practice, however, the opposite is true. Significantly, the meeting received little media attention in the region or beyond. It barely rated a mention in the Australian press: how different from the Keating era prior to 1996 when former foreign minister Gareth Evans appeared with maps depicting Australia at Asia's core, to widespread media acclaim. Singapore's *Straits Times* consigned coverage of the meeting to the Asia section of the government-sponsored broadsheet. Elsewhere, much of the Philippine press dismissed the summit as 'disappointing' ('A disappointing summit', 2004).

Such media coverage suggests ASEAN's peripheral rather than core role in regional growth and stability. For the real story that emerges from the ASEAN and ARF meetings is that the multilateral regional dispensation is in the process of being eclipsed by the larger and more powerful regional players from Northeast Asia, notably China and Japan. Meanwhile, the ASEAN grouping itself looks increasingly fragmented politically, economically and strategically, and Australia looks on ambivalently rather than with the unalloyed enthusiasm it once did, increasingly uncertain about what a proposed East Asian Community grouping might entail.

Since the financial meltdown of 1997–98, ASEAN's inability to address the region's economy, or security issues like East Timor's separation from Indonesia, piracy, smuggling or the regional franchises of al-Qaeda has been evident for all but ASEAN's scholar–bureaucracy and their western admirers to see. To address transnational problems, however, requires transnational strategies, which in turn require a major re-evaluation of the TAC which, *inter alia*, imposes upon signatories acceptance of the principle of non-interference in the internal affairs of member states. Ironically, of course, this is the source of the Association's attraction to the grouping's least democratic members, from developed Singapore and Malaysia, to poverty-stricken and authoritarian Myanmar, Cambodia, Laos and Vietnam, as well as to those in the emerging 'ASEAN Plus Three' forum, like China.

Consequently, any attempt to modify the Treaty of Amity and Cooperation meets with resistance. This was evident when democratizing Indonesia, which chaired the grouping in 2004, put forward the outline for a genuine ASEAN security community that would both promote human rights, democracy and transparent communication and also create a regional peacekeeping force. Rather than grasping the opportunity offered by such a bold approach to the security dilemmas confronting the region, member states, instead, regarded the Indonesian initiative suspiciously, construing it as an unacceptable bid by Indonesia to assert itself over the rest of ASEAN's membership (Wain 2004). At the 2004 Jakarta meeting, a suitable face-saving formula concealed the differences. Ministers agreed to the concept of a security community, while denying it any substance; or, as the convoluted ASEAN prose explained, the ministers agreed to engage in progressive security cooperation, but 'not in the form of a defense pact, military alliance or a joint foreign policy'; in other words, not in the form of a security community.

At the same time, whilst Indonesia is evidently keen to engender some greater regional coherence, it is equally concerned about the proposal for an East Asian summit that would give enhanced credibility to an enlarged East Asian community composed of ASEAN plus the Northeast Asian 'Three', namely, China, Japan and South Korea. Although both Singapore and Malaysia see China's growing market as a source of regional regeneration and welcome the prospect of deeper East Asian integration, other members of the grouping, notably Indonesia, but also Vietnam and the Philippines, are concerned by China's potential for exerting regional hegemony. Japan, meanwhile, which formally proposed an East Asian summit in December 2003, is increasingly worried by the thrall that China's market casts over Southeast Asia.

Given ASEAN's lack of common purpose, some of ASEAN's dialogue partners, irritated by its informality and indecision, have advertised a desire for a share in the leadership of the ASEAN Regional Forum. Chris Patten, in a state of post-bonding *tristesse*, expressed frustration with ASEAN-style diplomacy, observing that 'foreign policy isn't just about being nice to people and getting on. It's about trying to secure objectives' ('A disappointing summit', 2004).

Such demands will only grow more insistent as the weakness of ASEAN, both in security and in economic terms, becomes apparent. Indeed, as economic deals and security agreements within and outside the region occur increasingly on a bilateral or trilateral basis, which practically refutes the notion of an integrated economic and security community, Asia's regional groupings begin to look rather *less* than the sum of their parts. For, ultimately, state-interested *realpolitik* in Asia is played through the rhetorical shells of ASEAN's multilateralist arrangements, like the ARF and ASEAN Plus Three. Observing the growing incoherence of ASEAN's karaoke diplomacy, the *Manila Times* aptly concluded that 'Singing, rather than thinking, is Asia's dubious contribution to international conclaves' ('A disppointing summit', 2004). In karaoke and in ASEAN, imitation rather than originality or substance prevails.

NOTE

1. Interestingly, Condoleeza Rice wisely declined to attend the ASEAN gathering in Laos. This was the first time in over twenty years that the American Secretary of State had not attended the meeting.

Bibliography

'A deadly connection' (2002), *Sydney Morning Herald*, 16 November.

'A disappointing summit' (2004), *Manila Times*, 9 July.

Abdullah Haji Ahmad Badawi (1992), 'Laying the foundations for a new age in Southeast Asia', in Normah Mahmood and Thangam Ramnath (eds), *Southeast Asia: The Way Forward*, Kuala Lumpur: Institute of Strategic and International Studies.

Abeysinghe, T., H.G. Ng and L.Y. Tan (1994), 'ESU forecasts of the Singapore economy', in Anthony Chin and Ngiam Kee Jin (eds), *Outlook for the Singapore Economy*, Singapore: Trans Global Publishing.

Acharya, Amitav (1991), 'The Association of Southeast Asian Nations: security community or defence community?', *Pacific Affairs*, **64** (2).

Acharya, Amitav (1993), *A New Regional Order in South-East Asia: ASEAN in the Post-Cold War Era*, Adelphi Paper 279, Oxford: Oxford University Press/IISS.

Acharya, Amitav (1997a), 'Ideas, identity and institution-building: from the "ASEAN way" to the "Asia–Pacific way" ', *Pacific Review*, **10** (3).

Acharya, Amitav (1997b), 'The periphery as the core: the third world and security studies', in Keith Krause and Michael Williams (eds), *Critical Security Studies*, London: UCL Press.

Acharya, Amitav (1998a), 'Collective identity and conflict management in Southeast Asia', in Emanuel Adler and Michael Barnett (eds), *Security Communities*, Cambridge: Cambridge University Press.

Acharya, Amitav (1998b), 'Culture, security, multilateralism: the ASEAN way and regional order', in Keith Krause (ed.), *Culture and Security: Multilateralism, Arms Control and Security Building*, London: Frank Cass.

Acharya, Amitav (1999a), 'A concert of Asia?', *Survival*, **41** (3).

Acharya, Amitav (1999b), 'Realism, institutionalism, and the Asian economic crisis', *Contemporary Southeast Asia*, **21** (1).

Acharya, Amitav (1999c), 'Regionalism and the emerging world order: sovereignty, autonomy, identity', paper presented to Centre for the Study of Globalisation and Regionalisation Conference, 'After the global crises: what next for regionalism?', Scarman House, University of Warwick, 16–18 September.

Acharya, Amitav (2000), *The Quest for Identity: International Relations of Southeast Asia*, Singapore: Oxford University Press.

Acharya, Amitav (2001), *Constructing a Security Community in Southeast Asia: ASEAN and the Problem of Regional Order*, London: Routledge.

Acharya, Amitav (2002a), 'Dubya's dangerous and divisive doctrine', *Straits Times*, 16 October.

Acharya, Amitav (2002b), 'An opportunity not to be squandered', *Straits Times*, 12 November.

Acharya, Amitav (2003), Review of ASEAN's Diplomatic and Security Culture: Origins, Development and Prospects, *Contemporary Southeast Asia*, **25** (2).

Ahmed, Reme (2002a), 'KL arrests 23 Islamic militants in swoop', *Straits Times*, 5 January.

Ahmed, Reme (2002b), 'Asean adopts plan to fight terrorism', *Straits Times*, 21 May.

Ahmed, Reme (2002c), 'Asean ministers acknowledge defining terrorism is not crucial, fighting it is', *Straits Times*, 21 May.

Akamatsu, Kenichi (1962), 'Historical patterns of economic growth in developing countries', *Developing Economies*, 2, March–August.

'Al-Qaeda boss reported to have visited Australia' (2002), ABC Lateline,11 November.

'Al-Qaeda in Southeast Asia: evidence and response' (2002), CDI Terrorism Project, 8 February (www.cdi.org/terrorism/sea-pr.cfm).

'Al-Qaeda planned to kill Pope' (2002), *San Francisco Examiner*, 11 November.

'Al-Qaeda plot to bomb US ships foiled by MI6' (2002), *Daily Telegraph*, 13 January.

'Al-Qaeda's origins and links' (2003), BBC News, 16 May, (http://news.bbc.co.uk/1/hi/world/south_asia/1670089.stm).

Alagappa, Muthiah (1993), 'Regionalism and the quest of security: ASEAN and the Cambodian conflict', *Journal of International Affairs*, **46** (2).

Alagappa, Muthiah (2003), 'Constructing security order in Asia', in Muthiah Alagappa (ed.), *Asian Security Order*, Stanford: Stanford University Press.

Alatas, Ali (2001), ' "ASEAN Plus" three equals peace plus prosperity', Regional Outlook Forum, Institute of Southeast Asian Studies (Singapore), 2 January.

Albinski, Henry (1970), *Politics and Sovereignty in Australia: The Impact of Vietnam and Conscription*, Durham, NC: Duke University Press.

Ali, Anuwar (1994), 'Japanese manufacturing investment in Malaysia', in K.S. Jomo (ed.), *Japan and Malaysian Development: In the Shadow of the Rising Sun*, London: Routledge.

'Alien arrests bid to flush out "sleepers" ' (2002), *Bangkok Post*, 11 March.

Almonte, Jose, T. (1997), 'Ensuring the "ASEAN way" ', *Survival*, **39** (4).

Amnesty International (2002a), *Indonesia: Amnesty International Report 2002*, London: Amnesty International Publications.

Amnesty International (2002b), *Malaysia: Amnesty International Report 2002*, London: Amnesty International Publications.

Amsden, Alice H. (1989), *Asia's next Giant South Korea and Late Industrialization*, New York: Oxford University Press.

'An Australian view: a nation loyal to the throne' (1960), *Round Table*, 200, September.

'APEC economic leaders' declaration of Common Resolve' (1994), *The Indonesian Quarterly*, **22** (4).

Ariff, Mohamed (1994), 'APEC and ASEAN: complementing or competing', in Andrew Mack and John Ravenhill (eds), *Pacific Cooperation: Building Economic and Security Regimes in the Asia–Pacific*, St Leonards, NSW: Allen & Unwin.

Aron, Raymond (1966), *Peace and War: A Theory of International Relations*, trans. Richard Howard and Annette Baker Fox, Malabar, Florida: Kreiger.

'ASEAN makes bold moves for recovery' (1998), *Straits Times*, 17 December.

ASEAN Secretariat (2004), 'Declaration of ASEAN Concord 11 (Bali Concord 11) B 1' (www.aseansec.org/15159.htm), accessed 26 January 2004.

ASEAN Secretariat (2005), 'Trade' (www.ASEANsec.org/12021), accessed 12 February 2005.

'ASEAN: the game goes on' (1998), *Economist*, 1 August.

ASEAN–China Expert Group (2001), *Forging Closer ASEAN–China Economic Relations in the Twenty First Century*, Jakarta: ASEAN Secretariat, October.

Asher, Mukhul (1993), 'Planning for the future: the welfare system in a new phase of development', in Gary Rodan (ed.), *Singapore Changes Guard: Social, Political and Economic Directions in the 1990s*, Melbourne: Longman Cheshire.

Ashley, Richard (1996), 'The achievements of post-structuralism', in Ken Booth, Steve Smith and Marysia Zalewski (eds), *International Theory: Positivism and Beyond*, Cambridge: Cambridge University Press.

Asia Watch (1989), *Human Rights in Indonesia and East Timor*, New York: Asia Watch.

'Asia without British power: Australians adjust to the prospect' (1968), *Round Table*, 299, January.

'Asian help for Burma weakens sanctions' (1996), *Independent*, 12 July.

'Asia's competing capitalisms' (1995), *Economist*, 24 June.

'ASIO raids vs Australian Indonesian relations' (2002), ABC Lateline, 2 November.

'Australia and EEC: a critical view of the Common Market' (1961), *Round Table*, 205, December.

'Bad deal in Cambodia' 1996, *Economist,* 12 October.

Baker, Mark (2002a), 'Evidence points to web of extremists', *Age*, 9 November.

Baker, Mark (2002b), 'Angry Thais threaten writers over Hambali plot reports', *Sydney Morning Herald*, 14 November.

Baldwin, David (1997), 'The concept of security', *Review of International Studies*, **23** (1).

'Bali bombing – Australian and Indonesian Police' (2003), transcript of World Today Broadcast, ABC, 6 March (www.abc.net.au/worldtoday. s800527.htm).

'Bali opens terror trial in blast fatal to 200' (2002), *International Herald Tribune*, 12 May.

Ball, Desmond (1995), *Developments in Signals Intelligence in Southeast Asia*, Canberra: Australian National University Strategic and Defence Studies Centre.

Ball, Desmond (1998), *Burma's Military Secrets: Signals Intelligence from the Second World War to Civil War and Cyberwarfare*, Bangkok: White Lotus.

Barber, Benjemin (1996), *Jihad versus McWorld: How Globalism and Tribalism are Reshaping the World Order*, New York: Ballantine.

Barthes, Roland (1977), *Image, Music, Text*, trans. Stephen Heath, London: Fontana.

Barton, Greg (2002), 'An Islamist north Australia: Al Qaeda's vision', *Age*, 30 October.

'Bash a yank a day' (1973), *Australian Financial Review*, 26 June.

Battacharya, Amer and Mari Pangetsu (1993), *Indonesia: Development Transformation and Public Policy*, Washington, DC: World Bank.

Bauer, Raymond A. (1952), *The Man in Soviet Psychology*, Cambridge, MA: Harvard University Press.

Bauer, Raymond A. (1954), 'The psycho-cultural approach to Soviet studies', *World Politics*, **7** (1).

Bazi, Mohamad (2001), 'Bin Laden's logistical mastermind', *New York Newsday*, 21 September.

Beary, M.D. and J.P. Cobb (1981), 'Solitary psychosis: three cases of mono-symptomatic delusion of alimentary stench treated with behavioural psychotherapy', *British Journal of Psychiatry*, 138.

Beeson, Mark (ed.) (2002), *Reconfiguring East Asia: Regional Institutions and Organisations after the Crisis*, London: RoutledgeCurzon.

Bell, Coral (1966), 'The architecture of stability in South Asia', *World Today*, April.

Bell, Coral (1968), 'Security in Asia: reappraisals after Vietnam', *International Journal*, **XXIV** (1).

Bell, Coral (1996), 'The architecture of stability in South Asia', *World Today*, April.

Bell, Roger (1996), 'Bilateral relations: a new regional context', in Roger Bell, Tim McDonald and Alan Tidwell (eds), *Negotiating the Pacific Century: The 'New' Asia, the United States and Australia*, St Leonards, NSW: Allen & Unwin.

Berkeley, George (1937), *Principles of Human Knowledge* (text of first edition, 1710, with appendix by T.E. Jessop), London: A Brown.

Bhagwati, Jagdish (1996), 'Asia's chance to lead', *Asiaweek*, 29 November.

Bialer, Seweryn (1986), *The Soviet Paradox*, New York: Knopf.

Blainey, Geoffrey (1968), *The Tyranny of Distance: How Distance Shaped Australia's Destiny*, Melbourne: Macmillan.

'Blowback' (2001), *Jane's Intelligence Review*, 26 July.

Bobrow, Davis B., Steve Chan and Simon Reich (1996), 'Southeast Asian prospects and realities: American hopes and fears', *Pacific Review*, **9** (1).

Bonner, Raymond and Seth Mydans (2002), ' "Sleeper cells" in Singapore show *Al Qaeda's* long reach', *New York Times*, 26 January.

Booth, Ken (1987), 'New challenges and old mind-sets: ten rules for empirical realists', in Carl G. Jacobsen (ed.), *The Uncertain Course: New Weapons, Strategies and Mind-Sets*, Oxford: Oxford University Press/SIPRI.

Booth, Ken (1990), 'Security in anarchy', *International Affairs*, **67** (3).

Booth, Ken (1991a), 'Introduction: the interregnum: world politics in transition', in Ken Booth (ed.), *New Thinking About International Security*, London: HarperCollins.

Booth, Ken (1991b), 'Preface', in Ken Booth (ed.), *New Thinking About International Security*, London: HarperCollins.

Booth, Ken (1991c), 'Security and emancipation', *Review of International Studies*, **17** (4).

Booth, Ken (1995), 'Dare not to know: international relations versus the future', in Ken Booth and Steve Smith (eds), *International Relations Theory Today*, Cambridge: Polity.

Booth, Ken (1997), 'Security and self: reflections of a fallen realist', in Keith Krause and Michael Williams (eds), *Critical Security Studies: Concepts and Cases*, London: UCL Press.

Booth, Ken and Steve Smith (eds) (1995), *International Relations Theory Today*, Cambridge: Polity.

Booth, Ken and Russell Trood (eds) (1999), *Strategic Cultures in the Asia–Pacific*, London: Macmillan.

Borges, Jorge Luis (1962), *Ficciones*, New York: Grove Press.

Bosworth, Stephen (1991), 'The United States and Asia', *Foreign Affairs: America and the World 1991/1992*, **71** (1).

Bowie, Alasdair (1994), 'The dynamics of business–government relations in industrialising Malaysia', in Andrew MacIntyre (ed.), *Business and Government in Industrializing Asia Relations*, St Leonards, NSW: Allen & Unwin.

'Britain in Europe: an Australian view' (1962), *Round Table*, 209, December.

Broinowski, Alison (1992), *The Yellow Lady: Australian Impressions of Asia*, Melbourne: Oxford University Press.

Broinowski, Alison (2003), *Howard's War*, Melbourne: Scribe.

Brown, Geoffrey M. (1977), 'Attitudes to an invasion of Australia in 1942', *Journal of the Royal United Services Institute of Defence Studies*, March.

Bruns, Gordon (1971), 'An Australian view of British entry: economic gains and political dangers', *Round Table*, 244, October.

Brzezinski, Zbigniew (1962), *Ideology and Power in Soviet Politics*, New York: Praeger.

Brzezinski, Zbigniew, (1966), 'The Soviet system: transformation or degeneration?', *Problems of Communism*, January.

Brzezinski, Zbigniew (1976), 'Soviet politics', in Paul Cocks, Robert V. Daniels and Nancy Whittier Heer (eds), *The Dynamics of Soviet Politics*, Cambridge, MA: Harvard University Press.

Buchan, Alistair (1966), 'An Asian balance of power', *Australian Journal of Politics and History*, **12** (2).

Bull, Hedley (1975), 'The Whitlam government's perception of our role in the world', in B.D. Beddie (ed.), *Advance Australia – Where?* Melbourne: Oxford University Press.

Burns, Arthur Lee (1970), 'Who are the Australians? Class attitudes without the class', *Round Table*, 238, April.

'Bush backs independent 9-11 probe' (2002), CBSNews.com, 20 September (www.cbsnews.com/stories/2002/09/24/attack/printable523156.shtml).

Busse, Nikolas (1999), 'Constructivism and Southeast Asian security', *Pacific Review*, **12** (1).

Buzan, Barry (1988), 'The Southeast Asia security complex', *Contemporary Southeast Asia*, **10** (1).

Cairns, J.F. (1972), *The Eagles and the Lotus*, Melbourne: Landsdowne.

Calder, Kent E. (1993), *Strategic Capitalism: Private Business and Public Purpose in Japanese Industrial Finance*, Princeton: Princeton University Press.

Callick, Rowan (2005), 'Howard: Australia's Mr Asia', *Australian Financial Review*, 4–5 February.

Campbell, David (1989), *The Social Basis of Australian and New Zealand Security Policy*, Canberra: Research School of Pacific Studies, Australian National University.

Campbell, David (1998), *Writing Security: United States Foreign Policy and the Politics of Identity*, Manchester: Manchester University Press.

Campos, Juan (1991), 'Leadership and the principle of shared growth: insights into the Asian miracle', *Asian Journal of Political Science*, **1** (2).

'Capital market pariahs' (1998), *Financial Times*, 12 August.

Cerny, Philip G. (1997), 'Paradoxes of the competition state: the dynamics of political globalization', *Government and Opposition*, **32** (2).

Chalk, Peter (1997), *Grey Area Phenomena in Southeast Asia*, Canberra Papers on Defence and Strategy, 123, Canberra: Australian National University Press.

Chalk, Peter (2001), 'Separatism and Southeast Asia: the Islamic factor in Southern Thailand, Mindanao, and Aceh', *Studies in Conflict and Terrorism*, **24** (4).

'Challenges and prospects in the current international situation' (2003), One Day Seminar on 'ASEAN Cooperation', Indonesian Embassy, New York, 3 June.

Chalmers, Malcolm (1996), *Confidence Building in Southeast Asia*, Boulder: Westview.

Chalmers, Malcolm (1997) 'ASEAN and confidence building: continuity and change After the Cold War', *Contemporary Security Policy*, **18** (1).

Chan, Heng Chee (1976), *The Dynamics of One Party Dominance: The PAP at the Grassroots*, Singapore: Oxford University Press.

Chan, Steve and Cal Clark (1994), *Flexibility, Foresight and Fortuna in Taiwan's Development: Navigating Between Scylla and Charybdis*, London: Routledge.

Chanda, Nayan (1989), 'Civil war in Cambodia?', *Foreign Policy*, 76, Fall.

Chandrasekaran, Rajiv (2002), 'Indonesia a "big disappointment" in terror war', *Washington Post*, 24 March.

Chang, Gordon (2004), 'Tide of growth turns in China', *Australian*, 19 July.

Che Man, W.K. (1990), *Muslim Separatism: The Moros of the Philippines and the Malays of Southern Thailand*, Oxford: Oxford University Press.

Chee, Soon Juan (2001), *Your Future, My Faith, Our Freedom: A Democratic Blueprint for Singapore*, Singapore: Open Singapore Centre.

Cheeseman, Graeme (1996), 'Contending national, regional and global imperatives in Australia's post-Cold War thinking', *Korean Journal of Defense Analysis*.

Cheeseman, Graeme (1999a), 'Asian–Pacific security discourse in the wake of the Asian economic crisis', *Pacific Review*, **12** (3).

Cheeseman, Graeme (1999b), 'Australia: the white experience of fear and dependency', in Ken Booth and Russell Trood (eds), *Strategic Cultures in the Asia–Pacific*, London: Macmillan.

Chia, Siow Yue (ed.) (1994), *APEC: Challenges and Opportunities*, Singapore: Institute of Southeast Asian Studies.

Chiddick, John P. and Max E. Teichmann (1977), *Australia and the World: A Political Handbook*, London: Macmillan.

'China's creeping assertiveness' (1995), *Asia Wall Street Journal*, 10 November.

Christensen, Scott, David Dollar, Ammar Siamwalla and Pakorn Vichyanond (1993), *Thailand: The Institutional and Political Underpinnings of Growth*, Washington: World Bank.

Clark, Jonathan (2003), *Our Shadowed Present: Modernism, Postmodernism and History*, London: Atlantic Books.

Colbert, Evelyn (1984), 'Stand pat', *Foreign Policy*, 54, Spring.

Collins, Randall (1978), 'Some principles of long term social change: the territorial power of states', in Louis Kriesberg (ed.), *Research in Social Movements, Conflicts and Change*, Vol. 1, Greenwich, CT: JAI Press.

Collins, Randall (1986), *Weberian Sociological Theory*, New York: Cambridge University Press.

Conesa, Pierre (2002), 'Al-Qaida, the sect', *Le Monde Diplomatique*, 7 January (http://mondediplo.com/2002/01/07sect).

'Confessions of an al-Qaeda terrorist' (2002), *Time Magazine*, 15 September.

Connor, Walker (1972), 'Nation-building or nation-destroying?', *World Politics*, **24** (3).

Copeland, Dale C. (2000), 'The constructivist challenge to structural realism', *International Security*, **25** (2).

Cotton, James (1990), 'APEC: Australia hosts another Pacific acronym', *Pacific Review*, **3** (2).

Cotton, James (1998), 'The new insecurity in Asia', *Quadrant*, December.

Crouch, Harold (1993), 'Authoritarian trends: the UMNO split and the limits to state power', in Joel S. Kahn and Francis K.W. Loh (eds), *Fragmented Vision: Culture and Politics in Contemporary Malaysia*, St Leonards, NSW: Allen & Unwin.

Cumings, Bruce (1997), 'Boundary displacement: area studies and international studies during and after the Cold War', in Mark Seldon (ed.), *Bulletin of Concerned Asian Scholars: Special Edition: Asia, Asian Studies and the National Security State*, **1** (1) (http://www.csf.colorado.edu/bcas/sympos/current.htm).

Dalangin, Lira (2003), 'MILF: camp Abubakar upland military's next goal', *Newsbreak* (Philippines), 17 February (www.inq7.net/brk/2003/feb/17/brkpol_4-1.htm).

'Dancing girls and romance on road to terrorist attacks' (2002), *Sydney Morning Herald*, 25 June.

Darby, Philip (1973a), 'Stability mechanisms in South-East Asia: I. Prospects for regionalism', *International Affairs*, January.

Darby, Philip (1973b), 'Stability mechanisms in South-East Asia: II. Balance of power and neutralisation', *International Affairs*, April.

David, Jonah (1994), 'Don't count on me, Singapore', *National Review*, 16 May.

Denker, M.S. (1994), 'The evolution of Japanese investment in Malaysia', in K.S. Jomo (ed.), *Japan and Malaysian Development: In the Shadow of the Rising Sun*, London: Routledge.

Department of Defence (1972), *Australian Defence Review*, Canberra: Australian Government Publishing Service.

Desker, Barry and Kumar Ramakrishnan (2002), 'Forging an indirect strategy in Southeast Asia', *Washington Quarterly*, **25** (2).

Dibb, Paul (2001), 'Indonesia: the key to South-East Asian security', *International Affairs*, **77** (4).

Dibb, Paul, David Hale and Peter Prince (1999), 'Asia's Insecurity', *Survival*, **41** (3).

Dinnen, Sinclair (2004), 'Australia lends a fist', *Foreign Policy*, 141, March/April.

Djalal, Dini (2003), 'Asia's intelligence gap', *Foreign Policy*, March/April.

Dooley, Michael P., David Folkerts-Landau and Peter Garber (2004), *Direct Investment, Rising Real Wages and the Absorption of Excess Labor in the Periphery*, NBER Working Paper 10626, Cambridge, MA: National Bureau of Economic Research.

Dorsch, Jörn and Manfred Mols (1998), 'Thirty years of ASEAN: achievements and challenges', *Pacific Review*, **11** (2).

Doyle, Michael W. (1995), *UN Peacekeeping in Cambodia: UNTAC's Civil Mandate*, Boulder: Westview.

Doyle, Michael W. and Nishkala Suntharalingam (1994), 'The UN in Cambodia: lessons for complex peacekeeping', *International Peacekeeping*, **1** (2).

Dunn, J.A. (1989), 'The Asian auto imbroglio: patterns of trade policy and business strategy', in Stephen J. Haggard and Chung-in Moon (eds), *Pacific Dynamics: The International Politics of Industrial Change*, Boulder, CO: Westview.

East Asia Vision Group (2001), *Towards an East Asian Community: Region of Peace, Prosperity and Progress*, Seoul: Korea Institute for Economic Policy.

'East Asia wobbles' (1995), *Economist*, 23 December.

East Asian Strategic Review 2003 (2003), Tokyo: National Institute for Defense Studies/Japan Times.

Economist Intelligence Unit (1998a), *Country Report: Malaysia and Brunei 2nd Quarter 1998*, London: Economist Intelligence Unit Limited.

Economist Intelligence Unit (1998b), *Indonesia Country Report 1st Quarter 1998*, London: Economist Intelligence Unit Limited.

Eden, Lorraine and M.A. Molot (1993), 'Fortress or free market? NAFTA and its implications for the Pacific rim', in Richard Higgott, Richard Leaver and

John Ravenhill (eds), *Pacific Economic Relations in the 1990s: Cooperation or Conflict?*, St Leonards: Allen & Unwin.

Edwards, John (1996), *Keating: The Inside Story*, Melbourne: Penguin.

Emmerson, Donald K. (1987), 'ASEAN as an international regime', *Journal of International* Affairs, **41** (1).

Emmerson, Donald K. (1995), 'Region and recalcitrance: rethinking democracy through Southeast Asia', *Pacific Review*, **8** (2).

Emmerson, Donald K. and Sheldon W. Simon (1993), *Regional Issues in Southeast Asian Security: Scenarios and Regimes*, Seattle: National Bureau of Asian Research.

Esposito, John (1995), *The Islamic Threat: Myth or Reality?*, Oxford: Oxford University Press.

Evans, Gareth and Bruce Grant (1995), *Australia's Foreign Relations in the World of the 1990s*, Melbourne: Melbourne University Press.

'Ex-Fateha chief gets out of headscarf debate' (2001), *Straits Times*, 28 January.

Fairbank, John King (ed.) (1974), *Chinese Ways in Warfare*, Cambridge, MA: Harvard University Press.

Fallows, James (1994), *Looking at the Sun: The Rise of the New East Asian Economic and Political System*, New York: Pantheon.

'Fateha break up shows extremism not supported' (2001), *Straits Times*, 27 January.

'Fateha pol' (2002), *Berita Harian*, 23 January.

Ferguson, R. James (1999), 'East Asian regionalism: the challenge of political reform and systemic crisis in the late 1990s', paper presented to Centre for the Study of Globalisation and Regionalisation Conference, 'After the global crises: what next for regionalism?', Scarman House, University of Warwick, 16–18 September.

'Fightin' words' (1998), *Time Magazine Asia*, 2 November.

Fineman, Mark and Bob Drogin (2002), 'Indonesian cleric had role in skyjackings, officials say', *Los Angeles Times*, 2 February.

Finnemore, Martha and Kathryn Sikkink (2001), 'Taking stock: the constructivist research program in international relations and comparative politics', *Annual Review of Political Science*, 4.

Firdaus, Irwan (2002), 'Bali bombing suspect "studied under cleric linked to al-Qa'ida" ', *Independent*, 26 November.

Fisk, Robert (1993), 'Anti-Soviet warrior puts his army on the road to peace', *Independent*, 6 December.

FitzGerald, Stephen (1997), *Is Australia an Asian Country? Can Australia Survive in an East Asian Future?* Sydney: Allen & Unwin.

Fleron, Frederick and Erik Hoffman (1991), 'Sovietology and perestroika: methodology and lessons from the past', Harriman Institute Forum, September.

Foot, Rosemary (1996), 'Thinking globally from a regional perspective: Chinese, Indonesian and Malaysian reflections on the post-Cold War era', *Contemporary Southeast* Asia, **18** (1).

Foster, Leonie (1983), 'The Australian Round Table, the Moot and Australian nationalism', *Round Table*, 288, October.

'Four Corners: the Bali confessions – chronology' (2003) (www.abc.net.au/ 4corners/content/2003/20030210_baliconfessions_chronology.htm), accessed 17 July 2004.

Freidman, Thomas (2001), *The Lexus and the Olive Tree*, New York: Pan.

Freinhar, J.P. (1984), 'Delusions of parasitosis', *Psychosomatics*, **25** (1).

Friedberg, Aaron L. (1993), 'Ripe for rivalry: prospects for peace in a multipolar Asia', *International Security*, **18** (3).

Fukuyama, Francis (1992), *The End of History and the Last Man*, London: Hamish Hamilton.

Galston, William A. (1991), *Liberal Purposes: Goods, Virtues and Diversity in the Liberal State*, Cambridge: Cambridge University Press.

Garnaut, Ross (1994), 'Options for Asia–Pacific trade liberalization (a Pacific free trade area)', in Chia Siow Yue (ed.), *APEC: Challenges and Opportunities*, Singapore: Institute of Southeast Asian Studies.

Garnaut, Ross and Peter Drysdale with John Kunkel (1994), *Asia Pacific Regionalism: Readings in International Economic Relations*, Sydney: Harper.

Gelber, H.G. (1968), *The Australian–American Alliance: Costs and Benefits*, London: Penguin.

Gellner, Ernest (1985), *The Psychoanalytical Movement: The Coming of Unreason*, London: Grafton.

Gellner, Ernest (1994), *Conditions of Liberty: Civil Society and its Rivals*, London: Hamish Hamilton.

George, Cherian (2000), *Singapore: The Air Conditioned Nation – Essays on the Politics of Comfort and Control, 1999–2000*, Singapore: Landmark.

Giddens, Anthony (1998), *The Third Way: The Renewal of Social Democracy*, Cambridge: Polity Press.

Gilpin, Robert (2003), 'A postscript to the Asian Financial crisis: the fragile international economic order', *Cambridge Review of International Studies*, **1** (1).

Godement, François (1996), *The New Asian Renaissance: From Colonialism to the Post-Cold War*, London: Routledge.

Godement, François (1999), *The Downsizing of Asia*, London: Routledge.

Goh, Chok Tong (1998), 'The Asian economic crisis: challenges for the US', speech to United States Chamber of Commerce, Washington, DC, 22 September.

Goh, Evelyn (2003), 'Hegemonic constraints: the implication of 11 September for American power', *Australian Journal of International Affairs*, **57** (1).

Goldsmith, James (1994), *The Trap*, London: Macmillan.

Gomez, Edmund T. (1994), *Political Business Corporate Involvement of Malaysian Political Parties*, Townsville, QLD: James Cook University Press.

Gomez, James (2000), *Self-Censorship: Singapore's Shame*, Singapore: ThinkCentre.

Gomez, James (2002), *Internet Politics: Surveillance and Intimidation in Singapore*, Singapore: ThinkCentre.

Gordon, Bernard K. (1978), 'Japan, the United States and Southeast Asia', *Foreign Affairs*, April.

Government of Singapore (1991), *Singapore: The Next Lap*, Singapore: Times Editions.

Gowing, Peter (1974), *Muslim Filipinos*, Manila: Solidaridad.

Grant, Bruce (1968), 'Pacific signposts', *Meanjin Quarterly*, **27** (3).

Grant, Bruce (1970), 'Australian foreign policy', in *New Zealand and Australia: Foreign Relations in the 1970s*, papers read at the 1969 Conference of the New Zealand Institute of International Affairs, Wellington: Price Milburn.

Grant, Bruce (1972), *The Crisis of Loyalty: A Study of Australian Foreign Policy*, Sydney: Angus & Robertson.

Gray, Colin (1981), 'National style in strategy', *International Security*, **6** (2).

Gray, John (1995), *Enlightenment's Wake*, London: Routledge.

Gray, John (1998), *False Dawn: The Delusions of Global Capitalism*, London: Granta.

Green, Stephen and Ming He (2004), 'China's stock market: out of the valley', briefing paper, Royal Institute of International Affairs, London: February.

Greenwood, Gordon and Norman Harpur (eds) (1963), *Australia in World Affairs, 1945–1960*, Melbourne: F.W. Cheshire.

Grenville, Stephen (1998), 'The Asian economic crisis', talk to Australian Business Economists and the Economic Society (NSW Branch), Sydney, 12 March.

Gunaratna, Rohan (2004), 'Al Qaeda's origins, threat and its likely future', in David Martin Jones (ed.), *Globalization and the New Terror*, Cheltenham, UK and Northampton, MA, USA: Edward Elgar.

Haacke, Jurgen (2003), 'ASEAN's diplomatic and security culture: a constructivist assessment', *International Relations of the Asia Pacific*, **3** (1).

Haas, Michael (1989), *The Asian Way to Peace: A Story of Regional Cooperation*, New York: Praeger.

'Habibie, Estrada rethink KL visit' (1998), *Straits Times*, 2 October.

Haggard, Stephen J. (1990), *Pathways from the Periphery: The Politics of Growth in the Newly Industrializing Countries*, Ithaca: Cornell University Press.

Haimson, Leopold (1953), 'Soviet psychology and the Soviet conception of man', *World Politics*, **5** (3).

Halliday, Fred (1989), *The Making of the Second Cold War*, London: Verso.

'Hambali plotted terror campaign' (2003), *Star* (Malaysia), 1 January.

'Hambali: SE Asia's most wanted' (2002), BBC News/Asia–Pacific, 21 October (http://news.bbc.co.uk/1/low/world/asia–pacific/2346225.htm).

Hamid, Wan Hamidi (2000), 'Lost at the fringe', *Straits Times*, 30 July.

'Hangover cure' (2004), *Economist*, 24 September.

Hanoi Declaration (1998), 6th ASEAN Summit, 16 December, Southeast Asian Science Policy Advisory Network (www.icsea.or.id/sea-span/1198/RG1228LL.htm).

Hara, Kimi (1999), 'Rethinking the "Cold War" in the Asia–Pacific', *Pacific Review*, **12** (4).

Harding, Harry (1994), 'Asia policy to the brink', *Foreign Policy*, 96, Fall.

Harding, Harry (1998), 'Wanted: Asian–US cooperation', *Straits Times*, 22 October.

Harland, Bryce (1993), 'Whither East Asia?', *Pacific Review*, **6** (1).

Harnden, Toby (2002), 'US identifies key Sept 11 terrorist', *Daily Telegraph*, 15 July.

Harries, Owen (1975), 'Australia's foreign policy under Whitlam', *Orbis*, **XIX** (3).

Harris, Stuart (1994), 'Conclusion: the theory and practice of regional cooperation', in Andrew Mack and John Ravenhill (eds), *Pacific Cooperation: Building Economic and Security Regimes in the Asia–Pacific Region*, St Leonards, NSW: Allen & Unwin.

Harris, Stuart (1999), 'The regional response in Asia–Pacific and its global implications', paper presented to Centre for the Study of Globalisation and Regionalisation Conference, 'After the global crises: what next for regionalism?', Scarman House, University of Warwick, 16–18 September.

Hasluck, Paul (1967), Statement to House of Representatives, 17 August.

Head, Jonathan (2001), 'ASEAN stumbles over war on terror', BBC News 5 November (http://news.bbc.co.uk/hi/english/world/asia–pacific/newsid_1638000/1638522.stm).

Hefner, Robert (2000), *Civil Islam*, Princeton, NJ: Princeton University Press.

Hemmer, Christopher and Peter J. Katzenstein (2002), 'Why is there no NATO in Asia? Collective identity, regionalism and the origins of multilateralism', *International Organization*, **56** (4).

Henderson, Callum (1998), *Asia Falling? Making Sense of the Asian Currency Crisis and its Aftermath*, New York: McGraw-Hill.

Henderson, Jeannie (1999), *Reassessing ASEAN*, Adelphi Paper 328, Oxford: Oxford University Press/IISS.

Henson, Bertha (2002), 'PAP eases up to let MPs debate more freely', *Straits Times*, 23 March.

Herschede, Fred (1991), 'Trade between China and ASEAN: the impact of the Pacific rim era', *Pacific Affairs*, **64** (2).

Hewison, Kevin (1989), *Bankers and Bureaucrats: Capital and the Role of the State in Thailand*, New Haven: Yale University Southeast Asian Studies, Monograph Series, no. 34.

Hidalgo, C.C. (2000), 'Camp Abubakar: a symbol of Muslim pride', Codewan.com (Philippines), 17 May (www.codewan.com.ph/ CyberDyaryo/features/f2000_0515_01.htm).

Higgott, Richard (1988), 'Shared response to the market shocks?', *World Today*, January.

Higgott, Richard (1998), 'The Asian economic crisis: a study in the politics of resentment', *New Political Economy*, **3** (3).

Higgott, Richard and Kim Richard Nossal (1998), 'Australia and the search for a security community in the 1990s', in Emanuel Adler and Michael Barnett (eds), *Security Communities*, Cambridge: Cambridge University Press.

Hill, Hal (1994), 'The economy', in Hal Hill (ed.), *Indonesia's New Order: The Dynamics of Socio-Economic Transformation*, St Leonards, NSW: Allen & Unwin.

Hill, Hal and Joao M. Saldanha (eds) (2001), *Development Challenges for the World's Newest Nation*, Singapore: Institute of Southeast Asian Studies.

Hirst, Paul and Grahame Thompson (1996), *Globalization in Question*, Cambridge: Polity.

Hoan, Anh Tuan (1996), 'ASEAN dispute management: implications for Vietnam and an expanded ASEAN', *Contemporary Southeast Asia*, **18** (1).

Hoge, James F. (2004), 'The rise of Asia: a global power shift in the making: is the United States ready?', *Foreign Affairs*, **83** (4).

Holland, Tom (2000), 'Asia's new fissure', *Far Eastern Economic Review*, 29 June.

Hope, A.D. (1972), *Collected Poems*, Sydney: Angus & Robertson.

Horne, Donald (1964), *The Lucky Country: Australia in the Sixties*, London: Penguin.

Horne, Donald (1972), *The Australian People*, Sydney: Angus & Robertson.

Huff, W.G. (1994), *The Economic Growth of Singapore: Trade and Development in the Twentieth Century*, Cambridge: Cambridge University Press.

Huffman, Karen, Mark Vernoy and Barbara Williams (1987), *Psychology in Action*, New York: John Wiley and Sons.

Hughes, Christopher W. (1996), 'Japan's subregional security and defence linkages with ASEANs [sic], South Korea and China in the 1990s', *Pacific Review*, **9** (2).

Hughes, T.E.F (1967), 'Australia in free Asia: both economic and military efforts', *Round Table*, 266, April.

Human Rights Watch (2000), *Malaysia/Burma: Living in Limbo*, New York: Human Rights Watch (www.hrw.org/reports/2000/malaysia,maybr008.htm).

Human Rights Watch (2002), *Malaysia's Internal Security Act and Suppression of Political Dissent: A Human Rights Backgrounder*, New York: Human Rights Watch (www.hrw.org/backgrounder/asia/malaysia-bck-0513.htm).

Huntingdon, Samuel (1996), *The Clash of Civilizations and the Remaking of the World Order*, New York: Simon & Schuster.

Hutchison, Jane (1997), 'Pressure on policy in the Philippines', in Gary Rodan, Kevin Hewison and Richard Robison (eds), *The Political Economy of South-East Asia*, Melbourne: Oxford University Press.

Hutton, Will (1995), *The State We're In*, London: Granta.

Huxley, Tim (1991), 'Singapore and Malaysia: a precarious balance', *Pacific Affairs*, **4** (3).

Huxley, Tim (1996), 'Southeast Asia in the study of international relations: the rise and decline of a region', *Pacific Review*, **9** (2).

Ibrahim, Anwar (1996), *Asian Renaissance*, Singapore: Times Books International.

'Indonesia issues warning over ASIO raids' (2002), 6 November.

'Indonesian ambassador warns Bali probe "at risk" ' (2002), ABC Lateline 6 November.

Inoguchi, Takashi (1993), *Japan's Foreign Policy in an Era of Global Change*, London: Pinter.

International Crisis Group (2002), 'Al Qaeda in Southeast Asia: The Case of the "Ngruki Network" in Indonesia', Asia Briefing, Brussels, 8 August.

International Crisis Group (2003), 'Al-Qaeda in Southeast Asia: The Case of the "Ngruki Network" in Indonesia', 8 August 2002, re-issued 10 January 2003 (http://www.intl-crisis-group.org/projects/asia/indonesia/reports/A400733_08082002.pdf>).

International Monetary Fund (2003), *The Global Implications of the US Fiscal Deficit and of China's Growth*, Washington, DC: International Monetary Fund.

'Into the heart of darkness' (2002), *Age*, 16 November.

Ironmonger, Duncan S. (1973), 'Australia's new government: problems of economic policy', *Round Table*, 250, April.

'Is there an Al-Qaeda connection in Indonesia?' (2002), *Sunday Times* (Singapore), 20 January.

Jackson, P.A. (1991), 'Thai–Buddhist identity: debates on the Thaiphung Phra Rwang', in C.J. Reynolds (ed.), *National Identity and its Defenders: Thailand, 1939–1989*, Monash Papers on Southeast Asia, 25, Clayton, Melbourne: Monash University Press.

'Jakarta admits 76 rapes in May riots' (1998), *Straits Times*, 22 December.

'Jakarta takes terrorist link claims seriously' (2002), *Indonesian Observer*, 23 January.

James, Clive (2002), 'Don't blame the west', *Guardian*, 16 October.

Janis, Irving (1982), *Groupthink: Psychological Studies of Policy Decisions and Fiascoes*, Boston: Houghton Mifflin.

Japan Bank for International Cooperation (1999), *Exim Review*, **19** (1).

Jayakumar, S. (2004), Remarks by Singapore Foreign Minister Prof. S. Jayakumar to the Singapore media at the conclusion of the 37th ASEAN Ministerial Meeting, Jakarta, Ministry of Foreign Affairs, Press Statements and Speeches (http://app.mfa.gov.sg/selections/press/report_press.asp?3911), 30 June.

Jenkins, David (2002), 'Soeharto's Komando Jihad chickens come home to roost', *Sydney Morning Herald*, 14 October.

Jervis, Robert (1998), 'Realism in the study of world politics', *International Organization*, **54** (4).

Jesudason, James V. (1990), *Ethnicity and the Economy: The State, Chinese Business, and Multinationals in Malaysia*, Singapore: Oxford University Press.

Johnson, Chalmers (1982), *MITI and the Japanese Miracle: The Growth of Industrial Policy 1925–1975*, Stanford: Stanford University Press.

Johnson, Chalmers (1996), 'The Okinawan rape incident and the end of the Cold War in East Asia', *Quadrant*, March.

Johnson, Chalmers and E.B. Keehn (1994), 'A disaster in the making: rational choice and Asian studies', *National Interest* (Summer).

Johnstone, Christopher (1999), 'Strained alliance: US–Japan diplomacy in the Asian financial crisis', *Survival*, **41** (1).

Jomo, K.S. (1994), 'The proton saga: Malaysian car Mitsubishi gain', in K.S. Jomo (ed.), *Japan and Malaysian Development: In the Shadow of the Rising Sun*, London: Routledge.

Jones, Catherine (1990), 'Hong Kong, Singapore, South Korea and Taiwan: oikonomic welfare states', *Government and Opposition*, **25** (4).

Jones, David Martin (1998), *Political Development in Pacific Asia*, Cambridge: Polity.

Jones, David Martin (2001a), *The Image of China in Western Social and Political Thought*, London: Palgrave.

Jones, David Martin (2001b), 'Old attitudes dying hard in Asia', *Australian Financial Review*, 11 January.

Jones, David Martin and Mike Smith (1999), 'Tigers ready to roar?', *World Today*, **55** (10).

Jones, David Martin and Mike L. Smith (2002), 'The strange death of the ASEAN way', *Australian Financial Review*, 12 April.

Jones, David Martin and Mike Lawrence Smith (2003), 'Reinventing realism
– challenging Australia's foreign policy orthodoxy: a reply to Makinda',
International Relations of the Asia Pacific, **3** (1).

Jung, Carl G. (1983), *Jung: Selected Writings*, selected and introduced by
Anthony Storr, London: Fontana.

Kagan, Jerome and Julius Segal (1992), *Psychology: An Introduction*, 7th edn,
New York: Harcourt Brace Jovanovich.

Kahler, Miles (1990), 'Organizing the Pacific', in Richard A. Scalapino et al.
(eds), *Regional Dynamics: Security, Political and Economic Issues in the
Asia–Pacific Region*, Jakarta: Centre for Strategic and International
Studies.

Kahler, Miles (1992), 'Institution building in the Pacific', in Andrew Mack and
John Ravenhill (eds), *Pacific Cooperation Building Economic and Security
Regimes in the Asia–Pacific Region*, St Leonards, NSW: Allen & Unwin.

Kaldor, Mary (1999), *New and Old Wars: Organized Violence in a Global Era*,
Stanford: Stanford University Press.

Karram, Azza (2000), 'Islamisms, globalisation, religion and power', in
Ronaldo Munck and Purnaka de Silva (eds), *Postmodern Insurgencies:
Political Violence, Identity Formation and Peacemaking in Comparative
Perspective*, London: Macmillan.

Katzenstein, Peter, J. (1995), 'Introduction: Asian regionalism in comparative
perspective', in Peter J. Katzenstein and Takashi Shiraishi (eds), *Network
Power: Japan and Asia*, Ithaca, NY: Cornell University Press.

Katzenstein, Peter (1999), 'Regionalism in Asia', paper presented to Centre
for the Study of Globalisation and Regionalisation Conference, 'After the
global crises: what next for regionalism?', Scarman House, University of
Warwick, 16–18 September.

Kausikan, Bilhari (1993), 'Asia's different standard', *Foreign Policy*, 92.

Kawaui, Masahiro, Richard Newfarmer and Sergio Schmukler (2001), *Crisis
and Contagion in East Asia Policy*, Research Working Paper 2610,
Washington, DC: World Bank.

Keating, Paul (1996), *Australia, Asia and the New Regionalism*, Singapore:
ISEAS.

Keating, Paul (2000), *Engagement: Australia Faces the Asia Pacific*, Sydney:
Macmillan.

Kedourie, Elie (1975),'A new international disorder', in Hedley Bull and
Adam Watson (eds), *The Expansion of International Society*, Oxford:
Oxford University Press.

Kennedy, Paul (1989), *The Rise and Fall of the Great Powers: Economic
Change and Military Conflict from 1500 to 2000*, London: Fontana.

Khamchoo, Chaiwit (1991), 'Japan's role in Southeast Asia security: *plus ça
change*', *Pacific Affairs*, **64** (1).

Khoman, Thanat (1976), 'The new equation of world power and its impact on Southeast Asia', *Orbis*, **20** (3).

Khong, Yuen Foong (1997a), 'ASEAN and the Southeast Asia security complex', in Patrick Morgan and David Lake (eds), *Regional Orders: Building Security in a New World*, University Park, Pennsylvania: Pennsylvania University Press.

Khong, Yuen Foong (1997b), 'Making bricks without straw in the Asia–Pacific?', *Pacific Review*, **10** (2).

Khoo, Nicholas and Michael L. Smith (2002), 'The future of American hegemony in the Asia–Pacific: a concert of Asia or clear pecking order?', *Australian Journal of International Affairs*, **56** (1).

Kim, Kihwan and Danny M. Leipziger (1993), *Korea: A Case of Government Led Development*, Washington: World Bank.

Kingsbury, Damian (2001),'East Timor', in Patrick Heenan and Monique Lamontagne (eds), *The Southeast Asia Handbook*, London: Fitzroy Dearborn.

Kissinger, Henry (1995), *Diplomacy*, New York: Simon & Schuster.

Koh, Tommy (1998), 'Grouping will emerge victorious', *Straits Times*, 20 December.

Kolodziej, Edward (1992a), 'What is security and security studies: lessons from the Cold War', *Arms Control*, **13** (1).

Kolodziej, Edward (1992b), 'Renaissance in security studies: caveat lector!', *International Studies Quarterly*, **36** (4).

Krasner, Stephen (1996), 'The accomplishments of political economy', in Ken Booth, Steve Smith and Marysia Zalewski (eds), *International Theory: Positivism and Beyond*, Cambridge: Cambridge University Press.

Krasnov, Vladimir (1988), 'Images of the Soviet future: the émigré and samizdat debate', in Alexander Shtromas and Morton Kaplan (eds), *The Soviet Union and the Challenge of the Future*, New York: Paragon House.

Krause, Keith and Andrew Latham (1998), 'Constructing non-proliferation and arms control: the norms of western practice', in Keith Krause (ed.), *Culture and Security: Multilateralism, Arms Control and Security Building*, London: Frank Cass.

Krause, Keith R. and Michael C. Williams (eds) (1997), *Critical Security Studies: Concepts and Cases*, London: UCL Press.

Kremmer, Christopher (2003), 'Then there were two: Al Qaeda planner caught', *Sydney Morning Herald*, 3 March.

Krugman, Paul (1994), 'The myth of Asia's miracle', *Foreign Affairs*, (November/December).

Krugman, Paul (1999), *The Return of Depression Economics*, London: Penguin.

Kurlantzick, Joshua (2000), 'Love my nanny: Singapore's tongue tied populace', *World Policy Journal*, winter.

Kurlantzick, Joshua (2005), 'Paradise lost', *New Republic*, 21 February.

Kwa, Chong Guan and See Seng Tan (2001), 'The keystone of world order', *Washington Quarterly*, **23** (1).

Laothamatas, Anek (1992), *Business Associations and the New Political Economy of Thailand*, Boulder, CO: Westview.

Lardy, Nicholas (1998), 'China and the Asian contagion', *Foreign Affairs*, **77** (4).

Latham, Mark (1998), *Civilising Global Capital: New Thinking for Australian Capital*, St Leonards, NSW: Allen & Unwin.

Latif, Asad (2001), 'When total defence becomes a way of life', *Straits Times*, 21 November.

Latif, Asad (2002), 'Who will lead Muslim S'poreans?', *Straits Times*, 28 January.

Lebow, Robert Ned (1994), 'The long peace, the end of the Cold War, and the failure of realism', *International Organization*, **48** (2).

Lee, Kim Chew (2002), 'More to anti-terrorism pact than meets the eye', *Straits Times*, 25 May.

Lee, Kuan Yew (1992), 'Democracy, human rights and justice', *Sunday Times* (Singapore) 11 November.

Lee, Kuan Yew (1998), *The Singapore Story: Memoirs of Lee Kuan Yew*, Singapore: Times Academic Press.

Lee, Kuan Yew (2000), 'Need for balance on East Asia's way to world eminence', *International Herald Tribune*, 23 November.

Lee, Kuan Yew (2002a), 'The global threat posed by militant Islam today', *Straits Times*, 6 June.

Legro, Jeffrey (2000), 'The transformation of policy ideas', *American Political Science*, **44** (3).

Leifer, Michael (1973), 'The ASEAN states: no common outlook', *International Affairs*, **49** (4).

Leifer, Michael (1989), *ASEAN and the Security of South-East Asia*, London: Routledge.

Leifer, Michael (1995), 'The issue is ASEAN', *Far Eastern Economic Review*, 30 November.

Leifer, Michael (1996), *The ASEAN Regional Forum: Extending ASEAN's Model of Regional Security*, Adelphi Paper 302, Oxford: Oxford University Press/IISS.

Leifer, Michael (1999), 'The ASEAN peace process: a category mistake', *Pacific Review*, **12** (1).

Leifer, Michael (2000a), 'S'pore Indonesia ties', *Straits Times*, 7 January.

Leifer, Michael (2000b), 'Gentleman's agreement not kept', *Straits Times*, 7 January.

Leifer, Michael (2000c), *Singapore's Foreign Policy: Coping with Vulnerability*, London: Routledge.

Leifer, Michael and Dolliver Nelson (1973), 'Conflict of interest in the Straits of Malacca', *International Affairs*, April.

Levin, Norman D. (1991), 'Japan's defense policy: the internal debate', in Harry H. Kendall and Clara Joewono (eds), *Japan, ASEAN and the United States*, Berkeley: University of California Press.

Lewis, Jeffrey (1999), 'Asian vs. international: structuring an Asian Monetary Fund', *Harvard Asian Quarterly*, **3** (1), (www.fas.harvard.edu/~asiactr/haq/199904/9904a005.htm).

Liddell Hart, Basil (1935), *The British Way in Warfare*, London: Macmillan.

Lilla, Mark (2001), *The Reckless Mind: Intellectuals in Politics*, New York: New York Review of Books.

Lim, Kim Chew (2003), 'Long and bumpy road to Asian integration', *Straits Times*, 11 July.

Lim, Linda Y.C. (1995), 'Economic outlook 1996: ASEAN region', in Chan Heng Chee (ed.), *Regional Outlook Southeast Asia 1996*, Singapore: Institute of Southeast Asian Studies.

Lingle, Christopher (1994), 'The smoke over some parts of Asia obscures some profound concerns', *International Herald Tribune*, 7 October.

Lingle, Christopher (1996), *Singapore's Authoritarian Capitalism: Asian Values Free Market Illusions and Political Dependency*, Fairfax, VA: Locke Institute.

Low, Ignatius (2002), 'Wanted: an E. Asian "Community" ', *Straits Times*, 16 January.

Lyon, Peter (1968), 'Substitutes for SEATO?' *International Journal*, **XXIV** (1).

Lyon, Peter (1969), *War and Peace in South-East Asia*, London: Oxford University Press for the Royal Institute for International Affairs.

MacIntyre, Andrew (1994), 'Power, properity and patrimonialism: government and business in Indonesia', in Andrew MacIntyre, (ed.), *Business and Government in Industrializing Asia Relations*, St Leonards, NSW: Allen & Unwin.

MacIntyre, Andrew (1997), 'South-East Asia and the political economy of APEC', in Gary Rodan, Kevin Hewison and Richard Robison (eds), *The Political Economy of South-East Asia*, Melbourne: Oxford University Press.

Mack, Andrew and John Ravenhill (1994), 'Economic and security regimes in the Asia–Pacific region', in Andrew Mack and John Ravenhill (eds), *Pacific Cooperation: Building Economic and Security Regimes in the Asia–Pacific*, St Leonards, NSW: Allen & Unwin.

Mackie, James (1995), 'Economic systems of the overseas Chinese', in Leo Suryadinata (ed.), *Southeast Asian Chinese and China: The Politico-Economic Dimension*, Singapore: Times Academic Press.

Mackintosh, Malcolm (1993), 'The Soviet Union in the Pacific: force structure and regional relations', in T.B. Millar (ed.), *Asian-Pacific Security After the Cold War*, St Leonards, NSW: Allen & Unwin.

MacLeod, Alexander (1974) 'The new foreign policy in Australia and New Zealand: the record of the Labour governments', *Round Table*, 255, July.

Madani, Dorsati H. (2001), *Regional Integration and Industrial Growth Among Developing Countries: The Case of Three ASEAN Members*, Policy Research Working Paper 2697, Washington, DC: World Bank.

Mahbubani, Kishore (1994a), 'The United States: go East young Man', *Washington Quarterly*, **17** (2).

Mahbubani, Kishore (1994b), 'You may not like it Europe, but this Asian medicine could help', *International Herald Tribune*, 1 October.

Mahbubani, Kishore (1995a), 'The Pacific impulse', *Survival*, **37** (1).

Mahbubani, Kishore (1995b), 'The Pacific way', *Foreign Affairs*, **74** (1).

Makinda, Samuel (2001), 'Review of "Reinventing Realism: Australia's Foreign and Defence Policy in the Millennium" ', *International Relations of the Asia–Pacific*, **1** (2).

'Malay MPs call for "careful approach" to tudung issue' (2001), *Straits Times*, 27 January.

Martin, A.W. (1993), *Robert Menzies: A Life*, Volume 1, Melbourne: Melbourne University Press.

Matthews, Trevor and John Ravenhill (1994), 'Strategic trade policy: the Northeast Asian experience', in Andrew MacIntyre (ed.), *Business and Government in Industrializing Asia Relations*, St Leonards, NSW: Allen & Unwin.

McDougall, Derek (1989), 'The Hawke government's policies towards the USA', *Round Table*, 310, April.

McVey, Ruth (1992), 'The materialization of the Southeast Asian entrepreneur', in Ruth McVey (ed.), *Southeast Asian Capitalism*, Ithaca: Cornell University Press.

Mead, Margaret (1951), *Soviet Attitudes Toward Authority: An Interdisciplinary Approach to Problems of Soviet Character*, New York: McGraw-Hill

Mediansky, F.A. and A.C. Palfreeman (eds) (1988), *In Pursuit of National Interests: Australian Foreign Policy in the 1990s*, Sydney: Pergamon Press.

Mercer, Jonathan (1995), 'Anarchy and identity', *International Organization*, **49** (2).

Millar, T.B. (1968), *Australia's Foreign Policy*, Sydney: Angus & Robertson.

Miller, J.D.B. (1969), 'Lessons from Vietnam', *Australian Outlook*, **23** (1).

Miller, J.D.B. (1970), 'Australia in Vietnam: necessary assurance or burnt fingers?', *The Round Table*, 242, July.

Milosz, Czeslaw (1990), *The Captive Mind*, trans. Jane Zielonko, New York: Vintage International.

'Minister for Foreign Affairs, Alexander Downer' (2002), Transcript of ABC Radio AM on Bali arrests, 22 November (www.dftat.gov.au/media/transcripts/2002/021122_fa_bali.html).

'Ministers let their hair down' (2001), *Weekend Australian*, 28–9 July.

Ministry of Defence (2001a), 'Total defence' (http://mindef.gov.sg/td/introduction/c_intro.htm), accessed 23 November.

Ministry of Defence (2001b), 'Social defence' (http://mindef.gov.sg/td/aspects/o_c_psycho.htm), accessed 23 November.

Ministry of Defence (2001c), 'Psychological defence' (http://mindef.gov.sg/td/aspects/o_c_psycho.htm), accessed 23 November.

Ministry of Foreign Affairs (1998), 'A new initiative to overcome the Asian currency crisis: the New Miyazawa Initiative', 3 October (www.mof.go.jp/english/if/e1e042.htm).

Ministry of Foreign Affairs (1999), *Diplomatic Bluebook 1999: Japan's Diplomacy with Leadership Toward the New Century*, Tokyo: Ministry of Foreign Affairs (www.mof.go.jp/policy/other/bluebook/1999/I-c.html).

Mohamad, Mahathir (1970), *The Malay Dilemma*, Singapore: Asia–Pacific Press.

Mohamad, Mahathir (1999), *A New Deal for Asia*, Kuala Lumpur: Pelanduk.

Mohamad, Mahathir and Shintaro Ishihara (1995), *The Voice of Asia*, Tokyo: Kodansha International.

Moon, Chung-in (1994), 'Changing patterns of business–government relations and regime transition in South Korea', in Andrew MacIntyre (ed.), *Business and Government in Industrializing Asia Relations*, St Leonards, NSW: Allen & Unwin.

Morris, Meaghan (1998), 'White panic or Mad Max and the sublime', in Chen Kuan-Hsing (ed.), *Trajectories: Inter-Asian Cultural Studies*, London: Routledge.

Munro, Caroline (2002), 'Bashir goes on trial', *Daily Telegraph* (Australia), 11 May.

Murphy, Dan (2000), 'Stalled deal', *Far Eastern Economic Review*, 10 February.

'Muslims here reject Fateha chief's remarks' (2002), *Straits Times*, 24 January.

Mydans, Seth (2003), 'Suspect going on trial in Bali blast', *International Herald Tribune*, 12 May.

Nabers, Dirk (2003), 'The social construction of international institutions: the case of ASEAN + 3', *International Relations of the Asia Pacific*, **3** (3).

Nagatomi, Yuichiro (1995), 'Economic regionalism and the EAEC', *Japan Review of International Affairs*, **3** (9).

Naim, Moises (1998), 'Editor's note', *Foreign Policy*, Spring.

Nair, C.V. Devan (1976), *Socialism That Works ... the Singapore Way*, Singapore: Federal Publications.

Naisbett, John (1995), *Megatrends Asia: The Eight Asian Megatrends that are Changing the World*, London: Nicholas Brealey.

Narine, Shaun (1998), 'Institutional theory and Southeast Asia: the case of ASEAN', *World Affairs*, **161** (1).

Nathan, Dominic (2002), '15 nabbed here for terror plans', *Straits Times*, 6 January.

Nathan, K.S. (1991), 'Australia and South-East Asia: from cooperation to constructive engagement', *Round Table*, 319, July.

Nesadurai, Helen E.S. (1996), 'APEC: a tool for US regional domination', *Pacific Review*, **9** (1).

Neves, Felipe Ortiagão (2005), 'Questioning received wisdom: groupthink as an explanation for intelligence failure', unpublished MA dissertation, King's College, University of London.

Newsom, David (1995), 'Foreign policy and academia', *Foreign Policy*, 101.

O'Brien, Denis (2000), 'The talented Mr Horne', *Australian*, 1–2 April.

O'Brien, Patrick (1980), 'Constitutional conflict in Australia', *Conflict Studies*, March.

O'Neill, Robert (1973), 'Australian defence policy under Labor', *Journal of the Royal United Services Institute for Defence Studies*, September.

Oakeshott, Michael (1975), *On Human Conduct*, Oxford: Clarendon Press.

Oakeshott, Michael (1996), *The Politics of Faith and the Politics of Scepticism*, ed. Timothy Fuller, New Haven: Yale University Press.

'Obuchi's big bail-out' (1998), *Financial Times*, 14 October.

Office of Public Affairs (2003), 'Statement by the Treasury Department regarding today's designation of two leaders of Jemaah Islamiyah', KD-3796, Washington, DC, 24 January.

Ohmae, Kenichi (1991), *The Borderless World: Power and Strategy in the International Economy*, New York: Harper.

Öjendal, Joakim (2004), 'Back to the future? Regionalism in South-East Asia under unilateral pressure', *International Affairs*, **80** (3).

Okimoto, Daniel (1989), *Between MITI and the Market Japanese Industrial Policy in High Technology*, Stanford: Stanford University Press.

'On being Australian in 1959: the diggers come to town' (1959), *Round Table*, 197, December.

Onuf, Nicholas G. (1989), *A World of Our Making: Rules and Rule in Social Theory and International Relations*, Berkeley: University of California Press.

'Opening remarks by Prime Minister Goh Chok Tong at the dialogue with community leaders on the arrest of the second group of Jemaah Islamiyah members' (2002), Singapore Government Press Release, Media Relations

Division, Ministry of Information, Communications and the Arts, 14 October.

Orwell, George (2002), 'Writers and the Leviathan', *Politics and Letters*, Summer 1948, republished in George Orwell, *Essays*, New York: Alfred Knopf/Everyman Library.

Osborne, Milton (1995), *Southeast Asia: An Introductory History*, London: Allen & Unwin.

Pacific Economic Cooperation Council (1994), *Pacific Economic Outlook 1994–1995*, San Francisco: Asia Foundation.

Palen, Ronen (2000), 'A world of their making: an evaluation of the constructivist critique in international relations', *Review of International Studies*, **26** (4).

Paltridge, Shane (1966), 'Australia's defence policy', *Survival*, January.

'Par for the course' (1995), *Economist*, 26 December.

Park, M.K. (1987), 'Interest representation in South Korea: the limit of corporatist control', *Asian Survey*, **27** (8).

Park, Yung-Chul (2001), 'Finance and economic development in East Asia', *APEC Economic Outlook Symposium*, Hong Kong, 28–9 June.

Parreñas, Julius Caesar (1998), 'ASEAN and Asia–Pacific Economic Cooperation', *Pacific Review*, **11** (2).

Patrick, Hugh T. (1994), 'Comparisons, contrasts and implications', in Hugh T. Patrick and Yung Chul Park (eds), *The Financial Development of Japan, Korea and Taiwan: Growth, Repression and Liberalization*, Oxford: Oxford University Press.

Peou, Sorpong (2002), 'Realism and constructivism in Southeast Asian security studies today: a review essay', *Pacific Review*, **15** (1).

Pererira, Brendan (2000),'Bigotry rears its ugly head in multi-racial Malaysia', *Straits Times*, 29 July.

Perry, John Curtis (1985), 'Asia's telectronic highway', *Foreign Affairs*, 59.

Pettman, Ralph (1983), 'The radical critique and Australian foreign policy', in Peter J. Boyce and John R. Angel (eds), *Independence and Alliance: Australia in World Affairs*, Sydney: George Allen & Unwin.

Phillips, A.A.(1958), *The Australian Tradition: Studies in a Colonial Culture*, Melbourne: F.W. Cheshire.

Philpott, Simon (2001), 'Fear of the dark: Indonesia and the Australian national imagination', *Australian Journal of International Affairs*, **55** (3).

'PM reveals plan to crash jet into Changi' (2002), *Sunday Times* (Singapore), 7 April.

'Pointless?' (1996), *Economist*, 27 July.

Pomfret, John (2001), 'Chinese leader's hard line raises his political risks', *International Herald Tribune*, 9 April.

Popper, Karl (1959), *The Poverty of Historicism*, London: Routledge.

Popper, Karl (1985), *Popper Selections*, ed. David Miller, Princeton, NJ: Princeton University Press.

Popper, Karl (2002), *The Poverty of Historicism*, 2nd edn, London: Routledge.

Power, Andrew (1994), 'Prosperity and patrimonialism: business and government in Indonesia', in Andrew MacIntyre (ed.), *Business and Government in Industrializing Asia Relations*, St Leonards, NSW: Allen & Unwin.

Preiss, Michael (2004), 'Why China needs to develop a bond market', *China Brief*, **IV** (4).

Prest, Wilfred and J.O.N. Perkins (1962), 'Australia contemplates an enlarged EEC: economic changes for Australia', *Round Table*, 209, December.

Price, Charles (1975), 'Beyond white Australia: the Whitlam government's immigration record', *Round Table*, 260, October.

'Prognosis dismal for Asian flu' (1998), *Financial Times*, 2 October.

Pupphavesa, Wisarn and Maureen Crewe (1994), 'AFTA and NAFTA: Complementing or Competing?', in Chia Siow Yue (ed.), *APEC: Challenges and Opportunities*, Singapore: Institute of Southeast Asian Studies.

Quah, Stella R. and Jon Quah (1987), *Friends in Blue: the police and public in Singapore*, Oxford: Oxford University Press.

Quilty, Mary (1998), *Textual Empires: A Reading of Early British History of Southeast Asia*, Melbourne: Monash Asia Institute.

Radelet, Steven and Jeffrey Sachs (1997), 'Asia's reemergence', *Foreign Affairs*, **76** (6).

Rahim, Farah Abdul (2003), 'White paper sheds light on Singapore JI indoctrination process', Channel News Asia.com, 9 January (www.channel-newsasia.com/stories/singaporelocalnews/view/29264/1/.html).

Rahim, Lily (1998), *The Malay Dilemma: The Political and Educational Marginality of the Malay Community*, Singapore: Oxford University Press.

Ramesh, Thakur (1997), 'Australia and New Zealand: unequal partners on the periphery', in James Cotton and John Ravenhill (eds), *Seeking Asian Engagement: Australia in World Affairs 1991–1995*, Melbourne: Oxford University Press.

Rankin, Aiden (2000), 'A smug metropolitan consensus is conspiring against democracy', *Times*, 18 January.

Ravenhill, John (2002), 'A three bloc world? The new East Asian regionalism', *International Relations of the Asia–Pacific*, **2** (1).

Reading, Brian (1992), *Japan: The Coming Collapse*, London: Weidenfeld & Nicolson.

Redding, S. Gordon (1993), *The Spirit of Chinese Capitalism*, Berlin: Walter de Gruyter.

Rees-Mogg, William (1997), 'Blair could make it the year of the tiger', *Times*, 1 January.

'Regions in transition' (2000), summary of Asia–Europe Roundtable, the inaugural Asia–Europe Roundtable jointly organized by the Asia–Europe Foundation (Singapore), the Friedrich Ebert Siftung and the Singapore Institute of International Affairs, 29–31 August.

Reich, Robert B. (1991), *The Work of Nations: Preparing Ourselves for the 21st Century*, New York: Knopf.

Remington, Thomas (1992), 'Sovietology and system stability', *Post Soviet Affairs*, **8** (3).

Renouf, Alan (1979), *The Frightened Country*, London: Macmillan.

Republic of Philippines (1999), Directorate for Intelligence, 'Reference Folder on International Terrorism', National Headquarters, Philippine National Police, Camp Crame, Quezon City.

Ressa, Maria (2002), 'Infiltrating the MILF', *Newsbreak*, 28 October (www.inq7.net/nwsbrk/2002/oct/28/nbk_1-1.htm).

Rhee, Jong-chan (1994), *The State and Industry in South Korea: The Limits of the Authoritarian State*, London: Routledge.

Robison, Richard (1990), *Power and Economy in Suharto's Indonesia*, Manila: Journal of Contemporary Asia Publishers.

Robison, Richard (1996), 'Looking north: myths and strategies', in Richard Robison (ed.), *Pathways to Asia: The Politics of Engagement*, St Leonards, NSW: Allen & Unwin.

Robison, Richard and David S.G. Goodman (eds) (1996), *The New Rich in Asia: Mobile Phones, McDonalds and Middle-Class Revolution*, London: Routledge.

Rodan, Gary (2002), 'Keeping a tight grip on the internet', *Asian Wall Street Journal*, 13 June.

Rodner, M. (1995), 'APEC: the challenges of Asia–Pacific cooperation', *Modern Asian Studies*, **29** (2).

Rohwer, Jim (1996), *Asia Rising: How History's Biggest Middle Class Will Change the World*, London: Nicholas Brealey.

Roy, Denny (1994), 'Hegemon on the horizon? China's threat to East Asian security', *International Security*, **19** (1).

Roy, Oliver (2000), 'Islam, Iran and the new terrorism', *Survival*, **42** (2).

Rozman, Gilbert (1998), 'Flawed regionalism: reconceptualizing Northeast Asia in the 1990s', *Pacific Review*, **11** (1).

Rutland, Peter (1993), 'Sovietology: notes for a post-mortem', *National Interest*, Spring.

Saiful Azhar Adullah and Sheridan Mahavera (2002), 'Asean: plus 3 secretariat plan gets a boost', *New Straits Times*, 29 July.

Salleh, Ismail Muhammed and Saha Dhevan Meyanathan (1993), *Malaysia: Growth Equity and Structural Transformation*, Washington, DC: World Bank.

Schein, Edgar H. (1996), *Strategic Pragmatism: The Culture of the Singapore Economic Development Board*, Cambridge, MA: MIT Press.

Schmitt, Carl (1996), *The Concept of the Political*, trans. George Schwab, Chicago: University of Chicago Press.

Schwarz, Adam (1994), *Indonesia: A Nation in Waiting*, St Leonards, NSW: Allen & Unwin.

'Security plan built on solid ground', (2001), *Australian*, 1 August.

Segal, Gerald (1989), *Rethinking the Pacific*, Oxford: Clarendon.

Segal, Gerald (1992), 'Towards a Pacific century?', in John Baylis and N.J. Rengger (eds), *Dilemmas in World Politics: International Issues in a Changing World*, Oxford, Clarendon Press.

Seivers, Sara E. and Wei Shang-Jin (1999), 'The cost of crony capitalism', *Straits Times*, 4 July.

'Shared values' (2001), Singapore Infomap: The National Website (www.sg/flavour/values-bg.html), accessed 25 November.

Sheehy, Gail (1990), *The Man Who Changed the World*, New York: Perennial Library.

Shelley, Rebecca (2004), *Democratization in East Asia: the International Dimension*, London: Routledge.

Sheridan, Greg (1995), *Living with Dragons: Australia Confronts its Asian Destiny*, St Leonards, NSW: Allen & Unwin.

Sheridan, Greg (1997), 'Inside Asia', *Australian*, 17 November.

Sheridan, Greg (2003), 'Trade and terrorism', in *Asia: A Worldwide Special Report*, supplement of *Australian*, 8 September.

Shiina, Motoo (1995), 'Peace in East Asia: investing in the future', *Japan Review of International Affairs*, **9** (3).

Shinyo, Takahiro (1995), 'The conditions for arms control and disarmament in Asia and the Pacific', *Japan Review of International Affairs*, **9** (3).

Shtromas, Alexander and Morton A. Kaplan (eds) (1988), *The Soviet Union and the Challenge of the Future*, New York: Paragon House.

Sidel, John T. (2001), 'Review of "Quest for Identity: International Relations of Southeast Asia" ', *Survival*, **43** (4).

Simon, Sheldon (1978), 'The ASEAN states: obstacles to security cooperation', *Orbis*, **22** (2).

Simon, Sheldon (1987), 'ASEAN security prospects', *Journal of International Affairs*, **41** (1).

Simon, Sheldon (1998), 'Security prospects in Southeast Asia: collaborative efforts and the ASEAN Regional Forum', *Pacific Review*, **11** (2).

Simon, Steven and Daniel Benjamin (2000), 'America and the new terrorism', *Survival*, **42** (1).

Slisli, Fouzi (2001), 'The western media and the Algerian crisis', *Race and Class*, **41** (3).

Smith, P.J. (2005), 'Border security and transnational violence in Southeast Asia', in P.J. Smith (ed.), *Terrorism and Violence in Southeast Asia*, Armonk: M.E. Sharpe.

Snitwongse, Kusuma (1990), 'Meeting the challenges of a changing Southeast Asia', in Robert Scalapino, Seizebura Sato, Jusuf Wanandi and Soo-Joon Han (eds), *Regional Dynamics: Security, Political and Economic Issues in Southeast Asia*, Jakarta: Centre for Strategic and International Studies.

Snitwongse, Kusuma (1995), 'ASEAN's security cooperation: searching for a regional agenda', *Pacific Review*, **8** (3).

Snitwongse, Kusuma (1998), 'Thirty years of ASEAN: achievements through political cooperation', *Pacific Review*, **11** (2).

Snyder, Jack (1977), *The Soviet Strategic Culture: Implications for Limited Nuclear Options*, Santa Monica: RAND.

Soesastro, Hadi (2001), 'Whither ASEAN Plus Three?', Regional Trading Arrangements: Stocktake and Next Steps, Pacific Economic Cooperation Council, Trade Policy Forum, Bangkok, 12–13 June.

Solarz, Stephen J. (1990), 'Cambodia and the international community', *Foreign Affairs*, Spring.

Song, Byung-Nak (1990), *The Rise of the Korean Economy*, Hong Kong: Oxford University Press.

Soon, Teck Wong and Tan C. Suan (1993), *Singapore: Public Policy and Economic Development*, Washington, DC: World Bank.

Sopiee, Noordin (1992), 'The new world order: what Southeast Asia should strive for', in Normah Mahmood and Thangan Ramnath (eds), *Southeast Asia: The Way Forward*, Kuala Lumpur: Institute of Strategic and International Studies.

Star, Barbara (2002), 'Intelligence from Afghanistan breaks Singapore plot', CNN.com 11 January.

State Department (2002a), *Patterns of Global Terrorism 2002*, Washington, DC: Department of State (http://www.state.gov/s/ct/rls/pgtrpt/2002/html).

State Department (2002b), 'Admiral Blair says al-Qaeda has ties to groups in Asia', International Information Programs 22 March (http://usinfo.state.gov/topical/pol/terror/02032502.htm).

'States of denial' (1996), *Economist*, 10 August.

Strange, Susan (1997), *The Retreat of the State: The Diffusion of Power in the World Economy*, Cambridge: Cambridge University Press.

'Sweeping Asian terror alliance uncovered' (2002), CNN.com/World, 19 September (www.cnn.com/2002/WORLD/asiapcf/southeast/09/19/singapore.arrests/).

Symons, Fiona (2003), 'Analysis and roots of jihad', BBC News, 16 February (http://news.bbc.co.uk/1/hi/world/middle_east/1603178.stm).

t'Hart, Paul (1990), *Groupthink in Governments: A Study of Small Groups and Policy Failure*, Baltimore: Johns Hopkins University Press.

t'Hart, Paul, Eric K. Stern and Bengt Sundelius (eds) (1997), *Beyond Groupthink: Political Dynamics and Foreign Policy-Making*, Michigan: University of Michigan Press.

Tan, Amy (2002), 'Southeast Asia a potential Al-Qaeda sanctuary – FBI', Reuters Report 14 March..

Tan, Andrew (1998), *Armed Rebellion in the ASEAN States*, Canberra: Australian National University Strategic and Defence Studies Centre.

Tan, Andrew (2000a), *Intra-ASEAN Tensions,* discussion paper 84, London: Royal Institute for International Affairs.

Tan, Andrew (2000b), 'Armed Muslim separatist rebellion in Southeast Asia: persistence, prospects and implications', *Studies in Conflict and Terrorism*, **23** (4).

Taubert, A. (1991), 'Liberalism under pressure in Indonesia', *Southeast Asia Affairs 1991*, Singapore: Institute of Southeast Asian Studies.

Taylor, Lenore (1999), 'The lobby that loved Indonesia', *Australian Financial Review*, 16–17 October.

'Tentacles of terror' (2002), *Bulletin*, 13 February.

'Terrific Pacific' (1996), *Economist*, 20 July.

'Terror investigations strain Malaysian politics' (2002), BBC News, 22 January (www.bbc.co.uk/hi/english/world/asia–pacific/newsid_1775000/ 1775718.stm).

'Thailand wages battles against border smugglers' (2000), *Straits Times*, 7 July.

Thambipillai, Pushpa (1998), 'The ASEAN growth areas: sustaining the dynamism', *Pacific Review*, **11** (2).

Thayer, C.A. (2005), 'Al Qaeda and political terrorism in Southeast Asia', in P.J. Smith (ed.), *Terrorism and Violence in Southeast Asia*, Armonk: M.E. Sharpe.

'The Bali bomber's network of terror' (2003), BBC News/Asia–Pacific, 12 May (http:news.bbc.news.co.uk/1/world/asia–pacific/2499193.stm).

'The Baluch connection: is Khalid Sheikh Mohammed tied to Baghdad?' (2003), *Wall Street Journal*, 18 March.

'The Bank Bali scandal' (1999), *Business Times*, 30 August.

'The FBI's hijacker list' (2001), CBSNews.com, 27 September (www.cbsnews.com/archive/printable311329.shtml).

'The five shared values' (2001), Singapore Infomap: The National Website (www.sg/flavour/values-5.html), accessed 25 November.

'The Pacific needs pax Americana' (1996), *Daily Telegraph*, 17 April.

'The Pakistan connection' (2002), *Sunday Times* (Singapore), 7 April.

'The plot thickens, but mostly outside Singapore' (2002), *Straits Times*, 26 January.

'The trail to Kuala Lumpur' (2002), *Straits Times*, 29 January.

Theervit, Khien (1979), *Australian–Thai Relations: A Thai Perspective*, occasional paper 58, Singapore: ISEAS.

'Thoughts of chairman Lee' (2000), *Australian*, 11 November.

Tomasic, Dinko (1953), *The Impact of Russian Culture on Soviet Communism*, Glencoe, IL: The Free Press.

'Top al-Qaeda suspect captured' (2002), BBC News, 1 March (www.bbc.co.uk/1/hi/world/south_asia/2811473.stm).

Trood, Russell and Ken Booth (1999), 'Strategic culture and conflict management in the Asia–Pacific', in Ken Booth and Russell Trood (eds), *Strategic Cultures in the Asia–Pacific*, London: Macmillan.

Tsang, Donald (1998), 'Asia needs a bond market', *Asia Wall Street Journal*, 17–18 July.

Turley, William S. and Jeffrey Race (1980) 'The third Indochina war', *Foreign Policy*, 38, Spring.

Turner, Bryan (1994), *Orientalism, Postmodernity and Globalism*, London: Routledge.

'Twisted ties to terrorist network' (2002), *Sydney Morning Herald*, 16 October.

Valencia, Mark (1995), *China and the South China Seas Dispute*, Adelphi Paper 298, Oxford: Oxford University Press/IISS.

Vatikiotis, Michael (1993), *Indonesian Politics Under Suharto*, London: Routledge.

Wade, Robert (1990), *Governing the Market: Economic Theory and the Role of Government in East Asian Industrialization*, Princeton: Princeton University Press.

Wade, Robert (1992), 'East Asia's economic success: conflicting perspectives, partial insights, and shaky evidence', *World Politics*, **44** (1).

Wain, Barry (2004), 'ASEAN–Jakarta jilted: Indonesia's neighbours are not very supportive of its vision of a regional security community', *Far Eastern Economic Review*, 10 June.

Waldmen, Peter (2000), 'A look at four questions that we may never answer', *Asian Wall Street Journal*, 7–8 January.

Walt, Stephen (1999), 'Rigor or rigor mortis? Rational choice and security studies', *International Security*, **24** (4).

Walter, G. (1991), 'An unusual monosymptomatic hypochondriacal delusion presenting as self-insertion of a foreign body into the urethra', *British Journal of Psychiatry*, 159.

Walter, James (1980), *The Leader: A Political Biography of Gough Whitlam*, St Lucia, QLD: University of Queensland Press.

Wanandi, Jusuf (1999a), 'ASEAN's challenges for its future', *Global Beat*, Pacific Forum CSIS PacNet (3), 22 January 1999 (www.nyu.edu/globalbeat/asia/Wanandi012399.html).

Wanandi, Jusuf (1996), 'Building a community', *Asiaweek*, 29 November.

Wanandi, Jusuf (1999b), 'Moving East Asia forward again', Annual Meeting of the Trilateral Commission, Washington, DC (www.trilateral.org/annmtgs/trialtxts/t53/wan.htm).

Wanandi, Jusuf (2000), 'East Asian institution-building', Annual Meeting of the Trilateral Commission, Tokyo, 2000 (www.trilateral.org/annmtgs/trialtxts/t54/wan.htm), accessed 2 October 2003.

Wanandi, Jusuf (2002a), 'A global coalition against international terrorism', *International Security*, **26** (4).

Wanandi, Jusuf (2002b), 'A nation in denial for too long', *International Herald Tribune*, 5 November.

Wanandi, Jusuf (2002c), 'Indonesia: a failed state?', *Washington Quarterly*, **25** (3).

Wang, Jisi (1997), 'The role of the United States as a global and Pacific power: a view from China', *Pacific Review*, **10** (1).

Warhurst, John (1992), 'The Department of Prime Minister and Cabinet in Australia, 1972–90', *Round Table*, 324, October.

Way, Wendy (ed.) (2000), *Documents on Australian Foreign Policy: Australia and the Indonesian Incorporation of East Timor, 1974–1976*, Melbourne: Department of Foreign Affairs and Trade/Melbourne University Press.

'Weakness is strength in policy scapegoating' (1998), *Australian Financial Review*, 10 August.

Weigley, Russell (1973), *The American Way of War*, London: Macmillan.

Wendt, Alexander (1992a), 'Anarchy is what states make of it: the social construction of power politics', *International Organization*, **46** (2).

Wendt, Alexander (1992b), 'Collection identity formation and the international state', *American Political Science Review*, **88** (2).

Wendt, Alexander (1999), *Social Theory of International Politics*, Cambridge: Cambridge University Press.

White, Gordon (1993), *Riding the Tiger: The Politics of Economic Reform in Post-Mao China*, London: Macmillan.

Whitlam, E.G. (1985), *The Whitlam Government, 1972–1975*, London: Penguin.

Whitlam, E.G. (1997), *Abiding Interests*, St Lucia, QLD: University of Queensland Press.

Whitlam, Gough (1973a), *Australia's Foreign Policy: New Directions, New Definitions*, Canberra: Australian Institute of International Affairs.

Whitlam, Gough (1973b), speech to the House of Representatives, 13 December.

Wibisono, Christianto (1995), 'The economic role of the Indonesian Chinese', in Leo Suryadinata (ed.), *Southeast Asian Chinese and China: The Politico-Economic Dimension*, Volume 2, Singapore: Times Academic Press.

Wilcox, Wayne (1968), 'The prospective politics of insecurity and asymmetry in Asia', *International Journal*, **XXIV** (1).

Wilkinson, Marian (2002), 'We'll hit you: pre-Bali alert', *Sydney Morning Herald*, 16 October.

Wilson, Chris (2001), 'Indonesia and transnational terrorism', *Current Issues Brief 6*, Canberra: Department of the Parliamentary Library, 11 October 2001 (www.aph.gov.au/library/pubs/cib/2002-02/02cib06/.htm).

Wohlforth, William (1994), 'Realism and the end of the Cold War', *International Security*, **19** (4).

Wolf, Martin (1998a), 'Let lenders beware', *Financial Times*, 9 December.

Wolf, Martin (1998b), 'Threats of depression', *Financial Times*, 26 August.

Wolf, Martin (1998c), 'Serious yes, hopeless no', *Financial Times*, 7 October.

Wolf, Martin (2004), 'Emerging Asia feeds the twin US deficits', *Financial Times*, 12 August.

Wong, John (1977), *The ASEAN Economies*, Singapore: Economic Research Centre.

Woolcott, Richard (2003), *The Hot Seat: Reflections on Diplomacy from Stalin's Death to the Bali Bombing*, Sydney: HarperCollins.

World Bank (1993), *The East Asian Miracle: Economic Growth and Public Policy*, Oxford: Oxford University Press

World Bank (1994), *East Asia's Trade and Investment: Regional and Global Gains from Industrialization*, Washington, DC: World Bank.

World Bank (1996), *World Development Report*, Washington, DC: World Bank.

Worthington, Ross (2001), 'Between Hermes and Themis: an empirical study of the contemporary judiciary in Singapore', *Journal of Law and Society*, **28** (4).

Yahuda, Michael (1996), *The International Politics of the Asia–Pacific, 1945–1995*, London: Routledge.

Yearbook Australia 1982 (1982), Canberra: Bureau of Statistics.

Yeo, George (1995), 'A new greater East Asia co-prosperity sphere?', in Greg Sheridan (ed.), *Living with Dragons: Australia Confronts its Asian Destiny*, St Leonards, NSW: Allen & Unwin.

Yoshihara, Kunio (1988), *The Rise of Ersatz Capitalism in Southeast Asia*, Kuala Lumpur: Oxford University Press.

Yoshihara, Kunio (1994a), *Japanese Economic Development: A Short Introduction*, Kuala Lumpur: Oxford University Press.

Yoshihara, Kunio (1994b), *The Nation and Economic Growth: The Philippines and Thailand*, Kuala Lumpur: Oxford University Press.

Yoshihara, Kunio (1995), 'The ethnic Chinese and ersatz capitalism in Southeast Asia', in Leo Suryadinata (ed.), *Southeast Asian Chinese and China: The Politico-Economic Dimension*, Singapore: Times Academic Press.

Young, Alwyn (1992), 'A tale of two cities: factor accumulation and technical change in Hong Kong and Singapore', in Olivier Jean Blanchard and Stanley Fischer (eds), *NBER Macroeconomics Annual 1992*, Cambridge, MA: MIT Press.

Young, Alwyn (1995), 'The tyranny of numbers: confronting the statistical realities of the East Asian growth experience', *Quarterly Journal of Economics*, **CX** (3).

Zakaria, Fareed (1994), 'Culture is destiny: a conversation with Lee Kuan Yew', *Foreign Affairs*, 73, March/April.

PERIODICALS

Age
Asian Wall Street Journal
Asiaweek
Australian
Bangkok Post
Berita Harian
Bulletin
Business Times (Singapore)
Christian Science Monitor
Daily Telegraph (Australia)
Daily Telegraph (London)
Economist
Far Eastern Economic Review
Financial Times
Forbes Magazine
Fortune Magazine
Guardian
Independent
Indonesian Observer
International Herald Tribune
Jakarta Post
Le Monde Diplomatique
Los Angeles Times
Manila Times
Nation (Bangkok)
New Straits Times
New York Newsday
New York Times
News and View Indonesia

Newsbreak
Newsweek
San Francisco Examiner
Star (Malaysia)
Straits Times
Sunday Times (Singapore)
Sydney Morning Herald
Time Magazine
Time Magazine Asia
Times
Wall Street Journal
Washington Post
Weekend Australian

Index